DECISION
SUPPORT SYSTEMS

DECISION SUPPORT SYSTEMS
A Data-Based, Model-Oriented, User-Developed Discipline

edited by

William C. House
Professor, University of Arkansas

a petrocelli book
new york / princeton

Designed by Diane L. Backes
Typesetting by Backes Graphics

Printed in the United States of America
1 2 3 4 5 6 7 8 9 10

Library of Congress Cataloging in Publication Data

Main entry under title:

Decision support systems.

  Bibliography: p.
  Includes index.
  1. Management information systems. 2. Decision-making.
I. House, William C.
T58.6.D433   1983   658.4'0388   83-13081
ISBN 0-89433-225-2
ISBN 0-89433-208-2 (paperback)

Contents

PART TWO
Management Problem-Solving Styles, Manager-Analyst
Interaction, Interactive Model Implications and
Successful Model Applications

Preface

Existing management information systems have typically been built around transaction processing, structured problems, and static models. They have been widely criticized as being too data, accounting, and hardware oriented, limited to providing current internal information for lower-level managers. Operations Research/Management Science systems typically focus on structured problems and produce precise imperative or recommended solutions, using analytic, optimization, or simulation techniques. Throughout using organizations, emphasis has been placed on efficient use of hardware and software resources in information production activities and in developing efficient solutions to well-structured management decision problems.

Decision support systems (DSS) place more emphasis on utilizing information to improve human effectiveness and less stress on producing information in an efficient, cost-effective manner. Management skills and machine capabilities are carefully balanced so that information and judgment can be blended to achieve improved decision results. The objective is to support, not replace, judgment in such a manner that the strengths of both man and machine processes will be utilized to the fullest. Such systems create supportive tools under the control of users without automating the total decision process, predefining objectives, or imposing solutions. As such, they are valuable in helping incorporate the insight and judgment of the decision maker into the problem-solving phases of problem formulation, data selection, and alternative generation/evaluation. The decision support system has considerable potential for helping higher-level managers solve practical, unstructured problems where some structure is present and judgment is essential.

Keen and others suggest that decision support systems are most effective in situations where clearcut goals exist, procedures employed are well understood, a few users with common goals are benefitted, and the system can operate independently of other systems. Several authors, including Lankau, maintain that decision support systems should incorporate data from multiple sources (internal and external), permit accurate and representative modelling of decision environments, cut across functional communication lines, and provide user-friendly interface capabilities. Thus, these authorities assert that while decision support systems ideally are integrated, broad in scope, and extensive in modelling and display capabilities, they are best applied initially in narrow areas, to clearcut problem situations, with standardized procedures.

Ease of use and fast response to user needs are among the most desired DSS characteristics, requiring high quality, fast response terminals connected to user-oriented, on-line interactive systems. To achieve the desirable degree of ease of use, acquiring familiarization with system operating procedures and attaining skillfulness in system use is essential on the part of both non-technical users and systems analysts. Since system capabilities often vary widely, a dual mode of operation is desirable. A system-driven interaction mode with menus and helpful hints can be used by beginners while a user-driven interaction method or command mode may be utilized by experts. Either procedural or non-procedural languages can be employed with decision support systems based on user skills and desires. Data-based knowledge systems range from simple retrieval based on known problem characteristics to inferential retrieval based on stored logic likely to be applicable to selected types of problems.

Current decision support systems vary widely in their characteristics and capabilities, but the most common versions provide user-friendly data retrieval keyed to either simple inquiry or report generation requirements plus some modelling and graphics capabilities. A report generator added to a data base management system often provides the foundation for a decision support system. Internal data bases can be expanded to include more external data. Some type of mathematical modelling routines generally are included, frequently built around electronic spread sheet capabilities which allow different what-if assumptions to be tested. Statistical analysis and risk assessment routines can be added as well as graphic display programs if users desire. The various options included are designed to provide flexible decision support for unstructured problems, broadening earlier MIS capabilities.

An important decision organizations must make is whether to initially install easier-to-use systems with less scope, power and flexibility, or to implement more powerful software packages with expanded capabilities to handle a wide variety of decision problems. A second choice is between the use of non-procedural languages which require only the problem characteristics to be specified, and procedural languages which require that the user specify the exact procedures to be used. The technical expertise of users or analysts, the complexity of problems and procedures involved, and the willingness and ability of users to become involved with decision-oriented data processing will affect the choices to be made. As a practical matter, many decision support systems have had their inception in managerial use of financial planning languages and simple planning models to help answer what-if questions.

The development and implementation of decision support systems, as currently envisioned, will require changes in the orientation and philosophy of many organizational personnel (e.g., to delivering services rather than products, to greater user acceptance of responsibility for system implementation, and a secondary role for technical specialists). Many authorities, such as Gerrity, believe it is desirable to start with simple components, gradually phasing in more complex functions and sophisticated analysis as experience is gained in system use and continually focusing on end user requirements at all times. Other writers stress the importance of starting with key decision areas, well-defined subproblems, and user-identified critical decision success factors.

System developers must carefully balance two conflicting interests: The desirability of having a flexible, generalized system with considerable sophistication and complexity to handle a wide variety of decision problems versus the simplicity, low cost and limited risk of a less sophisticated system which focuses on specific and limited problem interests. Thus, a key tradeoff involves whether to start with an inexpensive, easy-to-use, low overhead system aimed at one-time problems requiring fast response, or to select a more expensive and extensive system with higher startup costs but larger and less expensive (per information unit) capabilities for expansion to handle larger numbers of diverse problems. Limitations of manpower, money, and hardware and software resources plus the diversity and criticality of user information needs and user levels of computer expertise will play important roles in the initial choice. Development of prototype systems of utilization of several different software packages for different applications may help cut costs, complexity, and risk.

In justifying the expense of developing and implementing decision support systems, more emphasis is being placed on their value to organizational decision makers than on cost savings and clerical activity automation factors stressed in earlier system selection. DSS payoffs include the improvement of management effectiveness by extending the range and depth of decision-making capabilities and increasing the value of management decisions to organizations by reducing the effort, time and cost required to carry out the decision process.

Many of the highly-touted management information systems of the sixties and seventies failed largely due to overemphasis of machine efficiency, accounting-oriented transaction processing, and fixed-format report generation. Decision support systems appear to have a better chance for successful implementation because they emphasize human effectiveness more than machine efficiency, provide flexible responses to queries about less well-structured but higher payoff problem environments, and encourage user involvement in system development. As a result of increasing user orientation and improved user-analyst coordination/communication, application implementation time and costs can often be reduced, systems become easier for non-technical personnel to use, and decision support systems often turn out to be more useful to a larger number of individuals than proved possible with earlier generation systems.

William C. House
Fayetteville, Arkansas

PART ONE

DECISION SUPPORT SYSTEMS: Characteristics, Compatibility with Decision Styles, Effective Design Criteria, and Interactive Systems Impact

INTRODUCTION
William C. House

The capabilities of decision support systems are difficult to define and generalize, in view of the fact that there is no consensus as to what characteristics a system should have to qualify as a DSS. Therefore, no generally accepted definition of such systems can be realistically stated at this point in time. The majority of current systems which are characterized as decision support systems do appear to be flexible, do deal principally with unstructured problems, and are at least partially interactive.

Data-oriented information systems of the 1950s and 1960s are slowly giving way to more model-oriented information systems in the 1970s and 1980s. These systems are more data integrated and more comprehensive in scope, both internally and externally, than their predecessors, and vary widely in the extent to which system outputs affect actual decisions. Data base management systems and financial planning models are key features of many decision support systems. In actual practice, many managers don't use the support systems frequently or directly, but make wide use of intermediaries, conceptualization guides, and memory aids.

A sizeable number of existing information systems don't fit the decision-making styles and processes of their users very well. Evolving systems seem to be more responsive to a variety of information needs than previous systems, to be deemphasizing instant interaction capabilities, and to be limiting conversational problem solving to structured applications. As decision support systems become more highly developed, it is reasonable to expect more flexible, comprehensive, and responsive outputs to meet a wide variety of decision styles, processes, and needs than practical or possible at present.

Vazonyi[1] maintains that decision support systems are a new form of technology which deals with unstructured decision problems and provides flexible support of decision makers with computer-based information. Four suggested design criteria for evolving support systems include representation forms; support of intelligence, design, and choice activities; memory aids, and decision-maker control. Decision support systems differ from operations research/management science in the formality of structures and the ability of managers to alter existing structures. However, formal optimization turns out to be an important but not indispensable aspect of operations research/management science.

The basic structure of statistical decision theory is expressed in states, acts, and outcomes. The decision maker has the formidable task of finding environmental states and alternative acts, specifying outcomes, and choosing the optimum solution. If parameters change, the optimum solution will change, and changes can be implemented and the effects explored through the process of sensitivity analysis. A frequent result is that insight turns out to be more important than finding optimal problem solutions.

Decision support systems can provide supporting data for the processes of exploring/structuring, interpreting, and implementing so essential in operations research/management science. Such systems can decrease the cost and time required to perform various decision-making phases, increase the applicability and efficiency of the process of structuring managerial situations, and improve processes for collaboration between manager, operations researcher, and information analyst. The decision support system provides possibilities of man-machine dialogs and flexible, reactive responses to meet changing conditions.

Sprague and Watson point out that while it is possible to indicate examples and characteristics of decision support systems, it becomes much more difficult to define and generalize DSS capabilities so as to improve understanding and acceptance of them. Decision support systems can be defined broadly as decision-aiding and decision-implementing systems or more narrowly as interactive, computer-based systems oriented toward unstructured decision making. Literal application of these definitions excludes too many systems which may actually support managerial decision making in some helpful way and includes too many others which are little more than glorified report generators.

Information systems evolution can be viewed more realistically in terms of systems technology (i.e., speed, capacity, cost) and systems performance (i.e., types of tasks done and information generated, degree of use of decision models, organizational levels served). Four levels of systems performance can be distinguished: Basic data processing systems, integrated data processing systems, management information systems, and decision support systems. These systems differ in the scope of activities covered, the degree of integration of functional activities, and the extent to which files are integrated and decision models are incorporated into the system.

Management information systems typically are based on integrated reporting and data base/data communications subsystems. Decision support systems, including a data base, a model base, and the decision maker, focus on the supporting of decision making rather than systems of information flows and reports. The data base subsystem draws from both internal and external sources and incorporates a variety of logical structures. A comprehensive decision support system will contain strategic, tactical, and operating models in its model base as well as model building blocks and subroutines. The decision-maker subsystem includes a terminal device and command language which will allow the decision maker to access and manipulate models and data in the decision support system. Existing DSS systems are slowly evolving toward a comprehensive information system which will directly support the decision-making process at all organizational levels in all areas.

Alter tackles the difficult and challenging task of defining decision support systems by examining case examples of seven types of decision support systems. In his framework, a basic distinction can be drawn between electronic data processing systems designed to automate transaction processing, record keeping, and business reporting; and decision support systems developed to aid in decision making and decision implementation.

The most useful taxonomy for categorizing various decision support systems seems to be the degree to which the system's outputs directly determine the decision to be made, ranging from simple or complex data retrieval to proposing or making decisions. Based on generic operations performed, seven types of systems can be identified and further categorized as data-oriented or model-oriented. *File-drawer* systems allow immediate access to data items, *data analysis* systems permit data manipulation using operators tailored to tasks to be performed, and *analysis information systems* provide access to a series of data bases and small models.

Four types of model-oriented systems can also be identified. *Accounting models* calculate the consequences of planned actions using accounting definitions whereas *representation models* estimate action consequences based on models that are at least partially nondefinitional. *Optimization models* generate optimal solutions within a series of constraints to provide guidelines for action while *suggestion models* carry out background calculations for suggested decisions involving structured tasks. The taxonomy developed appears to be useful as a guideline for designing systems, as a foundation for system implementation, and as a framework for communication and research.

Baxter maintains that traditional management information systems which emerged as an outgrowth of the automation of transaction processing failed because they didn't provide enough useful information for decision-making. If line managers can identify the most critical decisions they face and the major characteristics of such decisions, data processing specialists can help develop on-line programs which will provide support to managerial decision-making. Decision support systems are an integrated blending of information technology and managerial judgment designed to expand managerial decision-making capability. While management information systems are internal oriented, static, and report summary information on past events, decision support systems help improve manager's understanding of their responsibility areas by providing interpretive data which is more external oriented and evolutionary in nature.

The starting point for DSS is indoctrination of would be users, use of prototype systems which can be implemented in a short period of time, and coordination between line managers and computer specialists. Some organizations try to identify critical success factors in key decision areas through interviews of line managers. Current decision support systems seem to be more oriented toward unstructured and semistructured than structured decisions. The emphasis in DSS shifts from what information technology can provide in MIS to what the line manager really needs. Critical success factors plus computer model programs provide on-line decision support data which result in business decisions that produce business results. Feedback from past decisions and system flexibility aid the DSS in evolving into a larger, more comprehensive management tool.

Geoffrion and Powers present a clearcut concept and examples of management support systems which integrate data sources, mathematical models, and computers into management tools designed to cope with rapid environmental change and complex decision processes. More analytic and systematic decision-making methods are needed to augment brainpower as knowledge and information resources expand.

Management support systems include data files, models, problem solvers, and interface facilities. Data files consist of related data in computer readable form. Models demonstrate under trial assumptions how different alternatives affect system performance. Problem solvers are computer programs of varying complexity that execute models using evaluate, satisfy, and optimize commands. Interface facilities permit the user to communicate with data files, models, and problem solvers. Two related concepts are management information systems, which have only implicit models and problem solvers, and decision support systems that emphasize descriptive models for unstructured problem solving while management support systems utilize prescriptive models in structured problem solving.

Although management support systems can lead to large cost savings and profit increases, problems often occur with excessive data requirements, high development and maintenance costs, technical barriers to ease of use, job dissatisfaction, lack of credibility, unsatisfactory responsiveness, intended uses that don't materialize, and inability of systems to adapt to changing requirements. Technical difficulties with basic system components and insufficient user involvement can also cause trouble. Risks of failure can be reduced by setting modest objectives, modular development, and considering human factors. Receptivity toward new approaches, treating data as a critical resource, and utilizing available support system packages can accelerate system benefits.

Carlson stresses that the benefits of computer support for decision making generally take one of two forms: Displaced costs or added value. Computer systems have been used in supporting four types of decisions: strategic planning, management control, operational control, and operational performance. Several authorities have defined decision support systems as systems which support semi-structured and unstructured decisions for management control and strategic planning activities.

Two general categories of information systems, data-oriented and model-oriented, have had limited success in supporting decisions because of a mismatch between the decision-maker's requirements (in many cases), and Decision Support Systems Design/Performance. Decision-making processes may be viewed as rational (expected value), heuristic (satisfying), or dynamic consensus (successive limited comparisons). Decision support system requirements include support of multiple decisions, inclusion of different data processing requirements, and design of the system for more than one specific decision.

Observation of decision makers indicates that many of them rely on conceptualizations (e.g., pictures and charts), need memory aids, and expect to exercise direct, personal control over supporting activities. In addition, decision-making activities can be categorized in terms of intelligence, design, and choice (Simon) and wide differences in styles, skills, and knowledge are exhibited by various decision makers. Major problems with the design of existing systems arise because they do not provide representations needed for semi-structured and unstructured decisions, support too few basic decision-making activities, do not provide enough support for conceptualization and memory, and do not support a wide enough variety of decision-making skills, styles, and knowledge bases.

A decision support system is proposed that would provide physical representations, operations for intelligence, design, and choice, automated memory aids, and aids to direct personal control. Memory aids to support use of representations and operations include data bases, views, workspaces, libraries, links, triggers, and profiles. Control aids would include mechanical facilitators, training supporters, combined operations, and operation result changes. The design framework assumes an interactive, graphics environment, encompassing the use of a set of representations, operations with associated memory aids, control aids, and extensive user involvement. Decision makers would be allowed to select a sequence of operations, a variety of decision-making processes can be supported by each representation, and designer/users can segment the decision problem and identify intelligence, design, and choice activities.

As Sprague points out, decision support systems can be regarded as a natural outgrowth of the MIS systems as information technology has progressed, as a key subset of management information systems, or as a separate type of system which has been in a development process for years. DSS can also be defined on one extreme as an interactive computer system which would aid decision makers to utilize data and models in solving unstructured problems and on the other as any system which provides some contribution to decision-making. Observed characteristics of typical systems include orientation toward less structured problems, combined data access, retrieval functions, model use, ease of use by nontechnical users, and adaptability to environmental changes and varying decision styles.

In distinguishing among EDP, MIS, and DSS systems, EDP systems can be characterized by a focus on data processing at operational levels, efficient transaction processing on a batch basis, integrated files, and summary reports while MIS emphasizes information systems activities at middle management levels, structured information flows, functional integration of EDP tasks, and data-based inquiry and report generation. A DSS system is oriented toward top management levels, is user initiated and controlled, can support different decision making styles, and emphasizes flexibility, adaptability, and fast response. This evolutionary, connotational view of DSS has certain deficiencies, including implying that decision support is needed only at the top levels, ignoring the need to coordinate decisions at several levels, and indicating that decision support is the only needed requirement from the information system.

Toolsmiths create and combine information technology tools to support a DSS in the form of dialog management, data management, and model management capabilities. Further improvements are possible, especially in data base management capabilities and modeling languages. A better understanding of decision-making and related managerial activities is needed to help determine what outputs can and should be produced by any information system. Other development issues of concern for the future include who will do it, how should it be done, and how much can be done. Conclusions to be drawn include: DSS development efforts must be integrated with EDP and MIS systems, the three technology levels and people interrelationships must provide the development framework for an adaptive system, performance objectives determine types of support needed for various types of decisions supported, and the system must provide dialogue, data, and model management capabilities.

Alter emphasizes that current systems have limited interactive and conversational characteristics by conventional definitions. Although many authorities believe that numerous organizations have unstructured problems which can best be handled through interactive problem solving, most systems do little more than give answers or ask for answers. Major reductions in hardware, software, and modeling costs will be required in order for organizations to develop a mix of power and flexibility sufficient to support interactive problem solving.

Decision makers appear to be reluctant, in many instances, to use computer systems interactively because of the lack of natural language interfaces, incompatible work styles, status hangups, etc. This reluctance is further amplified by the existence of staff help to whom system usage can be delegated. It may be desirable to develop better man-machine interfaces, not to encourage greater managerial DSS use, but to encourage greater use through intermediaries who understand system details.

On-line computation and fast turnaround allow faster inquiry answers, minimize concentration interruptions and debugging annoyances, allow more alternatives to be considered, and permit monitoring of real time production processes. Convenience and efficiency rather than man-machine synergy are key features of man-machine interaction. Responsiveness, rather than interactiveness, in terms of power, accessibility, and flexibility, seems to be the key aspect of decision-support systems.

Keen, like Alter, stresses the need for systems with interactive problem-solving capabilities without the need for executives to directly operate computer terminals. Interactive systems provide managers with direct access to fast feedback computer systems. Decision-support systems tailored to managers' decision-making needs and processes are based on the assumption that computers must support but not replace managerial judgment, that such systems are best for semi-structured tasks, and that effective problem-solving is essentially interactive and is enhanced by man-machine dialogue.

PMS, BRANDAID, and GADS are examples of interactive systems used successfully by middle managers and specialists. The lack of true interactive problem solving, the existence of pause and reflect modes, and greater emphasis on accessibility than interactive conversation, suggests that decision-support systems may require some extension if they are to prove useful to top managers. Interactive computer systems require users, communication devices, software interaction interfaces, data, and models. Users often have a choice of one or more of interaction including programmer, expert, novice, or natural language modes.

Studies of existing interactive systems suggest that conversational problem solving is largely limited to more structured applications and that interaction is not a major factor in system use. Chauffeur-driven, intermediary systems may take on a variety of roles including exegesist, confidant, crusader, and teacher. The chauffeur must know the system in detail and assist the user in his planning and analysis functions.

Top management planning typically requires small data volumes, medium response times, data examination and presentation by lower management levels, examination of alternatives and options in a leisurely fashion, and exploratory decision making in undefined sequences. A modest proposal for top management decision-support systems would include such features as unstructured approaches, relevant responses, and timely but not instantaneous feedback. The APL language has proven very useful for planning in terms of quick program development, reduced error rates and lower turnaround time (but higher running time) than other languages. Less emphasis on interaction and more stress on employing skilled intermediaries directly in the planning process is very desirable. A range of strategies can be used in decision-support systems, making tradeoffs between software and intermediary interfaces based on the degree of task structure, number of system users, training difficulties, organization levels and extent of software overhead.

Carlson[2] discusses new approaches to computer systems that facilitate retrieval, manipulation, and collection of decision-making information, and support all decision-making stages—problem identification, choice of data and decision-making approaches, and alternative evaluation. Four main components of decision-support systems are good data representations, easy-to-use operations, adequate memory, and control aids. An important criterion of DSS usefulness is quick response to commands and easy access to decision locations.

Decision-support systems require three basic technologies: A computerized data base, computer time-sharing systems, and video displays. Current systems support data gathering, creation/comparison of alternatives, and explanation/selling of a decision. Increased interest in decision-support systems has been expanded due to declining computer storage costs and improvements in data entry/data management systems. Successful systems will require technology assembly into systems compatible with managerial styles, environments in which relevant data and decision-making processes cannot be specified in advance, system availability even if not used regularly, and capabilities for supporting decisions where compromise or time constraints are more important than optimal decisions or standard operating procedures.

Alter[3], in his discussion of decision-support systems used to improve managerial effectiveness, cites lack of familiarity with types of systems available, overconcentration on technical characteristics, and lack of user impetus to implement innovative systems as barriers to use of these systems. Computer systems can be categorized in terms of what the user does with them: Data item retrieval, ad hoc file analysis, pre-specified data aggregations, estimation of decision consequences, and propose or make decisions. Conventional EDP systems range from data-oriented to model-oriented and typically perform only standardized reporting functions.

Seven types of decision-oriented reporting systems are in existence including retrieval only, retrieval and analysis, multiple data bases plus analysis, decision evaluation (accounting models, simulation models), proposing decisions, and making decisions. Decision-support systems (in addition to standard EDP system goals) seek to improve managerial communication, facilitate problem-solving, promote individual learning, and increase organizational control. These systems also provide ammunition for personal persuasion and common negotiation bases, assisting managers in making and communicating decisions regarding tactics and strategy.

Davis points out that comprehensive and accurate requirements determination is essential in planning and implementing information systems applications. The three major difficulties in determining information requirements, including human information processing constraints, information requirement variety and complexity, and user-analyst interaction complexities, suggest several general strategies for determining information requirements that can be tailored to fit the specific conditions that exist.

Information requirements should be determined at two levels—overall information structure and detailed individual applications—with the scope and detail of the requirements and methods used differing at the two levels. A master development plan can be used to establish an overall information system structure, a comprehensive applications portfolio, clearly defined application boundaries, orderly application development, and data requirements for shared data bases.

The ability of humans as information requirements specifiers is limited by human capacity restrictions, human bias in data selection and use, and human problem solving behavior. Short term memory limitations, excessive use of adjustments from anchor points, a bias toward current information, over reliance on concrete data, incorrect inferences from too small samples, and bounded rationality are especially troublesome problems. The characteristics of utilizing systems and applications as well as the relevant experience of the user/developers are system or application dependent characteristics which affect the determination of requirements. Information determination requirements should assist systems designers in limiting and structuring the problem space, facilitate search efficiency within problem boundaries, aid in overcoming human biasing factors, and ensure complete, correct requirements determination.

Common strategies for information requirements determination include asking questions, derivation from existing systems, synthesis from existing systems, synthesis from characteristics of utilizing systems, and experimentation evolution from evolving systems. Some common asking methods include open or closed questions, brainstorming, and group consensus. Existing systems in using or other organizations, proprietary packages/systems, and literature descriptions are useful for deriving requirements in applicable situations. The characteristics of object systems that utilize the information provided by application systems are also a useful source of information requirements. Normative analysis, process analysis, strategy set transformation, and critical factors analysis are organization oriented approaches while decision analysis, socio-technical analysis, and input-output analysis are application oriented methods of deriving information requirements from object systems. An iterative, evolutionary discovery approach, which captures an initial set of requirements for system development, allows experimentation with a developing information system if conditions are appropriate for this method.

An effective procedure for strategy selection requires a contingency approach dependent on the environment and process of requirements determination in effect. The steps in this approach include identification of development process element characteristics that affect uncertainty (e.g., utilizing and application systems, users, analysts), evaluation of the effects of these characteristics on process uncertainty (i.e., requirements set stability, requirements specification ability of users, and analysts ability to uncover requirements), evaluation of the total effect of process and overall requirements uncertainties, selection of a primary requirements determination strategy, and choice of appropriate methods. Addition or reduction of uncertainty in the system development process is affected by the stability of system processes and management control, maturity in computer use, degree of applications complexity and integration, and experience of analysts and users in systems development.

Uncertainties with respect to requirements set stability, user requirements specification ability, and analysts requirements determination ability must be evaluated with respect to characteristics of utilizing systems, information system or applications, users, and analysts. Choosing a primary requirements determination strategy that takes these uncertainties into account indicates appropriate sets of methods and supplemental strategies most likely to be workable for given situations.

Footnotes

[1] See Andrew Vazonyi, " Decision Support Systems: The New Technology of Decision-Making," *Interfaces,* November, 1978, pp. 72–77 for a more complete discussion of this viewpoint.

[2] See E.D. Carlson, "Decision Support Systems: Personal Computing Systems for Managers," *Management Review,* January, 1977, pp. 4–11 for a more complete discussion of these ideas.

[3] See Steven Alter, "How Effective Managers Use Information Systems," *Harvard Business Review,* November-December, 1976, pp. 97–104 for further discussion of these important concepts.

1

BIT-BY-BIT: Toward Decision Support Systems

by Ralph H. Sprague, Jr. and Hugh J. Watson

About the authors:

Ralph H. Sprague, Jr. Professor and Chairman of the Decision Sciences Department at the University of Hawaii, recently spent his sabbatical year as Visiting Professor at Stanford University and Visiting Scientist at IBM Research Laboratory in San Jose. He has over fifteen years of teaching, research, and consulting experience in the information systems field. Much of his recent work deals with the development and evaluation of decision support systems.

Hugh J. Watson is a Professor of Management at the University of Georgia. His current research interests include computer simulation and computer-based information systems. He is a co-author of *Computers for Business: A Managerial Emphasis.*

Digital computers were first commercially introduced in 1954. Since that time computer technology and information systems performance have advanced spectacularly and seem certain to continue to do so. To managers and information specialists this rapidly changing field offers

Reprinted with Permission from California Management Review

tremendous professional, managerial, and organizational opportunities
—if they can stay abreast of it.

Around 1970 business journals began to publish articles on information systems whose characteristics and capabilities differed from
those of previous systems.[1] These systems could affect the management of many organizations, and managers should be familiar with
their capabilities, characteristics, design philosophy, elements, and
structure. We will refer to them as "decision support systems," (also
known as "management decision systems" and "strategic planning systems") since this terminology is frequently used and is a good description of the salient features of such systems. Consider a few examples.

- Getty Oil developed a Plan Analysis and Modelling System
  (PAMS) for use in supporting capital investment decision making.
  It allows managers to interrogate and analyze historical data with
  an Englishlike language, displaying the result in tabular or graphic
  form. The system also provides access to a large repertory of financial routines and models for generating future plans which are
  analyzed and displayed to aid in data decision making.[2]

- American Airlines developed an Analytical Information Management System (AAIMS) to support planning, finance, marketing,
  and operations functions. The system manages a large amount of
  historical data on the entire airline industry and provides managers with the ability to interactively access, analyze, compute,
  and display historical future data. It is used to facilitate studies
  and forecasts of load factors, market share, aircraft utilization,
  productivity measurement, and revenue/yield, among other
  things.[3]

- A large paper company has developed an interactive CRT based
  system for capacity planning and production scheduling. It is
  used almost exclusively by the chief analyst for the vice-president
  of production to create and evaluate alternative plans and schedules for all the production facilities nationwide. It draws on detailed historical data and utilizes forecasting and scheduling
  models to simulate overall performance under a variety of planning assumptions.

The above examples describe just a few of the systems for decision support that have begun to spring up in the literature. Evidence suggests

many firms are moving to develop systems such as these that have as their main focus the support of managerial decision making. In a recent survey 12 percent of the responding organizations reported the use of advanced systems that could be characterized as decision support systems (DSS).[4] A 1977 conference in California devoted to the presentation of implemented DSS drew an audience of over 200 to discuss eleven existing systems.[5] A study published that year described and classified fifty-six systems that support decision making.[6]

Although it is relatively easy to identify examples of such systems and describe their characteristics, it is much more difficult to define them and generalize their abilities in a way that will promote their development and use. The examples given above come from different industries and support different managerial tasks, yet they have some characteristics in common: They give managers access to a variety of data, facilitate the use of analytic techniques and models, and do so in a flexible, "fast response" manner to permit easy repeated use of the system. The nature of the systems performance in each of these three areas forms the basis of a descriptive model for decision support systems which can help assess their value to decision makers.

The inevitable problem with new terminology is that it means many things to many people. "DSS" is no exception. The definitions in recent literature cover a spectrum from narrow to broad. At the narrow end are those who say that a DSS is an interactive, computer-based system which supports managers in making unstructured decisions— decisions for which no procedure or structured approach has ever been defined. At the broad end of the spectrum, "Business computer applications can be stereotyped into two categories: electronic data processing (EDP) systems, and decision support systems (DSS). . . . EDP systems are designed to automate or expedite transaction processing, record keeping, and business reporting; DSSs are designed to aid in decision making and decision implementation."[7]

The first definition is too narrow, the second too broad. There are not enough computer-based systems that make a significant contribution to supporting unstructured decision making. There are too many systems making some kind of contribution to decision making, by producing a report on which managers base a decision, for instance. In neither case can we generalize from existing systems enough to be helpful in designing and developing new systems. The broad definition raises questions about the difference between DSS and management information systems (MIS), which for several years have been described as rising above mere processing of transaction data to serve the information needs of managers.

We propose a conceptualization of DSS in the middle range of the two extremes, a set of characteristics describing a DSS with a model classifying them. We hope to lend substance to the term DSS so that it does not become diluted to the point of uselessness or raise false hopes leading to the unfulfilled promises like those of the early days of MIS. We hope to give managers the ammunition to keep the systems designers and vendors honest—they owe us more than a new label or "buzz word"—and to show, by comparing existing systems with our model, where we should expect, even demand, improvements and additions to the systems claimed to be DSS.

INFORMATION SYSTEMS EVOLUTION

The evolution of information systems can be viewed in two separate but interrelated dimensions. The systems technology dimension identifies various computer generations based on attributes as computer speed, storage capacity, input-output speed, power of high-level languages, extent and speed of data communications, data-based management capability. "System performance dimension" refers to what is accomplished with the available technology, the types of tasks performed, the nature of the data base, the type of information generated, the use of decision models to provide information, and the organizational levels served by the information system.[8] The systems performance dimension can be divided into four levels: basic data processing systems, integrated data processing systems, management information systems, and decision support systems.

BASIC DATA PROCESSING SYSTEMS.

The most basic information systems perform only single data processing tasks. Each task is a self-contained job, like payroll. No common data base exists. A separate file is maintained for each job. The outputs from the information system are scheduled reports summarizing the transaction data that have been processed. These reports are available to all managerial levels but are of limited value to middle and top management because of the nature of their decision-making responsibilities (that is, management control and strategic planning). Typically, no decision support is available other than that derived from the summary reports.

INTEGRATED DATA PROCESSING SYSTEMS.

The integrated data processing stage sees the combination of data processing "jobs" into integrated "systems." Many of the tasks use more than one data file and the same input data are often used in more than one job. Almost all of the data processing activities still involve the processing of transaction data and the generation of reports that primarily support lower management decision making. Simple decision models, such as those for inventory control, are included in the information system at this stage.

MANAGEMENT INFORMATION SYSTEMS.

There are differences of opinions as to what constitutes these. Some view a MIS as a future integration of the processing of transaction data and the preparation of an expanded set of scheduled reports. Others believe a MIS should provide all organizational elements with the information needed to function effectively. What most people mean by a MIS is an information system with a partially integrated data base perhaps partitioned by major business functions like marketing, production, and personnel. Scheduled reports are supplemented by ones available on demand and serve the information needs of middle and top management. Attempts are made to structure appropriate information flows to upper management. Decision models are more common but they are usually "library programs" and not well-integrated into the information systems.

DECISION SUPPORT SYSTEMS.

In general these are information systems featuring an integrated system composed of decision models, data base, and decision maker to support decision making. T.P. Gerrity noted the growing thrust toward decision support in 1971:

To date, the primary impact of new information technology has been upon the lower levels and more structured tasks of the organization. There is, however, growing pressure to bring the power of the computer and management science directly to the aid of the decision maker facing complex and unstructured decision tasks. The aim is to develop Man-Machine Decision Systems (MMDS)—an effective blend of human intelligence, information technology and software (information processing techniques and management science models), which interact closely to solve complex problems.[9]

To support such systems, an enhanced data base, one which retains external and other internal data as well as transaction data, must be maintained. With such data available it is possible to "feed" the decision models embedded in the information system. These systems also contain mechanisms providing easy access to decision models and data base by the user.

TRENDS AND OBSERVATIONS

We recently conducted a nationwide survey to determine the state of information systems evolution in technology and performance dimensions.[10] Several observations and conclusions of that study are relevant here. Advances in one dimension must generally be accompanied by advances in the other for a sound evolution of information systems. Advances in systems performance have been more difficult than technological advances because they include changes in organizational structure and philosophy, revisions in personnel skills and attitudes, and a more sophisticated management. Additional advances in both dimensions will be required to move from a MIS which is based on integrated reporting and data base/data communication approaches, into a full decision support system.

Consider the technology of data bases and data communications (DB/DC) that seems to characterize much of the current advancement in the technology dimension. The DB/DC technology seems to be primarily concerned with:

- managing a large amount of data in physical storage;

- providing a variety of logical data structures independent of physical storage structure;

- supporting independence between data and applications programs to decrease programming maintenance and data redundance; and

- providing access to data in a flexible, user-oriented way, usually
  through a generalized report generator and information retrieval
  capabilities.

The DB/DC approach depends heavily on report generation and information retrieval for any advancement in systems performance. This
dependence is based on the implicit assumption that if the manager
can gain access to data to answer specific questions or can define a report to suit his needs and can get those answers or reports quickly, then
his decision-making needs have been met and the decisions are obvious.
This philosophy reflects the accounting-oriented, structured report
emphasis of much of MIS work. A system designed to improve management performance by supporting decision making must go further
than just providing access to data in a quick and flexible way. It must
provide a set of mechanisms for the use of models in the system that
draw on the data base and are closely integrated with it. It must provide a mechanism for the decision maker to interact with data and
models in a convenient, supportive manner. The DB/DC approach is
necessary, not sufficient, for decision support.

DECISION SUPPORT SYSTEMS

Decision support systems focus on the support of decision making
rather than the system of information flows and reports. These systems
consist of three major subsystems—a data base, a model base, and the
decision maker. Of primary importance is management of subsystems
and the interfaces between them, viewed here in terms of the capabilities of sophisticated software systems.

   The data base and model base are managed by software systems that
work closely together to facilitate the necessary flow of data. Both are
directed by a command language through a terminal that provides the
mechanisms by which the decision maker gains access to both data
and models, and manipulates them to support decision making. Figure
1.1 shows the three major components, software systems, and linkages.

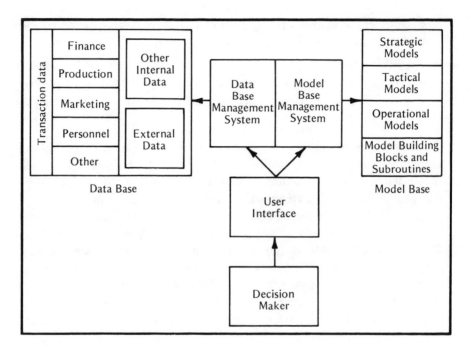

FIGURE 1.1 Components of a Decision Support System

THE DATA BASE SUBSYSTEM

The data base system consists of the data base and the software system for managing it. The capabilities of the data base management system will determine the characteristics of the data base itself. A data base that remains viable over time implies a network of data-gathering devices and communication linkages. Data must be captured at or near the source, transmitted to and stored in the data base. In most cases, communication linkages are also required from the data base to its ultimate destination, the decision maker.

The comprehensive data base for decision support must draw data from several sources. The traditional source is the basic data processing activities of the organization. Drawn from transactions processing, these data are usually summarized or compressed abstracts of the organization's performance at the operational level. Additional sources of internal data are also required. Subjective estimates from managers and engineering-related data are needed for some decision making but seldom available from normal data processing activities. Budgets, standards, and plans are important internal data, and external data sources are also needed, particularly for decision support at upper managerial levels.

To satisfy the retrieval and inquiry demands of a DSS, the data base must have a variety of logical structures. The record-oriented sequential file, the mainstay of data-processing systems for many years, is giving way to more complex structures that support multiattribute retrieval. In the molecular view of the data element or field, the data element is the building block on which logical structures are based. No longer does a set of data elements form a specific type of record in a specific file used by a limited number of computer programs. Instead, a data base is stored so it can be used in combination with others for many applications. The result is an integrated data base that is a general resource, drawn upon for reports, inquiries, and as input to decision models.

Like any other general corporate resource, the data resource must be carefully managed. The human functions of data base management are increasingly being performed by data base administrators. The software functions have been evolving with the development of data base management systems (DBMS). DBMS functions generally as generation, maintenance, access, and control.[11] Specifically, it creates, restructures and updates files, selects, retrieves and sorts data, and generates reports.[12] Discussions of the functions of data base management systems and the status of their development can be found in the literature.[13]

THE MODEL BASE SUBSYSTEM

The widely discussed disuse and misuse of models by managers[14] can often be traced to lack of a set of integrated models and an easy way to manage their use in the decision-making system. Lack of integration stems in part from the practice of separating management science and information systems groups in organizations.[15] A new approach to modeling rapidly gaining popularity includes managers using time-sharing, user-oriented languages to develop simple models which are subsequently refined. There are no high corporate models built from scratch, but small tentative models tested, integrated, revised and tested again. Through this approach "the manager is beginning to realize that the real value of the model comes not from must *using* it but from *creating* it."[16] The basic structure of this approach demands ways of supporting a large number of flexible, temporary models based on the current data base—a model base and a model base management system.

The models comprising the model base subsystem require comment. The rather inclusive DSS described here includes strategic, tactical, and operational models, also model building blocks and subroutines. The strategic models tend to be broad in scope with many variables expressed in compressed, aggregated form. Much of the data required to fuel the models is external and subjective rather than the familiar and readily available transaction data. The time horizons for the models are often measured in years, as are top management's strategic planning responsibilities. The models probably employ a numeric mode of analysis (such as with most simulation models), are probably deterministic, and are usually descriptive and custom-built for the particular organization.

The tactical models are commonly employed by middle management to assist in allocating and controlling the use of the organization's resources. The models are usually only applicable to a subset of the organization, like production, and there is some aggregation of variables. Their time horizon varies from one month to less than two years. Some subjective and external data is needed but the greatest requirements are for internal data. These models are much more likely to employ an analytic mode of analysis, are probably deterministic, are often used in optimality analysis, and are less likely than strategic models to be custom-built.

The operational models are usually employed to support the short-time horizon decisions (as those made daily, weekly) commonly found at lower organizational levels. These models normally use internal, objective data in their operation, are deterministic, and employ an analytic mode of analysis. They are often ready-built and used in optimization analyses. Table 1.1 illustrates the opportunities for strategic, tactical, and operational modeling.

In addition to strategic, tactical, and operational models for decision support, the model base contains model building blocks and subrou-

TABLE 1.1 Opportunities for Strategic, Tactical, and Operational Modeling

---

Strategic

Company objectives planning
Policy planning
Plant location selection
Environmental impact planning
Nonroutine capital budgeting

Tactical

Financial planning
Manpower requirements planning
Sales promotion planning
Plant layout determination
Routine capital budgeting

Operational

Credit scoring
Media selection
Production scheduling
Inventory control
Motion and time analysis
Quality control

---

tines from which other models can be constructed. Standard management science models such as linear programming and capital budgeting are included, as are traditional statistical routines like time series analysis, multiple regression, and analysis of variance. In form and size, these tools might range from a set of subroutines for use with a procedure-oriented language (IBM's Scientific Subroutine Package (SSP) in FORTRAN) to a set of self-contained programs with a common control procedure (the BMD package of statistical programs) to a large system for operating all models of a generic type (IBM's Mathematical Programming System (MPS)). These "packaged models" can be used separately for ad hoc decision support, or together to construct more comprehensive models.

The comprehensive set of models for decision support becomes a major corporate resource, just as the data base is a resource. Like the data base, this "model base" requires careful management. The parallels between these two resources and their management are quite extensive. Before the advent of data base management software, data files were defined for a specific purpose and used only by one (or a few) computer programs. This approach led to data redundancy and self-contained data processing jobs. Later evolutionary developments led to broader subsystems and shared data files, but it was not until the development of data base management systems that the full potential of the data base could be realized.

Without model management software, models have been built predominantly on a standalone basis for ad hoc decision analyses. The required data were defined and obtained to fit the model. Once built and used, the models were put on the shelf for future use. Not kept up-to-date, they were seldom used again. Evolutionary developments have seen the increased integration of models into information systems (as inventory models contained in an inventory management system). Recent developments have created broader model-based systems such as financial planning and forecasting systems. The realization of the full potential of a comprehensive and integrated set of models depends on the development of a model management software system.

The requisite functions of a model base management system (MBMS) are analogous to the functions of a DBMS as described earlier. They are:

- A flexible mechanism for building or generating models, perhaps through a type of model definition language.

- A way to redefine or restructure a model in response to changes in the modeled situation (as a change in the basic form of the model).

- A procedure for updating a model in response to change in data (as a revised parameter estimate without a change in structure).

- Operation of the model to obtain the decision support desired. Alternative forms include: periodic run of a well-established model, special results from an ad hoc model, the use of data analysis models, interactive rerun of a model or set of models, and the sequential run of a set of interrelated models according to a pre-defined procedure.

THE DECISION MAKER SUBSYSTEM

The view of the decision maker as an outsider using the system rather than a major subsystem of it often results in several shortcomings in perspective that affect DSS design. Too often systems designers focus on computer hardware and software to the exclusion of the decision-making tasks and the cognitive characteristics of the decision maker. There is usually an attempt to identify the system's requirement, but too little attention is paid to "ease the use" and other factors impor-tant if the user is considered part of the system.

Systems designers sometimes implicitly assume the decision maker acts alone. Few individuals charged with decision-making responsibili-ties operate without the advice and counsel of others. Often decision making is done by a group, a board or committee. The interaction of an individual decision maker with others is an important part of the decision-making process. More attention needs to be devoted to the decision maker, his tasks, cognitive preferences, abilities, and way of arriving at decisions, to the user as part of the system.

Two primary components of man-machine interface are the terminal device and the command language the user employs to interact with the system. Terminal device technology has advanced rapidly in the past few years. Today, visual display cathode ray tubes (CRT) are economical and common, though typewriter-like terminals still abound. The CRT, especially when equipped with graphic and color capabilities, is a po-tent element in aiding the decision maker in interacting with the DSS.

The command language allows the decision maker to gain access to and manipulate data and models in the DSS. It must be flexible enough to accommodate a wide range of decision-making styles, powerful enough to be human-oriented instead of computer or system-oriented. The command structure must be English-like to accommodate top managers lacking the knowledge or inclination to deal with computer languages, but must accommodate staff analysts working in finer de-tail. Ideally, the language would have the capability to run in "novice mode, expert mode, and programmer mode."[17] Finally, it must be hierarchical, with macro commands to choose which model to run, data to access, or procedures to implement. The net result is a language available to the full spectrum of decision makers from top-level managers to systems analysts.

CONCLUSIONS

The decision support systems described here have several important characteristics: a comprehensive data base and model base with a sophisticated software system for managing each, and a powerful command language to enable decision makers to interact with the data and models. DSS is still developing and though few existing systems possess all these features now, several are evolving toward such a structure.

Existing sytems have generally focused on one type of problem or decision-making situation which is more broadly defined than the typical decision model is built to serve. M.S. Scott Morton pioneered many of these ideas with his work on the design and testing of a manufacturing planning and control system.[18] (An extensive summary of this system and others appears in an important new book Morton coauthored with Peter Keen.)[19] Another popular target of DSS type systems has been financial planning and control, usually at the tactical level.[20]

Time sharing vendors are also beginning to recognize the importance of DSS. One system developed by Boeing Computer Services has many of the characterisitics in our DSS model. Called Executive Information System (EIS), it is one of the services on their time-sharing network, depicted as a set of six interrelated subsystems: report writing; graphics; financial applications; forecasting and statistics; modeling, what if, and simulation; and data base management. The first two subsystems allow the forematting of reports, graphs and charts in a flexible manner specified by the system's user. The third subsystem consists of a set of financial models such as capital investment analysis, purchase/lease analysis, and depreciation method comparison that can be used individually or incorporated in a more comprehensive user-written model. The fourth subsystem provides about the same kind of modeling capability as the third except it is for statistical models such as descriptive statistics, extrapolation based on constant or percentage changes over time, time series analysis, and analysis of variance.

The six subsystems fall neatly into the three major capabilities of the descriptive model. The third and fourth subsystems comprise the model building blocks and subroutines in our model base. The fifth subsystem consists of a modeling language, a set of commands to construct specific models, particularly suited to accounting models such as those generating pro forma financial statements, given forecasts and assumptions of sales and costs. This functions like the modeling language in the model-base management system. Finally, the data base subsystem manages a matrix-type data base to prepare financial reports by product, region, and branch, and for each of many time periods. The user accesses this integrated set of functions through a terminal, either typewriter or screen-type, using a high-level "language" corresponding to the command language in our conceptual framework.

Similar systems available from other time-sharing vendors also perform some of these functions. FOCUS is a language which emphasizes data retrieval and report formatting. EXPRESS is a language strong in creating customized user models. IBM helped develop a system at First National Bank of Chicago, now offered as a program product under the name TREND ANALYSIS/370,[21] that is particularly strong in the retrieval and full color graphic display of data, weaker in model usage support and flexible definition of displays.

Most of the current systems still function as packaged computer programs that are broadly defined but not full-range DSS. There is as yet no linkage of these systems into a data base system. Data is generally defined and prepared specifically for each application. The models are narrowly defined, the linkages between them minimal, the revisions procedures ad hoc. The desirable functions of model base management are still in the primitive stages.

Still there is encouraging progress. Evolutionary developments moving toward the type of DSS described here are in effect and will soon create the type of system that truly approaches the objective of comprehensive information systems—to directly support the decision-making process at all levels and in all areas of the organization.

REFERENCES

[1] G. Boer, "A Decision Oriented Information System," *Journal of System Management* (October 1972), pp. 36–39; R.L. Ferguson and C.H. Jones, "A Computer Aided Decision System," *Management Science* (June 1969), pp. B550–B561; W.R. King and D.I. Cleland, "Decision and Information Systems for Strategic Plan-

ning," *Business Magazine* (April 1973), pp. 29–36; M.S. Scott Morton, *Management Decision Systems: Computer Based Support for Decision Making* (Graduate School of Business Administration, Harvard University, 1971).

[2] D.O. Cooper, L.B. Davidson, and W.K. Denison, "A Tool for More Effective Financial Analysis," *Interfaces* (February 1975), pp. 91-103.

[3] R.L. Klass, "A DSS for Airline Management," *Data Base* (Winter 1977), pp. 3-8.

[4] H.J. Watson, R.H. Sprague, and D.W. Kroeber, "An Empirical Study of Information Systems Evolution," *Proceedings,* Tenth Hawaii International Conference on Systems Sciences, Western Periodicals, North Hollywood, California (1977).

[5] E. Carlson (ed.), "Proceedings of a Conference on Decision Support Systems," *Data Base* (Winter 1977).

[6] S. Alter, "A Taxonomy of Decision Support Systems," *Sloan Management Review* (Fall 1977), p. 39-56.

[7] Ibid., p. 39.

[8] H.J. Watson, R.H. Sprague, D.W. Kroeber, "Computer Technology and Information System Performance," *MSU Business Topics* (Summer 1977), pp. 17-24.

[9] T.P. Gerrity, "Design of Man-Machine Decision Systems: An Application to Portfolio Management," *Sloan Management Review* (Winter 1971), p. 59.

[10] Watson, Sprague and Kroeber, op. cit. (reference 4).

[11] D. Lefkovitz, *Data Management for On-Line Systems* (Rochelle Park, N.J.: Hayden), Chapter 1.

[12] G. Davis, *Management Information Systems: Conceptual Foundation, Structure and Development* (New York: McGraw Hill, 1974), p. 298.

[13] R.G. Canning, "The Cautious Path to a Data Base," *EDP Analyzer* (June 1973); R.G. Canning, "The Current Status of Data Management," *EDP Analyzer* (February 1974); R.G. Canning, "Problem Areas in Data Management," *EDP Analyzer* (March 1974); R.G. Canning, "What's Happening with CODASYL-Type BBMS," *EDP Analyzer* (October 1974); R.L. Nolan, "Computer Data Bases: The Future is Now," *Harvard Business Review* (September-October 1973), pp. 98-113.

[14] R.H. Hayes and R.L. Nolan, "What Kind of Corporate Modeling Functions Best," *Harvard Business Review* (May-June 1974), pp. 102-112; J.D.C. Little, "Models and Managers: The Concept of a Decision Calculus," *Management Science* (April 1970), pp. 466-485; R.H. Sprague, "System Support for a Financial Planning Model," *Management Accounting* (June 1972), pp. 29-34; R.H. Sprague and H.J. Watson, "MIS Concepts Part I," *Journal of Systems Management* (January 1975), pp. 34-37.

[15] N.L. Chervany and W.C. Perkins, "Organizational Relationships Between Management Science and Management Information Systems: Some Empirical Evidence," *Proceedings, 7th National AIDS,* Cincinnati, Ohio (November 5, 1975), pp. 216–218.

[16] Hayes and Nolan, op. cit., p. 110.

[17] P.G.W. Keen, "Interactive Computer Systems for Managers: A Models Proposal," *Sloan Management Review* (Fall 1976), pp. 1–17.

[18] M.S. Scott Morton, op. cit.

[19] P.G.W. Keen and M.S. Scott Morton, *Decision Support Systems: An Organizational Perspective* (Reading, Mass.: Addison-Wesley Publishing Company, 1978).

[20] R.H. Sprague, "System Support for a Financial Planning Model," *Management Accounting,* (June 1972), pp. 29–34.

[21] D. Nash, "Building EIS, A Utility for Decisions," *Data Base* (Winter 1977), pp. 43–45.

2

A Taxonomy of Decision Support Systems

by Steve Alter

About the author:

Steve Alter is a Professor at the University of Southern California.

INTRODUCTION

As evidenced by the title of a recent well-attended conference,[1] *decision support system* (DSS) is a buzzword whose time has arrived. Now that most corporations have survived the growing pains of learning to develop and use data processing systems, many of the most innovative new systems clearly fall under the general heading of decision support. Unfortunately, there is relatively little organized knowledge about DSSs. Although a certain amount of conjecture has been generated concerning the *nature* of decision support systems and the significance of various system characteristics, even the conjectures are often contradictory.

This article discusses a taxonomic scheme that was one of the main findings of an exploratory study of decision support systems[2] undertaken in response to this dearth of information. The purpose of the study was to gain a better understanding of the dynamics of these

Reprinted with permission from Sloan Management Review.

systems and the key issues leading to their success or lack of success. As will be discussed, one of the conclusions in this regard was that these key issues differ across various types of DSSs.

In embarking upon this research a definitional question arose immediately: What are decision support systems? How can they be recognized and distinguished from other systems? Taking the approach of looking first and defining later, the following general distinctions emerged. Business computer applications can be stereotyped into two categories: electronic data processing (EDP) systems and decision support systems (DSS). The main difference between DSS and EDP systems is related to their basic purposes. EDP systems are designed to automate or expedite transaction processing, record keeping, and business reporting; DSSs are designed to aid in decision making and decision implementation. While most DSSs are used to facilitate management, planning, or staff activities, EDP systems emphasize intrinsically clerical activities. Whereas the general orientation of EDP systems is toward mechanical efficiency, that of DDSs is more toward the overall effectiveness of individuals or organizations. The manner of usage is also quite different. Unlike the EDP user, who typically receives reports on a periodic basis, the DSS user often initiates each instance of system use, either directly or through a staff intermediary.

Although the DSS vs. EDP dichotomy is weakened by overlaps due to the multiple purposes and orientations of many systems, implementers and users who participated in the study had no real difficulty in identifying DSSs used in their organizations. Starting with detailed case studies of eight systems[3] a sample of fifty-six DSSs was eventually compiled. The data used in the analysis consisted of mini-case studies of each of the systems. Each mini-case was a structured story of the system in terms of interview responses to questions under the following headings:

- General background,
- System history and characteristics,
- Types of use and impact,
- Limitations and types of disuse or abuse,
- Factors in favor of or opposed to getting started, and
- Factors in favor of or opposed to successful implementation.

As the sample grew, it became increasingly clear that the *decision support system* is not a homogeneous category. Quite to the contrary, many of the systems in the sample differed vastly in what they did and how they did it. This led me to wonder why people who talk about DSSs often seemed to talk about DSSs *in general*. It appeared that this was much like talking about pets in general, without distinguishing between dogs and cats and piranha fish and turtles. I concluded that one of the main products of the research should be a taxonomy of decision support systems which differentiated the sample in a useful and understandable manner.

A first step in attempting to develop such a taxonomy was to examine the usefulness of commonly used system-labeling schemes such as:

- *Functional Area:* marketing, production, finance;
- *Decision Perspective:* operational control, management control, strategic planning;[4]
- *Problem Type:* structured vs. unstructured;[5]
- *Computer Technology:* interactive vs. batch;
- *Modeling Approach:* simulation vs. optimization.

Unfortunately, few significant conclusions seemed to emerge when the systems in the sample were grouped in terms of these schemes. For instance, financial projection systems for operational planning seem very similar in concept and structure to several systems for strategic planning. Likewise, the significance of interactive computation seemed to diminish greatly when decision makers were not hands-on users of systems. Difficulties in deciding whether one repetitive business problem was more versus less structured than another also reduced the usefulness of that distinction.

A TAXONOMY OF DECISION SUPPORT SYSTEMS

The taxonomy that seemed most useful in categorizing the systems in the sample was based on what can be called the *degree of action implication of system outputs* (i.e., the degree to which the system's outputs could directly determine the decision). This is related to a spectrum of generic operations which can be performed by decision support systems. These generic operations extend along a single dimension ranging from extremely data oriented to extremely model oriented:

- Retrieving a single item of information,
- Providing a mechanism for ad hoc data analysis,
- Providing prespecified aggregations of data in the form of reports,
- Estimating the consequences of proposed decisions,
- Proposing decisions, and
- Making decisions.

The idea here is that a decision support system can be categorized in terms of the generic operations it performs, independent of the type of problem, functional area, decision perspective, etc.

Clustered from this viewpoint, the fifty-six systems in the sample fell into seven reasonably distinct types which can be labeled as follows:[6]

File drawer systems allow immediate access to data items.

Data analysis systems allow the manipulation of data by means of operators tailored to the task and setting or operators of a general nature.

Analysis information systems provide access to a series of data bases and small models.

Accounting models calculate the consequences of planned actions based on accounting definitions.

Representational models estimate the consequences of actions based on models which are partially non-definitional.

Optimization models provide guidelines for action by generating the optimal solutions consistent with a series of constraints.

Suggestion models perform mechanical work leading to a specific suggested decision for a fairly structured task.

Figure 2.1 illustrates that this taxonomy can be collapsed into a simple dichotomy between data-oriented and model-oriented systems. Such a simplification loses a great deal of information, however, by grouping systems which differ in many significant ways.

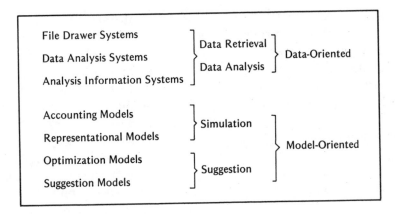

FIGURE 2.1 Data-Oriented vs. Model-Oriented Decision Support
System Types

Each of the seven types of DSS will be discussed briefly with refer-
ences to specific examples. The last section of the article will summarize
some of the differences in key issues across the various types.

FILE DRAWER SYSTEMS

File drawer systems are basically mechanized versions of manual
filing systems. The purpose of file drawer systems is to provide on-line
access to particular data items (e.g., status information concerning
entities ranging from overdue invoices and available seats on future
airplane flights through inventory items, stock portfolios, lots flowing
through a shop, etc.).

System A1 is a CRT-based inventory control system used in manufacturing complicated, high technology hardware on a one-of-a-kind
basis. Since a single missing part can halt the progress of this complex
assembly process, it is very important that the location and status of
all available parts are known at all times. In addition to day-to-day
use in finding and reallocating parts, the system is used by plant
management in a weekly meeting. At this meeting the current needs
of various projects are examined, and existing inventory is reallocated
or transferred from project to project to expedite a smooth work flow.

System A2 is a CRT-based shop floor information system which tracks the flow of production lots of integrated circuits through a manufacturing process which involves over fifty steps and suffers from a serious yield problem. The input to the system consists of daily work reports submitted by operators. The system stores this information and maintains a history of each lot by step. Included are the yield, the release date, identification of the person who did the work, and so on. In addition, various aggregations of productivity data by operators and by lot are provided. The data is accessed by means of thirteen standard retrieval commands. The system is used by section chiefs to monitor work flow and to detect yield problems and production bottlenecks.

Typically, the hands-on users of such systems are nonmanagerial personnel ranging from clerks to foremen who use the system to support their day-to-day operational tasks. The concept is a very simple one: people performing ongoing operational tasks should have immediate access to the information they need, and should be able to obtain the most current version of that information. In some cases, it is proprietary commercial information to which access is sold (e.g., commodity and service trading systems which provide availability information concerning ships for charter, lumber in stock, apartments for rent, etc.).

DATA ANALYSIS SYSTEMS

Data analysis systems are generally used by nonmanagerial line or staff personnel in analyzing files of current or historical data.

System B1 is a CRT-based analysis system in a bank. It is used by division comptrollers to generate customized monthly variance reports which are used in budget control sessions with responsible cost center managers. By allowing these comptrollers to screen, analyze, and annotate budget variances before they are sent to cost center managers, the system expedites the budget control process and facilitates communication between the involved parties. This system also contains planning aids which help division planners generate their one-year and five-year budgets by doing simple projections, comparisons, and extensions of line items.

System B2 is a generalized financial analysis system which is basically an interpretive language for use by financial analysts. It is used in an oil company to analyze investment opportunities and to consolidate plans at the corporate level. The purpose of the system was to improve upon a disorderly series of programs which did particular calculations and consolidations. It replaced all these programs with a unified system which could handle most financial analysis needs and which would produce reasonably consistent reports.

The data analysis systems in the sample fell into two categories: *tailored analysis systems* and *generalized analysis systems*. Tailored analysis systems are designed specifically to meet particular analysis requirements related to a definite job or task. The data in these systems is often historical, although current status information may be included. These systems allow analysts to manipulate the data and to produce analysis reports on an ad hoc basis. Generalized analysis systems are specialized programming languages whose purpose is to allow users to perform fairly general kinds of analysis of data bases and to program simple models. Such systems are viewed as off-the-shelf tools for use in many settings. Given a data base in an appropriate format, some of these systems provide the user with the capability to analyze the data by means of operations such as data retrieval, pictorial representation, summarization of the data, and calculations. Others are oriented more toward facilitating the creation of simple models. Unlike tailored analysis systems which address the special analysis needs of particular tasks, generalized analysis systems are designed to be readily transferable and relatively context free. The border between file drawer systems and tailored analysis sytems is fuzzy. Although there exist systems whose sole purpose is the retrieval of data items and other systems whose sole purpose is the analysis of files of information, systems also exist which attempt to serve both functions.

ANALYSIS INFORMATION SYSTEMS

Throughout the first twenty years of computer-based *management information systems*, one of the most common complaints was that these systems simply were not flexible enough to satisfy the changing information needs of managers. Typically, such management information systems were basically transaction processing and record keeping systems. Although these systems could be used conveniently to generate standard periodic reports, their requirements for efficiency precluded the generation of management information relevant to decisions or situations whose essential components varied over time. The purpose of *analysis information systems* is to provide management information through the use of a series of decision-oriented data bases and small models.

System C1 is a growing marketing information system in a consumer products company. Its data bases include internal sales, advertising, promotion, and pricing data, plus a number of proprietary marketing data bases which are purchased from marketing research firms. The system is used by staff personnel for many types of ad hoc reporting. In addition, it is used by a research group in developing methodologies for forecasting sales and analyzing the effectiveness of competitive actions. The data is accessed through a report generator and a statistical package.

System C2 is a sales analysis system developed at an industrial equipment company. In addition to detailed sales data, it contains internally generated and purchased information about customers and potential customers, plus forecasts from industry sector economic models. It is used for product planning through the development of growth forecasts by industry sector, and of corresponding forecasts for product growth within industry sectors. Viewed by its originators as a tool kit of data and small models for the purpose of supporting planning, an attempt is made to limit the system's use for day-to-day reporting and analysis.

The basic idea underlying these analysis information systems is to recognize the incongruities between transaction processing systems and decision-oriented information systems, and to proceed accordingly. Analysis information systems are designed to extract relevant data from EDP systems and to augment this data with external data. By maintaining this type of analysis data base, it is possible to access that data freely and without being constrained by the operational requirements of scheduling and running a large-scale corporate data center efficiently. In some cases, such systems are basically vehicles by which a staff man or staff group tries to have an impact on the ways in which decisions are made. The *modus operandi* is highly incremental: start with an existing data base and set of models, identify a new business problem, develop a solution that extends the system, and use the credit gained to expand the scope of future efforts.

ACCOUNTING MODELS

Accounting models use definitional relationships and formulas to calculate the consequences of particular actions.

System D1 is a voyage profitability estimator used by a shipping company via time sharing. This program performs a standard profit calculation which is used to decide what charter rate should be charged for a particular voyage. The formula that is used involves ship and voyage characteristics including tonnage, speed, rate of fuel consumption, port costs, and so on. Because much of this data is stored in advance, what formerly required fifteen to twenty minutes of calculations now requires three to five minutes of specification using the terminal. In addition to merely saving time, this makes it possible for charter clerks to explore tradeoffs between speed and fuel consumption.

System D2 is an on-line source and application of funds budget used for operational decision making and financial planning over a two year horizon in an insurance company. The inputs are cash flow projections from various lines of insurance and investment areas. The output is an overall cash flow by month. The system output is used at weekly meetings of an investment committee to help in allocating funds across investment areas and to minimize the amount of cash that is left idle in banks.

The accounting models in the sample were used to facilitate planning by generating estimates of income statements, balance sheets, or other outcome measures. The inputs to these systems were estimates by business unit (product, department, etc.) of various elements of costs and revenues. Using accounting definitions and estimated line items rather than actuals, these systems performed the kinds of extensions and additions that are performed by a clerk or a computer in producing a business statement. Such systems contained little or no sense of any mechanism whereby the firm's actions are related to outcomes in the market. For instance, it was typical to use sales as a fixed input rather than as a function of price or other competitive actions. On the other hand, one of the key attributes of these models was their understandability by managers.

REPRESENTATIONAL MODELS

Representational models include all simulation models which are not primarily accounting definitions (i.e., which use at least partially nondefinitional relationships in estimating the consequences of various actions, environmental conditions, or relationships). Whereas an accouting model might start with product sales and prices that were determined external to the system, a representational model might start with only price and then calculate sales based on a model representing the causal mechanism by which price determines sales. On the boundary between accounting definitions and representational models are sytems such as E1—some of whose statements are definitions, while others are cost accounting approximations to the relationships between variables.

System E1 is used by a large chemical company to simulate and cost out flows of materials among a hierarchy of mining sites, production facilities, inventory depots, and sales locations. The purpose of the model is to provide a quick and reliable method for evaluating a variety of yearly budgeting alternatives at a variety of planning levels. Based on individual models of each point in the flow pattern, the system calculates volumetric outputs and costs which are then aggregated upward. This helps rationalize the development of yearly budgets by allowing management to examine the profit impact of alternatives involving changes in volumes, prices, distribution patterns, production costs, transportation modes, inventory levels, raw materials sources, etc.

System E2 is an aggregate market response model which relates levels of advertising, promotions, and pricing to levels of sales for a particular brand. The model is used by a consumer product company to track the marketplace and the effects of competitive actions. The model was developed in a team setting by reconciling an analysis of historical information with individuals' subjective opinions concerning response parameters.

It is possible to classify simulation models in terms of the uncertainty inherent in the relationships in the models themselves. Thus, simulation models can be viewed along the following dimension: (1) accounting definitions, (2) models in which the form of the relationship is accurate while parameter values may be inaccurate, and (3) models in which the form of the relationship may not be a good representation of the underlying process. Clear-cut accounting models are on one end of the spectrum, and representational models are on the other end. Many models fall between the two extremes.

The location of a model along the above continuum has many implications for its potential usefulness and acceptance. Accounting models are typically viewed as specialized adding machines that perform calculations a person would otherwise perform manually. Much of the effort in building such a model involves the clarification of accounting definitions and relationships that are internal to the company. On the other hand, representational models are frequently viewed as attempts to develop an understanding of the possible relationship between future actions and future outcomes. Much of the effort in building these models involves the creation of approximate relationships that attempt to roughly describe the linkages between actions and outcomes. In using an accounting model, the accuracy of the model itself should not be an issue; rather, the main questions should concern the quality of the estimated values provided as inputs. In using a representational model, one of the main issues is whether or not the model is a reasonable representation of the situation being studied. At the same time, an important part of the benefit of such a model comes from the increased understanding that is gained by trying to develop explicit relationships describing how part of the business environment works. Related to accuracy, but only partially, are the credibility and acceptance of a model. In many cases, representational models tend to have credibility problems. Because they are approximations, it is often possible to question important relationships and to wonder whether these relationships produce misleading results. At the same time, however, representational models that pass the test of credibility can be a very valuable source of understanding concerning the interaction between internal and external forces in the future.

OPTIMIZATION MODELS

Optimization models are used in studying situations that can be described mathematically as complicated puzzles whose goals involve combining the pieces in a way that attains a specific objective such as maximizing profit or minimizing cost.

System F1 aids in determining the start dates of three-week, twenty-member training classes in a training school for personnel who exhibit a high attrition rate. The inputs to the model include the company's forecasted service demands, current staffing levels, the acceptance level of shortfall during peak periods, and so on. Constrained by these inputs and some complex rules concerning consecutive start dates and school administration, the system uses a smoothing algorithm to generate a set of start dates with relatively (although not necessarily *optimally*) low cost. The system is used iteratively in developing an understanding of the effect on the current year's plan of potential modifications in policy inputs such as the maximum shortfall acceptable during peak periods.

System F2 was a linear programming model used by a consumer products company faced with short-run supply problems. For many of the raw materials the company used, both availability and supply had suddenly begun to fluctuate. One way to make the best of a bad situation was to respond to these fluctuations by adjusting product recipes in a way that met production requirements at minimum cost. It took a staff analyst two weeks to set up a small linear programming model that produced an optimal set of product recipes based on somewhat simplified assumptions concerning the flexibility of production facilities. The system was used sporadically over the course of a year as a way of providing guidelines for production adjustments.

The systems classified here as optimization models are used as analysis tools rather than as a way of generating a definitive answer that can be acted upon directly. In other words, this approach for supporting decisions can be used in situations that have enough structure to develop an optimizating model than can be used as part of the analysis. Many applications of optimization techniques such as linear programming are of this type. There are other types of applications, however, in which there exists enough structure that a model can produce a direct suggestion of action. These models will be described in the next section.

SUGGESTION MODELS

Suggestion models generate suggested actions based on formulas or mathematical procedures which can range from decision rules to optimization methods. The purpose of such systems is to expedite or bypass other procedures for generating the suggestion. In a sense, suggestion systems are even more structured than optimization systems, since their output is pretty much *the answer*, rather than a way of viewing tradeoffs, the importance of constraints, and so on.

System G1 performs some complicated calculations which are needed in adjusting the rates on particular group insurance policies based on the historical relationship between premiums and claims for those policies. The system was developed to eliminate part of the clerical burden associated with renewal underwriting and to help assure that rate calculations are consistent and accurate. Using the system has become part of the job of a large number of underwriters in an insurance company. Instead of calculating renewal rates by hand and in a relatively undisciplined manner, the underwriter fills out coded input sheets for the system, which calculates a renewal rate under a series of standard statistical and actuarial assumptions that may or may not apply to the policy. Upon receiving the output, the underwriter reviews the accompanying documentation and decides whether these calculations correctly represent the situation. If not, the coding sheet is modified in an appropriate manner and resubmitted.

System G2 was used to expedite the assembly of a standard piece of electronic equipment over the course of a one-year production contract. Each unit of equipment contained ten diodes, each of which had a particular resonant frequency. Due to problems in producing the diodes, this measurable frequency varied from one diode to the next. Due to peculiarities of the electronics, 200 among the millions of different combinations of diodes of particular frequencies could be used in any unit of the equipment. The weekly input to the system was the inventory on hand of each type of diode. Using linear programming, the system maximized the number of units produced with this inventory. The output of the model fed a program which generated a separate circuit diagram for each unit to be assembled. In this way, a complicated manual matching problem (analogous to little league scheduling) was automated.

The suggestion models in the sample were a potpourri of applications which had a single common theme (i.e., performing a calculation whose output was a specific recommendation for action). These applications differed greatly in impact and significance. The user of an optimal bond bidding model stated that it had increased the profits of his bank because neither he nor any other person could possibly match the model's performance in generating solutions to an intrinsically combinatoric problem of choosing bond coupon rates which satisfy a series of complicated constraints at minimal cost to the bond underwriter. The developer of a system which calculated rates for group insurance policies felt that this system had probably saved money by preventing rate errors which had occasionally gone unnoticed. The implementer of a system which forecasts production requirements by product line and type felt that this system had an important impact on production planning since only very aggregate forecasts had been available previously. On the other hand, most of the remaining suggestion systems in the sample had their primary impact through saving time and/or aggravation by allowing someone to avoid spending several hours each week doing a task manually (and somewhat less optimally).

COMPARATIVE FINDINGS

By merely asking what type of operation a decision support system performs, it was possible to classify each of fifty-six DSSs into one of seven categories. The categories range from type A, systems whose basic purpose was to retrieve simple aggregations of raw data, through type G, systems whose basic purpose was to suggest actions based on formulas or mathematical procedures. Aside from performing different types of operations, do the various types of DSS actually differ in significant ways?

Figure 2.2 summarizes some of the important characteristics of the systems of each type encountered in the sample. Each entry in Figure 2.2 is an attempt to describe in a single qualitative phrase the commonalities or predominant values of each characteristic within the systems of each type. (The sample contained seven, eight, three, eleven, six, and nine mini-cases of systems in categories A through G respectively.) Without getting into an elaborate methodological discussion, there is clearly some question of whether or not these mini-cases constitute a sufficient basis for generalizations by type. On the other hand, many of the commonalities by the system type in the data were relatively striking (e.g., in many instances, most or all of the occurrences of a particular problem were within one type of system or two types with a similar characteristic).

To the extent to which its summary characterizations are accurate, Figure 2.2 indicates that systems of various types do differ in many significant ways. Consider, for instance, the notion of the *key role* in

CHARACTER-ISTICS	DECISION SUPPORT SYSTEM TYPES						
	A FILE DRAWER	B DATA ANALYSIS	C ANALYSIS INFORMATION	D ACCOUNTING	E REPRESEN-TATIONAL	F OPTIMIZATION	G SUGGESTION
TYPE OF TASK	operational	operational or analysis	analysis	planning	planning	planning	operational
HANDS-ON USER	non-managerial line personnel	non-managerial line personnel or staff analyst	staff analyst	staff analyst or manager	staff analyst	staff or nonmanagerial line personnel	nonmanagerial line personnel
DECISION MAKER	non-managerial line personnel	non-managerial line personnel manager, or planner	manager or planner	manager, planner, or line personnel	manager	manager or nonmanagerial line personnel	nonmanagerial line personnel

FIGURE 2.2 Characteristics of Particular Decision Support System Types

CHARACTER-ISTICS	DECISION SUPPORT SYSTEM TYPES						
	A FILE DRAWER	B DATA ANALYSIS	C ANALYSIS INFORMATION	D ACCOUNTING	E REPRESEN-TATIONAL	F OPTIMIZATION	G SUGGESTION
KEY ROLE	hands-on user	hands-on user	intermediary	intermediary, feeder	intermediary	intermediary	hands-on user
KEY USAGE PROBLEM	user motivation and training	can people figure out what to do with the system	how effective is the intermediary	integration into planning process	under-standing	understanding	user motivation and under-standing
SYSTEM INITIATOR	managerial	entre-preneurial	entrepreneurial	user or managerial	entre-preneurial	mixed	mixed

FIGURE 2.2 Characteristics of Particular Decision Support System Types (continued)

CHARACTERISTICS	DECISION SUPPORT SYSTEM TYPES						
	A FILE DRAWER	B DATA ANALYSIS	C ANALYSIS INFORMATION	D ACCOUNTING	E REPRESEN- TATIONAL	F OPTIMIZATION	G SUGGESTION
KEY DESIGN IMPLE- MENTATION PROBLEM	defining the data; procedural changes	deciding how to use system; assessing impact on decisions	focusing usage and develop- ment; control mix of projects	getting people to participate seriously in planning process	richness vs. understand- ability	richness vs. linearity and understanding	designing rules sensibly
KEY CHANGE ISSUE	changing in- formation sources and procedures	unfreezing job image and way of approach- ing prob- lems	using system as a vehicle for change	unfreezing procedures people are familiar with	unfreezing ways of approaching problems	unfreezing ways of approaching problems	unfreezing standard procedures; avoiding a fear reaction
KEY TECHNICAL PROBLEM	system crashes; re- trieval from large data base	flexible retrieval from broad data base; generality vs. power	flexible retrieval from broad data base	checking con- sistency of intention, meaning of numbers	modeling technology	modeling and solution technology	task modeling

FIGURE 2.2 Characteristics of Particular Decision Support System Types (continued)

successful system usage. Since the planning and analysis systems (C through F) were often used through intermediaries who structured and performed much of the analysis, the success of these systems was especially dependent on the ability of the intermediary to maintain effective communication with decision makers. In the systems for operational tasks (especially A and G), intermediaries were not a main issue because the hands-on user was the decision maker.

The key usage problem varied greatly across the sample. In the systems for operational tasks (A and G), user motivation and training were major issues, especially since the system development efforts were often initiated by the user's superiors. In the data analysis systems (B), a recurrent problem was that system implementers and proponents incorrectly assumed that potential users would figure out how to apply the systems; in the more successful cases, either users were trained to use the system in a relatively repetitive manner or the implementers themselves were the users. For the representational and optimization models (E and F), the key impediment to successful usage was a lack of understanding of how the model worked and what it really represented. This was a direct consequence of the fact that the users of these models were typically intermediaries rather than decision makers.

Although the implementation patterns of the systems varied greatly, it was interesting that most of the data analysis systems, analysis information systems, and representational models (B, C, and E) were initiated by internal or external entrepreneurs. These individuals often found themselves in a position of attempting to sell their innovative ideas to managers and potential users. On the other hand, the need for most of the file drawer systems and accounting models (A and D) was identified by users or their superiors. One possible inference is that these latter types of DSS are more easily visualized and appreciated by nontechnical personnel.

Key design and implementation problems varied by system type. Since the file drawer systems (A) were all used by a large number of people, and often involved procedural changes in the way data was collected and reported on a day-to-day basis, the process of defining the data and handling the procedural changes was especially important. The data analysis systems (B) were typically viewed as a way of making it convenient to analyze specialized data bases. In addition to the previously mentioned problem of deciding how to use these systems in changing situations, it was often difficult to assess the degree to which the analysis had a significant impact on decisions. The analysis information systems (C) in the sample were entrepreneurial efforts that grew incrementally; a key issue noted by the developer in each case was that of focusing usage appropriately and controlling the mix of projects that were undertaken. The purpose of most of the accounting models (D) in the sample was to compute the combined result of planning inputs submitted by people in different parts of the company; a significant problem for these systems was to get people to participate seriously in the planning process by submitting numbers that were well thought out. The tradeoff between richness and understandability was a key issue for both representational models and optimization models (E and F); as these models became richer and more detailed, they also became more difficult to explain. For suggestion models (G), the key design issue was whether or not it was actually possible to develop a standard method or set of rules for computing a suggested decision. In half of the sample cases, the specification of the method was considered a major breakthrough.

Systems of different types brought different kinds of change. File drawer systems, accounting models, and suggestion models (A, D, and G) brought changes in organizational procedures and information handling methods. The successful use of data analysis systems (B) by line rather than staff personnel seemed to require major changes in the user's job image. The success of advanced models (primarily E and F) often required changes in the way people thought about situations and solved problems.

Finally, the main technical challenges varied in a manner quite consistent with the generic operation performed by the system. In the data-oriented systems, the main technical challenge involved attainment of an appropriate balance between flexibility and efficiency in retrieval from a data base. In model-oriented systems, developing the model itself was the main technical challenge since current modeling methods are insufficient for many types of analysis of the future.

CONCLUSIONS AND IMPLICATIONS

This article has attempted to support the hypothesis that a particular taxonomy is appropriate and useful. Since there is no statistical methodology for supporting such a hypothesis, the article has proceeded by proposing an organizing principle (generic operations), describing a taxonomy based on that principle, describing two examples of each type of system, and comparing the types of systems in terms of key characteristics. If it has been demonstrated that the taxonomy is an appropriate classification scheme, the question that remains is whether or why it is useful. I believe that the taxonomy is useful in a number of ways:

- As a guideline for designing systems,
- As a guideline for implementing systems, and
- As a framework for communication and research.

A GUIDELINE FOR DESIGNING SYSTEMS

One of the main implications of the taxonomy itself is that there are many different ways to use computers in supporting decision making. In designing a DSS, one of the first steps is to choose the type of system that will be developed. A potential use of the taxonomy is as a guideline in this process. In other words, a system designer might attempt to sketch out a system of each type as a potential *solution* to the *system design problem,* and would then combine the most useful features of each solution into his final design. Thus, the taxonomy would provide a substantive framework which would help in generating quite different approaches for supporting a particular decision. Whether this would actually be a fruitful exercise is a researchable question that has not yet been explored. Be this as it may, the sample did contain indirect supporting evidence in the form of several cases which at least suggest that the exercise of generating alternative designs might be useful. In one of these cases, a consultant felt very strongly that a representational model was needed for advertising decisions, whereas several users were more worried about the unavailability of data. After a period of trial and error, an effective procedure was developed in which a staff specialist provided briefings based in part on his use of a representational model (E) and in part on his use of a data analysis system (B). In another case, a plan to build a very expensive detailed simulation model (E) for raw materials allocation was abandoned when a staff man in a different department demonstrated that the same analysis could be done inexpensively with a rather simple optimization model (F). In a third case, a portfolio analysis system was installed to help portfolio managers think about portfolios from many different viewpoints (e.g., risk profiles, industry breakdowns, detailed sorted listings, etc.). After initial experience with this data analysis approach (B), it became clear that many portfolio managers wanted displays of what a portfolio would look like if particular decisions were made. To handle these *what if* inquiries, an accounting model (D) was added to the system. As a result, system usage increased. In all three cases, the consideration of different types of systems led to a better overall solution.

The taxonomy also provides insight for system user groups and system development groups concerning the types of systems that are currently installed and are on the drawing boards in their organizations. If none or few of the types of DSS are being used, the taxonomy provides a reference point in asking why existing applications encompass only a limited number of approaches for supporting decisions. One possible conclusion is that for this particular organization, computer-based decision support simply does not have high priority. Alternatively, the users may not be familiar with the different approaches that can be used, and the designers may have been reluctant to try to initiate types of systems that are new and untested in the organizational setting. The fact that most of the B, C, and E systems in the sample were initiated by internal or external entrepreneurs gives added credence to the notion that people whose main activities are not computer-related may have a very limited appreciation of how computers can aid in decision making. For these individuals, the taxonomy may be valuable as a framework for understanding the technical approaches that are or are not being suggested or used by resident systems groups.

A GUIDELINE FOR IMPLEMENTING SYSTEMS

The comparative findings in the previous section indicate that key implementation issues vary across the different types of DSS. These findings complement the growing body of knowledge concerning the general topic of implementation.[7] This knowledge is useful because it provides guidelines for implementers and alerts them to early warning

signals that may be symptomatic of incipient implementation difficulties. The comparative findings provide an additional framework for
anticipating and avoiding potential problems. For instance, while implementing a data analysis system, a designer should be especially
concerned about the user's willingness and/or ability to figure out how
to apply the system in novel situations. In developing an accounting
model, the implementer should put special effort into assuring that
the input estimates are well thought out. In developing a representational model or optimization model, the implementer should be concerned about possible misunderstandings of what the model means
and how it can or cannot be used.

Although it is obviously impossible to assure implementation success rates should benefit from organized knowledge about implementation if this information can be used to anticipate and avoid potential
problems. To the degree to which the various types of DSS really are
quite different, it is not only desirable, but also necessary to accumu-
late and analyze empirical data about the various types of systems.
From the viewpoint of the MIS or DSS researcher, a stronger restate-
ment might be as follows: unless taxonomies of this sort are taken
into account in the research design, contradictory or inconclusive results can be *expected* because taxonomic contingencies (rather than
noise per se) may well swamp the effects being studied.

A FRAMEWORK FOR COMMUNICATION AND RESEARCH

Finally, the taxonomy provides a framework for communication
and research. In light of the continual state of confusion that has sur-
rounded terms such as management information system (which usually
is not used by management), interactive system (which rarely interacts
with decision makers), distributed processing (which has many meanings currently), the need for understandable taxonomies in the computer applications field should be clear. The findings described here—
both the taxonomy itself and the fact that DSSs of various types differ
in many important ways—illustrate that the term *decision support
system* can have vastly different connotations for different people.
Consider, for instance, the respective viewpoints of a user of a file
drawer system and of a user of a very large optimization model. Whereas
the file drawer user might conclude that the essence of decision support
lies in on-line access to data, the optimization user might feel that on-

line access is completely beside the point since each run of his DSS might require two hours of preparation and setup. Rather, he would probably identify accurate and complete modeling as the key issue in producing a useful DSS. Although the opinions of both users might be appropriate with regard to their own systems, neither conclusion would be appropriate for all or even most DSSs. Thus, whether it is this particular taxonomy or another, a classification scheme for DSSs is needed merely to help users and implementers communicate their experience in this emerging area.

Footnotes

[1] Conference on Decision Support Systems, San Jose, California, January 24–26, 1977, sponsored by IBM San Jose Research Laboratory, Sloan School of Management, M.I.T., Wharton Business School, and ACM-SIGBDP.

[2] See Alter [2].

[3] See Alter [1].

[4] See Gorry and Scott Morton [3].

[5] See Simon [8], Gorry and Scott Morton [3], and Mason and Mitroff [5].

[6] Mason [4] describes a parallel but more abstract taxonomy suggested by Churchman.

[7] See [6], and Schultz and Slevin [7].

REFERENCES

[1] Alter, S. "Eight Case Studies of Decision Support Systems." Mimeographed. Cambridge, MA: Center for Information Systems Research, Sloan School of Management, M.I.T., 1974.

[2] Alter, S. "A Study of Computer Aided Decision Making in Organizations," Ph.D. dissertation, M.I.T., 1975.

[3] Gorry, G. A., and Scott Morton, M.S. "A Framework for Management Information Systems," *Sloan Management Review*, Fall 1971, pp. 55–70.

[4] Mason, R. "Basic Concepts for Designing Management Information Systems," In *Information for Decision Making: Quantative and Behavorial Dimensions*, compiled by A. Rappaport, pp. 2–16, Englewood Cliffs, NJ: Prentice-Hall, 1970.

[5] Mason, R., and Mitroff, I. "A Program for Research on Management Information Systems," *Management Science* 19 (1973): 475–487.

[6] "Special Issue on Implementation," *Management Science,* in press.

[7] Schultz, R., and Slevin, D. *Implementing Operations Research/Management Science,* New York: American Elsevier, 1975.

[8] Simon, H. *The New Science of Management Decision,* New York: Harper and Row, 1960.

3

Line Managers Move from MIS to DSS for Decision-Making Help

by John D. Baxter

Decision Support Systems are the 'in' thing as Management Information Systems seem to fade. In DSS, the line manager is 'king.'

Line managers who have been around long enough, remember the golden promises made to them back in the 60s that the computer was going to change their lives. It was going to completely change the way they managed their companies.

They were told that the age of push-button management was just around the corner.

Well, here it is in the early 80s, and push-button management is a long way off. Maybe, it is further off than ever. As one about-to-retire top executive noted recently, "Doing a good job of managing seems tougher than ever these days. Companies are more diversified, the economy is more jumbled, the constraints on management are tighter and the competition comes at you from more sides than ever."

So, where is that great promise and buzz word of the 60s—Management Information Systems (MIS)?

In a word, it seems to have flopped. As one information systems expert now puts it, "The MIS craze of several years ago ended—for all practical purposes—in expensive failure."

Reprinted with permission from Iron Age.

The key reason for the failure of MIS is cited by information systems consultant John M. Thompson.

"Initially," he says, "people looked at MIS as an outgrowth of the computer's transaction process function and experience—the automation of payrolls, accounts receivables, inventory controls and so on. The attitude was that a great pile of corporate data had been amassed, so why not have executives use it for managing.

"But," he adds, "this information simply was unsuited for management use in making decisions. Managers were left data rich and information poor."

Mr. Thompson is a vice president of Index Systems, Inc., a Cambridge, MA, consulting and systems development firm.

So, management today, in the opinion of a number of experts, instead of standing triumphantly atop a mountain of data with a clear overview and control of all company operations, finds itself buried under that very mountain of data.

"Suffocation by statistics" is the autopsy report on MIS made by one management systems 'pathologist.'

Where does all this leave management today?

Enter DSS—Decision Support Systems. DSS is now pushing onto center stage in the evolving drama of the computer in industry.

A skeletal description of DSS in practice is where a company line manager identifies for a data processing manager the most critical on-job decisions he makes. The data processing manager then sets up an on-line computer program of relevant information to specifically give support to the line manager in making those decisions.

Notably, DSS can help managers at all company levels and in companies of just about any size.

Is DSS just another buzz word, or another failure about to happen?

That's for managers in industry to determine—by testing in the field. That's where claims and performances are sorted out. That testing is now going on, and reportedly, is picking up steam. DSS use in growing, more companies are turning to it, and quite a few are said to be finding it a significant improvement over MIS in giving on-job, decision making support to line managers.

Thomas P. Gerrity, president of Index Systems, and one of the pioneers in the development of DSS at the Massachusetts Institute of Technology, says, "I have been involved in DSS for the past 15 years or so, but it is only in the last two or three years that it has really taken off. After a long, slow growth, it has suddenly gone straight up."

Mr. Gerrity explains that there is good reason for the recent surging in interest in DSS.

"The technology is there now," he says. This is in reference chiefly to distributed data processing (a network of local data processing terminals tied into a central computer), and on-line information capability (where a 'dialogue' between user and computer is possible).

"And very importantly," he adds, "the pressure has been mounting on managers to make sense out of the overwhelming amount of data they are buried under these days. The time for DSS is right."

Mr. Thompson defines DSS as "a blending of information technology and management judgment which provides an understanding and a decision-making capability better than either could reach independently."

The key point there, he stresses, is "decision-making capability."

Mr. Thompson quickly adds another key point: "DSS starts with the line manager and his job."

The consultant makes a quick sum-up of differences between MIS and DSS:

"MIS informs you about what **has** happened; DSS is a learning tool that helps a manager get a handle on what **is** happening in his particular area of responsibility. MIS is summary data; DSS is interpretive—what's going on **behind** the numbers.

"MIS is static—it consists of reports a manger uses every Monday morning. DSS is evolutionary—as a manager learns more of his job and the way he makes decisions, he changes the system. MIS tends to be internal—it looks at just internal company data and gives summary results. DSS looks at a blend of internal and external data."

The starting point in a DSS program in a company is indoctrination into such systems for those who are to take part in it.

Indoctrination in a company comes usually from a consultant or from an information systems specialist or manager who has had DSS experience or courses in 'B' schools or seminars.

Notably, a number of experts who have set up DSS programs in manfacturing plants stress that the task does not have to be costly and long-drawn-out. Too, they point out that results—at least on a limited basis—can be quickly realized. These points are so because it is possible—and often even preferable—to get into DSS in a toe-wetting prototype approach.

A man highly experienced in setting up DSS programs in manufacturing companies is Adam Crescenzi, a vice president of Index Systems. He notes that "very properly" the attitude of line managers he approaches on DSS is "show me first before I believe it."

In two recent DSS programs set up with his help in manufacturing operations, the first step was to build a prototype of a system.

"Prototype," he explains, "means something we can do rather quickly—a three or four-month time frame—so that we can see something working in the system. It may not be the ideal thing, but a line manager can actually interact with the data on the terminal and get out some useful information to support him in decisions he faces."

Mr. Crescenzi reports that both the line managers and the executives who have to approve budgets to cover DSS costs, like the prototype approach. Line managers, for their part, see some results quickly, and the budget-approvers are in a position to say, We are giving DSS a try, and at the least amount of cost. If we want to throw it out four months from now, we can throw it out and we haven't made too big an investment.

Many companies settle on the prototype. Mr. Crescenzi states that in the last two cases he used a prototype DSS approach in manufacturing companies, "the prototypes became the permanent systems." He adds that that is not unusual.

A key element in a company DSS program—following proper indoctrination by those who are to take part in it—is a meeting between a line manager and a representative from the company's computer services group. (See box here on the DSS cycle.)

The purpose of this meeting, and usually a number of others to follow, is to pinpoint those deicsions and goals most critical to the line manager's job responsibilities. Also pinpointed, is the information support needed by the line manager to help attain these goals. The essence of the meeting is in-depth questioning of the line manager by the data processing specialist.

There are variations in such meetings as to techniques used to uncover a line manager's goals and information needs. The consultants at Index Systems frequently use the popular interviewing method called, Critical Success Factors.

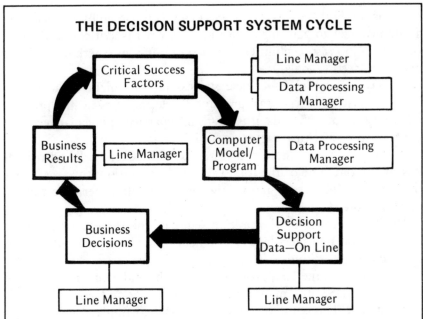

THE DECISION SUPPORT SYSTEM CYCLE

1. Line Manager and Data Process Manager (or other information specialist) confer. Data manager questions line executive in depth to assist that executive in pinpointing goals most critical to success of Line Manager's job. Also pinpointed, is the information support needed by the Line Manager to help attain these goals. (Typically, at start of a DSS program, a limited number of goals and data are sought.)

2. The Data Process Manager compiles needed information data and sets up a computer model or program for on-line access to that information by the Line Manager.

3. The Line Manager draws on the on-line computer model/program for decision support information as he requires it.

4. The Line Manager blends the decision support information now provided him with his judgment and intuition to make decisions relating to the critical success factors of his job.

5. Results of Line Manager's decisions are usually improved when he uses a soundly-conceived Decision Support System. The system, typically, evolves into a large, more comprehensive management tool as feedback from results of past decisions is evaluated.

The system is flexible: inputs are expanded or changed as critical success factors of Line Manager's job change.

NOTE: This is a highly simplified illustration of DSS and does not purport to include all the steps and procedures involved in developing a sound DSS program—ranging from setting of priorities to measurement of program costs and benefits.

"This method," explains Mr. Gerrity, "is triggered by interviewing a line manager to gain his or her idea on what is 'critical' to the success of his job responsibilities. It is a common-sense method of seeing needs and setting goals."

He says examples of critical success factors might include such things as pricing tactics, fast product development cycle and product reliability. In other words, it is anything a particular line manager may perceive to be a critical factor on his job.

"This method is simple and fast," says Mr. Gerrity. "And regardless of the outcome of the total DSS implementation, the fact is that the interview process is almost always a valuable experience for the parties involved."

Mr. Thompson adds that a knowledge of the three basic kinds of decisions that managers face can be helpful to those involved in DSS. (See box on basic kinds of decisions.)

Notably then, the DSS process starts with—and centers on—the line manager. In DSS, the manager is king, information technology is his silent servant. This is unlike the case in MIS where in-place technology—hardware and software—governs what is fed back to line managers.

A somewhat typical case might illustrate the DSS process.

The interview (line manager and data processing specialist) uncovers, that in the judgment of a line manager, pricing is a critical success factor. After agreement on the most pertinent data needed in making decisions on pricing, the data processing manager might then build a price-change program or model. This program/model might well be based on company sales, production and inventories following previous company price changes. Also included, might be data on competitors' prices following past company price changes.

This is, of course, a simplified DSS illustration. But DSS is not a greatly complicated technique. And it is flexible and evolves easily and naturally.

It is getting easier than ever for companies to get started on DSS. One reason is because of a fast-growing, commercially-available information and process information from that data into a computer terminal in what Mr. Thompson calls, "a very flexible and user-friendly way. You don't have to be a programmer to use it."

He also terms development of these program packages as "new and exciting." They have been available in most cases for less than a year.

BASIC KINDS OF DECISIONS

Structured Decisions—These largely involve situations where no choice, or very little choice or alternative, is possible. The decision situation here is largely self-evident once the facts and numbers are known. Managers make these decisions chiefly in areas of operations, rarely in cases of strategic planning. It is in dealing with the more highly structured decisions where MIS has been used mostly in recent years—"where a bunch of numbers crank out the answers," notes one information analyst.

Semi-Structured Decisions—These involve **both** data and a manager's intuition and judgment and are the kind most commonly faced by line managers. Examples: In operations control, decisions on expediting; in management controls, decisions on master scheduling; in strategic planning, decisions on optimum plant size and location. DSS can greatly assist line managers in making these kinds of decisions; MIS can help but little.

Unstructured Decisions—These involve no data reference source. They represent decisions based entirely on a manager's intuition and judgment. These kind of decisions are involved mostly in the area of company strategic planning, not often in areas of management operations and control. Line managers face unstructured decisions chiefly in dealing with people —workers, other managers, bosses and so on.

What is strikingly new, according to the consultant, is the rapid acceptance of these software kits. But he points out that these kits are not DSS. They are only tools to help a user to build a DSS program.

It is easy to see that the technologies and procedures of DSS could readily be expanded to cover aspects of management beyond decision-making. In fact, the original idea of those who pioneered DSS was a full management support system—MSS.

Says Mr. Thompson, "When we ask what are the critical things that a manager need support on, and what can we do to supply that support, that's management support, not just decision support." He sees DSS as "clearly, a sub-set of MSS.

"It depends on what a manager's job is, and what he needs for support," sums up Mr. Thompson.

So, start looking beyond DSS to MSS. That latter may be the ultimate blending of a manager's judgment and intuition and the power of the computer.

But still, push-button management is a long way off. Today, nobody is saying that DSS or MSS looks anything like a magic push-button. But those things can be a big help to managers.

4

Management Support Systems

by Arthur M. Geoffrion and Richard F. Powers

About the authors:

Arthur M. Geoffrion is professor of management at the University of California, Los Angeles.

Richard F. Powers is president of Insight, Inc., a management consulting firm based in Alexandria, Virginia.

Computers can help managers make better decisions more easily, but the road to a functioning management support system is fraught with peril.

United Airlines tried it and their salesmen's productivity went up 8 percent. The Kelly-Springfield Tire Company tried it and had direct annual savings of $8,4000,000. The R & G Sloane Manufacturing Company tried it and saw their profits go up 13 percent. Hunt-Wesson Foods, Inc., tried it and had annual savings in seven figures.

Reprinted with permission from The Wharton Magazine

Results like these are being achieved by a growing number of managers who are turning to *management support systems* to help to meet the challenges of their jobs. These systems integrate the modern capabilities of data sources, mathematical models, and computers into potent managerial tools.

Management support systems are being developed at a time of great managerial challenge owing to rapid environmental change and the increasing complexity of managerial decision-making. Today's manager must cope with such destabilizing influences as rapid technological change, inflation and monetary instability, rampant governmental intervention, and diminishing supplies of energy and natural resources, not to mention the parade of special problems to which any business is heir. An avalanche of pertinent data is available to most managers, but pervasive uncertainties and the sheer complexity of analysis seem to frustrate its effective use.

There is a clear and present need for more analytic and systematic methods of decision-making. Fortunately, the rapid advances being made in computer technology and in management science-operations research, and the increased receptivity to computers by today's managers, have been paving the way for the evolution of management support systems. These systems have been making great strides in spite of such deterrents as organizational inertia, cost, and fear of failure.

In broader terms, an historical process of profound significance to the world of management is under way: *Just as energy-driven machines augmented muscle power in the Industrial Revolution, so will information-driven management support systems increasingly augment brain power in the on-going Information Revolution.*

The Information Revolution has been widely noted as a hallmark of emerging postindustrial societies. Sociologist Daniel Bell puts it this way: "The crucial point about a postindustrial society is that knowledge and information become the strategic and transforming resources of the society, just as capital and labor have been the strategic and transforming resources of industrial society . . . the new information technology becomes the basis of a new intellectual technology in which theoretical knowledge and its new techniques (such as systems analysis, linear programming, and probability theory), hitched to the computer, become decisive for industrial and military innovation." One of the primary embodiments of this new intellectual technology is the management support system.

What exactly *is* a management support system? It consists of four components: *data files*, a *model*, a *solver*, and *interface facilities.* These must be integrated together within a unified framework, and organized so as to support managerial decision-making within a prescribed domain over an extended period of time. Some definitions are in order:

A *data file* is a list of related facts or data in computer-readable form. The data files needed for a management support system usually go well beyond what is readily available through standard reports and the existing computerized data base (if any). They can contain information like the selling price of a certain product, the number of pieces produced per hour, or the estimated setup time of a certain type of machine. The effort required to develop these files typically consumes the better part of the total effort needed to build a complete system.

A *model* is a careful description of a real system (that is, a portion of a company). It shows how, under trial assumptions, alternative managerial choices will influence system performance. The term "model" usually conjures up visions of mathematical symbols and computers, but models can also be described in conventional terms—narrative, diagrams, lists, and the like—for easy managerial understanding. For example, a statement like "Each month's ending inventory of each product equals the initial inventory plus production minus sales" is perfectly acceptable. A great many such statements typically will be necessary. Managers need not be concerned with the subsequent translation into symbols necessary to gain access to the power of mathematics and computers.

The *trial assumptions* mentioned above relate to factors that influence the relationships between managerial choices and performance measures; for example, the assumed cost of capital. *Managerial choices* are either decisions (like whether to build a new plant in Atlanta) or policies which guide decisions (like the level of customer service targeted for the Boston distribution center). *System performance measures* are the indices by which managerial choices will be judged (for instance, next year's after-tax profits).

Even the most perfect model will be useless unless a suitable *solver* is available to manipulate it. Model and solver go hand-in-glove. A solver is a computer program for exercising a model by executing any of a repertoire of commands.

The three principal types of commands, in order of increasing sophistication, are: *evaluate, satisfy,* and *optimize.* "Evaluate" means that the system performance measures are to be evaluated under fully specified managerial choices. This is also known as simulation. A "satisfy" command allows some freedom in the managerial choices, and directs that this latitude be used to satisfy stipulated conditions. "Optimize" takes "satisfy" to its logical conclusion by requiring, in addition, that a particular performance measure be driven to the best possible value (for example, minimum total system cost). This requires an optimization technique such as linear programming.

The more complex the model or the more sophisticated the command, the more advanced must be the solver technology for satisfactory performance. The technical difficulties involved can be awesome. Some of the most spectacular failures of management support systems over the years can be attributed directly to inadequate solver technology. These embarrassments, plus the intellectual challenge of the technical problems encountered in solver design, have spurred a great deal of research. Technical progress has been quite impressive over the decade, particularly in the area of optimization.

An *interface facility* is, from a manager's point of view, a means of communicating with the data files, the model, and the solver. It can be manual, computer-based, or a combination of the two. Such facilities enable the manager to communicate changes in trail assumptions or managerial objectives, to communicate commands to the solver, and to obtain reports summarizing the results derived by the solver. Usually there are also interface facilities that enable the support system to tap independently-maintained data sources elsewhere in the organization.

The management support system concept is related to two prior concepts still enjoying wide currency. One is the *management information system*, which usually consists of data files and interface facilities catering to the information needs of management. Models and solvers, as these terms are used here, tend to be absent or only implicit (for instance, they may take the form of essentially preprogrammed decision rules). The other concept, the *decision support system*, usually has the same four components as a management support system. The distinction is a matter of relative emphasis and intent. The decision support system tends toward descriptive models for analysis in an unstructured problem setting, whereas management support systems (as we define the term) tend toward prescriptive models for synthesis in a more structured problem setting.

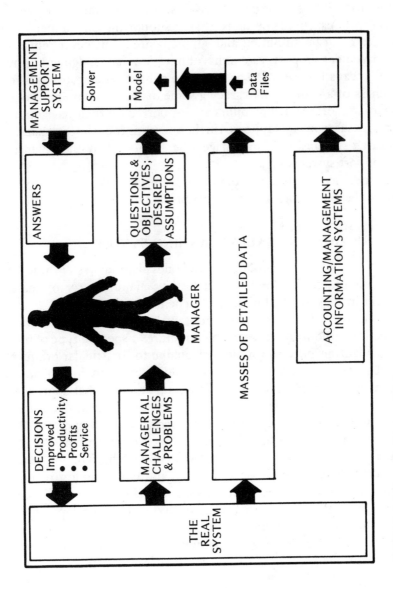

FIGURE 4.1 How the System Works

Figure 4.1 shows the components of a management support system (except for interface facilities) and also the role of the whole system as a tool for guiding managerial decisions. It is important to recognize that this role can never be more than a supporting one; a manager's capabilities can be amplified and supplemented, but never replaced. All management support systems have limitations, and judgmental powers will always be needed. The aim is to enhance the professional effectiveness of a manager by carrying some of the burdens and providing sharper tools. As airline pilots are supported by their navigational systems, as surgeons are supported in the operating room by their patient-monitoring systems, so can managers be supported by their management support systems.

Two specific cases drawn from our personal experience will serve to illustrate the definitions and concepts presented above.

A PRODUCTION AND SALES PLANNING SYSTEM

Our first example is the production and sales planning system at R & G Sloane Manufacturing Company, a leading manufacturer of plastic pipes and fittings for the building and chemical industries.

Each of R & G Sloane's several thousand different products is made by injection molding, a process which requires a specific type of mold base to adapt an injection molding machine to a particular product's mold. There are about ninety types of mold bases, a new copy of any of which may require several months to obtain at a cost that approaches the cost of a molding machine. Good utilization of the available mold bases as well as of molding machines is therefore very important. The basic problem is to plan the production, inventories, and sales of each product on a monthly basis over a twelve-month horizon in the face of seasonal demand, limited availability and compatibility of injection molding machines and mold bases, and various policy constraints imposed by management. The aim is to maximize total company profits over the planning horizon.

Several factors contribute to making this problem a very complex and difficult one:

- Sheer size, with thousands of different products to coordinate, a hundred machines and a few hundred mold bases;

- The influence of seasonality, which requires building pre-season inventories large enough to cover sales when demand outstrips production capability and yet not so large as to incur excessive investment and storage costs;

- The need to balance setup costs against inventory investment and storage costs—many short runs keep inventory levels down but incur high production costs, while long runs lead to low production costs but high inventory levels;

- The need to anticipate which mold bases and machine sizes will be heavily loaded at what times of the year, which makes it difficult to allocate them properly among competing uses; and

- The differences in profit contribution among products, which complicate the setting of production priorities and sales strategies when demand exceeds manufacturing capabilities.

A management support system was devised to deal with all of these complexities simultaneously. It has the four components mentioned earlier, each particular to R & G Sloane:

The *data files* are the joint responsibility of nearly every major functional department of the company, including cost accounting, customer service, data processing, industrial engineering, inventory control, marketing, scheduling, and tooling. Data are maintained on individual products (designated mold base type, parts per hour, standard cost, selling price, current inventory level, etc.), on molding machines (variable operating cost, uptime estimate, fixed overhead rate, etc.), on mold bases (setup time, machine compatibility, uptime estimate, etc.), on demand forecasts, inventory holding costs, setup costs, product lines, and a variety of other necessary details.

The *model* is equivalent to a large collection of simple statements like "The total production of all products requiring mold base type 109 in January is limited by the estimated availability of mold base by the estimated availability of mold base type 109." Altogether there are about 30,000 such statements involving 50,000 decision variables.

The *solver* was specifically designed and implemented to be able to optimize profits for this model. Technically, this requires the ability to solve routinely a mixed integer programming problem with about 12,000 integer variables.

Most of the *interface facilities* (for instance, programs to tap company files) are used by technical support personnel rather than by the managers themselves. Managers make their needs known to technically trained intermediaries who translate these needs into specifications for computer runs, make the runs, and assist in interpreting the results.

Most of the computer output is designed for direct management examination. The principal output reports are the master product schedule, master machine group schedule, cost summary, setup summary, inventory summary, and the master summary reports by product line and marketing division.

To illustrate: the master mold base schedule gives, for each mold base type for each month of the planning horizon, 1) the mold base days available, 2) mold base days used, 3) the percent utilization, and 4) for fully utilized bases, the marginal rate at which total profit is estimated to increase if availability could be increased.

The comprehensiveness of this support system makes possible a wide variety of uses. For production management it can perform a master scheduling function, allocate limited machine and mold base capacity, and plan seasonal inventories. For sales and marketing management it can allocate sales when the demand outstrips the capacity, support profitability studies, and illuminate the consequences of alternative product mix, pricing, and promotion strategies. And for investment and financial management it can facilitate the annual profit planning exercise, improve the management of assets, and help make decisions concerning the acquisition or sale of injection molding machines and mold bases.

The system has been in operation for more than two years and was recently noted in *Business Week.* The greatest difficulties experienced have been in routinizing the timely provision of necessary data, and in conceptualizing "what if" data scenarios at a sufficient level of detail and realism. The main benefits have come from improved inventory management, better resource utilization, and more timely decisions to buy and sell major assets. The vice-president of operations credits the system for an increase in operating profits during a recent year of 13 percent.

The distribution planning system at Hunt-Wesson Foods is the oldest support system with which we have been associated. It has been in regular use and in almost constant evolution for a full decade. Hunt-Wesson credits the system with achieving an ongoing annual savings of $3 million.

Hunt-Wesson Foods produces and nationally markets a broad line of canned goods and edible oil products. As with most food companies, distribution costs consume a substantial fraction of each sales dollar. This raises certain perennial questions, such as: How many distribution centers should there be, of what size, and where? Which customers should each distribution center service? Which plants should supply which distribution centers with which products? And how much of each product should be produced in each plant?

Management wishes to answer these questions simultaneously so as to minimize the sum of all costs associated with production, freight, inventory, and the distribution centers. This must be carried out with proper regard for the constraints imposed by limited production capacities, throughput limitations at the distribution centers, customer service standards, demand forecasts, and various business policies such as continuing to single-source all customers.

Prior to the development of the current system, the traditional methods which had been used to deal with these questions had begun to break down. Notes the director of the corporate facilities planning department, "As each new distribution center was fitted into the existing system, a sense of uncertainty was building . . . about the distribution system as a whole." It was this sense of uncertainty that led to the initiation of a project to develop a comprehensive optimization-based support system.

The first version of such a system began operating in 1971. Its innovative design marked the beginning of a new generation of support systems for distribution planning, and it has continued to evolve over the years in response to new demands and opportunities for use. The four components are briefly summarized below:

The *data files* are updated periodically by personnel in accounting, data processing, marketing, operations research, production, traffic, and other functional specialties. Data are maintained on raw material sources (volumes, prices), on production plants (capacities, unit production costs), on distribution centers (capacities, costs), on customers (location, volume), on transporation (permissible links, freight rates), and on other pertinent details.

WHY DOES IT WORK?

What makes management support systems so effective? Here are four general answers to this question.

They can cope with the rapid changes in today's business environment because, being computer based, information flows and computations take place at electronic speeds. The limiting factor is how promptly data files can be updated as external conditions change.

They can cope with the ever-tightening limits to growth because optimization techniques are designed specifically to deal with limits and constraints, to make allocations, and to maximize performance or efficiency. The use of optimization to achieve better resource allocation and improve efficiency can only ac-celerate as key resources become scarcer and more expensive, and as reduced growth stops camouflaging inefficiency.

They can cope with the increasing complexity of managerial decision-making because an explicit conceptual framework permits truly systematic analysis aided by the logical power of modern mathematics and the awesome processing power of computers.

They enable riskless experiments. Just as airplanes are first "flown" in a wind tunnel, so can a wide range of business decisions be "tested" using a management support system. Such experiments clarify the potential effects of decision alternatives without risk of damaging failure.

The *model* presently involves 34 product groups, 18 plants and refineries, 53 candidate distribution center locations, 289 zones of customer demand, and about 70,000 alternative transportation links.

A specially designed *solver* has undergone many refinements over the years, and today permits the calculation of optimal solutions from scratch in just a few minutes on an IBM 3033.

The *interface facilities* of most concern to a manager are the mechanisms for requesting computer runs, and the output reports. At Hunt-Wesson, the former function has been reduced, for most runs, to filling in the blanks and circling multiple choice options on a standardized request form. The output reports include computer-generated maps and histograms as well as conventional tables. Three levels of management-oriented reports are generated: master summaries, first-level detail reports in which products are aggregated, and second-level detail reports in which products are not aggregated.

The original primary motive for developing this system was to guide the development of the company's network of distribution centers. This it has done quite successfully. Each year since 1971 the system has been used to rebalance the network by analyzing the need for and timing of changes such as the opening of new distribution centers, relocating existing ones, and modifying service areas. Four new distribution centers have been added to the original twelve, one has been relocated, and numerous improvements have been made in assignment of customers to particular distribution centers.

Interestingly, the range of issues addressed with the system has expanded substantially over the years. New ways are continually being found to use the system as a tool both for tactical short-range planning and for strategic long-range facility planning. It has been used, for example, to evaluate the impact of major volume or product changes on the entire distribution network, to study possible expansions or relocations of production capacity, and to assess acquisitions of new product lines.

EASIER SAID THAN DONE

The question now arises, if management support systems lead to such large savings and increases in profits, why doesn't every company have them? The answer, of course, is that it's not that simple: management support systems are not foolproof, nor are they always easy to implement in an organization. Also, a lot depends on the attitudes and actions of the managers themselves. We shall discuss several common concerns of managers who are investigating the idea of a management support system for their companies.

First of all, management support systems tend to have voracious appetites for data. Specific data requirements are, of course, dictated by the model. It is the art of modeling to find the right compromise between the data requirements, model realism, and solvability. Some of the knotty questions that arise are these: How much of the required data can be accessed by machine rather than by manual procedures? How much of it is actually inaccessible for all practical purposes? How reliable are the data sources and how laborious will it be to deal with discrepancies, gaps, and incomparabilities? How badly distorted are available data by the special needs of their local genesis, accounting fictions, or government reporting requirements? How much work will be required to refine the original data into truly pertinent information?

For all but the most modest management support systems, coping with data requirements consumes the lion's share of time, money, and tolerance for psychological stress. It is the tail that wags the dog. Many an otherwise well-conceived system has foundered on the shoals of data development. Such failures are seldom documented in print, but the dangers of excessive data requirements are almost universally recognized.

It is therefore a matter of considerable importance that progress is being made toward meeting the legitimate needs of data development. Progress can be seen on several fronts: the increasing availability of commercial remotely computer-accessible data banks, the continuing movement toward data base management and information systems, and the recent gradual emergence of powerful software packages designed to extract and refine data from a wide variety of organizations for use in a specific type of management support system.

No manager needs encouragement to pay attention to costs, nor to beware the tendency for system enthusiasts to underestimate them. Unfortunately, it is difficult to offer any general guidelines as to what a management support system should cost. The range is very wide; many substantial systems are built in less than a year for an all-inclusive cost between $50,000 and $100,000, while extremely ambitious ones may cost up to several millions of dollars and some of the simplest may cost only a few thousand dollars. Annual maintenance and enhancement costs usually are a modest fraction of the initial development costs.

Not to be overlooked are the intangible costs in managerial strain and aggravation associated with undertaking a major project of this type. And instituting a new system like this could be costly in terms of personnel who are unable or unwilling to cope with the change. It often takes a masterful touch to avoid alienating those who must eventually use these systems. Although it may sometimes seem so during the development phase, management support systems are not built for the sheer joy of technical achievement. They are working tools. Like all tools, they should be engineered with the human user in mind. An ideal support system is straightforward, easy to understand in functional terms, easy to interface with, and devoid of tedious or anxiety-producing requirements.

Few systems measure up to this ideal. The usual mistake is to design a management support system as though the original technical creators will be the only users. The result is predictable when the user group broadens: lack of confidence, frustration, and eventually flagging interest if not outright rejection.

Managers should be concerned with human engineering on two levels. At a purely technical level, they should insist that the system's interface facilities follow the well-known principles of user-friendly software design—that is, the use of natural language wherever possible, the lack of rigid format for input, extensive error traps and diagnostics, familiar-looking reports, and so on. Making the system approachable by nontechnical personnel should be a first priority.

The second level of concern is with the psychological impact on job satisfaction. The management support system should be perceived to add to overall job satisfaction rather than to detract from it. Thus, some systems will endear themselves as beasts of burden which offer liberation from tedious chores. In the experience of Getty Oil, for instance, "Financial analysts are now spending much less time at a desk calculator, and they are giving much more thought to the bigger problems that the company faces."

Other systems will endear themselves for their ability to assimilate subjective judgment and turn it into useful advice. An example is the system used at United Airlines to help plan the use of salesmen's time. One salesman who participated in a field trial of the system commented: "It was amazing to have quick answers to the perennial questions, How often should I call? Should I try to double the revenue in a low producer or attempt to gain additional dollars in a large account? . . . We've all guessed in the past. Under [the new system] we guess to an extent, but the guesses have a system." Another participating salesman opined: "The best thing about [the new system] is the opportunity I have to express my knowledge of my accounts, and then ultimately to see this develop into an overall program that aids me in planning my workday, workweek, and beyond."

GAINING CREDIBILITY

It has been said, and wisely so, that "most managers would rather live with a problem they can't solve than use a solution they don't understand." It follows that a management support system must do more than give good results. It must earn credibility in the eyes of managers.

A common approach to establishing management credibility is to argue in terms of the management support system itself: how extensive its data files are, how realistic its model is, how sophisticated its solver is, and how much human and computer resources have been expended on it. Our observation is that most experienced managers are unimpressed by such arguments.

A much more effective approach is to begin by demonstrating that the system yields results with good face validity over a fairly wide range of situations. For example, do the results look reasonable? Are they similar to accepted results or current practice? Do they pass the scrutiny of common sense?

Affirmative answers to such questions *prove* nothing. We are not talking about establishing the "true" validity of system results. We *are* talking about a hurdle to be overcome if functional managers are to take their management support system seriously. If they don't, all is lost.

A manager should keep in mind that face validity may not always come easily: a management support system sometimes yields surprising or even counterintuitive solutions that turn out to be valid. This can happen, in part, because people tend to think in terms of past experience and fairly simple patterns of reasoning, while management support systems have no prior mental set and can utilize highly complex patterns of reasoning. At Chevron U.S.A., for example, some of the popular rules of thumb used by even experienced truck dispatchers have proven to be very uneconomical.

Another illustration is provided by the experience of Swift Chemical Company. As part of its operation, phosphate rock of different quality grades is mined and blended to satisfy delivery contracts specifying a nominal quality grade. Each contract specifies a penalty (or premium) for shipping below (or above) nominal grades. The traditional practice prior to the development of a management support system was to ship at or above nominal grade in order to avoid revenue penalties. It was a great surprise when the system indicated that most contracts should be shipped well *below* the nominal contract grades.

The system accepted lower revenues in the near term because an inflexible policy of shipping at or above nominal grade has overwhelming longer term effects: Unbalanced consumption of high grade rock led to higher inventory costs for the surplus low grade rock, higher spot purchase costs of high grade rock from competitors to supplement the firm's own sources, and lost sales due to shortages. The management support system's radical solution was soon confirmed in practice. Profits soared. After the excess inventory of low grade rock was worked off, management was pleased to note that the system again favored shipping many contracts at or above nominal contract grade.

THE PROBLEM OF RESPONSIVENESS

From time to time one hears stories about lack of responsiveness of management support systems to the fast-moving concerns of management. In some cases it is said that the need would be long past by the time a proper management support system could be built. In other cases a system may be in place, but is said to be glacial in its rate of response.

Generally, managers cannot expect system responsiveness to be impressive if the system has first to be built. That usually takes several months or more (this is not meant to deny the ability of most staff groups to do one-shot ad hoc analyses on very short notice). But one can expect reasonable responsiveness once the system is in place unless this dimension has been neglected in the design.

Management support systems have the potential to analyze new issues as they arise with a speed and thoroughness well beyond what is possible with traditional procedures. For example, the truck dispatching system in use by Chevron works in seconds from a computer terminal and is run hundreds of times each day. The financial analysis system used by Getty Oil enables rapid and thorough analysis of sudden new capital requirements. And the manager of sales forecasting, merchandise distribution, and inventory at the Kelly-Springfield Tire Company praises his system's ability to help him "put my finger on trouble spots in minutes rather than in hours. It puts everybody in a position to make decisions more quickly and more correctly than ever before."

Another interesting fact that mangers should keep in mind is that management support systems often turn out to have uses quite different from those originally intended. This point was mentioned earlier, in our discussion of Hunt-Wesson Foods' system. Getty Oil's financial planning and analysis system provides another good example: originally built to improve the company's investment analysis methods and to facilitate long range planning, the system now has "hundreds of applications . . . from project analysis to a corporate model, from price forecasting to acquisition and divestment analysis." At least fifteen separate management groups use the system, often for purposes originally unforeseen.

A management support system without a considerable measure of evolutionary adaptability is likely to have a short life. Our experience is that target issues tend to change with surprising rapidity. A system that can deal only with the original set of issues will soon be obsolete.

Some of the steps that can be taken to enhance evolutionary adaptability are: make the system implementation highly modular, avoid solver designs which are overdependent on special problem structure that might change in the future, require the documentation to be thorough and up to date, arrange for long term access to people as highly qualified as those who conceived and built the original system, and have a program to broaden the base of managerial support beyond those whose needs were responsible for the initiation of system development.

Finally, it must be admitted that, in spite of all the progress to date, achieving a fully successful management support system is still a difficult undertaking. The possibility of disastrous failure must be reckoned with. So long as this is so, management must assess the risk and weigh it against the possible rewards of success. The reasons for the possible abortion or early demise of management support system projects are many. Perhaps the most common are technical difficulties and resistance to change.

Technical difficulties may arise in one or more of the four basic system components. It may prove impractical to acquire the necessary data; the model may be misguided or insufficiently realistic; the solver may not be up to the demands made of it; or inadequate interface facilities may fatally impede use of, or the necessary vitalizing information flows to and from, the system.

Management support systems can fail even when the systems themselves are technically successful. Most such failures involve resistance to change. Chief among the reasons for such resistance (and fortunately, by now widely recognized) is the ostracism likely to be suffered by any system when the target user group is not directly involved in nearly all stages of its development. We have already discussed possible pitfalls relating to human engineering and credibility. Also to be considered is resistance born of politics, a mismatched organizational reward system, individual fears concerning job security, and various other causes of resistance to innovation of any type.

Experience teaches that risk of failure is greatly diminished when modest initial project objectives are set, the level of technical sophistication attempted is not too high, organizational aspects are considered as carefully as technical aspects, and artificial deadlines are avoided.

IMPLICATIONS FOR MANAGEMENT PERSONNEL

While the avowed mission of a management support system is literally to support management, it can also induce changes well beyond what one would expect of a "support" tool. The longer-term implications merit careful consideration.

To begin with, system development and maintenance is inherently a technical effort requiring technical people. If the organization lacks sufficient people with the necessary specialized skills—almost a certainty unless the organization already has extensive experience in this field—it will have to recruit or otherwise gain access to them.

In addition, not all managers are equally comfortable using quantitative tools. It is safe to predict that some will adapt much better than others to the demands and opportunities associated with a management support system. Over a period of time, the system may act as a kind of Darwinian selection mechanism influencing career paths. Managers who work well with the system and excel with its help will tend to receive greater rewards.

A management support system can influence not only hiring, firing, and career paths, but also the management infrastructure itself. It can, for example, be either a divisive or cohesive force with respect to inter-functional coordination. This depends on how comprehensive its scope is: A narrow scope will tend to accentuate the local advantages to the particular business function addressed at the expense of other functions, whereas a broader scope will tend to bring about the coordination of related business functions in an integrated "total system" manner. Here is an example of how a sufficiently comprehensive system can provide structure and central focus to cooperative activities involving many parties:

At British Airways European Division, half a dozen or more separate planning groups used to monitor and plan flight schedules, revenues, costs, load factors, fleet changes, route traffic potentials, market shares, and financial impacts. Their "planning systems had evolved gradually and piecemeal. Each element of the planning process had a set of computer programs of its very own . . . . The monitoring systems and various parts of the planning systems used different computers. Data flow between the computers was slow, difficult, and unreliable. . . Schedule changes occurred so rapidly that by the time an economic assessment was available, it could bear little relation to the up-to-date plans." Now nearly all planning is done in an integrated way by a single on-line management support system. The result is much improved coordination among the essential business functions, with major profit increases to prove it.

TANGIBLE AND INTANGIBLE BENEFITS

Clearly, the possible tangible benefits of a management support system are manifold. But how does it add up in dollars and cents? It is difficult to generalize. Often the percentage of direct cost savings is quite small, which reinforces one's natural inclination to reserve the approach for applications with a relatively large cost base. Our own experience is most extensive in the area of distribution planning, where annual cost savings typically range between 5 percent and 15 percent. The first year's savings are usually enough to pay for the initial system development costs several times over.

Occasionally a company will release aggregate cost and benefit figures, rather than figures relating to individual projects. Standard Oil of Indiana did this recently: "During the last three years, the average annual cost of the Operations Research Department was about $1.2 million; average annual benefits were $9.0 million, as attested to by the users who paid for the services."

However, not all benefits may be "tangible" in the usual sense of direct improvements in profit or service. The generation of insights and improved organizational understanding deserve to rank high among the benefits of investing in management support systems. The manager who funded such systems in a high technology firm offers this observation, typical of many we have heard: "Probably more than anything else, models have contributed to our understanding of our business. The process of creating a model specification and of understanding the fact that there are interrelationships within our business . . . has proven of at least an equal value to the application of the models thus created."

In addition, two other possible kinds of indirect benefits should be noted. The first is use of management support systems in connection with adversary proceedings. For example, the optimal flight crew scheduling system at Flying Tiger Line has been used during pilot union negotiations to help management evaluate the economic implications of various proposed work rule changes. The second indirect benefit is use as an instrument of advocacy. The evidence marshaled with the help of a management support system, not to mention the aura of authority surrounding the system itself, can be impressively persuasive. We know distribution managers who have used a comprehensive distribution planning system to gain finance committee approval for needed new facilities previously denied, and we know of an electric utility which has touted its support system to regulatory authorities as evidence of the maximal operating efficiency needed to qualify for rate increases and other favors.

Few organizations have come close to exploiting the full potential of management support systems. The modest suggestions which follow may help accelerate the process:

- Be receptive toward new approaches. New management support systems are best spawned in a climate of openness, broad perspective, and free exchange of ideas. An important step is getting to know and staying in touch with people having a professional interest in management support systems, especially a company's own management science and information systems staffs (by whatever name they use—one survey found 47 different names for 109 such staff groups). These people have a built-in incentive to help identify new opportunities. Student project teams from local universities may also be valuable for this purpose.

- Take advantage of pertinent seminars, short courses, and other educational opportunities. Education is a bridge between what is accomplished. This bridge is especially important for a field like management support systems where the science of the possible is advancing so rapidly.

- Keep in mind that data are a critical resource. Management support systems typically require large volumes of reliable, timely data, preferably in machine-readable form. Organizations which treat operating and accounting business data as the critical resource that it is have a significant advantage. This means taking steps such as: designing new business sytems and procedures with an eye toward data capture for subsequent analysis as a legitimate (if secondary) function; working toward making coding schemes, data formats, and paperwork procedures simpler, more standardized, and more logical; and providing for routine, careful, and well-documented data archives on mass storage media.

- Consider available management support systems packages. Although every manager tends to believe that his particular problem is unique, in fact there is a great deal of commonality among the problems faced in different organizations. It is often possible to build efficient and flexible computer software for a well-defined class of applications. Such software needs only some custom tailoring for each new application. This sort of development has occurred in such areas as material requirements planning, vehicle routing, inventory control, and distribution system planning.

Relying on an existing software package may offer such advantages as lower cost, superior technical quality and performance, and documentation well beyond what would be affordable for a single application. Some disadvantages to this approach are that it is often difficult for managers to distinguish among the superficially similar claims made on behalf of competing packages (the differences may well be profound, but require highly competent technical analysis to discern), and also that it is easy to surrender, to the supplier of the package, some of the crucial managerial responsibilities for understanding the capabilities and limitations of the resulting support system and for creatively directing its effective use.

5

A Framework for the Development of Decision Support Systems

by Ralph H. Sprague, Jr.

About the author:

Ralph H. Sprague, Jr. Professor and Chairman of the Decision Sciences Department at the University of Hawaii, recently spent his sabbatical year as Visiting Professor at Stanford University and Visiting Scientist at IBM Research Laboratory in San Jose. He has over fifteen years of teaching, research, and consulting experience in the information systems field. Much of his recent work deals with the development and evaluation of decision support systems.

INTRODUCTION

We seem to be on the verge of another "era" in the relentless advancement of computer based information systems in organizations. Designated by the term Decision Support Systems (DSS), these systems are receiving reactions ranging from "a major breakthrough" to "just another 'buzz word'."

One view is that the natural evolutionary advancement of information technology and its use in the organizational context has led from EDP to MIS to the current DSS thrust. In this view, the DSS picks up

Reprinted with permission from MIS Quarterly.

where MIS leaves off. A contrary view portrays DSS as an important subset of what MIS has been and will continue to be. Still another view recognizes a type of system that has been developing for several years and "now we have a name for it." Meanwhile, the skeptics suspect that DSS is just another "buzz word" to justify the next round of visits from the vendors.

The purpose of this article is to briefly examine these alternative views of DSS, and present a framework that proves valuable in reconciling them. The framework articulates and integrates major concerns of several "stakeholders" in the development of DSS: executives and professionals who use them, the MIS managers who manage the process of developing and installing them, the information specialists who build and develop them, the system designers who create and assemble the technology on which they are based, and the researchers who study the DSS subject and process.

DEFINITION, EXAMPLES, CHARACTERISTICS

The concepts involved in DSS were first articulated in the early '70's by Michael S. Scott Morton under the term "management decision systems".[32] A few firms and scholars began to develop and research DSS, which became characterized as *interactive* computer based systems, which *help* decision makers utilize *data* and *models* to solve *unstructured* problems. The unique contribution of DSS resulted from these key words. That definition proved restrictive enough that few actual systems completely satisfied it. Some authors recently extended the definition of DSS to include any system that makes some contribution to decision making; in this way the term can be applied to all but transaction processing. A serious definitional problem is that the words have a certain "intuitive validity;" any system that supports a decision, in any way, is a "Decision Support System."

Unfortunately, neither the restrictive nor the broad definition helps much, because they do not provide guidance for understanding the value, the technical requirements, or the approach for developing a DSS. A complicating factor is that people from different backgrounds and contexts view a DSS quite differently. A manager and computer scientist seldom see things in the same way.

Another way to get a feeling for a complex subject like a DSS is to consider examples. Several specific examples were discussed in The

Society for Management Information Systems (SMIS) Workshop on DSS in 1979.[35] Alter examined fifty-six systems which might have some claim to the DSS label, and used this sample to develop a set of abstractions describing their characteristics.[1, 2] More recently, Keen has designated about thirty examples of what he feels are DSS and compares their characteristics.[26]

The "characteristics" approach seems to hold more promise than either definitions or collections of examples in understanding a DSS and its potential. More specifically, a DSS may be defined by its capabilities in several critical areas—capabilities which are required to accomplish the objectives which are pursued by the development and use of a DSS. Observed characteristics of a DSS which have evolved from the work of Alter, Keen, and others include:

- they tend to be aimed at the less well structured, underspecified problems that upper level managers typically face;

- they attempt to combine the use of models or analytic techniques with traditional data access and retrieval functions;

- they specifically focus on features which make them easy to use by noncomputer people in an interactive mode; and

- they emphasize flexibility and adaptability to accommodate changes in the environment and the decision making approach of the user.

A serious question remains. Are the definitions, examples, and characteristics of a DSS sufficiently different to justify the use of a new term and the inference of a new era in information systems for organizations, or are the skeptics right? Is it just another "buzz word" to replace the fading appeal of MIS?

DSS VERSUS MIS

Much of the difficulty and controversy with terms like "DSS" and "MIS" can be traced to the difference between an academic or theoretical definition and "connotational" definition. The former is carefully articulated by people who write textbooks and articles in journals. The latter evolves from what actually is developed and used in practice, and is heavily influenced by the personal experiences that the user of the term has had with the subject. It is this connotational definition of EDP/MIS/DSS that is used in justifying the assertion that a DSS is an evolutionary advancement beyond MIS.

This view can be expressed using Figure 5.1, a simple organizational chart, as a model of an organization. EDP was first applied to the lower operational levels of the organization to automate the paperwork. Its basic characteristics include:

- a focus on data, storage, processing, and flows at the operational level;
- efficient transaction processing;
- scheduled and optimized computer runs;
- integrated files for related jobs; and
- summary reports for management.

In recent years, the EDP level of activity in many firms has become a well-oiled and efficient production facility for transactions processing.

The MIS approach elevated the focus on information systems activities, with additional emphasis on integration and planning of the information systems function. In *practice,* the characteristics of MIS include:

- an information focus, aimed at the middle managers;
- structured information flow;
- an integration of EDP jobs by business function, such as production MIS, marketing MIS, personnel MIS, *etc.;* and
- inquiry and report generation, usually with a database.

The MIS era contributed a new level of information to serve management needs, but was still very much oriented to, and built upon, information flows and data files.

According to this connotational view, a DSS is focused still higher in the organization with an emphasis on the following characteristics:

- decision focused, aimed at top managers and executive decision makers;
- emphasis on flexibility, adaptability, and quick response;

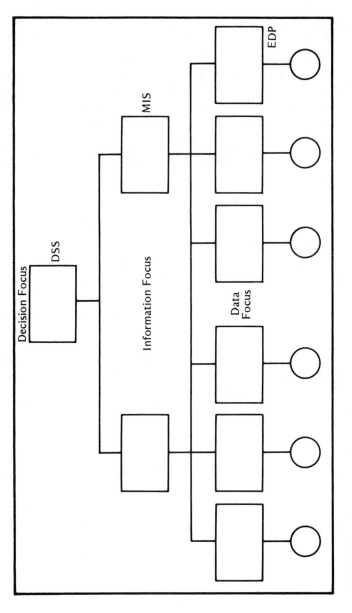

FIGURE 5.1 The Connotational View

- user initiated and controlled; and
- support for the personal decision making styles of individual managers.

This connotational and evolutionary view has some credence because it roughly corresponds to developments in practice over time. A recent study found MIS managers able to distinguish the level of advancement of their application systems using criteria similar to those above.[27] Many installations with MIS type applications planned to develop applications with DSS type characteristics. However, the "connotational" view has some serious deficiencies, and is definitely misleading in the further development of a DSS.

- It implies that *decision support* is needed only at the top levels. In fact, *decision support* is required at all levels of management in the organization.

- The decision making which occurs at several levels frequently must be coordinated. Therefore, an important dimension of *decision support* is the communication and coordination between decision makers across organizational levels, as well as at the same level.

- It implies that *decision support* is the only thing top managers need from the information system. In fact, decision making is only one of the activities of managers that benefits from information systems support.

There is also the problem that many information systems professionals, especially those in SMIS, are not willing to accept the narrow connotational view of the term "MIS." To us, MIS refers to the entire set of systems and activities required to manage, process, and use information as a resource in the organization.

THE THEORETICAL VIEW

To consider the appropriate role of a DSS in this overall context of information systems, the broad charter and objectives of the information systems function in the organization is characterized:

Dedicated to improving the performance of knowledge workers in organizations through the application of information technology.

- Improving the performance is the ultimate objective of information systems—not the storage of data, the production of reports, or even "getting the right information to the right person at the right time." The ultimate objective must be viewed in terms of the ability of information systems to support the improved performance of people in organizations.

- Knowledge workers are the clientele. This group includes managers, professionals, staff analysts, and clerical workers whose primary job responsibility is the handling of information in some form.

- Organizations are the context. The focus is on information handling in goal seeking organizations of all kinds.

- The application of information technology is the challenge and opportunity facing the information systems professional for the purposes and in the contexts given above.

A triangle was used by Robert Head in the late '60's as a visual model to characterize MIS in this broad comprehensive sense.[22] It has become a classic way to view the dimensions of an information system. The vertical dimension represented the levels of management, and the horizontal dimension represented the main functional areas of the business organization. Later authors added transactional processing as a base on which the entire system rested. The result was a two dimensional model of an MIS in the broad sense—the total activities which comprise the information system in an organization. Figure 5.2 is a further extension of the basic triangle to help describe the concept of the potential role of a DSS. The depth dimension shows the major technology "subsystems" which provide support for the activities of knowledge workers.

Three major thrusts are shown here, but there could be more. The structured reporting system includes the reports required for the management and control of the organization, and for satisfying the information needs of external parties. It has been evolving from efforts in EDP and MIS, in the narrow sense, for several years. Systems to support the communication needs of the organization are evolving rapidly from advances in telecommunications with a strong impetus from office automation and word processing. DSS seems to be evolving from the coalescence of information technology and operations research/management science approaches in the form of interactive modeling.

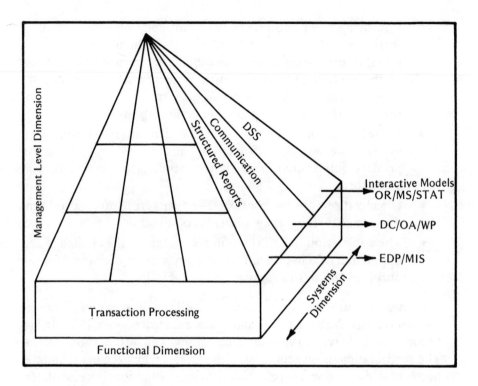

FIGURE 5.2 The Complete View

To summarize this introductory section, a DSS is not merely an evolutionary advancement of EDP and MIS, and it will certainly not replace either. Nor is it merely a type of information system aimed exclusively at top management, where other information systems seem to have failed. A DSS is a class of information system that draws on transaction processing systems and interacts with the other parts of the overall information system to support the decision making activities of managers and other knowledge workers in the organizations. However, there are some subtle but significant differences between a DSS and traditional EDP or so-called MIS approaches. Moreover, these systems require a new combination of information systems technology to satisfy a set of heretofore unmet needs. It is not yet clear exactly how these technologies fit together, or which important problems need to be solved. Indeed, that is a large part of the purpose of this article.

It is apparent, however, that a DSS has the potential to become another powerful weapon in the arsenal of the information systems professional to help improve the effectiveness of the people in organizations.

THE FRAMEWORK

The remainder of this article is devoted to an exploration of the nature of this "thrust" in information systems called "DSS." The mechanism for this exploration is another of the often maligned but repeatedly used "frameworks."

A framework, in the absence of theory, is helpful in organizing a complex subject, identifying the relationships between the parts, and revealing the areas in which further developments will be required. The framework presented here has evolved over the past two years in discussions with many different groups of people.[1] It is organized in two major parts. The first part considers: (a) three levels of technology, all of which have been designated as a DSS, with considerable confusion; (b) the developmental approach that is evolving for the creation of a DSS; and (c) the roles of several key types of people in the building and use of a DSS. The second part of the framework develops a descriptive model to assess the performance objectives and the capabilities of a DSS as viewed by three of the major stakeholders in their continued development and use.

THREE TECHNOLOGY LEVELS

It is helpful to identify three levels of hardware/software which have been included in the label "DSS." They are used by people with different levels of technical capability, and vary in the nature and scope of task to which they can be applied.

SPECIFIC DSS

The system which actually accomplishes the work might be called the *Specific DSS*. It is an information systems "application," but with characteristics that make it significantly different from a typical data processing application. It is the hardware/software that allows a specific decision maker or group of decision makers to deal with a specific set of related problems. An early example is the portfolio management system [20] also described in the first major DSS book by Keen and Scott Morton.[23] Another example is the police beat allocation system used on an experimental basis by the City of San Jose, California.[9] The latter system allowed a police officer to display a map outline and call up data by geographical zone, showing police calls for service, activity levels, service time, *etc.* The interactive graphic capability of the system enabled the officer to manipulate the maps, zones, and data to try a variety of police beat alternatives quickly and easily. In effect, the system provided tools to *amplify* a manager's judgment. Incidentally, a later experiment attempted to apply a traditional linear programming model to the problem. The solution was less satisfactory than the one designed by the police officer.

DSS GENERATOR

The second technology level might be called a *DSS Generator.* This is a "package" of related hardware and software which provides a set of capabilities to quickly and easily build a Specific DSS. For example, the police beat system described above was built from the Geodata Analysis and Display System (GADS), an experimental system developed at the IBM Research Laboratory in San Jose.[8] By loading different maps, data, menu choices, and procedures or command strings, GADS was later used to build a Specific DSS to support the routing of IBM copier repairmen.[42] The development of this new "application" required less than one month.

Another example of a *DSS Generator* is the Executive Information System (EIS) marketed by Boeing Computer Services.[6] EIS is an integrated set of capabilities which includes report preparation, inquiry capability, a modeling language, graphic display commands, and a set of financial and statistical analysis subroutines. These capabilities have all been available individually for some time. The unique contribution of EIS is that these capabilities are available through a common language which acts on a common set of data. The result is that EIS can be used as a DSS Generator, especially for a Specific DSS to help in financial decision making situations.

Evolutionary growth toward DSS Generators has come from special purpose languages. In fact, most of the software systems that might be used as Generators are evolving from enhanced planning languages or modeling languages, perhaps with report preparation and graphic display capabilities added. The Interactive Financial Planning System (IFPS) marketed by Execucom Systems of Austin, Texas [18], and EXPRESS available from TYMSHARE [44], are good examples.

DSS TOOLS

The third and most fundamental level of technology applied to the development of a DSS might be called *DSS Tools*. These are hardware or software elements which facilitate the development of a specific DSS *or* a DSS Generator. This category of technology has seen the greatest amount of recent development, including new special purpose languages, improvements in operating systems to support conversational approaches, color graphics hardware and supporting software, *etc.* For example, the GADS system described above was written in FORTRAN using an experimental graphics subroutine package as the primary dialogue handling software, a laboratory enhanced rasterscan color monitor, and a powerful interactive data extraction/database management system.

RELATIONSHIPS

The relationships between these three levels of technology and types of DSS are illustrated by Figure 5.3. The DSS Tools can be used to develop a Specific DSS application directly as shown on the left half of the diagram. This is the same approach used to develop most traditional applications with tools such as a general purpose language, data access software, subroutine packages, *etc.* The difficulty with this approach for developing DSS applications is the constant change and flexibility which characterize them. A DSS changes character not only in response to changes in the environment, but to changes in the way managers want to approach the problem. Therefore, a serious complicating factor in the use of basic tools is the need to involve the user directly in the change and modification of the Specific DSS.

APL was heavily used in the development of Specific DSS because it proved to be cheap and easy for APL programmers, especially the APL enthusiasts, to produce "throw-away" code which could be easily revised or discarded as the nature of the application changed. However, except for the few users who became members of the APL fan club, that language *did not* help capture the involvement of users in the

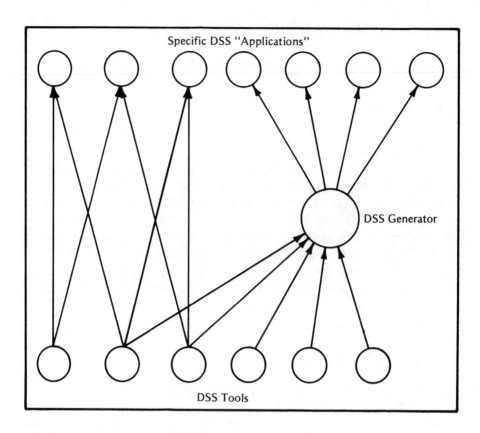

FIGURE 5.3 Three Levels of DSS Technology

building and modification of the DSS. The development and use of DSS Generators promises to create a "platform" or staging area from which Specific DSS can be constantly developed and modified with the cooperation of the user, and without heavy consumption of time and effort.

EVOLVING ROLES IN DSS

All three levels of technology will probably be used over time in the development and operation of a DSS. Some interesting developments are occurring, however, in the roles that managers and technicians will play.

Figure 5.4 repeats part of the earlier diagram with a spectrum of five roles spread across the three levels.

- The *manager or user* is the person faced with the problem or decision—the one that must take action and be responsible for the consequences.

- The *intermediary* is the person who helps the user, perhaps merely as a clerical assistant to push the buttons of the terminal, or perhaps as a more substantial "staff assistant" to interact and make suggestions.

- The *DSS builder* or facilitator assembles the necessary capabilities from the DSS Generator to "configure" the specific DSS with which the user/intermediary interacts directly. This person must have some familiarity with the problem area and also be comfortable with the information system technology components and capabilities.

- The *technical supporter* develops additional information system capabilities or components when they are needed as part of the Generator. New databases, new analysis models, and additional data display formats will be developed by the person filling this role. It requires a strong familiarity with technology, and a minor acquaintance with the problem or application area.

- The *toolsmith* develops new technology, new languages, new hardware and software, improves the efficiency of linkages between subsystems, *etc.*

Two observations about this spectrum of roles are appropriate. First, it is clear that they do not necessarily align with individuals on a one-to-one basis. One person may assume several roles, or more than one person may be required to fill a role. The appropriate role assignment will generally depend on:

- the nature of the problem, particularly how narrow or broad;

- the nature of the person, particularly how comfortable the individual is with the computer equipment, language, and concepts; and

- the strength of the technology, particularly how user oriented it is.

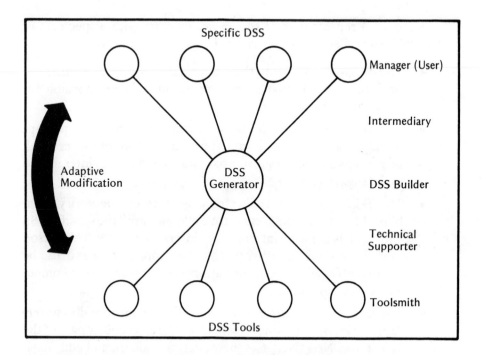

FIGURE 5.4 Three Levels of DSS with Five Associated Roles for Managers and Technicians

Some managers do not need or want an intermediary. There are even a few chief executives who take the terminal home on weekends to write programs, thereby assuming the upper three or four roles. In fact, a recent survey of the users of IFPS shows that more than one third of them are middle and top level managers.[45] Decisions which require group consensus or systems design (builder) teams are examples of multiple persons per role.

Secondly, these roles appear similar to those present in traditional systems development, but there are subtle differences. The top two are familiar even in name for the development of many interactive or online systems. It is common practice in some systems to combine them into one "virtual" user for convenience. The user of the DSS, however, will play a much more active and controlling role in the design and development of the system than has been true in the past. The builder/technical support dichotomy is relatively close to the information specialist/system designer dichotomy discussed in the ACM curriculum recommendations.[3] Increasingly, however, the DSS builder resides in the functional area and not in the MIS department. The toolsmith is similar to a systems programmer, software designer, or computer scientist, but is increasingly employed by a hardware or software vendor, and not by the user's organization. The net result is less direct involvement in the DSS process by the information systems professional in the EDP/MIS department. (Some implications of this trend are discussed later.) Moreover, the interplay between these roles is evolving into a unique development approach for a DSS.

THE DEVELOPMENT APPROACH FOR DSS

The very nature of a DSS requires a different design technique from traditional batch, or online, transaction processing systems. The traditional approaches for analysis and design have proven inadequate because there is no single comprehensive theory of decision making, and because of the rapidity of change in the conditions which decision makers face. Designers literally "cannot get to first base" because no one, least of all the decision maker or user, can define in advance what the functional requirements of the system should be. A DSS needs to be built with short, rapid feedback from users to ensure that development is proceeding correctly. It must be developed to permit change quickly and easily.

ITERATIVE DESIGN

The result is that the most important four steps in the typical systems development process—analysis, design, construction, implementation—are combined into a single step which is iteratively repeated. Several names are evolving to describe this process including breadboarding [31], L'Approache Evolutive [14], and "middle out".[30] The essence of the approach is that the manager and builder agree on a small but significant subproblem, then design and develop an initial system to support the decision making which it requires. After a short period of use, for instance, a few weeks, the system is evaluated, modified, and incrementally expanded. This cycle is repeated three to six times over the course of a few months until a *relatively* stable system is evolved which supports decision making for a cluster of tasks. The word "relatively" is important, because although the frequency and extent of change will decrease, it will never be stable. The system will always be changing, not as a necessary evil in response to imposed environmental changes, but as a conscious strategy on the part of the user and builder. In terms of the three level model presented earlier, this process can be viewed as the iterative cycling between the DSS Generator and the Specific DSS as shown in Figure 5.4. With each cycle, capabilities are added to, or deleted from, the Specific DSS from those available in the DSS Generator. Keen depicts the expansion and growth of the system in terms of adding verbs which represent actions managers require.[24] Carlson adds more dimension by focusing on representations, operations, control, and memories as the elements of expansion and modification.[11] In another paper, Keen deals substantively with the interaction between the user, the builder, and the technology in this iterative, adaptive design process.[25]

Note that this approach requires an unusual level of management involvement or management participation in the design. The manager is actually the iterative designer of the system; the sytems analyst is merely the catalyst between the manager and the system, implementing the required changes and modifications.

Note also that this is different from the concept of "prototyping"; the initial system is real, live, and usable, not just a pilot test. The iterative process does not *merely* lead to a good understanding of the systems performance requirements, which are then frozen. The iterative changeability is actually *built into* the DSS as it is used over time. In fact, the development approach *becomes the system.* Rather than developing a system which is then "run" as a traditional EDP system, the DSS development approach results in the installation of an adaptive process in which a decision maker and a set of information system "capabilities" interact to confront problems while responding to changes from a variety of sources.

THE ADAPTIVE SYSTEM

In the broad sense, the DSS is an adaptive system which consists of all three levels of technology in place and operating with the participants (roles), and the technology adapting to changes over time. Thus, the development of a DSS is actually the development and installation of this adaptive system. Simon describes such a system as one that adapts to changes of several kinds over three time horizons. [34] In the short run, the system allows a *search* for answers within a relatively narrow scope. In the intermediate time horizon, the system *learns* by modifying its capabilities and activities, *i.e.*, the scope or domain changes. In the long run, the system evolves to accommodate much different behavior styles and capabilities.

The three level model of a DSS is analogous to Simon's adaptive system. The Specific DSS gives the manager the capabilities and flexibility to *search*, explore, and experiment with the problem area, within certain boundaries. Over time, as changes occur in a task, the environment, and the user's behavior, the Specific DSS must *learn* to accommodate these changes through the reconfiguration of the elements in the DSS generator, with the aid of the DSS builder. Over a longer period of time, the basic tools evolve to provide the technology for changing the capabilities of the Generators out of which the Specific DSS is constructed, through the efforts of the toolsmith.

The ideas expressed above are not particularly new. Rapid feedback between the systems analyst and the client has been pursued for years. In the long run, most computer systems *are* adaptive systems. They are changed and modified during the normal system life cycle, and they evolve through major enhancements and extensions as the life cycle is repeated. However, when the length of that life cycle is shortened from three to five months, or even weeks, there are significant implications. The resulting changes in the development approach and the traditional view of the systems life cycle promises to be one of the important impacts of the growing use of a DSS.

PERFORMANCE OBJECTIVES AND CAPABILITIES

Most of the foregoing discussion has dealt with some aspects of the technological and organizational contexts within which a DSS will be built and operated. The second part of the framework deals with what a DSS must accomplish, and what capabilities or characteristics it must have. The three levels of hardware/software technology and the corresponding three major "stakeholders" or interested parties in the development and use of a DSS can be used to identify the characteristics and attributes of a DSS.

At the top level are the *managers or users* who are primarily concerned with what the Specific DSS can do for them. Their focus is the problem solving or decision making task they face, and the organizational environment in which they operate. They will assess a DSS in terms of the assistance they receive in pursuing these tasks. At the level of the DSS Generator, the *builders* or designers must use the capabilities of the generator to configure a Specific DSS to meet the manager's needs. They will be concerned with the capabilities the Generator offers, and how these capabilities can be assembled to create the specific DSS. At the DSS tool level, the *"toolsmiths"* are concerned with the development of basic technology components, and how they can be integrated to form a DSS Generator which has the necessary capabilities.

The attributes and characteristics of a DSS as viewed from each level must be examined. From the manager's view, six general performance objectives for the Specific DSS can be identified. They are not the only six that could be identified, but as a group they represent the overall performance of a DSS that seems to be expected and desirable from a managerial viewpoint. The characteristics of the DSS Generator from the viewpoint of the builder are described by a conceptual model which identifies performance characteristics in three categories: dialogue handling or the man-machine interface, database and database management capability, and modeling and anlytic capability. The same three part model is used to depict the viewpoint of the "toolsmith," but from the aspect of the technology, tactics, and architecture required to produce those capabilities required by the builders.

MANAGER'S VIEW: PERFORMANCE OBJECTIVES

The following performance requirements are phrased using the normative word "should." It is likely that no Specific DSS will be required to satisfy all six of the performance requirements given here. In fact, it is important to recall that the performance criteria for any Specific DSS will depend entirely on the task, the organizational environment, and the decision maker(s) involved. Nevertheless, the following objectives collectively represent a set of capabilities which characterize the full value of the DSS concept from the manager/user point of view. The first three pertain to the type of decision making task which managers and professionals face. The latter three relate to the type of support which is needed.

1. *A DSS should provide support for decision making, but with emphasis on semi-structured and unstructured decisions.* These are the

types of decisions that have had little or no support from EDP, MIS, or management science/operations research (MS/OR) in the past. It might be better to refer to "hard" or underspecified problems, because the concept of "structure" in decision making is heavily dependent on the cognitive style and approach to problem solving of the decision maker. It is clear from their expressed concerns however, that managers need additional support for certain kinds of problems.

2. *A DSS should provide decision making support for managers at all levels, assisting in integration between the levels whenever appropriate.* This requirement evolves from the realization that managers at *all* organizational levels face "tough" problems as described in the first objective above. Moreover, a major need articulated by managers, is the integration and coordination of decision making by several managers dealing with related parts of a larger problem.

3. *A DSS should support decisions which are <u>inter</u>dependent as well as those that are <u>in</u>dependent.* Much of the early DSS work inferred that a decision maker would sit at a terminal, use a system, and develop a decision *alone.* DSS development experience has shown that a DSS must accommodate decisions which are made by groups or made in part by several people in sequence. Keen and Hackathorn [24] explore three decision types as:

Independent. A decision maker has full responsibility and authority to make a complete implementable decision.

Sequential Interdependent. A decision maker makes part of a decision which is passed on to someone else.

Pooled Interdependent. The decision must result from negotiation and interaction among decision makers.

Different capabilities will be required to support each type of decision—personal support, organizational support, and group support respectively.

4. *A DSS should support all phases of the decision making process.* A popular model of the decision making process is given in the work of Herbert Simon.[33] He characterized three main steps in the process as follows:

Intelligence. Searching the environment for conditions calling for decisions. Raw data is obtained, processed, and examined for clues that may identify problems.

Design. Inventing, developing, and analyzing possible courses of action. This involves processes to understand the problem, generate solutions, and test solutions for feasibility.

Choice. Selecting a particular course of action from those available. A choice is made and implemented.

Although the third phase includes implementation, many authors feel that it is significant enough to be shown separately. It has been added to Figure 5.5 to show the relationships between the steps. Simon's model also illustrates the contribution of MIS/EDP and MS/OR to decision making. From the definition of the three stages given above, it is clear that EDP and MIS, in the narrow sense, have made major contributions to the intelligence phase, while MIS/OR has been primarily useful at the choice phase. There has been no substantial support for the design phase, which seems to be one of the primary potential contributions of a DSS. There also has been very little support from traditional systems for the implementation phase, but some early experience has shown that a DSS can make a major contribution here also.[42]

5. *A DSS should support a variety of decision making processes, but not be dependent on any one.* Simon's model, though widely accepted, is only one model of how decisions are actually made. In fact, there is no universally accepted model of the decision making process, and there is no promise of such a general theory in the foreseeable future. There are too many variables, too many different types of decisions, and too much variety in the characteristics of decision makers. Consequently, a very important characteristic of a DSS is that it provide the decision maker with a set of capabilities to apply in a sequence and form that fits each individual cognitive style. In short, a DSS should be process independent, and user driven or controlled.

6. *Finally, a DSS should be easy to use.* A variety of terms have been used to describe this characteristic including flexibility, user friendly, nonthreatening, ***etc.*** The importance of this characteristic is underscored by the discretionary latitude of a DSS's clientele. Although some systems which require heavy organizational support or group support may limit the discretion somewhat, the user of a DSS has much more latitude to ignore or circumvent the system than the user of a more traditional transaction system or required reporting system. Therefore, a DSS must "earn" its users' allegiance by being valuable and convenient.

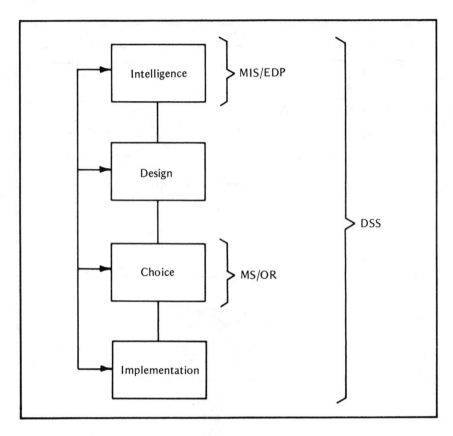

FIGURE 5.5 Phases of Decision Making

THE BUILDER'S VIEW: TECHNICAL CAPABILITIES

The DSS Builder has the responsibility of drawing on computer based tools and techniques to provide the decision support required by the manager. DSS Tools can be used directly, but it is generally more efficient and effective to use a DSS Generator for this task. The Generator must have a set of capabilities which facilitate the quick and easy configuration of a Specific DSS and modification in response to changes in the manager's requirements, environment, tasks, and thinking approaches. A conceptual model can be used to organize these capabilities, both for the builders and for the "toolsmith" who will develop the technology to provide these capabilities.

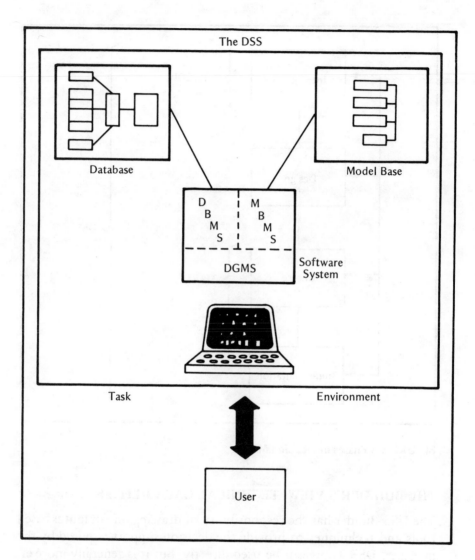

FIGURE 5.6 Components of the DSS

The old "black box" approach is helpful here, starting with the view of the system as a black box, successively "opening" the boxes to understand the subsystems and how they are interconnected. Although the DSS is treated as the black box here, it is important to recall that the overall system is the decision *making* system, consisting of a manager/user who uses a DSS to confront a task in an organizational environment.

Opening the large DSS box reveals a database, a model base, and a complex software system for linking the user to each of them as shown in Figure 5.6. Opening each of these boxes reveals that the database and model base have some interrelated components, and that the software system is comprised of three sets of capabilities: database management software (DBMS), model base management software (MBMS), and the software for managing the interface between the user and the system, which might be called the dialogue generation and management software (DGMS). These three major subsystems provide a convenient scheme for identifying the technical capability which a DSS must have. The key aspects in each category that are critical to a DSS from the Builder's point of view, and a list of capabilities which will be required in each category must now be considered.

THE DATA SUBSYSTEM

The data subsystem is thought to be a well understood set of capabilities because of the rapidly maturing technology related to databases and their management. The typical advantages of the database approach, and the powerful functions of the DBMS, are also important to the development and use of a DSS. There are, however, some significant differences between the Database/Data Communication approach for traditional systems, and those applicable for a DSS. Opening the Database box summarizes these key characteristics as shown in Figure 5.7.

First is the importance of a much richer set of data sources than are usually found in typical non-DSS applications. Data must come from external as well as internal sources, since decision making, especially in the upper management levels, is heavily dependent on external data sources. In addition, the typical accounting oriented transaction data must be supplemented with non-transactional, non-accounting data, some of which has not been computerized in the past.

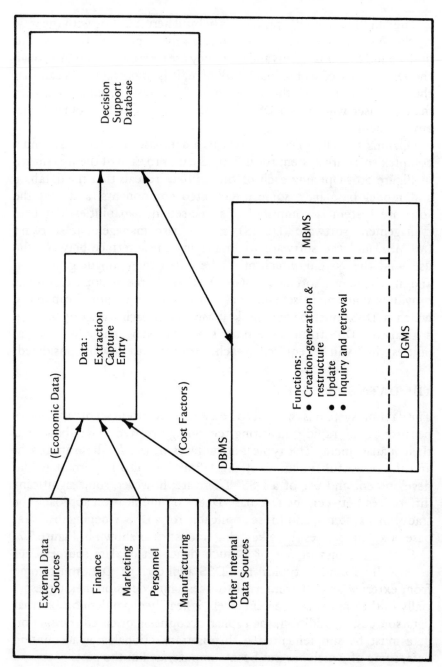

FIGURE 5.7 The Data Subsystem

Another significant difference is the importance of the data capture and extraction process from this wider set of data sources. The nature of a DSS requires that the extraction process, and the DBMS which manages it, be flexible enough to allow rapid additions and changes in response to unanticipated user requests. Finally, most successful DSS's have found it necessary to create a DSS database which is logically separate from other operational databases. A partial set of capabilities required in the database area can be summarized by the following:

- the ability to combine a variety of data sources through a data capture and extraction process;

- the ability to add and delete data sources quickly and easily;

- the ability to portray logical data structures in user terms so the user understands what is available and can specify needed additions and deletions;

- the ability to handle personal and unofficial data so the user can experiment with alternatives based on personal judgment; and

- the ability to manage this wide variety of data with a full range of data management functions.

THE MODEL SUBSYSTEM

A very promising aspect of a DSS is its ability to integrate data access and decision models. It does so by imbedding the decision models in an information system which uses the database as the integration and communication mechanism between models. This characteristic unifies the strength of data retrieval and reporting from the EDP field and the significant developments in management science in a way the manager can use and trust.

The misuse and disuse of models have been widely discussed.[21, 28, 36, 39] One major problem has been that model builders were frequently preoccupied with the structure of the model. The existence of the correct input data and the proper delivery of the output to the user was assumed. In addition to these heroic assumptions, models tended to suffer from inadequacy because of the difficulty of developing an integrated model to handle a realistic set of interrelated deci-

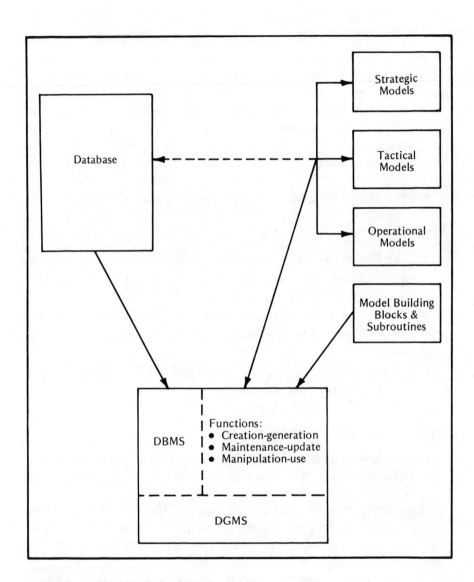

FIGURE 5.8 The Models Subsystem

sions. The solution was a collection of separate models, each of which dealt with a distinct part of the problem. Communication between these related models was left to the decision maker and intellectual process.

A more enlightened view of models suggests that they be imbedded in an information system with the database as the integration and communication mechanism between them. Figure 5.8 summarizes the components of the model base "box." The model creation process must be flexible, with a strong modeling language and a set of building blocks, much like subroutines, which can be assembled to assist the modeling process. In fact, there are a set of model management functions, very much analogous to data management functions. The key capabilities for a DSS in the model subsystems include:

- the ability to create new models quickly and easily;
- the ability to catalog and maintain a wide range of models, supporting all levels of management;
- the ability to interrelate these models with appropriate linkages through the database;
- the ability to access and integrate model "building blocks;" and
- the ability to manage the model base with management functions analogous to database management (*e.g.*, mechanisms for storing, cataloging, linking, and accessing models).

For a more detailed discussion of the model base and its management see [37, 38, 46].

THE USER SYSTEM INTERFACE

Much of the power, flexibility, and usability characteristics of a DSS are derived from capabilities in the user system interface. Bennett identifies the user, terminal, and software system as the components of the interface subsystem.[5] He then divides the dialogue, or interface experience itself into three parts as shown in Figure 5.9:

1. *The action language*—what the user *can do* in communicating with the system. It includes such options as the availability of a regular keyboard, function keys, touch panels, joy stick, voice command, *etc.*

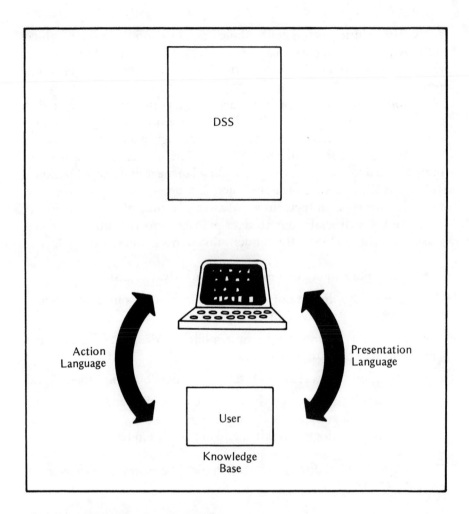

FIGURE 5.9 The User System Interface

2. *The display or presentation language*—what the user *sees.* The display language includes options such as character or line printer, display screen, graphics, color, plotters, audio output, *etc.*

3. *The knowledge base*—what the user *must know.* The knowledge base consists of what the user needs to bring to the session with the system in order to effectively use it. The knowledge may be in the user's head, on a reference card or instruction sheet, in a user's manual, in a series of "help" commands available upon request, *etc.*

The "richness" of the interface will depend on the strength of capabilities in each of these areas.

Another dimension of the user system interface is the concept of "dialogue style." Examples include the questions/answer approach, command languages, menus, and "fill in the blanks." Each style has pro's and con's depending on the type of user, task, and decision situation. For a more detailed discussion of dialogue styles see [13].

Although this just scratches the surface in this important area, a partial set of desirable capabilities for a DSS generator to support the user/system interface includes:

- the ability to handle a variety of dialogue styles, perhaps with the ability to shift among them at the user's choice;
- the ability to accommodate user actions in a variety of media;
- the ability to present data in a variety of formats and media; and
- the ability to provide flexible support for the users' knowledge base.

THE TOOLSMITH VIEW: THE UNDERLYING TECHNOLOGY

The toolsmith is concerned with the science involved in creating the information technology to support a DSS, and the architecture of combining the basic tools into a coherent system. The same three part model can be used to describe the toolsmith's concerns because the tools must be designed and combined to provide the three sets of capabilities.

Each of the three areas—dialogue, data handling, and model handling—has received a fair amount of attention from toolsmiths in the past. The topic of DSS and the requirements it imposes has put these efforts in a new perspective revealing how they can be interrelated to increase their collective effectiveness. Moreover, the DSS requirements have revealed some missing elements in existing efforts, indicating valuable potential areas for development.

DIALOGUE MANAGEMENT

There has been a great deal of theoretical and some empirical work on systems requirements for good man/machine interface. Many of these studies are based on watching users' behavior in using terminals, or surveying users or programmers to ascertain what they want in interactive systems.[10, 16] A recent study examines a series of interactive applications, many of which are DSS's, to assess the *type* of software capabilities required by the applications.[43] This study led directly to some creative work on the software architecture for dialogue generation and management systems (DGMS) as characterized in the model of the previous section.[12] This research uses a relation as the data structure for storing each picture or "frame" used in the system, and a decision table for storing the control mechanism for representing the potential users' option in branching from one frame to another.

DATA MANAGEMENT

Most of the significant work in the database management area during the past several years is aimed at transaction processing against large databases. Large DBMS's generally have inquiry/retrieval and flexible report preparation capabilities, but their largest contribution has been in the reduction of program maintenance costs through the separation of application programs and data definitions. On the other hand, DBMS work has generally had a rather naive view of the user and the user's requirements. A DSS user will not be satisfied merely with the capability to issue a set of retrieval commands which select items from the database, or even to display those selected items in a report with the flexible definition of format and headings. A DSS user needs to interact repeatedly and creatively with a relatively small set of data. The user may only need 40-100 data variables, but they must be the *right ones;* and what is right may change from day to day and week to week. Required data will probably include time series data which are not handled comprehensively by typical DBMS's. Better ways are needed to handle and coordinate time series data as well as mechanisms for capturing, processing, and tagging judgmental and probabilistic data. Better ways are also needed for extracting data from existing files and capturing data from previously non-computerized sources. The critical area of data extraction with fast response, which allows additions and deletions to the DSS database from the large transaction database was a major contribution of the GADS work.[8,29] In short, the significant development in database technology needs to be focused and extended in some key areas in order to directly serve the needs of a DSS.

MODEL MANAGEMENT

The area of model creation and handling may have the greatest potential contribution to a DSS. So far, the analytic capability provided by systems has evolved from statistical or financial analysis subroutines which can be called from a common command language. More recently, modeling languages provide a way of formulating interrelationships between variables in a way that permits the creation of simulation or "what if" models. As we noted earlier, many of the currently viable DSS Generators have evolved from these efforts. Early forms of "model management" seem to be evolving from enhancements to some modeling languages, which permit a model of this type to be used for sensitivity testing or goal seeking by specifying target and flexibility variables.

The model management area also has the potential for bringing some of the contributions of artificial intelligence (AI) to bear on a DSS. MYCIN, a system to support medical diagnosis, is based on "production rules," in the AI sense, which play the role of models in performing analytic and decision guidance functions.[15] A more general characterization of "knowledge management" as a way of handling models and data has also been tentatively explored.[7] More recent work proposes the use of a version of semantic networks for model representation.[17] Though this latter work is promising, AI research has shown the semantic network approach to be relatively inefficient with today's technology. Usable capabilities in model management in the near future are more likely to evolve from modeling languages, expanded subroutine approaches, and in some cases, AI production rules.

ISSUES FOR THE FUTURE

At this stage in the development of the DSS area, issues, problems, and fruitful directions for further research/development are plentiful. At a "task force" meeting this summer, thirty researchers from twelve countries gathered to discuss the nature of DSS's and to identify issues for the future. Their list, developed in group discussions over several days, was quite long.[19] The issues given here, phrased as difficult questions, seem to be the ones that must be dealt with quickly, lest the promise and potential benefits of DSS's be diluted or seriously delayed.

WHAT'S A DSS?

Earlier it was noted that some skeptics regard DSS as "just another buzz word." This article has shown that there is a significant amount of content behind the label. The danger remains, however, that the bandwagon effect will outrun our ability to define and develop potential contributions of a DSS. The market imperatives of the multi-billion dollar information systems industry tend to generate pressures to create simple labels for intuitively good ideas. It happened in many cases, but not all, of course, with MIS. Some companies are still trying to live down the aftereffects of the overpromise/under-undelivery/ disenchantment sequence from the MIS bandwagon of the late '60's. Eventually, a set of minimal capabilities or characteristics which characterize a DSS should evolve. In the short range, a partial solution is education—supplying managers with intellectual ammunition they can use in dealing with vendors. Managers should and must ask sharp, critical questions about the capabilities of any purported DSS, matching them against what is really needed.

WHAT IS REALLY NEEDED?

After nearly two decades of advancements in information technology, the real needs of managers from an information system are not well understood. The issue is further complicated by the realization that managers' needs and the needs of other "knowledge workers" with which they interact, are heavily interdependent. The DSS philosophy and approach has already shed some light on this issue by emphasizing "capabilities"—the ability for a manager to do things with an information system—rather than just "information needs" which too often infer data items and totals on a report.

Nevertheless, it is tempting to call for a hesitation in the development of DSS's until decision making and related managerial activities are fully understood. Though logically appealing, such a strategy is not practical. Neither the managers who face increasingly complex tasks, nor the information systems industry which has increasingly strong technology to offer, will be denied. They point out that a truly comprehensive theory of decision making has been pursued for years with minimum success.

A potential resolution of this problem is to develop and use a DSS in a way the reveals what managers can and should receive from an information system. For example, one of Scott Morton's early suggestions was that the system be designed to capture and track the steps taken by managers in the process of making key decisions, both as an aid to the analysis of the process, and as a potential training device for new managers.

The counterpart of the "needs" issue is the extent to which the system meets those needs, and the value of the performance increase that results. Evaluation of a DSS will be just as difficult, and important, as the evaluation of MIS has been. The direct and constant involvement of users, the ones in the best position to evaluate the systems, provides a glimmer of hope on this tough problem. Pursuit of these two tasks together may yield progress on both fronts with the kind of synergistic effect often sought from systems efforts. The iterative design approach and the three levels of technology afford the opportunity, if such a strategy is developed from the beginning.

WHO WILL DO IT?

A series of organizational issues will revolve around the roles and organizational placement of the people who will take the principle responsibility for the development of DSS's. Initiative and guidance for DSS development efforts frequently come from the user area, not from the EDP/MIS area. Yet current technology still requires technical support from the information systems professional. The DSS builder may work for the vice president of finance, but the technical support role is still played by someone in the MIS department. To some extent, the demand for a DSS supports the more general trend to distribute systems development efforts out of the MIS department into the user department. The difference is that many DSS software systems, or generators, specifically attempt to directly reach the end user without involvement of the MIS group. The enlightened MIS administrator considers this a healthy trend, and willingly supplies the required technical support and coordination. Less enlightened DP administrators often see it as a threat. Some companies have set up a group specifically charged with developing DSS type applications. This strategy creates a team of "DSS Builders" who can develop the necessary skills in dealing with users, become familiar with the available technology, and define the steps in the developmental approach for DSS's.

HOW SHOULD IT BE DONE?

One of the pillars on which the success of DSS rests, is the iterative development or adaptive design approach. The traditional five to seven stage system development process and the system life cycle concept have been the backbone of systems analysis for years. Most project management systems and approaches are based on it. The adaptive design approach, because it combines all the stages into one quick step which is repeated, will require a redefinition of system development milestones and a major modification of project management mechanisms. Since many traditional systems will not be susceptible to the iterative approach, a way is also needed for deciding when an application should be developed in the new way instead of the traditional way. The outline of the approach described earlier is conceptionally straightforward for applications that require only personal support. It becomes more complicated for group or organizational support when there are multiple users. In short, DSS builders will need to develop a set of milestones, checkpoints, documentation strategies, and project management procedures for DSS applications, and recognize when they should be used.

HOW MUCH CAN BE DONE?

The final issue is a caveat dealing with the limitations of technical solutions to the complexity faced by managers and decision makers. As information systems professionals, we must be careful not to feel, or even allow others to feel, that we can develop or devise a technological solution to all the problems of management. Managers will always "deal with complexity in a state of perplexity"—it is the nature of the job. Information technology can, and is, making a major contribution to improving the effectiveness of people in this situation, but the solution will never be total. With traditional systems, we continually narrow the scope and definition of the system until we know it will do the job it is required to do. If the specification/design/construction/implementation process is done right, the system is a success, measured against its original objectives. With a DSS, the user and his systems capabilities are constantly pursuing the problem, but the underspecified nature of the problem insures that there will never be a complete solution. Systems analysts have always had a little trouble with humility, but the DSS process requires a healthy dose of modesty with respect to the ability of technology to solve all the problems of managers in organizations.

CONCLUSION

The "Framework for Development" described above attempts to show the dimensions and scope of DSS in a way that will promote the further *development* of this highly promising type of information system.

1. The relationships between EDP, MIS and DSS show that DSS is only one of several important technology subsystems for improving organizational performance, and that DSS development efforts must carefully integrate with these other systems.

2. The three levels of technology and the interrelationships between people that use them provide a context for organizing the development effort.

3. The iterative design approach shows that the ultimate goal of the DSS development effort is the installation of an *adaptive system* consisting of all three levels of technology and their users operating and adapting to changes over time.

4. The performance objectives show the types of decision making to be served by, and the types of support which should be built into, a DSS as it is developed.

5. The three technical capabilities illustrate that development efforts must provide the DSS with capabilities in dialogue management, data management, and model management.

6. The issues discussed at the end of the article identify some potential roadblocks that must be recognized and confronted to permit the continued development of DSS.

In closing, it should now be clear that DSS is more than just a "buzz word," but caution must be used in announcing a new "era" in information systems. Perhaps the best term is a "DSS Movement" as user organizations, information systems vendors, and researchers become aware of the field, its potential, and the many unanswered questions. Events and mechanisms in the DSS Movement include systems development experience in organizations, hardware/software developments by vendors, publishing activities to report experience and research, and conferences to provide a forum for the exchange of ideas among interested parties.

It is clear that the momentum of the DSS Movement is building. With appropriate care and reasonable restraint, the coordinated efforts of managers, builders, toolsmiths, and researchers can converge in the development of a significant set of information systems to help improve the effectiveness of organizations and the people who work in them.

REFERENCES

[1] Alter, S. "A Taxonomy of Decision Support Systems," *Sloan Management Review*, Volume 19, Number 1, Fall 1977, pp. 39–56.

[2] Alter, S. *Decision Support Systems: Current Practice and Continuing Challenges*, Addison-Wesley Publishing Co., Reading, Massachusetts, 1980.

[3] Ashenhurst, R.L. "Curriculum Recommendations for Graduate Professional Programs in Information Systems," *ACM Communications*, Volume 15, Number 5, May 1972, pp. 363–398.

[4] Barbosa, L.C. and Hirko, R.G. "Integration of Algorithmic Aids into Decision Support Systems," *MIS Quarterly*, Volume 4, Number 1, March 1980, pp. 1–12.

[5] Bennett, J. "User-Oriented Graphics, Systems for Decision Support in Unstructured Tasks," in *User-Oriented Design of Interactive Graphics Systems*, in S. Treu (ed.), Association for Computing Machinery, New York, New York, 1977, pp. 3–11.

[6] Boeing Computer Services, c/o Mr. Park Thoreson, P.O. Box 24346, Seattle, Washington, 98124.

[7] Bonezek, H., Hosapple, C. W., and Whinston, A. "Evolving Roles of Models in Decision Support Systems," *Decision Sciences*, Volume 11, Number 2, April 1980, pp. 337–356.

[8] Carlson, E.D., Bennett, J., Giddings, G., and Mantey, P. "The Design and Evaluation of an Interactive Geo-Data Analysis and Display System," *Information Processing-74*, North Holland Publishing Co., Amsterdam, Holland, 1974.

[9] Carlson, E.D., and Sutton, J.A. "A Case Study of Non-Programmer Interactive Problem Solving, *IBM Research Report RJ1382*, San Jose, California, 1974.

[10] Carlson, E.D., Grace, B.F. and Sutton, J.A. "Case Studies of End User Requirements for Interactive Problem-Solving Systems," *MIS Quarterly*, Volume 1, Number 1, March 1977, pp. 51–63.

[11] Carlson, E.D. "An Approach for Designing Decision Support Systems," *Proceedings*, 11th Hawaii International Conference on Systems Sciences, Western Periodicals Co., North Hollywood, California, 1978, pp. 76–96.

[12] Carlson, E.D. and Metz, W. "Integrating Dialog Management and Data Management," *IBM Research Report RJ2738*, February 1, 1980, San Jose, California.

[13] Carlson, E.D. "The User-Interface for Decision Support Systems," unpublished working paper, IBM Research Laboratory, San Jose, California.

[14] Courbon, J., Drageof, J., and Jose, T. "L'Approache Evolutive," *Information Et Gestion No. 103*, Institute d'Administration des Enterprises, Grenoble, France, January-February 1979, pp. 51–59.

[15] Davis, R. "A DSS for Diagnosis and Therapy," *DataBase*, Volume 8, Number 3, Winter 1977, pp. 58–72.

[16] Dzida, W., Herda, S., and Itzfeldt, W.D. "User-Perceived Quality of Software Interactive Systems," *Proceedings*, Third Annual Conference on Engineering (IEEE) Computer Society, Long Beach, California, 1978, pp. 188–195.

[17] Elam, J., Henderson, J., and Miller, L. "Model Management Systems: An Approach to Decision Support in Complex Organizations," *Proceedings*, Conference on Information Systems, The Society for Management Information Systems, Philadelphia, Pennsylvania, December 1980.

[18] Execucom Systems Corporation, P.O. Box 9758, Austin, Texas, 78766.

[19] Fick, G. and Sprague, R.H., Jr., (eds.). *Decision Support Systems: Issues and Challenges*, Pergamon Press, Oxford, England, forthcoming in 1981.

[20] Gerrity, T.P., Jr. "Design of Man-Machine Decision Systems: An Application to Portfolio Management," *Sloan Management Review 12*, Volume 12, Number 2, Winter 1971, pp. 59–75.

[21] Hayes, R.H. and Noland, R.L. "What Kind of Corporate Modeling Functions Best?" *Harvard Business Review*, Volume 52, May-June 1974, pp. 102–112.

[22] Head, R. "Management Information Systems: A Critical Appraisal," *Datamation*, Volume 13, Number 5, May 1967, pp. 22–28.

[23] Keen, P.G.W. and Scott Morton, M.S. *Decision Support Systems: An Organizational Perspective*, Addison-Wesley Publishing Company, Reading Massachusetts, 1978.

[24] Keen, P.G.W. and Hackathorn, R.D. "Decision Support Systems and Personal Computing," Department of Decision Sciences, The Wharton School, The University of Pennsylvania, Working Paper 79-01-03, Philadelphia, Pennsylvania, April 3, 1979.

[25] Keen, P.G.W. "Adaptive Design for DSS," *Database*, Volume 12, Numbers 1 and 2, Fall 1980, pp. 15–25.

[26] Keen, P.G.W. "Decision Support Systems: A Research Perspective," in *Decision Support Systems: Issues and Challenges*, Pergamon Press, Oxford, England, 1981.

[27] Kroeber, H.W., Watson, H.J., and Sprague, R.H., Jr. "An Empirical Investigation and Analysis of the Current State of Information Systems Evolution," *Journal of Information and Management*, Volume 3, Number 1, February 1980, pp. 35–43.

[28] Little, J.D.C. "Models and Managers: The Concept of a Decision Calculus," *Management Science*, Volume 16, Number 8, April 1970, pp. B466–485.

[29] Mantey, P.E. and Carlson, E.D. "Integrated Geographic Data Bases: The GADS Experience," IBM Research Division, *IBM Research Report RJ2702*, San Jose, California, December 3, 1979.

[30] Ness, D.N. "Decision Support Systems: Theories of Design," presented at the Wharton Office of Naval Research Conference on Decision Support Systems, Philadelphia, Pennsylvania, November 4–7, 1975.

[31] Scott, J.H. "The Management Science Opportunity: A Systems Development Management Viewpoint," *MIS Quarterly*, Volume 2, Number 4, December 1978, pp. 59–61.

[32] Scott Morton, M.S. *Management Decision Systems: Computer Based Support for Decision Making*, Division of Research, Harvard University, Cambridge, Massachusetts, 1971.

[33] Simon, H. *The New Science of Management Decision*, Harper and Row, New York, New York, 1960.

[34] Simon, H. "Cognitive Science: The Newest Science of the Artificial," *Cognitive Science*, Volume 4, 1980, pp. 33–46.

[35] Society for Management Information Systems, *Proceedings of the Eleventh Annual Conference*, Chicago, Illinois, September 10-13, 1979, pp. 45–56.

[36] Sprague, R.H. and Watson, H.J. "MIS Concepts Part I," *Journal of Systems Management,* Volume 26, Number 1, January 1975, pp. 34–37.

[37] Sprague, R.H. and Watson, H.J. "Model Management in MIS," *Proceedings, 7th National AIDS,* Cincinnati, Ohio, November 5, 1975, pp. 213–215.

[38] Sprague, R.H. and Watson, H. "A Decision Support System for Banks," *Omega-The International Journal of Management Science,* Volume 4, Number 6, 1976, pp. 657–671.

[39] Sprague, R.H. and Watson, H.J. "Bit by Bit: Toward Decision Support Systems," *California Management Review,* Volume XXII, Number 1, Fall 1979, pp. 60–68.

[40] Sprague, R.H. "Decision Support Systems—Implications for the Systems Analysts," *Systems Analysis and Design: A Foundation for the 1980's,* Elsevier-North Holland, New York, New York, 1980, in press.

[41] Sprague, R.H. "A Framework for Research on Decision Support Systems," in *Decision Support Systems: Issues and Challenges,* Fick, G. and Sprague, R.H. (eds.), Pergamon Press, Oxford, England 1981, in press.

[42] Sutton, J. "Evaluation of a Decision Support System: A Case Study with the Office Products Division of IBM," San Jose, California: *IBM Research Report FJ2214* 1978.

[43] Sutton, J.A., and Sprague, R.H. "A Study of Display Generation and Management in Interactive Business Applications," *IBM Research Report No. RJ2392,* IBM Research Division, San Jose, California, November 9, 1978.

[44] TYMSHARE. 20705 Valley Green Driver, Cupertino, California, 95014.

[45] Wagner, G.R. "DSS: Hypotheses and Inferences," Internal Report, EXE-CUCOM Systems Corporation, Austin, Texas, 1980.

[46] Will, Hart J. "Model Management Systems," in *Information Systems and Organizational Structure,* E. Grochla and H. Szyperski (eds), Walter de Gruyter, New York, New York, 1975, pp. 467–483.

6

An Approach for Designing Decision Support Systems

by Eric D. Carlson

About the author:

Eric D. Carlson is a member of the staff at the IBM Research Laboratory in San Jose, CA. The paper, originally given at the 11th Hawaii International Conference on System Sciences, represents the author's synthesis of ideas developed by members of the decision support systems project at the San Jose laboratory. John Bennett and Jim Sutton provided many useful suggestions for early versions of the paper.

Studies of specific decisions and general studies of decision making have indicated the potential benefits of computer support for decision making. These potential benefits can be divided into two categories: displaced cost and added value.

Displaced cost results from reduced costs for data gathering, computation and data presentation in support of decision making. In these mechanical tasks, the dollar value of computer support is measurable.

Added value results from investigating more alternatives, doing more sophisticated analysis of alternatives, using better methods of com-

Reprinted with permission from Database

paring alternatives, making quicker decisions and so on. Often it is difficult to identify the added value because it does not occur on a routine basis. Measuring added value is complicated by the difficulty of linking increased profits or other monetary measures to a change in the decision making process, such as more alternatives considered.

Small improvements in decision making can result in high added value. For example, an airline's computer-supported decision to redeploy aircraft on one route is reported to have increased profit $300,000 in one month.[31] Such potential benefits continue to stimulate management's interest in computer support for decision making.[10]

Computer hardware and software vendors also have an interest in the development of computer support for decision making because such support can help justify large data bases, data base management systems, additional computing power, new programming languages, time sharing and terminals.[5] Computer support for decision making can encourage customer executives to take a personal interest in computers and can help the computer salesperson encourage "management involvement" in data processing.

The use of computers in decision making can be described in terms of various types of decisions (see Table 6.1). Following R.N. Anthony [3] , decisions can be classified as:

Strategic Planning: decisions related to setting policies, choosing objectives and selecting resources.

Management Control: decisions related to assuring effectiveness in acquisition and use of resources.

Operational Control: decisions related to assuring effectiveness in performing operations.

Operational Performance: decisions that are made in performing the operations.

H.A. Simon [29] classifies decisions as structured (programmable) or unstructured (nonprogrammable) depending on whether or not the decision making process can be described in detail before making the decision. A decision may be unstructured because of novelty, time constraints, lack of knowledge, large search space, need for nonquantifiable data and so on. G.A. Gorry and M.S. Scott Morton [17] combine Anthony's and Simon's categories, and the combination can be extended as shown in Table 6.1.

TABLE 6.1 Different Types of Decisions and Degree of Decision Structure (From Gorry and Scott Morton)

	Operational Performance	Operational Control	Management Control	Strategic Planning
Structured	Payroll Production	Accounts Receivable	Budget Analysis	Tanker Fleet Mix
	Airline Reservations	Inventory Control	Short Term Forecasts	Site Location
	Dispatching	Production Scheduling	Long Term Forecasts	Mergers
Unstructured	Solving A Crime	Cash Management	Budget Preparation	Product Planning

Gorry and Scott Morton claim that most existing computer support for decision making is for structured decisions, that some progress has been made in supporting semistructured decisions and that almost no computer support is used for unstructured decisions. They argue that it is the semistructured and unstructured decisions (especially management control and strategic planning) which are of the greatest concern to decision makers. They call systems which are intended to support these types of decisions decision support systems (DSS). Thus DSS are a subset of management information systems (MIS), since MIS include all systems which support any management decision making.

Because DSS have high potential value for both users and suppliers of computer services, one would expect to find many DSS in use. Yet the literature on the applications of computers in government and business indicates very little use of DSS. The lack of use is apparent even though there have been many attempts to develop such systems.

A survey of 56 DSS by S.L. Alter at M.I.T. divided them into two general categories: data-oriented systems and model-oriented systems. [2] Data-oriented systems provide functions for data retrieval, analysis and presentation. Both generalized and special-purpose software packages are included in this category. Systems in this category are usually developed by persons with data processing or computer science backgrounds. The model-oriented systems provide accounting, simulation or optimization models to help make decisions. These systems usually are developed by persons with management science backgrounds.

There are many opinions on why data-oriented systems and model-oriented systems have not had much success in supporting decision making. In general, the main problem seems to be a mismatch between DSS design or performance and the requirements of decision makers or decision making. The causes of the mismatch may be technical (for example, poor response times) or nontechnical (for example, different personal preferences). Because of the mismatch, many systems which are developed ceased to be used or are used for routine report generation rather than for direct support of decision makers.

This paper proposes a framework for designing DSS which is intended to help reduce the differences between the requirements of decision making and decision makers and the capabilities of the DSS. The framework is based upon a review of case studies of decision making and of DSS and upon five years of experience with the design, implementation and evaluation of a prototype DSS used in 16 applications with more than 200 users.[7, 18]

REQUIREMENTS FOR DSS

To understand DSS, we attempted to analyze the decisions and users for which such systems are intended. In particular, we reviewed and performed case studies of decision making to identify specific requirements of decision making and decision makers. There are many possible interpretations of these studies. The observations presented here are those which we have found useful in the design of DSS.

Three examples of paradigms of decision making illustrate the variety of decision making processes. The first example is the rational (economic) paradigm which postulates that decision processes attempt to maximize the expected value of a decision by determining payoffs, costs and risks for alternatives.[11] A second paradigm asserts that the decision making process is one of finding the first cost-effective alternative by using simple heuristics rather than optimal search techniques. [12] A third paradigm describes decision making as a process of successive limited comparisons to reach a consensus on one alternative.[20]

Additional evidence of the variety of decision making processes can be found in studies of decision making. L.A. Gordon and his associates [16], identified 40 processes in looking at nine types of decisions. H. Mintzberg and associates, [25] analyzed 25 decisions and identified seven basic processes with many variations. Carlson and Jim Sutton [8] observed different processes among individuals working on the same decision. Because of the variety of decision making processes, we conclude that a DSS is more likely to be used and to be cost effective if it supports multiple processes.

Another observation on decision making which we have found useful is that different types of decisions have different data processing requirements.[17] That is, a structured, operational control decision would have different requirements than a semistructured one and so on. For example, strategic planning decisions tend to require more varied, more aggregate and more qualitative data than management control decisions. And structured decisions tend to utilize more data transformations than unstructured decisions.

A specific decision may be of a different type in different organizations, at different times or for different decision makers. If a DSS is designed for a specific type of decision, any change in the type of decision requires a change in the DSS to accommodate changes in data processing requirements. Therefore we conclude that designing a DSS for a specific type of decision reduces the number of decisions it can support and leads to increased cost if there is a change in the type of decision which it is intended to support.

TYPES OF DECISION MAKERS

Studies of decision makers have ranged from recording their daily activities to observing their use of DSS. Five observations from such studies are important in our analysis of existing DSS and in our approach to DSS design.

First, decision makers have trouble describing a decision making process, but they do seem to rely on conceptualizations, such as pictures or charts, when making or explaining a decision.[8] In some cases the conceptualizations are not physically represented, but we can infer their existence as a basis for verbal communication (for example, "bottom line," "payoff curve," "quick ratio"). Thus a DSS should not require that a decision maker be able to describe the decision making process before the DSS is built, and DSS should help a decision maker conceptualize a problem.

Second, decision makers' activities can be categorized even though the decision making processes may be difficult to explain. H.A. Simon has used three categories for describing decision making activities:

intelligence, design and choice.[29] Intelligence, or problem finding, includes activities such as comparisons of current status with goals or standards, exception reporting, preliminary computations and so on. Design encompasses activities related to development of alternatives. Choice covers activities related to evaluating and selecting from the alternatives.

Studies of decision making which use this paradigm indicate that intelligence, design and choice activities are interleaved and interative, but that these activities can be identified.[27] Identifying intelligence, design and choice activities should be a useful method for selecting operations to be provided in a DSS. One must be careful, however, not to assume that these activities, and therefore the operations, will always be carried out in the same sequence.

A third observation is that decision makers need memory aids.[26] These memory aids may be physical, such as scratch paper, memos or reports. They may be mental rules that a decision maker applies. Or they may be reminders from a decision maker's staff. By observing the memory aids used by decision makers, we can identify memory aids which DSS should provide to be compatible with the needs of decision makers. A DSS may also provide additional memory aids or faster memory aids.

The fourth common observation about decision makers is that there are differences in their styles, skills and knowledge.[23] One possible explanation of the wide variety of decision-making processes is that the variety results from these differences. Therefore, if a DSS is designed to support a particular process, it would probably support particular styles, skills and knowledge rather than supporting the variety which is observed to exist. Decision makers would have to conform to the style, skills and knowledge assumed by the DSS.

Another approach is to try to design the DSS to match a specific decision maker's style, skill and knowledge. Because of the variety among decision makers, this approach is likely to require that the DSS be redesigned (or tailorable) for each decision maker, and that there be techniques for characterizing a decision maker's style, skills and knowledge. Such techniques are still not reliable or well known.[30]

Thus we conclude that if a DSS is to support varying styles, skills and knowledge, it should not attempt to enforce or to capture a particular pattern. Rather, the DSS should help decision makers use and develop their own styles, skills and knowledge. If this requirement can be met, the cost effectiveness of DSS should improve because several decision makers could make effective use of the same DSS.

Finally, a fifth observation is that decision makers expect to exercise direct, personal control over their support.[13, 24] This observation suggests that the decision maker should be able to personally control what the DSS does. This requirement does not necessarily imply that the decision maker needs to personally operate the DSS.[18] It implies that the decision maker must understand what the DSS can do and be able to interpret its outputs. With such an understanding, the decision maker can direct and evaluate the operation of a DSS and can integrate the information provided by the DSS with other information sources.

The correlation between our observations on the requirements of decision makers and the proposed DSS components is shown in Table 6.2. There are important parallels between the observed requirements (left column of Table 6.2) and the proposed DSS components (right column). The requirements indicate characteristics of decision makers and decision making which can be observed (and recorded) in a "systems analysis" preceding the design of a DSS. The DSS components identify the computer support which can be provided for each of these characteristics.

Note the expected differences between the requirements and the components as illustated by the examples under each of the four parallel headings (for example, a map outline contains less information than a city map). There are two reasons for the expected differences. First, a DSS will be only one of many alternatives for providing support for decision makers. Second, technology and costs limit the support that a DSS can provide.

For these reasons the DSS representations will not be as detailed as the decision makers' conceptualizations; the DSS operations will support only some of the decision making activities; the DSS memory aids will be activated differently than those to which the decision maker is accustomed, and using the DSS control aids will require learning new skills, making some changes in styles and adding to the decision maker's knowledge base.

We postulated earlier that the lack of use of DSS was caused by a mismatch between the requirements of decision makers and decision making and the support provided by DSS. The mismatch can be analyzed and illustrated using the parallels shown in Table 6.2. For ex-

TABLE 6.2 Decision Makers' Requirements and Proposed DSS Components

Decision Makers Use	*DSS Provides*
1. Conceptualizations	1. Representations
A city map	A map outline
Relationship between assets and liabilities	A scatterplot of assets vs. liabilities
2. Different Decision Making Processes and Decision Types, All Involving Activities for Intelligence, Design and Choice	2. Operations for Intelligence, Design and Choice
Gather data on customers	Query the data base
Create alternative customer assignments for salesmen	Update list to show assignments
Compare alternatives	Print summary statistics on each alternative
3. A Variety of Memory Aids	3. Automated Memory Aids
List of customers	Extracted data on customers
Summary sheets on customers	Views of customer data
Table showing salesmen and their customer assignments	Workspace for developing assignment tables
File drawer with old tables	Library for saving tables
Scratch paper	Temporary storage
Staff reminders	DSS messages
4. A Variety of Styles, Skills and Knowledge Applied Via Direct, Personal Control	4. Aids to Direct, Personal Control
Accepted conventions for inter-personal communication	Conventions for user-computer communication
Orders to staff	Training and explanation in how to give orders to the DSS
Standard operating procedures	Procedures formed from DSS operations
Revise orders or procedures	Override DSS defaults or procedures

ample in our analysis of existing DSS, such as the 56 described by Alter[2], we identified the following problems:

1. Existing DSS do not provide decision makers with familiar representations which support conceptualization. In addition the decision maker often is forced to deal with concepts (for example, flow charts) and representations (for example, printouts) which are unfamiliar and have little to do with the way the decision maker usually conceptualizes the decision.

2a. Existing DSS tend to segment intelligence, design and choice activities, whereas decision makers tend to integrate them. For example, Alter's data-oriented systems primarily support intelligence activities, but not design or choice, and the model-oriented systems primarily support design and choice and assume intelligence has been completed.

b. Existing DSS tend to support a single decision-making process.

3a. Existing DSS provide long-term memory aids (for example, data base), but do not provide short-term memory aids. For example, the scratch paper and staff reminders to which a decision maker is accustomed usually are not available in most DSS.

b. Existing DSS impose additional memory requirements, such as learning the names of the data in the DSS, and often the DSS does not provide memory aids to support these requirements.

4a. Existing DSS do not provide enough control aids to help the decision maker learn the new skills (for example, signing onto a computer terminal), styles (for example, automated support rather than manual) and knowledge base (for example, learning what the operations do) which a DSS introduces.

b. Existing DSS replace direct control with indirect control where one or more intermediaries interpret the DSS capabilities and outputs for the decision maker. This type of control introduces well-known communication problems.[13, 22]

The proposed framework for DSS design is intended to help overcome these problems. The parallels in Table 6.2 indicate where support is needed and highlight the design challenges in providing support which reduces the expected differences between the requirements of decision makers and the capabilities of the DSS. By using the framework we do not expect to overcome all the differences nor to totally replace manual support with automated support. We do expect to be able to reduce the differences to an acceptable level and to provide support which results in displaced cost or added value.

A DSS DESIGN FRAMEWORK

Any activity in a decision-making process takes place in the context of some conceptualization of the information which is used in the activity. The conceptualization may be a chart, a picture, a few numbers, an equation and so on. The conceptualization may be mental, but in most cases it is physically represented on scratch paper, blackboards, graph paper, foils and so on. A physical representation is particularly important when the decision maker wants to communicate some aspect of the decision to another person. Table 6.3 gives examples of representations associated with some intelligence, design and choice operations used in analyzing bad debts. Table 6.4 gives examples of intelligence, design and choice operations associated with a graph representation. Table 6.5 lists instances of representations.

Representations provide a context in which users can interpret DSS outputs and invoke the DSS operations. Representations also can be

---

TABLE 6.3 Representations for Analyzing Bad Debts

Intelligence

A *list* of customers with bad debts
A *graph* of bad debts over time
Cross tabulation statistics on
   attributes of customers

Design

A *scatter plot* of customers by two
   attributes associated with bad debts
   used to partition customers into risk
   groups

Choice

A *pie chart* of percentage of loans by
   customer risk groups used to
   evaluate the partition
A *report* on simulated bad debt losses
   for each alternative risk group
   partition

TABLE 6.4 Operations Associated with a Graph Representation

Intelligence

   Identify data to be graphed
   Scale the graph
   Plot data on graph

Design

   Draw polygons to partition the lines
    on the graph
   Forecast future data based on each
    partition

Choice

   Print summary statistics for each
    partition
   Display each partition on the graph

TABLE 6.5 Instances of Representations

Histograms	Balance sheets
Scatter plots	Spread sheets
Line graphs	Schedule boards
Mags	Engineering drawings
Surfaces	Architectural drawings
Pert charts	Aerial photographs
Organization charts	Seismic plots
Data entry forms	Scratch paper
Tabular reports	Memos

---

used to supply parameters for the DSS operations. For example, a point selected on a graph or locations on a map can identify a key value which will be used to retrieve detailed information. Or subdividing a list of employees or reconnecting groups on an organization chart can serve as an input mechanism for a manpower scheduling algorithm.

As described previously, intelligence, design and choice [29] is a well-known paradigm which can help classify the operations which are used in decision making. The categories are "complete" in that all decision-making operations can be classified into one or more of the three categories. Scott Morton [28] used these categories to describe a specific decision-making process before and after introduction of a DSS. T.P. Gerrity Jr. [15] illustrated how intelligence, design and choice could be used to analyze existing and proposed decision-making processes and how the categories could be used in identifying operations for a DSS.

Table 6.6 lists some general decision-making operations usually associated with intelligence, design and choice. Table 6.7 illustrates the use of the categories to describe the operations used in a specific decision-making process for allocating policemen to areas of a city.[8] Note that an operation may be used in more than one activity and that there is no prespecified ordering of the operations. The operations may involve complicated decision aids, such as simulation models or forecasting algorithms.

Several types of memory aids can be provided in a DSS to support the use of representations and operations. The following are examples:

A data base extracted from sources that are internal and external to the organization.

Views (aggregations and subsets) of the extracted data base.

Workspaces for displaying the representations and for preserving intermediate results as they are produced by the operations.

Libraries for saving workspace contents for later use.

Links for remembering data from one workspace or library that is needed as a reference when operating on the contents of another workspace.

Triggers to remind a decision maker that certain operations may need to be performed.

Profiles to store default and status data.

TABLE 6.6 General Decision Making
Operations for Intelligence, Design
and Choice

Intelligence

Gather data
Identify objectives
Diagnose problem
Validate data
Structure problem

Design

Gather data
Manipulate data
Quantify objectives
Generate alternatives
Assign risks or values to alternatives

Choice

Generate statistics on alternatives
Stimulate results of alternatives
Explain alternatives
Choose among alternatives
Explain choice

An extracted data base is a memory for data compiled from sources which the decision maker thinks may be relevant to the decision (see [6] for a detailed discussion of extracted data bases). Views are memory aids containing specifications for partitions (groupings), subsets or aggregations of data in the extracted data base which may be relevant to the decision alternatives. A decision can often be represented as a view. For example, a manpower allocation decision can be represented as a partition of a manpower data base where each group in the partition is allocated to a particular task. A hiring decision can be represented as a subset of an applicant data base where the subset is the list of those applicants to be hired.

Workspaces act as transient memory aids which provide a vehicle for accumulating results of the operations on the representations. For

**TABLE 6.7 Intelligence, Design and
Choice Operations in a Police Manpower
Allocation Decision**

Intelligence

Gather data on calls for police service
Divide city into small geographic zones
Select subset of data
Aggregate subset by zones
Validate data by checking familiar
   zones
Plot data values on map of zones

Design

Set objectives for combining zones
   into police beats
Develop quantitative measures for
   some of the objectives
Plot data values on map of zones
Combine zones into police beats
   based on objectives

Choice

Print summary statistics on each
   police beat alternative
Plot aggregate data on maps of police
   beat alternatives
Modify alternatives
Select an alternative
Plot data on map for chosen alter-
   native to explain choice to others

---

example, a "spread sheet" workspace could be used to develop product plans. A library associated with each workspace provides long-term memory for useful intermediate or final results created in the workspace. Many times information from one workspace or library may be needed in another workspace or library.

For example, a customer list may be used to identify a customer for whom the decision maker wants a graph of assets over time. Or a starting point on a may may be needed as an input to an algorithm that performs a districting operation on the map. Links are memory aids for information needed to make such associations. When a user identifies a customer's record in a list, or a point on a map, the link memory preserves the relevant data (for example, customer identification number, or the x,y coordinates of the point) for later use.

Triggers are memory aids used to invoke operations automatically or to remind the user to invoke operations. A trigger may be a message telling the user that before a profit forecasting operator can be invoked, rates of return must be assigned to various projects. Or a trigger may be a message which is displayed quarterly reminding the user to invoke the profit forecasting operation.

The profile memory aids store initial defaults for using the DSS, such as the axes labelling for a graph or the number of columns in a report. These defaults may be user-specific to help personalize use of the DSS for a decision maker. A "log" used to record a user's actions for backup or "replay" can be considered as a profile memory.

The representations, operations and memories of a DSS are intended to support a variety of decision making processes and a variety of types of decisions. The DSS control aids are intended to help decision makers use representations, operations and memories to synthesize a decision-making process based on their individual styles, skills and knowledge. The control aids may be crucial to the success of the DSS because they help the decision maker direct the use of the DSS and because they must help the decision maker acquire the new styles, skill and knowledge needed to make effective use of the DSS.

There are a variety of control aids which can be helpful. One type is aids which facilitate the mechanics of using the DSS. Examples are menus or function keys for operation selection, standard conventions for user-system interactions (such as editing or accessing libraries) which are enforced across representations and operations and use of the representations as the context for operation selection.

A second type includes aids to support training and explanation for using the DSS. These aids help the decision maker learn how to control the DSS. Natural language error messages, "help" commands and a training method which permits the decision maker to "learn-by-doing" are examples of this type of control aid.[19]

Decision maker control of the DSS also can be supported with aids which permit combining operations associated with one or more representations into procedures. A "procedure construction language" for combining the DSS operations using standard programming language control techniques, such as iteration and case statements, is one example of this type of control aid. Procedure construction also is a mechanism for adding new operations.

Another type of control aid is operations which help the decision maker change the results of other operations, such as the ability to edit results of a forecasting model. Finally, control aids can include operations for changing any DSS default values. For example, a DSS which provides operations to automatically draw a graph with a default scale and axes labelling conventions should provide operations to change these defaults.

USING THE DESIGN FRAMEWORK

The DSS design framework is a tool for focusing the systems analysis (of decision making) preceding the design of the DSS and for structuring the actual DSS design. We will assume an interactive, graphics environment in describing the use of representations, operations, memory aids and control aids as a DSS design framework, but such an environment is not required.

Both interactive systems and computer graphics expand the options available to the DSS designer. Interactive graphics should help provide control aids because user-system communication options are enhanced. Interactive graphics also enables a wide range of representations to be used in the DSS. Both Gerrity[15] and Scott Morton[28] present arguments for the use of interactive graphics for DSS.

Figure 6.1 illustrates the results of a hypothetical analysis for a DSS for investment decision making in which a flow chart of the existing or desired decision process is used as a tool for analysis. The focus is on the decision-making process, particularly the inputs, operations and

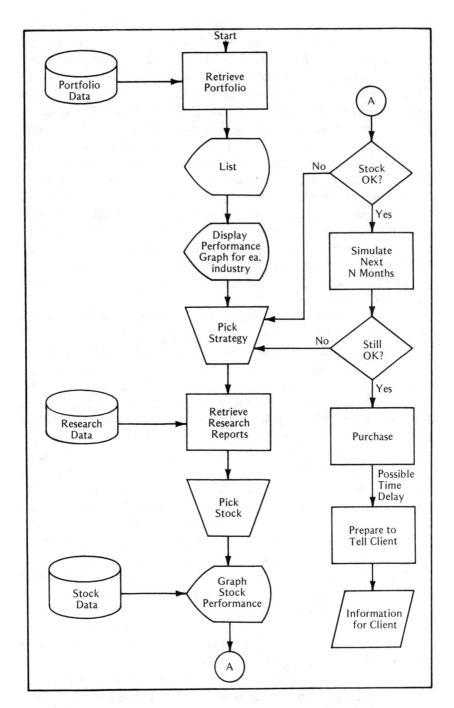

FIGURE 6.1 Analysis of an Investment Decision Using a Flowchart

outputs of each task. For different decision-making processes, the flow chart would be different. The same set of inputs, operations and outputs might appear, but their relationships would be different.

If the flow chart, or any other tool which focuses on the process, is used as a framework for the DSS design, the resulting DSS is likely to mimic the process captured in the flow chart. That is, the DSS is likely to impose a sequencing of tasks. If the decision-making process changes, the DSS has to be changed. Or if different decision makers who have different processes want to use the DSS, they will have to conform.

Figure 6.2 illustrates a schematic resulting from using the proposed DSS framework to analyze the same decision making. The representations and operations are chosen as in the process-oriented analysis, but they become the basis for the DSS structure. The representation-based approach attempts to make the DSS into a decision-making scratch pad which decision makers can use for a variety of decision-making processes.

In the representation-based DSS design, the memory and control aids help the user develop the decision-making process. If the decision maker wants to follow a specific process, such as the one flowcharted in Figure 6.1, this process can be "programmed" in the procedure construction language and executed under the decision maker's control.

Thus a DSS design based on Figure 6.2 is more general than the one based on Figure 6.1 because it can support a variety of decision-making processes. The DSS designed using Figure 6.2 might also be useful for other decisions, such as mergers and acquisitions, where the same representations and operations are used but the processes differ. The cost of the generality is that the DSS designed using Figure 6.2 may be more difficult to use than the one designed using Figure 6.1 because the user must learn to develop a process with the DSS. The memory and control aids are intended to help reduce this difficulty.

To show how the four components in the framework fit together, this example discusses a design using one representation, a scatterplot (see Figure 6.3). Results of operations on the scatterplot are displayed in the workspace. These results may be a scatterplot of data, a scatterplot of data filtered through a view or transformations of a scatterplot (for example, scaling). The scatterplot can be displayed and modified in the workspace by using the operations.

The operations are commands which the user selects, such as draw plot, label axes, scale, print summary statistics and so on. Intelligence,

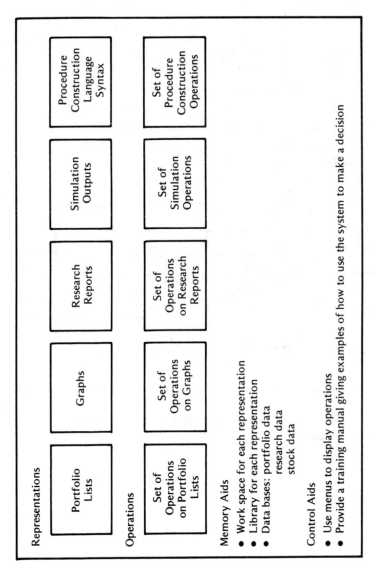

FIGURE 6.2 DSS Schematic Resulting From Using the DSS Design Framework to Analyze an Investment Decision

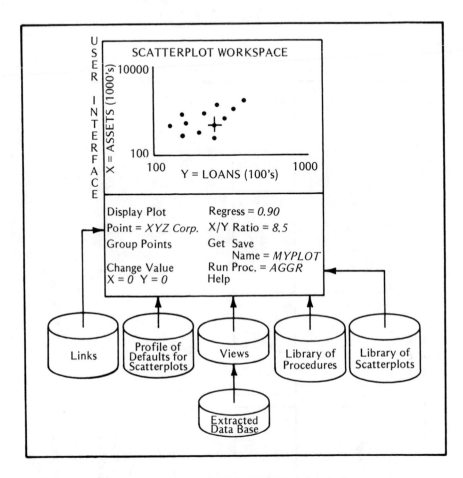

FIGURE 6.3 Relationships Among DSS Design Components for a Single Representation

design and choice activities identified in the systems analysis for the DSS could serve as a guide in selecting the operations to be provided.

Intelligence operations might include displaying data using a scatterplot and identifying the "keys" and numeric values of points on it. Design operations might include creating groups of points on the scatterplot and making temporary ("what if") changes in values of points on the scatterplot. Choice operations might include fitting a regression curve to the scatterplot and computing ratios based on values of points selected from the scatterplot.

Another method of identifying operations is to list possible transformations of the scatterplot representation, for example, plot points, label axes, scale axes, plot regression line, identify points on plot, compute ratios for a point on the plot, save plot and so on.

A library allows the user to name, save and retrieve the contents of a workspace. Thus, an interesting scatterplot can be named, saved and retrieved using the library facilities. A procedure library, which is associated with a representation (for example, an alphanumeric syntax used to construct procedures) can be accessed to execute "macro" operations which may or may not be associated with the scatterplot. For example, a sequence of labelling, scaling and drawing operations which produce a scatterplot may become a procedure. Or there may be a procedure which aggregates data for use in displaying a scatterplot.

The extracted data base contains the data which can be accessed for a scatterplot, and the view memory stores specifications for subsets (for example, customers with more than $100,000 in loans) and aggregations (for example, combine domestic and foreign customers). The link memory is used to store data which might be useful with another representation.

For example, the customer identification number associated with a point on the scatterplot could be stored in the link memory for use in retrieving a summary report about that customer. The profile memory would contain initial defaults for the scatterplot workspace, such as axes labelling and scaling, scatterplot colors or symbols used in the scatterplot. Defaults are required when the user wants a new scatterplot but forgets to specify some parameters.

Specific control aids include the menus which present the set of operations available to a user and a "help" operation for learning how to use other operations. Note that the memory aids often serve as control aids. For example, the procedure library can serve as a control aid for invoking a sequence of operations to create a scatterplot. The default memory can help reduce the time and effort needed to display a scatterplot (such as providing axes scaling and labelling for draw scatterplot). The workspace and library memories make it easier to recreate a scatterplot.

The representation (as displayed in the workspace) is the context in which operations are used, and the memory and control aids help the decision maker invoke the operations and use the results of the operations. If the parallels shown in Table 6.2 are valid, it is the combination of the four components which will help the decision maker make effective use of the DSS. That is, for any one of the four components to help improve decision making, the other three components seem necessary.

It seems likely that every DSS will require more than one representation. Figure 6.4 shows a DSS design framework consisting of four representations: tables, graphs, maps and a procedure construction language. Each representation has operations for intelligence, design and choice and an associated workspace for presenting the results of applying the operations to the representations. For each representation there are workspace, library and profile memory aids.

The operations in each representation can access an extracted data base, possibly through a view. Views can be constructed using a representation (for example, select points on a graph to specify subsetting) or via the procedure language.

With multiple representations, link memory is very important. Information presented on a graph may lead to questions best answered using a map (for example, "Where is that high crime area?"), or using a table (for example, "Give me a list of total crimes for each zone"). Links can help the user transfer data among representations. Control aids are provided by modules which give error messages and provide training sequences and by user-system communication conventions. Note that the control aids cover all representations, operations and memory aids.

Every DSS will have a specific set of representations, operations, memory aids and control aids. The generality of the DSS will depend on the skill of the designers in selecting these elements based on the analysis preceding the DSS design. The framework can provide a guide for selecting useful elements for combining them into a DSS. Our

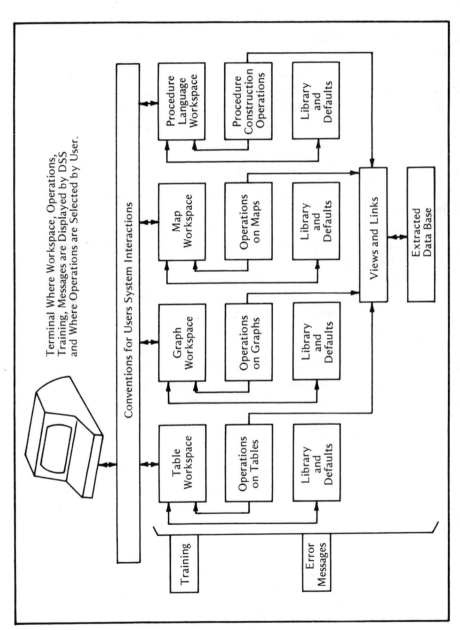

FIGURE 6.4 Relationships Among DSS Design Components for Multiple Representations

experience with one DSS indicates that one set of representations, operations, memories and control components can support a variety of users, decisions and decision-making processes.[7, 8, 18]

As a detailed example of the use of the framework, consider the design of the user interface for an interactive DSS to draw scatter-plots. Table 6.8 gives an example of a process-oriented interface ("20 questions") for a scatterplot. The interface leads the user through all the operations possible for this representation. Each time a scatterplot is drawn, the same process must be followed.

The interaction requires that the decision maker have a mental picture of what is going to appear (for example, what is the x-axis, does the data need to be scaled?). Once the scatterplot is drawn, any changes require that the procedural interaction be repeated. Figure 6.5 gives an example of the same set of operations, presented in the context of the scatterplot representation and supported by a set of memory and control aids.

The representation makes it convenient for the user to respond only to those of the "20 questions" which are relevant, does not require that changes to answers be made in a particular order, does not require that all questions be answered each time the scatterplot is drawn and presents the parameters (that is, the questions) with the scatterplot (that is, the result of the answers to the questions).

Exactly the same capabilities (inputs, operations and outputs) are provided in each interface. The process-oriented interface is based on the assumption that leading the user through a process makes the capabilities easier to use. The representation-oriented interface is based on the assumption that context makes the capabilities easier to use.

The final example is a comparison of a DSS containing the four proposed components with data-oriented and model-oriented DSS in a case study of DSS for a police manpower allocation decision. The problem was to decide on a scheme for allocating police manpower to areas (beats) of a city.

The decision was first attempted using a data-oriented DSS. Reports were generated on calls-for-service, workload, response times and so on. The relevant data was plotted manually on maps, and police management used the maps to develop and evaluate alternative decisions. The result was an allocation plan which was more expensive and further from the quantitative objectives (for example, balanced workload) than the existing plan.

TABLE 6.8 Process-Oriented Interface for Creating a Scatterplot

System:	*Choose function 1 = Table, 2 = Graphs, 3 = Plots*
User:	3
System:	*Do you want a tutorial? (Y or N)*
User:	N
System:	*Enter data name for X axis*
User:	$ LIABILITIES
System:	*Enter data name for Y axis*
User:	$ ASSETS
System:	*Do you want default scaling? (Y or N)*
User:	Y
System:	*Do you want default labels? (Y or N)*
User:	Y
System:	*Do you want descriptive statistics? (Y or N)*
User:	Y
System:	*Select stats 1 = Mean, 2 = Median, 3 = Range, 4 = Std. Dev., 5 = Var.*
User:	1 3 4
System:	*Do you want to execute a procedure? (Y or N)*
User:	N
System:	*Do you want to save results? (Y or N)*
User:	N

System then erases display screen and draws scatterplot

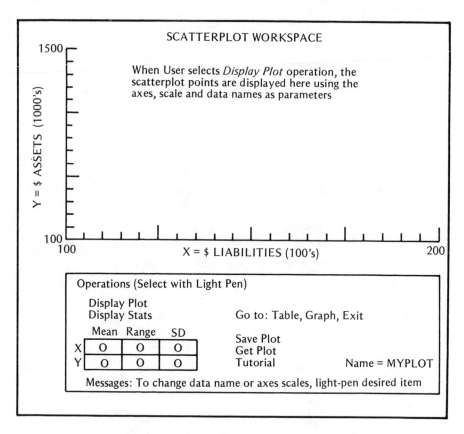

FIGURE 6.5 Representation-Oriented Interface for Creating a Scatterplot

Next, a consultant was asked to help make the decision using a model-oriented DSS to determine an "optimal" plan. The consultant interviewed decision makers, developed objective functions, collected the "relevant" data, developed an allocation model and ran the model to make the decision. The resulting plan was rejected by police management because it violated several qualitative objectives which could not be incorporated into the model.

A DSS with a design similar to the one shown in Figure 6.4 was provided for the decision makers. The DSS was used by the decision makers to develop a manpower allocation plan, a variation of which is still in use. This plan required fewer police officers and was closer to the objectives (quantitative and qualitative) than the plans produced with the data-oriented and model-oriented DSS.

Obviously we cannot prove that the DSS design framework caused one DSS to be more successful than the other two. In follow-up interviews with the police officers who used the DSS, however, each of the four components was referred to in some way by each officer as being a reason why this DSS was used and why it was valuable.

CONCLUDING ARGUMENTS

In spite of the current problems in developing DSS, the isolated successes and the potential for displaced cost and added value from DSS indicate high payoffs if the problems can be solved. Our observations from studies of decision making and decision makers indicated four major problems in the designs of existing DSS:

- Existing DSS do not provide the representations which decision makers need for semistructured and unstructured decisions.

- Existing DSS usually support only one or two of the three basic activities (intelligence, design and choice) of decision making.

- Existing DSS do not provide enough support (and introduce additional requirements) for conceptualization and memory, two areas where decision makers are observed to need help.

- Existing DSS require specification of the decision-making process in advance and do not support a variety of styles, skills and knowledge; thus they do not help decision makers exercise the personal control to which they are accustomed when making semistructured or unstructured decisions.

To overcome these problems we propose that DSS be designed to provide representations as the context for system use, operations on the representations to support intelligence, design and choice activities, a variety of memory aids to support use of the representations and operations and aids for controlling the representations, operations and memories.

At this stage we cannot prove that this approach is more useful or more cost effective than other approaches. We can, however, provide arguments as to why we believe the proposed approach is better. It is easier for a DSS designer to identify representations and the associated operations which are used in decision making than to identify completely all possible decision-making processes.

Instead of designing a DSS as a set of operations which result in representations, the DSS should be designed as a set of representations with associated operations. The operations-based approach is more likely to impose a sequencing of the operations (for example, a process) on the decision maker, and yet we see that to support a variety of processes, a large number of possible sequencings must be provided. The representation-based approach is more likely to let the decision maker select the sequencing of the operations, and a new sequencing (that is, a new process) is less likely to require programming modifications to the DSS. Moreover, one set of representations and operations can support a variety of decision-making processes because the differences among processes are more in the sequencing of operations and the decision maker's interpretation of representations than in the set of representations or operations to be used in the process.

The representations also may help DSS designers and users segment the decision problem and identify the relevant intelligence, design and choice operations. Providing operations for intelligence, design and choice activities helps the DSS support the entire decision-making process and makes it easier for the decision maker to integrate these activities.

The different types of memory aids act as note pads or file drawers for decision makers. They make it possible to retrieve useful results without having to repeat the operations which produced the results. They reduce the memory load on the decision maker, reduce the complexity of using representations and operations so that the decision maker can concentrate on interpretation, help personalize use of the DSS and help the DSS support a variety of decision-making processes. Providing control aids helps the decision makers direct the use of the representations, operations and memory aids according to their own styles, skills and knowledge.

User involvement is often cited as an objective for successful DSS design and use. All four components of the proposed approach for DSS design are intended to encourage user involvement. The representations provide a familiar frame of reference for designing and using the DSS. Operations for intelligence, design and choice provide support for common decision-making activities. Memory aids help develop and store useful results. Control aids help the decision maker personally direct the use of the DSS.

Further research is needed to substantiate the preceding arguments. Yet the success of a prototype system with the four components [7] and of systems which have similar components [e.g. 15, 28] indicate the potential value of using the proposed approach for DSS design.

REFERENCES

[1] Ackoff, R.L. Management misinformation systems. *Management Science* 14, 4 (December 1967), B147–B156.

[2] Alter, S.L., A study of computer-aided decision making in organizations. Unpublished dissertation, Massachusetts Institute of Technology, Cambridge, Mass., June 1975.

[3] Anthony, R.N. *Planning and Control Systems: A Framework for Analysis* Graduate School of Business Administration Harvard University, Boston, Mass., 1965.

[4] Brady, R.H. Computers in top-level decision making. *Harvard Business Review,* July-August 1967, 67–76.

[5] Canning, R.G. (ed.). APL and Decision Support Systems. *EDP Analyzer 14,* 5 (May 1976), 1–12.

[6] Carlson, E.D., Using large data bases for interactive problem solving. *Proceedings of the International Conference on Very Large Data Bases 1,* 1. ACM, New York. 1976, 499–501.

[7] Carlson, E.D., et al. The design and evaluation of an interactive geo-data analysis and display system. *Information Processing 74.* North Holland Publishing Company, Amsterdam, 1974, 1057–1061.

[8] Carlson, E.D. and Sutton, J.A. A case study of nonprogrammer interactive problem solving. IBM Research Report RJ1382. IBM Research Division, San Jose, CA, April 1974.

[9] Churchill, N.C., Kempster, J.H. and Uretsky, M. *Computer-Based Information Systems for Management: A Survey.* National Association of Accountants, New York, 1969.

[10] "Corporate war rooms plug into the computer" *Business Week,* August 23, 1976, 65–66.

[11] Cyert, R.M. and March, J.G., *A Behavioral Theory of the Firm.* Prentice-Hall, Englewood Cliffs, N.J., 1963.

[12] Cyert, R.M., Simon H.A., and Throw. Observation of a business decision. *Journal of Business 29,* (1956) 237-248.

[13] Eason, K.D. Understanding the naive computer user. *The Computer Journal 19,* 1 (February 1976), 3-7.

[14] Emery, J.C. An overview of management information systems. *DATA BASE 5,* 2-4 (December 1973), 1-11.

[15] Gerrity, T.P. Jr., Design of man-machine decision systems: an application to portfolio management. *Sloan Management Review 14,* (Winter 1971), 59-75.

[16] Gordon, L.A., Miller D., and Mintzberg, H. *Normative Models in Managerial Decision Making.* National Association of Accountants, New York, 1975.

[17] Gorry, G.A. and Scott Morton, M.S. A framework for management information systems. *Sloan Management Review 13,* (Fall 1971), 55-70.

[18] Grace, B.F. A case study of man/computer problem-solving: observations on interactive formulation of school attendance boundaries. IBM Research Report RJ1483, IBM Research Division, San Jose, Ca., February 1975.

[19] Grace, B.F. Training users of a decision support system. IBM Research Report RJ1790. IBM Research Division, San Jose, CA., May 1976.

[20] Lindblom, C.E. The Science of muddling through, *Public Administration Review 19,* (1959), 79-88.

[21] Little, J.D.C. Models and managers: the concept of a decision calculus. *Management Science 16,* 8 (April 1970), B-466-B-485.

[22] Lucas, H.C. *Why Information Systems Fail.* Columbia University Press, New York, 1975.

[23] McKenney, J.L. and Keen P.G.W. How managers minds work. *Harvard Business Review,* May-June 1974, 79-90.

[24] Mintzberg, H. *The Nature of Managerial Work.* Harper and Row, New York 1973.

[25] Mintzberg, H., Raisinghani, D., and Théorēt, A. The structure of "unstructured decision processes. *Administrative Science Quarterly,* 21 (June 1976), 246-275.

[26] Newell, A. and Simon, H.A. *Human Problem Solving.* Prentice-Hall, Inc. Englewood Cliffs, N.J., 1972.

[27] Nickerson, R.S. and Feehrer, C.E. Decision making and training. BBN Report No. 2982. Bolt Beranek and Newman, Inc., Cambridge, Mass., July 1975.

[28] Scott Morton, M.S. *Management Decision Systems.* Graduate School of Business Administration, Harvard University, Boston, Mass., 1971.

[29] Simon, H.A. *The New Science of Management Decisions.* Harper and Row, New York, 1960.

[30] Stabell, C.B. Individual differences in managerial decision making processes. Unpublished Ph.D. dissertation. M.I.T. Sloan School of Management, September 1974.

[31] Time Sharing Information Services, Inc., American Airlines Information Management System: Development, history, and return on investment. *Time Sharing Today* 3, 4 and 5 (July-August 1972), 1-15.

7

Why is Man-Computer Interaction Important for Decision Support Systems

by Steve Alter

About the author:

Steve Alter is a professor at the University of Southern California, Los Angeles.

INTRODUCTION

This paper attempts to shed some light on the whole issue of man-computer interaction. The basic point of this paper is that we should not allow our traditional jargon to shape our current thoughts about the on-line tools we use now and the interactive tools we may use in the future.

Ever since it became feasible to provide computing environments which could support on-line terminals, management scientists have enjoyed extolling the virtues of their latest interactive decision support systems. In this climate of opinion, I set out to write a Ph. D. thesis [1] on the development and use of such systems in current busi-

Reprinted with permission from Interfaces.

ness organizations. Early on, it became clear that something was drastically wrong. The ill-defined, but somehow anticipated "synergy" of man and machine just didn't seem to pan out in a sufficiently dramatic way to justify all the attention and anticipation. Although a substantial number of systems did deliver computing power in an on-line environment, the impact of man-computer interaction on the end result was almost always extremely difficult for users to define.

WHAT IS MAN-COMPUTER INTERACTION?

A logical starting point in discussing man-computer interaction is to cite an obvious feature of interactive, conversational decision support systems that is ignored by the prevailing rhetoric, namely, that such systems are neither interactive nor conversational in any "interesting" sense of the words. Using Webster's definition of interaction, i.e., mutual or reciprocal action or influence, even batch JCL error diagnostics such as:

IEF6591 MISPLACED SYSCHK DD STATEMENT

might be considered instances of interaction. At the risk of unfairness in the opposite direction, one might attempt to judge the level of man-machine interaction in current decision support systems in terms of a subset of Bales' [2] categories of interaction by members of human groups:

— gives answers,

— gives opinions or suggestions,

— gives orientation,

— asks for orientation,

— asks for opinions or suggestions,

— asks for answers.

Except in some highly specialized applications such as logical circuit design, the main categories of response by existing systems are "gives answers" and "asks for answers." "Gives answers" occurs when the answers are requested in a very specific, unambiguously defined question. "Asks for answers" occurs when the user's unambiguous request triggers a menu of pre-specified questions which must be answered in order to provide data needed to generate a pre-specified report. Calling this either interaction or conversation certainly stretches the meanings of these words, if not their definitions.

As John Bennett points out [3], however, human-to-human interaction may not be a good way to judge man-computer interaction. If possible at all, the man-to-man model of interaction between equals will not describe man-computer interaction outside of research settings for many years to come. "Slave-master" and "tool-craftsman" are better models of the kinds of interaction that are feasible now and in the near future.

WHAT IS INTERACTIVE PROBLEM SOLVING?

Underlying the notion that man-machine interaction is important is the idea that there are many "unstructured" problems that can be handled best through the process of "interactive problem solving." This process usually involves one or more people (preferably decision makers) sitting at a computer terminal working on a problem in an attempt to find the best possible way to visualize the problem and the best possible course of action.

Reports of such behavior were extremely rare in interviews concerning each of 56 different systems.[1] In the most common usage pattern for on-line systems, most of the thinking occurred off-line. Typically, the on-line system users came to the terminal with a prior idea of which reports they would request or how they would test the effects of a range of values of particular variables. In most of the instances where interactive problem solving was mentioned, the purpose was that of developing a report which would look good to someone else rather than of trying to find an answer which the user would act upon. A prime example:

When asked whether he ever made direct use of a case tracking system, the head of an adjudication group in a government regulatory agency said that he remembered only one instance. This was when he spent a lunch hour trying to generate a report which made his group's recent performance appear as favorable as possible in spite of some unfortunate delays and problems which made the standard report look rather bad.

This sort of usage seemed especially remarkable to me because it far outweighed the types of interactive problem solving I had expected to find.

It should be stressed that no conclusion concerning the potential utility of interactive problem solving can be drawn from the data in the sample. It is at least conceivable that future decision support systems will routinely exhibit a mix of power and flexibility sufficient for supporting interactive problem solving as defined above. For this to occur, however, major reductions in the costs of programming, modeling, and data storage, manipulation, and display will be required. Only at that point, however, will it be possible to understand the true significance of interactive problem solving for the usual run of managerial decision making.

WHY ARE DECISION MAKERS HESITANT TO USE COMPUTER INTERACTIVELY?

There has been much conjecture on this topic. A remarkably diverse collection of reasons have been cited, e.g., the lack of a natural language interface, the special style of work habits of managers, and even status hang-ups concerning typing. My conclusion is that most existing interactive decision support systems simply don't do anything which would entice an executive to use them at all.

For business problems which have enough structure to allow the evaluation of alternatives using models, it would seem that it should be possible to list feasible values of parameters, list the dimensions of the objective function, and then simply perform a series of runs using these values. For repetitive business situations in which problems can be identified using pre-specified exception reports, interaction would not be needed. Although interaction would be useful in exploring novel problems and/or unfamiliar situations (given that the appropriate data and models had somehow found their way into the system previously), it is reasonable to wonder whether the identity of the person hunched over the hot, smoking computer terminal should really matter very much on the average (assuming adequate competence and knowledge).

Consistent with this view, usage patterns for a particular commercial media analysis system led to a plausible assumption concerning the identity of direct users. The hands-on users of this media analysis system broke out as follows: Around 50% were secretaries or very junior analysts who simply typed specifications for previously requested reports and returned the output to their superiors. Another 35% of the users were empowered to make a limited range of substantive analysis decisions. Whenever the output revealed situations which looked especially interesting, they could pursue those situations by requesting additional reports. Up to 15% of the users were full project directors who had total freedom in the use of the system. The smaller the user organization, the more likely it was that a managerial individual would work directly with the system, principally because he didn't have a large amount of staff help. The generalization, which seemed to hold across the sample, was that the likelihood of direct decision support system usage by a decision maker is inversely proportional to the amount of staff help that is available. If much staff help is available, staff people will tend to be the users of (current) decision support systems while the decision makers attend to other chores. Whether this trend will be reversed by future decision support systems remains a matter of conjecture.

WHY SHOULD DECISION MAKERS USE COMPUTERS INTERACTIVELY?

It is a common belief that the direct use of decision support systems by decision makers should be encouraged. Be this as it may, the interviews in [1] revealed eight to ten anecdotes about the misuse of systems by people who were sold on a system's capabilities without really understanding either the capabilities or the associated limitations of the system. The common theme running through these examples was that there is a great danger of misuse of a system when it is not under the control of someone who understands the details. Given that we have trouble building models that are genuinely robust, and given that masses of historical data are difficult to interpret or even interrogate without models of some sort, *it seems to me that the direct use of decision support systems by nonexperts should be discouraged rather than encouraged.*

In contrast to suggestions that better man-machine interfaces are the key to greater managerial usage of decision support systems, this would imply that the goal of developing better man-machine interfaces in order to entice direct usage by busy managers may be entirely inappropriate. If managers have neither the time nor the inclination to learn the assumptions and practical details underlying a decision support system, then they should be encouraged to use it only through intermediaries who *do* understand the details.

Better man-computer interfaces are sorely needed, but not primarily by managers (at this point in the development of the technology).These improved interfaces are needed to help experts communicate with computers directly and precisely in well-defined terms related to the business problem at hand and not involved with distracting computer implementation features such as file configuration, data structure, decimal vs. binary representation of numbers, subroutine linkage conventions, and so on. The research in this area would not worry about cosmetic features of a language (e.g., error tolerance, English-like appearance, acceptance of ambiguous questions), but rather, about the precision, terseness, scope, power, and flexibility of the language in its application to the problem domain by experts (who might well be staff intermediaries working very closely with managers).

RETREAT FROM THE BRINK OF HERESY: Well-known Advantages of On-line Computation

On the other hand, on-line access to computers has a number of advantages which are well known:

1. Rapid turnaround allows computer users to obtain answers to isolated questions more or less immediately rather than tomorrow or next month. This means that reservation clerks can obtain up-to-the-minute information concerning openings. It also means that staff analysts can respond quickly to the new policy proposed in the executive committee and may, for example, even be able to generate pro forma statements before a meeting ends.

2. Rapid turnaround helps the computer user avoid the annoyance of interrupted concentration while waiting for the output. This is especially important in expediting the analysis of a data base and in testing complicated models.

3. Rapid turnaround allows people to consider more alternatives. On-line access to models makes it more feasible to play with them and to

do a certain amount of fine tuning of plans. When asked whether this capability led to significant improvments or insights, almost every respondent said that he could not quantify the improvement, but felt that it was not negligible.

4. Rapid turnaround alleviates annoyances related to debugging. Everyone who has used a batch system appreciates the pain of returning the next day only to find that he had asked the wrong question or had received no results at all due to a misplaced comma or other minute grammatical error.

5. On-line computation is essential for applications which involve monitoring and controlling production processes in real time.

These advantages of on-line computation are very real. Disappointingly, however, they are usually related to convenience and efficiency rather than the man-machine synergy I was always looking for. Although impressive capabilities leading toward man-machine synergy have been displayed by military command and control systems and special purpose systems developed in research settings, most of the practical benefits of on-line computation in decision support systems in business organizations seem to have occurred through more mundane mechanisms.

HOW ON-LINE-NESS CAN AFFECT SUBSTANCE

The most clear-cut impact of on-line-ness encountered in [1] occurred in a number of cases in which an on-line decision support system was seen as an impartial resource that could be used to focus and clarify a negotiation process. One of the earliest examples of this sort of usage is described by Scott Morton.[5] He built a CRT-based information system that was used in monthly planning meetings in evaluating the impact of alternative schedules on both marketing and production performance for a large household appliance. Prior to the system, the production and marketing managers had had a difficult time reconciling their mutually contradictory goals. The ongoing use of the model helped them appreciate their mutual dependency and greatly facilitated the development of plans that were satisfactory to both parties. A more recent example which has been used in many public sector settings is the GADS system developed by IBM Research, San Jose.[4] In one application, several teams of police personnel developed and evaluated alternative combinations of police "beats" with the ultimate goal of aggregating 248 city zones to 40 beats which were both balanced and equitable. The system provided instantaneous evaluations in terms of call-for-police-service statistics, while the user teams brought to bear their personal knowledge of the geography and character of each neighborhood. The result was a group problem solving climate in which computerized facts and personal knowledge and judgment could be brought to bear freely and productively. A final example encountered in [1] was an on-line shop floor information system. This system contained detailed historical information by lot and production step which could be displayed through standard retrieval commands concerning productivity by combinations of operator, machine, lot, production step, and so on. Aside from its use by production foremen in monitoring work flow and pinpointing yield problems, it became an implicit arbiter of day-to-day disputes concerning who had worked on what lot, when and why it was late or below standards. In all three of these cases, the fact that the system was on-line affected the substance of a group negotiation or problem solving process. Of particular significance was the fact that the system facilitated communication by clarifying where things stood, separating questions of judgment from questions of fact, and helping people focus on the same things at the same time.

WHERE DOES THIS LEAVE US?

The preceding sections can be summarized as follows:

1. Current interactive systems are not really interactive.

2. There is some question whether current systems can do anything which should entice executives to use them.

3. It is conceivable that nonexperts should be discouraged rather than encouraged to use on-line systems without the active help of expert intermediaries.

4. On-line systems have clearly brought their users significant benefits of efficiency and convenience.

5. Interactive computing sometimes has a major substantive impact in group planning processes.

Where does this leave us with regard to the impact of man-computer "interaction" on the decision support systems that are used today?

The first and most obvious point is that regardless of the identity or role of the hands-on user, responsive and well-engineered tools or systems are preferred to cumbersome, unresponsive, unmanageable tools or systems. In terms of the benefits listed above, on-line computational tools are often more responsive, more manageable, and more useable than off-line tools, especially in nonrepetitive situations.

The second point is that interaction for its own sake is not the main issue. Nominally interactive decision support systems encountered in [1] exhibited a wide range of successful patterns. Several were used directly by managers. Many were used by staff analysts in response to or in anticipation of requests by managers. In four or five instances, it was stated explicitly that the manager was never shown a computer output and that he was hardly aware that a computer had been used in developing what he perceived as a normal staff analysis. Across this range of usage patterns, the key issue was not whether the user of manager could talk to a computer to get the answers he needed, but rather, whether a combination of people, data, models, and technical tools could provide these answers in a convenient, timely, and cost-effective manner.

What is important in decision support systems is primarily "responsiveness" rather than "interactiveness," where responsiveness is a combination of:

1. power—the degree to which the system (including its human elements) can answer the most important questions;

2. accessibility—the degree to which the system can provide these answers in a timely and consistent manner;

3. flexibility—the degree to which the system can adapt to changing needs and situations.

From this perspective, the type of interface, the scope and type of model, the identity of the user, and many other issues are in some sense a series of design decisions whose overall objective is to attain a cost effective degree of responsiveness. For many decision situations, the best responsiveness for the price is attained by hiring staff people to do analyses more or less outside of the company's computer systems. For many others, strong reliance upon computer technology is simply a better choice. For a third group, there are no truly satisfactory choices because the most important questions (e.g., what really will happen next year?) seem to defy any formal or systematic combination of human intelligence and computer technology.

Ever since the notion of "interactive" computing was conceived in the 1950s, there has been a great sense of anticipation in the jargon surrounding this field. In reality, interactive computing has been a great boon in terms of the convenience and efficiency of computer users; occasionally, it has had a direct impact on the quality of decision making processes; in some cases, it may have created an environment in which some sort of man-computer synergy could occur; it hasn't been a panacea—YET.

REFERENCES

[1] Alter, Steven, "A Study of Computer Aided Decision Making in Organizations," unpublished Ph.D. thesis, MIT, 1975.

[2] Bales, Robert and Strodtbeck, Fred, "Phases in Group Problem Solving," *Journal of Abnormal and Social Psychology*, Vol. 46, pp. 485–495, 1951.

[3] Bennett, John, personal correspondence.

[4] Carlson, Eric et al., "The Design and Evaluation of an Interactive Geo-Data Analysis and Display System," in *Info Processing '74*, Amsterdam: North Holland, 1974, pp. 1057–1061.

[5] Scott Morton, Michael, *Management Decision Systems*, Boston: Division of Research, Harvard Business School, 1971.

8

INTERACTIVE COMPUTER SYSTEMS FOR MANAGERS: A Modest Proposal

by Peter G. W. Keen

About the author:

Peter G. W. Keen is assistant professor of organizational psychology at the Alfred P. Sloan School of Management, Massachusetts Institute of Technology.

INTRODUCTION

Until recently most managers had no direct contact with computer systems. They received standardized reports produced by their organization's data processing operations and might also commission special studies implemented by a technical staff. In many companies this situation has not changed, but in others the decentralization of the computer resource made possible by development of time-sharing, advance telecommunications and minicomputers has encouraged the creation of "interactive" systems. Managers in these companies can access the computer from a terminal, enter their requests or commands

Reprinted with permission from Sloan Management Review

directly, and receive feedback which is virtually immediate. The system software can be designed to allow a man-machine dialogue which transforms the computer into a personalized problem-solving tool.

Interactive systems facilitate the use of the computer's analytic power and data retrieval capabilities by managers as part of their ongoing decision-making process. There have been many lyrical visions of a man-machine symbiosis; Licklider defines a "procognitive" system which will give the decision maker access to a store of knowledge and analytic power that will immensely expand his problem-solving activities.[1] While this vision remains a distant (and for some a disturbing) ideal, the past few years have seen a rapid growth in the use of interactive computer technology. In particular, the concept of "Decision Support Systems" (DSS) has exploited the opportunity provided by time-sharing to tailor computer systems to managers' decision-making needs and processes.[2]

The DSS approach is based on several assumptions about effective decision making and the role of the computer within the problem-solving process.

- The computer must *support* the manager but not *replace* his judgment. It should not try to provide the "answer" nor impose a predefined sequence of analysis.

- The main payoff from computer support is in *semistructured* tasks. This imprecise term describes situations where parts of the analysis have sufficient potential for systematization for the computer to be of value, but where the decision maker's insight and judgment are needed to control the process.

- Effective problem solving is essentially *interactive* and is enhanced by a dialogue between man and machine. The user explores the problem situation, responds to feedback from the system, and exploits both his own strengths of experience and insight (often intuitive) and the system's analytic and informational power.

This article focuses on the last of these assumptions. The concept of interactive problem solving is a central tenet of faith in the DSS movement. It has led to a reliance on time-sharing and the design of software interfaces that are humanized and easy to use. Its application has also been fairly successful in making the computer relevant to managers and in replacing their indirect, essentially passive use of information systems with a highly active involvement.

There is a general tendency in the evangelical computer field to make dramatic claims. The DSS faith by comparison is relatively modest. It aims at developing systems for managers within a limited range of tasks, and it emphasizes the primacy of the manger in both the use of the system and the overall decision process. Several systems already exist which have been used over a lengthy period of time by middle-level managers for complex jobs. Empirical studies are available for the following three examples:

1. PMS is a portfolio management system used by investment managers in a bank's trust department.[3] This system provides graphical capabilities for data retrieval, analysis of customer portfolios, and search routines.

2. BRANDAID is a marketing planning model for evaluating pricing, promotion, and sales force decisions.[4] BRANDAID is based on a highly flexible interactive software interface that allows fast development of complex models.

3. GADS is an experimental DSS developed by IBM Research, San Jose.[5] This is a general purpose system which constructs and displays computerized maps for use in designing police force beats, planning urban growth, and assigning school district boundaries.

Experience with these and similar systems demonstrates that managers can and will use the computer as a problem-solving aid. Nonetheless, the movement has been limited to DSS usage by middle managers and staff specialists; senior managers still make minimal direct use of computer systems. In addition, there seems to be relatively little *interactive* problem solving. DSS frequently are run in a "pause-and-reflect" mode. Rather than a man-machine dialogue, most sessions at the terminal involve the entry of a few input commands which produce limited output that the user then takes away to analyze. The key value of time-sharing is the *accessibility* it allows, rather than its facilitation of interactive conversation.

Both of these conclusions have some important implications. They suggest that the DSS approach may need extension if the computer is to be made useful and usable by top managers. Also, the article of faith of interactive problem solving needs closer examination. These two topics are the subject of the rest of this article.

SYSTEMS FOR TOP MANAGERS: THE UNDERLYING ISSUE

The description of the DSS movement in terms of faith is deliberate. The whole history of information systems has been dominated by evangelical aims and assertions. This was the main cause of such recurrent fads of the 1960s as "the Total System," "Real-time, Online Planning Systems," and "Global Corporate Data Base." True believers make vast claims for a new technology or methodology and build expectations that are too often unreachable. Yet, faith does have its merits; the believers' commitment and energy are the vital driving forces behind the complex, risky, and unpredictable incursion of the computer on modern society.

The dominant evangelical aim has long been to bring the computer to top-level decision making. This aim has not been met. The term "Management Information System" (MIS) is largely a misnomer, since routinized historical analysis of sales, accounting, and inventory data is of only peripheral relevance to strategic planning. (A recent study of how executives in multinational corporations gather strategic intelligence summarized the use of the computer under the category "Other" which accounts for 5 percent of information sources.[6]) Hall's survey across a wide range of organizations, reported in an article "Strategic Planning Systems: Are Top Managers Really Using Them?" concludes that they are obviously not.[7] The unwillingness of executives to use a computer terminal is legendary.

These examples indicate that we do not as yet have effective strategies for the design and implementation of computer systems for senior-level decision makers. However, the aim remains and rests on faith—*surely* the computer can be made useful to top managers. The DSS approach defines a set of assumptions that have helped to make the computer relevant for middle managers in a limited range of applications. Its concepts and experience provide a base for accomplishing the wider aim. The key issues seem to be a more flexible conception of "interactive" and a broader definition of the man-machine interface that makes interaction possible. In particular, the problem-solving needs of the senior manager may best be met by the use of a staff specialist as an intermediary rather than through the direct use of a software interface.

INTERACTIVE SYSTEMS: SOME DEFINITIONS

Any interactive computer system requires:

- A user (This is not a trite point; the DSS approach stresses the fact that the "system" is man-with-machine.);

- A communication device, generally a terminal;

- The software interface which allows interaction;

- Data and models.

The interface is generally tailored to the user. Increasing attention has been paid to "human engineering" and to accommodating inexperienced as well as expert users. This is seen as critical to overcoming managers' fear or dislike of the computer. From the users' viewpoint, the *interface* is the *system* and the main issue in design is how the system should appear to the user. The same system may be presented in a variety of modes. Selection of the specific modes of interface which are made available to the user involves many tradeoffs between efficiency and software overhead costs.

The example below shows three interface modes. Each one utilizes a linear programming algorithm which requires user specification of such parameters as selling price and estimated sales. The program itself retrieves production and cost data from a permanent set of data bases. (The user inputs in each of the sessions are italicized.)

- *Programmer mode:*

  run LPX
  ? f/2   (output file will be on unit 2)
  ? 23.50 500k 200k end   (input data)
  ? link lpz-plx,rpt2,rpt4   (creates special program lpz from library of routines)
  ? save lpz   (stores lpz in permanent form)
  ? run/debug   (runs the program in "debug" mode, which allows the programmer to interrupt the run and access machine level data and commands)

Programmer mode is obviously not for the inexperienced user. It has some clear advantages if the program needs to be changed often, if a particular problem to be solved requires interpreting exactly what logical routines and data facilities are needed, or if the efficient running of the program depends on careful choice of routines and input methods.

- *Expert mode:*

run LPX
ready
input
price? *23.5*
sales? *500,000*
safety stock? *200,000*
check input? *no*   (asks if the user wishes to print out input data)
LPX running   (system automatically runs the program)
reports? *help*   (asks user which reports he wishes to have printed out; user replies by asking for list of options)
reports available   SOLN—summary of LP solution
                     COST—summary of cost data
                     SENSY—sensitivity analysis of solution
reports? *SOLN COST*

Dialogues in this style are limited only by the ingenuity of the system designer. They may, however, require more programming and running time than the underlying linear program and reporting routines. They are highly general and must be tailored to the user. Most DSS interfaces are of this style.

- *Novice mode:*

run LPX
please enter input data
selling price ($) ? *23.50*
estimated sales at this price (in units) ? *500,000*
desired inventory safety stock (in units) ? *200,000*

input data complete; check figures, type "y" if OK, type "c" if
data incorrect
price   23.50   OK? *y*
sales   500,000 OK? *y*
safety stock   200,000 OK? *y*
LPX now running; please wait
do you wish to see the solution in detail? *no*
reports available are;   COST summarizes cost coefficients and
                        totals
                        SENSY performs sensitivity analysis
type the name of the report(s) you would like (separate names by
comma or blank) ? *COST*

The Novice mode is polite, long-winded, and structures the users'
dialogue. It tries to minimize the skills and knowledge needed to
run the system and generally includes routines to check for errors
and to advise or prompt the user.

Many systems combine these modes. The user is often asked at the
start whether he wants the Expert or Novice styles. It is not uncommon
for a designer to embed an existing system which requires Programmer
level interactions within an Expert interface.

There is a fourth possible mode of interaction that at present cannot
even be approximated through software. This is an English language
or *Natural mode.* For the example problem above, a Natural mode
query would be:

Try out the LP, with Marketing's best estimates for next year. See how
sensitive the output is to changes in demand. I'll review it with you and we
can plan what else to look at.

While there has been substantial research effort in the field of "artificial
intelligence" to develop natural-language processing, software designs
capable of answering even well-structured rephrasings of the two sen-
tences above are a far away (evangelical) dream. The Natural mode
has obvious advantages—especially from the speaker's viewpoint—but
also has some important drawbacks. It is potentially ambiguous where
mathematical formulation is often more precise, coherent, and effi-

cient. In the absence of a Natural mode the speaker can translate his thoughts (at some cost and payoff) into the Expert or Novice mode. He may also use a staff specialist to translate them into the Programmer mode. This latter approach may be very efficient in certain circumstances; however, the intermediary must understand both the speaker's frame of reference and knowledge and the computer system's technical details.

THE TURNAROUND TEST: A MEASURE OF "INTERACTIVITY"

The DSS assumptions equate "interactive" with "conversational" for both the problem-solving process and the system technology. The Turnaround Test provides a broader definition.[8] Once a manager defines a request, the system is interactive if the turnaround (the processing of the request and the generation of any output reports) does not interrupt his problem-solving process and if he does not perceive any unreasonable delay. A few brief examples may clarify both what degree of interactive response is needed for particular problems and what type of system interface may be most suitable.

- Airline reservations, inventory status querying, and credit analysis are types of applications where a response to questions must be virtually immediate, since a thirty-second response time will be seen as irritatingly slow. The dialogue involved is entirely predictable and requires limited options. The system designer can thus develop a Novice or Expert interface that is both easy to use and efficient. The use of Natural interface would be inappropriate; it would be verbose and unnecessary. Here, interactive *is* equivalent to conversational. For example, the user can interpret and respond to the system output within a few seconds and with little need for reflection.

- Strategic planning and policy analysis are problem areas where a dialogue is rarely possible. The user must plan his questions or commands and will generally submit only a few at a time. He will often not need an instantaneous response. Once he has received the information he will need to pause and reflect. The system (most probably a specialist plus a computer) is interactive if the manager can ask questions naturally and if the output is returned in a "reasonable" period of time. (Reasonable may mean a few seconds for a query such as: "What was the average return for each subsidiary last year?" but days for: "Get me a breakdown of estimated competitive response in each region for all the products we've developed over the past two years.")

- Investment management problems have been analyzed by PMS, a system which was designed to be conversational. In this application one could justify either a Natural mode in which a staff intermediary is used or the Expert mode actually employed. Since PMS has many users, there is an obvious economy in a software interface, since skilled staff experts are scarce and expensive. Nonetheless, much of the use of PMS is through a "chauffeur," a typist or junior staff member who takes the investment manager's requests and puts them into the terminal.

These examples, particularly the second, suggest a wide range of strategies. Conversational problem solving seems mainly confined to the more structured applications. In the investment management example, usage is sometimes conversational but often pause-and-reflect. Time-sharing is needed for both instances, but mainly for the accessibility it allows. The strategic planning example suggests the design for an "interactive" system shown in Figure 8.1. The concept is very different from the DSS approach. Here, there may be no single prewritten program. One of the main roles of the intermediary is to build—very quickly—the needed system from a general library of data and functions available. If such building is possible, then the system can accommodate a much wider range of user requests and needs. The user requires very little knowledge of the systems' capabilities and routines; for him the intermediary *is* the system.

A later section of this article reviews the "incredibly rapid acceptance" of APL, a language that provides the flexibility and power needed for the intermediary to be able to pass the Turnaround Test.[9] APL is a language of hieroglyphs, incomprehensible to almost all managers and almost all professional programmers. It represents a very different strategy from the DSS approach, which has relied on bringing the terminal to the user and making the interface language similar to English and simple to use. Redefining the meaning of interactive suggests that

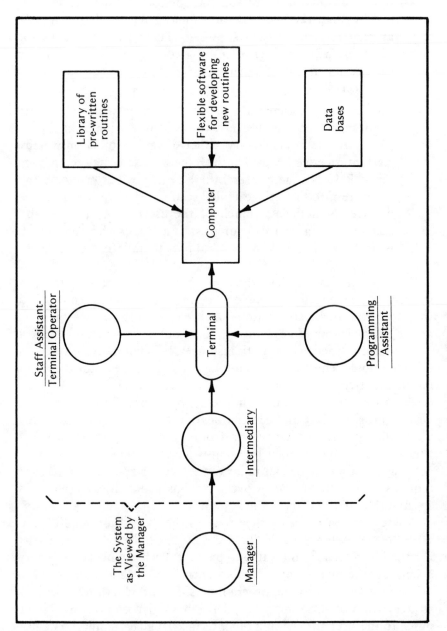

FIGURE 8.1 An "Interactive" System for Strategic Planning

an intermediary-plus-APL interface may be most effective for top management decision support (until the "millennium" of natural language processing and knowledge-based systems).

SOME SUPPORTING EVIDENCE: A REVIEW OF DSS USAGE

There are too few surveys of innovative computer systems in organizations. Alter's study of fifty-six systems in use provides a complex discussion of computer-aided decision making that, as the author comments, challenges many of the DSS articles of faith.[10] The systems examined by Alter range from "file drawers" (retrieval systems for inventory control or shop floor information) to "suggestion models" (optimal inventory allocation, required level of new sales by product, and calculation of contract activity levels). Alter's findings implicitly demonstrate the value of decentralizing the computer resource through time-sharing in that none of the systems were built by the organization's centralized EDP group.

Alter concludes that even where the system was specifically designed to support conversational usage:

> It was surprising that very few situations were encountered which could be described as "interactive problem-solving," i.e. a process involving a single person (especially a decision maker) sitting at a terminal for a prolonged length of time, adaptively exploring a problem space in an effort to find the best possible action. More typical user behavior involved performing a preconceived set of runs which tested the effect of various values of particular variables . . . In those relatively rare instances where interactive problem solving occurred to the greatest extent, the purpose was typically one of developing a report which would look good to someone else.

He suggests that "normal business problems just don't come packaged in a form which really requires interactive problem solving." He also points out that fast turnaround was seen as a major value of most systems.

Andreoli and Steadman provide similar conclusions to Alter's in a study of the PMS system.[11] PMS which is currently in use in several organizations is a complex, innovative DSS that has *gradually* had substantial impact on the decision processes of its users. Andreoli and Steadman examined PMS after it had been in operation for several years and the teething pains involved in such a major innovation had been worked through. They summarized the use of PMS:

> The system's repertoire of facilities, designed as an integrated set of tools to help the manager through the steps of an "intelligence, design, choice," decision making process, have in fact been dismembered and used individually in a non-interactive fashion on those tasks for which the managers feel the highest need.

(Alter, in an earlier study of PMS in the same organization, concluded similarly that "interaction was not a major factor in system use."[12])

THE GADS EXPERIENCE: THE CHAUFFEUR-DRIVEN SYSTEM

These observations of PMS are supported and extended by the various experiments and case studies carried out by the IBM Research Laboratory at San Jose using the GADS system. In several of the experiments, a "chauffeur" acted as intermediary. Holloway classifies the possible methods of organization this allows in Table 8.1.[13] Plan 1 (X handles all three tasks) is the method generally assumed in the DSS approach. Plan 4 (each task is handled by a separate person) is essentially the organization required if time-sharing is unavailable and the user must go through the centralized EDP group. Plans 2 and 3 (system operation is performed by a person other than the information consumer) correspond to the use of the intermediary outline above. In Plan 2 (X consumes the information and controls the process, while Y merely runs the system) the manager-user defines what is to be done and how; the chauffeur's role is limited. Andreoli and Steadman's observations indicate the PMS is often run in this fashion, rather than in the Plan 1 style which was intended by the designer. Plan 3 (X is limited to information consumption) involves a much more active role for the chauffeur, who structures the manager's requests and defines the necessary system commands and inputs.

Holloway and Grace discuss the advantages of each plan. Grace, whose studies focus on training novices to use GADS, concludes that Plan 2 is particularly effective for "one-shot" usage or in situations where the decision maker is under severe time pressure. Plan 2 minimizes the amount of knowledge of the system that he must have.[14]

TABLE 8.1 Organization for Analysis and Evaluation of the Problem

Function Performed by Each Person (X, Y, or Z)	Alternative Organization			
	Plan 1	Plan 2	Plan 3	Plan 4
Information Consumption	X	X	X	X
Process Control	X	X	Y	Y
System Operation	X	Y	Y	Z

Grace also comments on the "self-image" of most novices; they do not expect to directly use a system and also have a low tolerance for training. She describes several highly effective training devices that reduce the cost (to the novice) and the time involved in learning to use the system, but she suggests that the chauffeur-driven modes may facilitate highly effective problem solving in particular situations.

Holloway similarly compares the difference in "model validation" caused by the direct and chauffeur-driven modes. A major advantage of Plan 1 is that the user can psychologically and analytically validate the outputs from the system since he controls the whole problem-solving sequence. In addition, Plan 3 sometimes results in a "perceived uneven information flow" caused by lack of direct involvement with the system operation. At the same time, even short delays in response time (e.g. thirty seconds) are very frustrating to Plan 1 users.

Bennett, in a more theoretical study based on the GADS experience, points to the many roles that the chauffeur-intermediary may take on.[15] He can be:

- An *exegesist* who explains the system,

- A *confidant* who helps the user lose his fear of the computer and lack of self-confidence,

- A *crusader* "selling" both the system and the analytic strategies underlying it and stressing its long-term benefits,

- A *teacher* who provides individualized training and helps the user explore the possibilities of the system.

Bennett summarizes the intermediary as the integrating agent—the interface between man and machine. He argues that in several of the GADS applications, the intermediary was a vital catalyst.

A key implication of the GADS studies is that the intermediary may be almost essential in *introducing* the system, especially to users such as school administrators who, as Grace points out, do not expect to run the system themselves. As Bennett indicates, however, the intermediary is expensive and hard to find (in the GADS experiments, the chauffeur was generally one of the research team). He must know the system in detail and at the same time be able to help the user structure his analysis and planning. Where there are many users involved, the cost is surely prohibitive. Where the problem involved is not one-shot, the fixed cost of learning the system is likely to be quickly repaid. Nonetheless:

- Both the direct and the chauffeur-driven modes result in effective system usage.

- Top management decision making *is* generally *one-shot.*

SOME CHARACTERISTICS OF TOP MANAGEMENT PLANNING

Carter has discussed the question of computer systems for top managers from the manager's viewpoint.[16] He argues that the terminal and the executive will remain strangers to each other for the foreseeable future, since:

- Most of the executive's decision making requires "neither large amounts of detail nor immediate response."

- It is usually the responsibility of lower management levels to examine data and present key facts and conclusions to the executive.

- "The immediacy of executive decisions is usually less than for line managers and (he) can examine more alternatives and more options in a more leisurely fashion."

Obviously, Carter's argument eliminates the need for interactive problem solving.

One of the strengths of the DSS approach has been its focus on semi-structured problems which in many ways imply semi-structured, semi-interactive problem solving. It has carefully avoided building systems for unstructured corporate planning (though Meador and Ness provide a case study that suggests an interactive DSS can help an adventurous manager think through his assumptions and needs more clearly in strategic analysis).[17] Top management decision making is largely exploratory, tentative, and with no predefinable sequence. The problem definition changes and evolves. A system such as GADS or PMS, however flexibly designed, cannot accommodate this lack of structure. A DSS for strategic planning must thus be very different from the interactive systems with a software interface that have been described above.

DECISION SUPPORT FOR TOP MANAGERS:
THE MODEST PROPOSAL

The "system" is what the manager sees it to be. He is concerned with the Turnaround Test; a decision aid is interactive if he can maintain his necessarily unstructured approach to unstructured problems, get responses in terms and forms relevant to his needs, and receive results within a reasonable time period.

In the past few years, computer-based planning systems that meet these requirements *have* been developed, albeit, in a fragmented and somewhat informal manner. Many, perhaps most, use APL (the programming language developed by Iverson at IBM in the early 1960s).[18] APL allows *very* quick development of program although the running time for a completed program is much higher than for other standard languages. APL uses powerful operators that perform mathematical or logical functions that would require a whole sequence of FORTRAN or COBOL statements. The compactness and precision of APL make errors less frequent and thus reduce the amount of debugging needed. It is a fairly difficult language to learn, although once one adjusts to its hieroglyphs it is easy to reach reasonable facility with the simpler operators.

Several major companies have adopted APL for exactly the ad hoc applications that are a main aspect of top management decision making. IBM uses it for most of its financial planning.[19] *EDP Analyzer*

(May 1976) reports on use by Xerox, American Airlines and Massey-Ferguson.[20] APL requires expert intermediaries, but makes possible a level of responsiveness—of turnaround—unattainable at present by other means. It permits controllers, for example, to ask for analysis of exceptional items on standardized reports. The APL planning staff then develops a program generally within a few days. Babad describes a financial planning system for an insurance company that had been written in FORTRAN; the system was inflexible and development and testing had occupied several years of effort.[21] An earlier version had to be scrapped. However, using APL, Babad and his colleagues were able—in nine weeks—to implement a completely new system that was versatile and powerful and that has since been increasingly adopted as a management decision aid. He stresses that the success of this effort, after so many earlier failures, was due to the combination of a skilled designer interacting closely with users and the "much higher productivity" of APL.

Other examples of the marvels of APL are quickly being revealed; they often invite skepticism. In a seven month period, Dr. Luis Contreras and a staff of five specialists of ALFA corporation, a large Mexican conglomerate, built an APL-based corporate planning system of astonishing complexity.[22] This system is *used* by the company's top executives. It includes retrieval and analysis facilities for most functional areas of the company and has a powerful library of user-oriented routines for simulation and data presentation. Contreras described his system at a meeting of the TIMS/ORSA society and met with substantial disbelief that it was possible to implement such a system.

This article is not intended as a paean to APL, although of course the author has *seen the light* and joined the *one true faith*. There are several software systems under development that may provide the same power and flexibility of APL within a few years. The issue here is that, given some tool that allows rapid development or amendment of programs, the skilled intermediary can provide a top manager with a system that is interactive in the sense of the Turnaround Test. This DSS uses a very different style of interface from that of the human engineered, conversational GADS or PMS; *it abandons the assumption of interactive problem solving.*

The proposal of this article is indeed modest. It argues that we shift our direction away from bringing the manager to the computer. Instead of developing software interfaces that are easy to use and moving towards the ideal of English as the language for communicating with the computer, the Modest Proposal (MP) recommends that—in the short term at least—we use a specialized language such as APL even though it is incomprehensible and intimidating to managers. We hide the computer. The manager who works through the intermediary need not know if the "system" is a library of APL routines or a roomful of clerical slaves.

The MP requires a specialist who is a skilled mathematical programmer (APL is not for the mathematical virgin) and who also *understands* the management decision-making process from the *manager's* perspective. His role is one of *support;* he is an implementer and *not* a technician.[23] His task is to integrate man with machine. In recent years, graduate schools of management have (at least) been training students who have the matrix of skills necessary for this role; they are technically literate and are aware of the context of technique and the need for a management perspective.

In practical terms, the MP implies an initiative by the senior manager. The "interactive" intermediary must be made a part of the corporate planning team which is directly involved in the planning process. The manager must also accept that the computer has a supportive role to play. The starting point for developing the DSS will obviously be to generate the "primitive" data bases and functions, the library of routines that form the basis for the system that the intermediary draws on, extends, and modifies. ALFA, the Mexican corporation mentioned earlier, has only recently completed this step. Many of the APL routines are general-purpose reporting or analysis functions, designed around the senior executives' expressed needs. If one were building a traditional interactive system, these modules would be linked through the DSS software interface. In the ALFA case, there has been exactly this development, but in general the system is continuously evolving and special requests or problem situations require additional APL programming. The ALFA staff members report directly to the top management team. They are *planners,* not programmers.

More broadly, the MP implies a range of strategies for decision support, at all levels of the organization. The tradeoffs between software and an intermediary as the interface seem to depend on the following major factors.

- *Degree of structure in the task to be supported*—Structure makes interactive dialogue possible, even desirable. Conversely, in tasks that lack the structure and the opportunity for *predefining* the general sequence of the man-machine dialogue, the intermediary is the only practicable interface. However, he can be effective only if he can provide the necessary turnaround.

- *Number of system users*—If the system is to support many users, then there is likely to be substantial saving of effort and response time if the user accesses the system directly.

- *Difficulty in training*—The intermediary eases the burden of training. This may be especially important for top managers. Bennett's argument in support of the integrating agent stresses his value in reducing resistance to a complex and unfamiliar innovation.

- *Level in the organization*—Once we have a generation of managers who were exposed to direct use of computers in elementary school, we can obviously expect executives to be more willing to sit at a terminal and type or use a light pen. At the moment, many managers are simply unwilling to use a system. Once again, it should be stressed that the system is what they see it to be and if the economic payoff justifies the cost, then there may be an immediate payoff in using the intermediary.

- *Software overhead*—This fifth issue is implicit in the others. Some DSS interfaces are harder to build than the underlying system. The user dialogues cannot be predefined and the problem structure is too broad to allow an adequately general interface. The intermediary may be costly, but at the same time he may be much cheaper, more reliable and efficient than a pseudo-English command-driven interface that irritates managers because it prevents them from assessing a problem in the way they wish.

The simple recommendation underlying the MP is that we think of the systems we implement as a combination of interface and routines. There are often far more choices available than we may assume. If interactive problem solving is recognized as applicable only to relatively structured situations, then the system is explicitly designed as a skilled integrator and a flexible, responsive technology. That, after all, is exactly what the concept of decision *support* implies.

CONCLUSION

This article has, of course, overargued its case. The choices discussed above are not "either/or." In fact, as Bennett suggests, it may be desirable to use the intermediary to introduce the system and gradually encourage the manager to experiment directly with the DSS. Nonetheless, there is a tendency in the DSS movement, under whose banner the author is wholeheartedly enrolled, to assume that *use* of a *system* requires interactive problem solving. The suggestions made here might be seen as a step backwards, towards the "Expert" owning the system and usurping the manager's role. The concept of decision *support* is central here; the intermediary is a *planner* and directly linked into the management decision-making process. The technology he draws on is a means and not an end. In the examples of corporate strategic planning, he *is* the system from the viewpoint of the senior executive. The emergence of APL as a language that makes his role more feasible is of secondary relevance, although without some such aid he cannot provide the speed of response and quality of analysis that take his role beyond that of the traditional staff advisor.

The proposal here is *modest*. It requires an act of faith by the top manager rather than any new technical innovations. The software and hardware it assumes already exist in most companies. Two steps are involved: the potential intermediary must recognize that supporting the management decision process is the central issue, not the design of computer systems and the manager must define the intermediary as part of his own planning team and not as a technician. Perhaps as a third step, they should both buy an APL manual.[24]

Footnotes

[1] See Licklider [18].

[2] See Keen and Scott Morton [17].

[3] See Gerrity [10], Stabell [22], and Andreoli and Steadman [2] for a description of the systems and managers' response to it.

[4] See Little [19].

[5] See Carlsen and Sutton [5], Grace [11], and Holloway and Mantey [14].

[6] Unpublished study; personal communication.

[7] See Hall [12].

[8] This is analogous to the famous Turing test; a machine will have achieved real thought if and only if an observer cannot tell by asking questions if it is a machine or a person. See Feigenbaum and Feldman [9].

[9] See Ness [21].

[10] See Alter [1].

[11] See Andreoli and Steadman [2].

[12] See Alter [1].

[13] See Holloway and Mantey [14].

[14] See Grace [11].

[15] See Bennett [4].

[16] See Carter [6].

[17] See Meador and Ness [20].

[18] See Iverson [15].

[19] The IBM financial planning system is commerically available.

[20] See *EDP Analyzer* [8].

[21] See Babad [3].

[22] See Contreras [7].

[23] See Keen [16].

[24] See Hellerman and Smith [13] for an excellent recent text on APL.

REFERENCES

[1] Alter, S.A. "A Study of Computer-Aided Decision Making in Organizations." Ph.D. dissertation, Massachusetts Institute of Technology, 1975.

[2] Andreoli, P., and Steadman, J. "Management Decision Support Systems: Impact on the Decision Process." Master thesis, Massachusetts Institute of Technology, 1975.

[3] Babad, J.M. "The Monetary System—Implementation and Experience: A Case Study." In *The Implementation of Computer-based Decision Aids,* edited by P.G.W. Keen. Center for Information Systems Research, Massachusetts Institute of Technology, 1975.

[4] Bennett, J. "Integrating Users and Decision Support Systems." Paper presented to the Society for Management Information Systems, 1975.

[5] Carlsen, E.D., and Sutton, J.A. "A Case Study of Non-Programmer Interactive Problem-Solving." San Jose, Ca.: IBM Research Report RJ 1382, 1974.

[6] Carter, N. "The Executive and the Terminal." Paper presented to the Society for Management Information Systems, 1975.

[7] Contreras, L. Presentation to the National Conference of TIMS/ORSA, 1976.

[8] *EDP Analyzer,* vol. 14 no. 6, May 1976.

[9] Feigenbaum, E.A., and Feldman, J.F. *Computers and Thought,* New York: McGraw-Hill, 1963.

[10] Gerrity, T.P., Jr. "Design of Man-Machine Decision Systems: An Application to Portfolio Management." *Sloan Management Review,* Winter 1971, pp. 59–75.

[11] Grace, B.F. "A Case Study of Man/Computer Problem-Solving." San Jose Ca.: IBM Research Report RJ 1483, 1975.

[12] Hall, W. "Strategic Planning Models: Are Top Managers Really Finding Them Useful?" *Journal of Business Policy,* vol. 3 no. 2, pp. 33–42.

[13] Hellerman, H., and Smith, J.A. *APL/360.* New York: McGraw-Hill, 1976.

[14] Holloway, C.A., and Mantey, P.E. "Implementation of an Interactive Graphics Model for Design of School Boundaries." Stanford University Graduate School of Business, Research Paper 299, 1976.

[15] Iverson, K.E. *A Programming Language.* New York: John Wiley & Sons, 1962.

[16] Keen, P.G.W. "A Clinical Approach to the Implementation of OR/MS/MIS." Sloan School of Management Working Paper 780-75.

[17] Keen, P.G.W. and Scott Morton, M.S. *Decision Support Systems: An Organizational Perspective.* Reading, Ma.: Addison-Wesley, forthcoming.

[18] Licklider, J.C.R. "Man-Computer Symbiosis." *IRE Transaction on Human Factors in Electronics,* HFE 1, 1960, pp. 4–10.

[19] Little, J.D.C. "Brandaid." *Operations Research,* May 1975.

[20] Meador, C.L., and Ness, D.N. "Decision Support Systems: An Application to Corporate Planning." *Sloan Management Review,* Winter 1974, pp. 51–68.

[21] Ness, D.N. "Decision Support Systems Theories of Design." Paper presented at the Wharton ONR Conference on Decision Support Systems, September 1975.

[22] Stabell, C.B. "Individual Differences in Managerical Decision Making Processes: A Study of Conversational Computer System Usage." Ph.D. dissertation, Massachusetts Institute of Technology, 1974.

9

Strategies for Information Requirements Determination

by G. B. Davis

Memory Spectrum

About the author:

G. B. Davis is with the School of Management, University of Minnesota, Minneapolis, Minnesota.

An information system should meet the needs of the host organization it serves. The requirements for the information system are thus determined by the characteristics and procedures of the organizational system. But correct and complete information requirements are frequently very difficult to obtain. Simply asking prospective users of the information systems to specify the requirements will not suffice in a large percentage of cases. There are three major reasons for the difficulty in obtaining a correct and complete set of requirements:

1. The constraints on humans as information processors and problem solvers.

2. The variety and complexity of information requirements.

3. The complex patterns of interaction among users and analysts in defining requirements.

The constraints on humans as information processors and problem solvers are important in understanding fundamental human difficulties in responding to requests for requirements. This paper will emphasize these basic constraints while recognizing that the basic constraints based on human limitations are expanded and extended by the other two factors.

The three reasons for difficulty in arriving at correct and complete requirements for information systems suggest that there should not be a single approach to requirements determination that is applied to all projects. Instead, there should be several general approaches or strategies that may be used. These strategies reflect the best approaches to use considering the alternative set of conditions that may apply.

Within the broad outlines of a strategy for information requirements determination, one or more methodologies may be selected from among a number of such methodologies that have been developed for use in eliciting and documenting information requirements. Broad claims often are made about a methodology's use under all conditions. Rather than being universal, however, a methodology tends to work best with one of the broad strategies. Thus, having selected a strategy, the analyst needs to decide which of the alternative methodologies is appropriate to the strategy.

This paper seeks to bring more order into the information requirements determination process by clarifying the two levels of requirements needed, by explaining the difficulties of information requirements determination in terms of some fundamental limitations of humans as information processors and problem solvers, and by proposing a contingency theory for selecting a strategy for information requirements determination.

THE TWO LEVELS OF INFORMATION REQUIREMENTS

There are two levels at which information requirements need to be established in order to design and implement computer-based information systems:

1. The organizational information requirements to define an overall information system structure and to specify a portfolio of applications and data bases.

2. The detailed information requirements for an application.

The requirements determination process is similar for the two levels, and the same set of requirements determination strategies apply to both. However, the scope and detail differences in requirements suggest that some methods of requirements determination are more suitable for the less-detailed, broader-scope, organization-level information requirements, whereas other methods may be more suitable for the more detailed application information requirements. Some methodologies can be applied to requirements determination at both levels.

An overall plan or master plan is necessary for the formal information system in an organization (often termed a management information system). The master plan is important to information system development for reasons such as the following:

1. The plan defines an overall information system structure or architecture.

2. The plan establishes a portfolio of applications that will provide complete coverage of needs.

3. Clear, well-defined boundaries are established for individual applications. The interfaces among applications are defined so that applications can interact as part of the larger system.

4. The plan specifies an orderly development of applications based on organizational priorities and the necessary physical development sequence.

5. If the overall system architecture includes shared data bases, sets of data requirements are defined.

Information requirements determination at the organizational level is a key element in developing an information system master plan. The information requirements determination process obtains, organizes, and documents a complete set of high-level requirements. The requirements are factored into subsystems (a portfolio of applications) that can be scheduled for development. The boundaries and interfaces of the application subsystems are defined at this level, but there are no detailed requirements.

An application is a subsystem of the information system. It is the planning and management unit for development, operations, and maintenance. An application system provides information processing for an organizational unit or organizational activity. The organizational unit or organizational activity is the utilizing system or object system for the information system. The objectives and boundaries of the application and requirements for interfacing with other applications are established by the information system master plan. The information requirements determination process at the application level defines and documents specific information content plus design and implementation requirements.

There are essentially two types of information system application requirements: social and technical. The social or behavioral requirements specify objectives and assumptions such as the following:

- Job design objectives
- Work organization design objectives
- Individual role assumptions
- Responsibility assumptions
- Organizational policies

The technical requirements specify the outputs, inputs, stored data, and processes. A significant part of the technical requirements are associated with data—its structure and format. Data represents things and events, and data structure models the users' and developers' understanding of the structure of things and events. The format of data is the window by which users of the data see things and events. Format is thus constrained by the structure. Format is important in directing attention, showing relationships, providing readability, and assisting in deriving results and implications.

The use of data bases has increased the importance of the data structure requirements because the data structure is relatively permanent, whereas format is relatively easy to change. Five general information requirements for design of a data structure are given below. The first four of these requirements provide information for design of a logical data structure; the fifth requirement is necessary for the selection of a suitable physical data structure.

1. Identification of things and events included within the scope of the object system

2. Relationships among things and events

TABLE 9.1 Requirements for presentation format

Presentation format specification	Comments
Layout of data	The layout of data has a significant influence on information use. The order of presentation, the location on the page or screen, and use of boxes, arrows, and underlines affect the utilization of data on output media.
Directions and labels on data	Directions for use and labels on data can aid and encourage (or discourage) use or misuse.
Level of summarization of data	Summarized data is generally more useful in decision making, but detailed data is needed to provide users with assurance that summarization has not obscured important characteristics.
Processes performed on data	Output should be processed with subtotals, percentages, differences, measures of central tendency, etc., if users need to perform these processes.
Selection/query paths for data	The methods that are provided for selecting data and obtaining results from queries will affect the use and misuse of data.
Tracing data and processing trail pointers	It should be possible for a user to trace from a report back to the constituent data items or from a data item forward to its inclusion in summaries. Also, it should be possible to verify any computations or classifications of data.
Data connections and relationships	It should be possible for a user to explore related data if use of the initial output suggests it.

3. Attributes of things and events

4. Validation criteria for data items

5. Characteristics of use of data structure

Usable information content for human users of information is dependent not only on the availability of the data (via the data structure), but also on the presentation format. Significant differences in use of data, in errors in use, and in perceived value of the data can result from differences in presentation format. Examples of requirements relative to format and comments on the need for each are given in Table 9.1.

CONSTRAINTS ON HUMANS AS SPECIFIERS OF INFORMATION REQUIREMENTS

Humans appear to be so versatile with respect to information use that human constraints or limitations are frequently ignored. Yet, these limitations mean that "asking" users their information requirements will not necessarily yield a complete and correct set of requirements. These limitations are (1) humans as information processors, (2) human bias in selection and use of data, and (3) human problem-solving behavior.

Humans make use of three memories in information processing: [1, 2] external, long-term, and short-term. External memory consists of external media such as a pad of paper or a chalkboard. A visual display device can also be used as external memory. The human brain has both long-term and short-term memory. Long-term memory has essentially unlimited capacity. It requires only a few hundred milliseconds to read (recall) from it, but the write time (commit to memory) is fairly long. The short-term memory is human processor memory. It is very fast, but small in capacity. A computer analogy is register or cache memory. The short-term memory is used in human information processing for operations such as compute and compare. Its limitations may affect human ability to define requirements.

The capacity of short-term memory has been characterized as "seven plus or minus two."[3] The 7 ± 2 refers to chunks of data. A chunk may range from a single character to a visual image. Thus, a telephone number of seven digits may fill short-term memory during dialing, or the images of seven faces may be stored during human processing to select a person.

The limits of short-term memory affect the information requirements obtained whenever the process being used to elicit requirements uses only short-term memory (such as an interview unaided by external storage). The user being interviewed cannot hold a large number of items in short-term memory for discussion or analysis purposes and is therefore limited in processing responses. The short-term memory limitation may also affect the number of requirements that users define as important. In various processing activities using short-term memory, the user may have selectively emphasized a few items of information and recorded these in long-term memory as being the most important. These few may be the only ones recalled when a question is asked.

The short-term memory limitations can be significantly reduced by the use of external memory to store data being processed and by the use of methodologies that systematically elicit and record small numbers of data chunks.

There is substantial evidence to show that humans are not unbiased in their selection and use of data.[4, 5] Some of the behavior resulting in bias is summarized in Table 9.2. The net effect on the determination of information requirements is a significant bias toward requirements based on current procedures, currently available information, recent events, and inferences from small samples of events. The analyst and user who understand these biases may compensate for them; a significant method of compensation is to provide a structure for problem solving.

Problem-solving concepts from Newell and Simon are task environment and problem space.[6] The task environment is the problem as it exists; the problem space is the way a particular decision maker represents the task to work on it. The information requirements task environment is the determination of information requirements for an organization or for an application. The problem space in this case is how a particular analyst or a particular user formulates a representation to use in working on the problem of information requirements. Having a structure for thinking about a problem allows a more efficient solution procedure. Methodologies for information requirements determination provide such a structure for the problem space (Figure 9.1).

A concept related to the problem space is bounded rationality. Humans have a limited capacity for rational thinking; they must generally construct simplifications in order to deal with it. Rationality is

TABLE 9.2 Human bias in selection and use of data

Human biasing behavior	Explanation and effect on information requirements determination
Anchoring and adjustment	Humans tend to make judgments by establishing an anchor point and making adjustments from this point. Information requirements from users will tend to be a result of an adjustment from an anchor of the information currently available.
Concreteness	Decision makers tend to use only the available information in the form it is displayed. They tend not to search for data or transform or manipulate data that is presented. For information requirements determination, this means that requirements provided by users will be biased by the information they already have about their requirements and the form of this information.
Recency	Humans are influenced more by recent events than by events of the past. In defining information requirements, users will be biased by those events that happened recently. An information need that was experienced recently will be given greater weight than a need based on a less recent event.
Intuitive statistical analysis	Humans are not good as intuitive statisticians. For example, humans do not intuitively understand the effect of sample size on variance and therefore draw unwarranted conclusions from small samples or a small number of occurrences. This is an important limitation because many organizational phenomena occur at a fairly low rate. Also, there is a tendency to identify causality with joint occurrence and assign cause where none exists. These limits of humans in processing low-occurrence data and in identifying causality may result in misjudging the need for information.

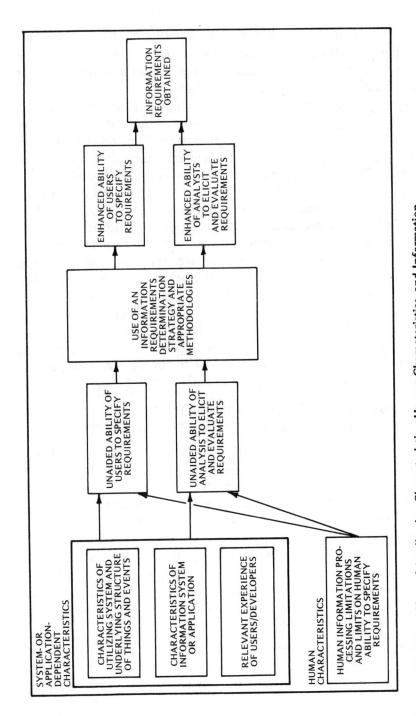

FIGURE 9.1 Effect of Application Characteristics, Human Characteristics, and Information Determination Strategies and Methodologies on Information Requirements Obtained

thus bounded or limited by use of a simplified model that does not correspond exactly to the real situation. Other limitations on the problem space are human processing capabilities and other factors such as training, prejudice, custom, and attitude.

Procedures for determining information requirements apply bounded rationality. They tend to use a somewhat simplified model of the organization and its information requirements. The completeness and correctness of the requirements obtained are thus limited not only by the model, but also by the training, prejudice, custom, and attitude of users and analysts involved in the process. The effect of bounded rationality on information requirements analysis is demonstrated in the behavior of system analysts. A characteristic of proficient system analysts is that they have learned to use a general model to bound the problem space and aid in an efficient search for requirements; poorly rated analysts have a poorly developed model and, therefore, a poorly developed search procedure in the problem space.[7] Also, the highly rated analysts consider organizational and policy issues in establishing requirements; the low-rated analysts do not include these issues in their problem space. The results suggest the need for analyst training in formulating and using a problem space and in considering important nondata issues such as context, organizational policy, and roles.

METHODS AND METHODOLOGIES FOR USE IN INFORMATION REQUIREMENTS DETERMINATION

A *method* is defined as an orderly or systematic procedure; a *methodology* is a set of methods and techniques. The terms are frequently used interchangeably.

Based on human limitations, an information requirements determination methodology should meet certain needs:

1. Assist an analyst to constrain and structure the problem space. It is estimated that analysts spend 75 percent of their time on this activity.[8]

2. Assist in searching efficiently within the problem space. It should aid in discovering requirements that are not obtained by anchoring and adjustment and in overcoming short-term memory limitations in human information processing.

3. Assist in overcoming biasing factors such as recency, concreteness, and small samples.

4. Provide assurance that requirements are complete and correct.

Methodologies differ in the amount of structure provided. Some provide conceptual structure but little process and documentation structure; others provide detailed structure for all tasks and all documentation. The importance of detailed structure may vary with different circumstances. For example, analysts and users with little experience and expertise may find detailed structure very useful; analysts and users experienced in the application area and able to define requirements may find detailed structure in a methodology to be inhibiting and frustrating.

STRATEGIES FOR INFORMATION REQUIREMENTS DETERMINATION

A strategy was defined earlier as an approach for achieving an objective. Strategies are general approaches; methods and methodologies are the detailed means for doing it. There are four strategies for determining information requirements: (1) asking, (2) deriving from an existing information system, (3) synthesis from characteristics of the utilizing system, and (4) discovering from experimentation with an evolving information system.

In a specific case, one of the strategies may be used as the primary strategy; others may be used as supplementary strategies. The set of four strategies is applicable both to organizational information requirements determination and to application requirements. For each strategy, there are a number of methods and methodologies that are in use (or have been proposed). In the discussion of strategies, some methods or methodologies will be used as illustrations; no attempt will be made to provide a comprehensive list.

In addition to strategies and methods for eliciting requirements, there are also strategies and methods for obtaining assurance that requirements are complete and correct and that systems as implemented meet those requirements.[9] A complete strategy for information system analysis, design, and implementation should include both an eliciting strategy and a quality assurance strategy. The selection of an assurance strategy has been described elsewhere; this paper focuses only on the strategy for eliciting or determining the information requirements. It is not directed at life cycle or other methodologies for assurance.

TABLE 9.3 Methods for asking users to define information requirements

Asking method	Description	Conditions suggesting use
Closed questions	Each question has a defined set of possible answers. Respondent selects from the set of responses.	When set of factual responses are known or respondent may not be able to recall all possibilities. Analyst must have knowledge of possible responses.
Open questions	No answers provided. Respondent is allowed to formulate response.	When feelings or opinions are important or when respondent has knowledge and ability to formulate responses.
Brainstorming	Group method for eliciting wide variety of suggestions by open flow of ideas.	Used to extend boundaries of problem spaces of participants and elicit nonconventional solutions.
Guided brainstorming	The IDEALS method[10] is an example. Participants are asked to define ideal solutions and then select the best feasible ideal solution.	Used to guide brainstorming to "ideal" solutions. Useful where participants have system knowledge, but may be locked into an anchoring and adjustment behavior.
Group consensus	Delphi method and group norming are examples. The participants are asked for their estimates or expectations regarding significant variables.	Used to arrive at "best" judgmental estimate of variables that are difficult or impossible to estimate quantitatively.

ASKING

In a pure asking strategy, the analyst obtains information requirements solely from persons in the utilizing system by asking them the requirements. From a conceptual standpoint, the asking strategy assumes that users have a satisfactory way to structure their problem space and that users can overcome or compensate for biases due to concreteness, recency, and small sample size. Anchoring by users in formulating responses is assumed to yield satisfactory results. These conditions may hold in very stable systems that provide users with a well-defined structure or in systems whose structure is established by law, regulation, or other outside authority. There are a variety of methods for carrying out an asking strategy. Table 9.3 summarizes some methods with comments on conditions that suggest their use.

If a pure asking strategy is followed, one or more of the asking methods is used to elicit requirements, and analysis is limited to consistency checks as requirements are documented. The asking methods listed in Table 9.3 can also be used in conjunction with other strategies.

DERIVING FROM AN EXISTING INFORMATION SYSTEM

Existing information systems that have been implemented and have an operational history can be used to derive requirements for a proposed information system for the same type of organization or for the same type of application. The types of existing information systems that are useful in deriving requirements are

1. Existing system that will be replaced by the new system

2. Existing system in another, similar organization

3. Proprietary system or package

4. Descriptions in textbooks, handbooks, industry studies, etc.

With regard to human problem-solving behavior, deriving from an existing information system is an explicit use of anchoring and adjustment. Users and analysts explicitly choose an existing system as an anchor and adjust the requirements from it. Deriving information requirements from an existing information system or application has also been termed a data analysis approach[11] since the data inputs and outputs of the existing system are the focus of analysis. Personnel in the utilizing system are asked to specify changes from the existing data outputs.

If the information system is performing fairly standard operations and providing fairly standard information for utilizing systems that are stable, the use of an existing system as an anchor is conceptually appropriate. In application systems for some well-defined functions such as payroll, data analysis of an existing system can be a useful primary method. In the early application of computers to organizational transactions and accounting systems, derivation of requirements from the processing performed on the data provided by the existing system was used widely. Also, data analysis of existing systems may be useful as the major method in situations where the objective is to improve processing functions but not the basic information content.

Some analysts use data analysis of the existing system as a secondary method for deriving requirements. In this case, to avoid being overly influenced by the concreteness of the existing system, they prefer to delay its use until after their primary analysis method has provided an initial set of requirements.

SYNTHESIS FROM CHARACTERISTICS OF THE UTILIZING SYSTEM

Information systems provide information services to facilitate the operation of systems (object systems) that utilize the information. The requirements for information thus stem from the activities of the object system. This suggests that the most logical and complete method for obtaining information requirements is to develop them from an analysis of the characteristics of the utilizing system. This approach may overcome the biases of anchoring, concreteness, recency, and small sample size by providing an analytical structure for the problem space of the user or analyst. Since requirements are derived from an analysis of the utilizing system, existing reports, recent events, or numbers of occurrence are not significant. The object system analysis is therefore appropriate when the utilizing system is changing or the proposed information system is different from existing patterns (in its content, form, complexity, etc.) so that anchoring on an existing information system or existing observations of information needs will not yield a complete and correct set of requirements.

Several methods have been proposed for performing information requirements determination from object system analysis. Although

TABLE 9.4 Characterization of methods for information requirements determination

Method	Primary requirements orientation	
	Organization	Application
1. Normative analysis	X	
2. Strategy set transformation	X	
3. Critical factors analysis	X	
4. Process analysis	X	
5. Decision analysis		X
6. Socio-technical analysis		X
7. Input-process-output analysis		X

useful at both organizational level and application level, each method has a primary orientation. They can be characterized as shown in Table 9.4.

Normative analysis methods are based on the fundamental similarity of classes of object systems. These fundamental characteristics lead to a prescribed or normative set of requirements. Analysis then concentrates on tailoring the normative requirements to meet nonstandard needs. An example of a normative methodology is Business Information Analysis and Integration Technique (BIAIT^{TM}).

BIAIT was developed in the 1970s by Burnstine.[12] The starting point for analysis is an order, the driving force in an organization. An order may be to supply a space, a skill, or a thing. Seven questions are asked with respect to the order:

1. Bill or accept cash?
2. Deliver in future or immediately?
3. Need history of customer buying behavior?
4. Negotiated or stipulated price?
5. Rent or sell?
6. Track product sold or not?
7. Made to order or provided from stock?

These seven questions about an order, each with two possible answers, define 2[7] or 128 theoretical combinations of responses, but there are about 60 feasible combinations. The responses define a cell that has associated with it four lists of generic requirements:

1. Common business functions

2. Information processing requirements

3. Business objectives

4. Occupations

The generic model is customized and labeled with the function names unique to the industry and business. The prescribed generic requirements are examined to see if and how they apply. From the customized model, reports, measurements, and data requirements can be derived.

A normative methodology such as BIAIT can be used at the organizational requirements level, at subsystem level, and application level. The methodology operates at a fairly high level and is probably most useful for organizational-level requirements or for categories of standard application requirements.

The advantages of a normative prescriptive method are the structure it imposes on the process and the completeness that can be obtained. It is especially useful for an analyst who does not have a good knowledge of the organization or application being studied, since it results in an examination of the normally prescribed information needs. The disadvantage of a normative method for deriving information requirements lies in the generality of the result. Normative requirements usually require adjustment and tailoring to fit specific organizational needs.

Strategy set transformation is a methodology primarily for obtaining organization-level information requirements.[13] The information requirements are derived from the objectives of the organization. For example, if an organizational objective is to improve profits and the selected strategy is to change the sales mix to a larger proportion of higher gross margin products, the information system application derived from this objective is a gross margin analysis report.

Critical factors analysis is a method for eliciting the significant decisions or other factors that can be used in deriving information requirements. Essentially, the method structures the problem space for finding decision requirements. An example of critical factors analysis is the Critical Success Factors (CSF) method. It can be used at both the organization and application level.

Critical Success Factors[14] is a method of eliciting requirements by asking users to define the factors that are critical to success in performing their functions or making decisions. A small number of critical factors usually emerges from this eliciting process. It requires relatively little effort to arrive at the critical factors.

Another approach to synthesis of requirements, called process analysis, focuses on business processes. The idea underlying this approach is that business processes (groups of decisions and activities required to manage each of the resources of the organization) are the basis for information system support. Processes remain relatively constant over time, and the requirements derived from the processes will reflect the nontransient needs of the organization. An example of process-based methodology is Business Systems Planning (BSP). The method is primarily for developing organizational information requirements as part of developing an information system master plan.

BSP is a comprehensive IBM methodology[15] well supported by manuals and instruction. Information requirements are derived from the object system in a top-down fashion by starting with business objectives and then defining business processes. Business processes are used as the basis for data collection and analysis. In interviews to clarify processes, executives are also asked to specify key success factors and to identify problems. Logically related categories of data are identified and related to business processes. This information is used in defining a proposed information architecture. Based on current status and proposed architecture, application priorities are established and migration to data bases planned.

For information requirements determination, decision analysis is performed by steps such as the following: [16]

1. Identify and prescribe decision.

2. Define decision algorithm or decision process. Various documentation methods may be used. Examples are decision flowcharts, decision tables, and decision trees.

3. Define information needed for the decision process.

Decision analysis has been shown to be very useful in clarifying the information requirements with users in cases where the decision process is fairly well-defined. For unstructured, poorly understood decision processes, decision analysis does not appear to perform any better than a data approach. Also, decision analysis does not apply to all applications or all information included in applications.[17]

The socio-technical analysis approach[18] consists of two parts: social analysis and technical analysis. The social analysis is to determine system requirements relative to the social system of the organization, including requirements for the system design and requirements for implementation. The social analysis is performed by studying patterns of social interaction and group behavior in the current system. Analysis methods may include group discussion and group problem-solving processes. Technical analysis is an analysis of variances and control loops that require information.

Socio-technical analysis is oriented to application-level analysis. It is especially appropriate for applications that involve many participants, that include both primary users and secondary users (such as data preparation personnel), or where the application will significantly change the work environment, the social interaction, or the job design.

Input-process-output analysis is a system approach. A system is defined in terms of its inputs, outputs, and transformation processes for receiving inputs and producing outputs. The system approach starts in a top-down fashion on an object system. Subsystems of the object system are analyzed to achieve further subdivision into subsubsystems, etc., until information processing activities are defined as separate activities within a subsystem.

The advantage of analysis based on inputs, processes, and outputs of systems is that it is systematic and comprehensive. By starting at a high level and factoring into subsystems, we can have reasonable assurance of completeness. Analysis can be carried to as low a level of detail as desired. A very comprehensive example of such an approach is the ISAC method. Data flow diagrams are a second example. A more limited methodology is Accurately Defined Systems (ADS).

The Information Systems Work and Analysis of Changes (ISAC)[19] method was developed by a research group at the Royal Institute of Technology and University of Stockholm, Sweden. It is being used in organizations, primarily in Scandinavia. The method is supported by instruction manuals and layouts for graphs, tables, and other documents. The method begins with an analysis (using a system graph) of the activities in the object system. Subsystems are then analyzed in the same way down to the level at which information processing appears as an activity. The information activities are analyzed as systems and subsystems using graphs termed activity graphs. Associated with the activity graphs are tables summarizing need for change, system objectives, social considerations, and properties of the system. The information system and subsystems from the activity graphs are analyzed for information flow and precedence using a system graph called an information graph. These graphs are supplemented by tables for properties, processes, and tasks. The information system is then analyzed in terms of data structures, equipment, program structures, operations, and manual routines.

Data flow diagrams,[20] when used at a high level of analysis, are a graphic method for defining inputs, processes, and outputs and for factoring systems into subsystems. The factoring process is top-down and can be carried to the level of program module specification.

ADS[21] was developed at NCR. It uses a set of five forms with "where from" referencing to define and check completeness of application requirements in terms of outputs, inputs, history data, logic, and computations.

DISCOVERING FROM EXPERIMENTATION WITH AN EVOLVING INFORMATION SYSTEM

Traditional procedures for information requirements determination are designed to establish a complete and correct set of requirements before the information system is designed and built. In a significant percentage of cases, requirements cannot be established correctly and completely. Information system applications based on elicited correct requirements are rejected by users or receive substantial rework to make them fit user needs. There are various reasons why requirements cannot be obtained. Users may not be able to formulate information requirements because they have no existing model (normative, prescriptive, or experiential) on which to base requirements. They may find it difficult to deal in abstract requirements or to visualize new systems. Users may need to anchor on concrete systems from which they can make adjustments.

TABLE 9.5 Conditions suggesting use or nonuse of iterative discovery method for information requirements determination

Conditions suggesting iterative discovery method	Conditions not supporting iterative discovery method
There is no well-defined model of information requirements. Experience of users and/or analysts is insufficient to define requirements. Users' need for information is evolving (such as in managerial or decision support applications).	There is an existing well-understood, well-defined model of the utilizing system and its information requirements. There is need for stability in an information system because of number of users, complex interfaces with outside systems, etc. Examples are major transaction processing systems.

Another approach to information requirements determination is, therefore, to capture an initial set of requirements and implement an information system to provide those requirements. As the users employ the system, they request additional requirements. The system is designed for ease of change. In essence, after an initial set of requirements provide an anchor, additional requirements are discovered through system use. The general approach has been described as prototyping or heuristic development.[22]

The iterative discovery method for information requirements determination has considerable appeal. However, upon examination, it has both advantages and disadvantages and appears to be more suitable under some circumstances than for others (Table 9.5).

SELECTING AN INFORMATION REQUIREMENTS DETERMINATION STRATEGY

Four strategies have been described for determining information requirements, with each strategy having a number of methods that may be employed. In order to provide operational potential to the strategy classification, this section will present an approach to the selection of an appropriate primary strategy. The selection procedure represents a contingency theory, i.e., the strategy selected is contingent on characteristics of the requirements determination environment and process.

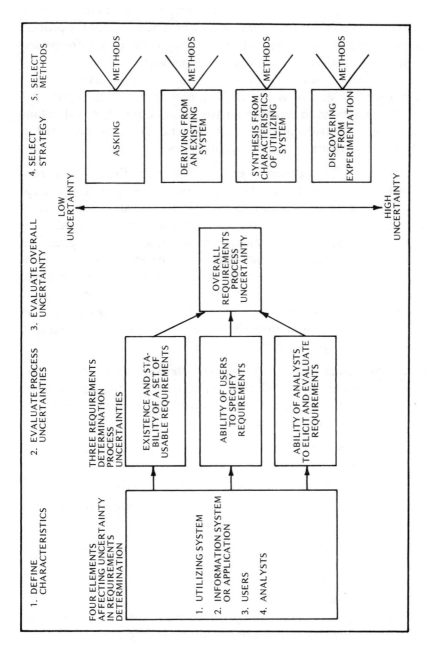

FIGURE 9.2 Selection of an Information Requirements Determination Strategy

The underlying basis for selecting a strategy is uncertainty as to the three requirements determination processes. The bases for the process uncertainty are characteristics of the utilizing system, the information system or application, the users, and the analysts.

The approach to selecting an information requirements determination strategy consists of five steps (Figure 9.2). The steps represent a series of evaluations to establish a basis for selection. The evaluations are not precise, but do provide for judgment. The steps are listed in Table 9.6 and explained in more detail below.

Step 1: Identify Characteristics of Elements in the Development Process that Affect Uncertainty. There are four elements in the development process that are relevant to the selection of an information requirements determination strategy: the utilizing system, the information system or application system, the users, and the analysts. The characteristics of these elements determine the expected level of uncertainty with respect to requirements determination as seen in Table 9.7. In other words, for each of the elements in the development process, there are characteristics that reduce expected uncertainty as to requirements determination; there are opposing characteristics that increase expected uncertainty.

Step 2: Evaluate the Effect of the Characteristics on Process Uncertainty. The characteristics of the four elements in the development process affect uncertainty of information requirements determination by affecting three process uncertainties, which are

1. Uncertainty with respect to existence and stability of a usable set of requirements.

2. Uncertainty with respect to users' ability to specify requirements.

3. Uncertainty with respect to ability of analysts to elicit requirements and evaluate their correctness and completeness.

The first uncertainty can arise from a number of characteristics of the utilizing system. Some examples are

- Lack of a well-understood model of the utilizing system. This lack may be reflected in confused objectives, unclear organization, and poorly defined operating procedures.

TABLE 9.6 Steps in selecting a strategy and methods for information requirements determination

---

1. Identify those characteristics of the four elements in the development process that affect uncertainty of information requirements determination:

   Utilizing system
   Information system or application
   Users
   Analysts

2. Evaluate the effect of the characteristics of the four elements in the development process on three process uncertainties:

   Existence and availability of a set of usable requirements
   Ability of users to specify requirements
   Ability of analysts to elicit and evaluate requirements

3. Evaluate the combined effect of the process uncertainties on overall requirements uncertainty.

4. Select a primary requirements determination strategy based on the overall requirements uncertainty.

Uncertainty	Strategy
Low	Asking
	Deriving from an existing system
	Synthesis from characteristics of utilizing system
High	Discovering from experimentation

5. Select one or more methods from the set of methods to implement the primary strategy.

TABLE 9.7 Characteristics of elements in the development process

Elements in development process	Examples of characteristics that:	
	Reduce uncertainty	Increase uncertainty
Utilizing system	Stable, well-defined system not in process of change	Unstable, poorly understood system in process of change
	Programmed activities or decisions	Nonprogrammed activities or decisions
Information system or application system	Traditional, simple set of requirements	Complex or unusual set of requirements
	Clerical support system	Management support system
Users	One or few users High user system experience	Many users Low user system experience
Analysts	Trained and experienced with similar information system	Little prior training or experience with similar information system

- Lack of stability in structure and operation of the utilizing system.
- Lack of stability in use of information system. Nonprogrammed activity has a low level of predefined structure, and, therefore, changes in user personnel may create unstable use patterns.
- A large number of users can affect the existence and stability of requirements if all users can specify requirements and there is no mechanism to arbitrate differences or achieve consensus.

The second process uncertainty is a result not only of human limitations in developing specifications but also of characteristics of the information system or application. Examples are

- Lack of user model of the utilizing system.
- Lack of structure for activity or decision being supported.

- Change in the utilizing system.

- Changes in the use of information.

- A complex system.

- A large number of users which will affect level of participation and users' feelings of responsibility in specifying requirements.

- Type of users doing the specifications. Clerical users may be able to specify procedure requirements, but not overall content; managers may be better in specifying content than procedures.

- Lack of user experience in the utilizing system and lack of experience in type of application being proposed.

The third uncertainty is related to the personal characteristics of the analysts, their general level of training, and prior experience with the same or similar applications. The characteristics of the application that affect users described above also effect analyst performance.

The level of knowledge and experience needed by users and analysts tends to differ for different requirements determination strategies. As illustrated in Figure 9.3, an asking strategy requires a higher level of user knowledge and experience than an experimental strategy.

Step 3: Evaluate the Combined Effect of the Process Uncertainties on Overall Requirements Uncertainty. The expected overall requirements uncertainty could be estimated directly from the characteristics of the object system, the information system, the users, and the analysts. However, it is useful to make this evaluation in two steps—first evaluating the effect of the characteristics of the four elements affecting the requirements determination uncertainty on three process uncertainties and then evaluating the three process uncertainties to arrive at an estimated overall level of requirements process uncertainty.

The expected overall level cannot be estimated with certainty, but the insight gained in the three-step evaluation allows a reasonable basis for selection of a strategy.

Steps 4 and 5: Select a Primary Requirements Determination Strategy and One or More Methods. The strategy is selected based on the level of requirements determination uncertainty.

When a strategy has been selected, one or more methods are selected for use. The selection of a primary strategy and associated method(s) does not preclude the use of a secondary strategy and other supple-

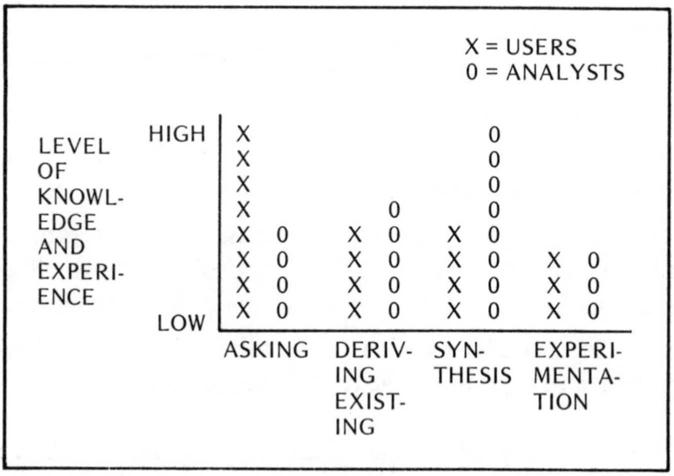

```
                                        X = USERS
                                        0 = ANALYSTS

                HIGH |  X                        0
LEVEL                |  X                        0
OF                   |  X                        0
KNOWL-               |  X              0         0
EDGE                 |  X   0     X    0     X   0
AND                  |  X   0     X    0     X   0     X   0
EXPERI-              |  X   0     X    0     X   0     X   0
ENCE                 |  X   0     X    0     X   0     X   0
                LOW  |_____
                        ASKING   DERIV-  SYN-      EXPERI-
                                 ING     THESIS    MENTA-
                                 EXIST-            TION
                                 ING
```

FIGURE 9.3 Relative Estimated Level of Knowledge and Experience by Users and Analysts to Employ the Four Requirements Determination Strategies

mentary methods, but it does assist the analyst in understanding how to deal with the expected level of uncertainty as to requirements.

In order to clarify the concept of uncertainty and its effect on information requirements determination, the use of the selection approach will now be illustrated for both the organizational information requirements and application requirements.

THE CONTINGENCY APPROACH APPLIED TO ORGANIZATIONAL INFORMATION REQUIREMENTS DETERMINATION

The set of characteristics that apply to organizational-level requirements determination include the items in Table 9.8.

The characteristic of organizational maturity in use of a computer-based information system reflects the fact that organizations exhibit a learning process. It is not feasible to implement a complex information system in an organization until participants have "learned" on a less complex system. The learning includes organizational and procedural discipline necessary with computer-based systems.

Three examples illustrate the use of the contingency concept for selection of an information requirements determination strategy for the organizational-level information requirements.

TABLE 9.8 Characteristics for organizational-level requirements

Elements in process	Characteristics affecting requirements determination uncertainty
Utilizing system	Stability of system processes Stability in management and control Maturity in use of information systems
Information system	Extent to which higher-level management applications are included in scope of systems Complexity and level of integration of information
Users	Level of experience in utilizing system Experience in planning information systems
Analysts	Experience in planning information systems

1. Company A is a small company with a stable technology that has not used computers before. It expects to apply computer processing first to accounting and inventory control. It has an analyst with two years experience. In the listing below and in those of the succeeding examples, the second column indicates whether an item adds or reduces uncertainty.

Stable system processes	Reduces
Stable management control	Reduces
Low maturity in computer use	Adds
Clerical level applications	Reduces
Complexity and integration low	Reduces
Experience of analysts	—
Experience of users low	Adds

Based on these characteristics, process uncertainties are classified in the following ways:

Low uncertainty as to existence and stability of requirements

Moderate uncertainty as to user ability to specify requirements

Moderate to low uncertainty as to analyst ability to elicit and evaluate requirements

The overall evaluation is moderate to low uncertainty. Given this level of uncertainty, a requirements strategy might be to derive an initial set of organizational requirements from the existing manual systems.

2. Company B has used computers for traditional accounting but would now like to have management-support applications, decision-support applications, query capabilities, and planning applications.

Stable system processes	Reduces
Management control changing	Adds
Fairly mature in use of computers	Reduces
Management-level applications	Adds
Complexity and integration high	Adds
Experience of users low	Adds
Experience of analysts moderate to high	Adds

An evaluation of these characteristics suggests a moderate to high uncertainty in existence and stability of requirements, a fairly high uncertainty as to user ability to specify requirements, and a moderate to high uncertainty as to analyst ability to elicit and evaluate requirements. Overall, there is a moderately high degree of uncertainty as to requirements determination. The fairly high level of uncertainty suggests a strategy of synthesizing organizational information needs from characteristics of the utilizing system.

3. Company C has a very unstable environment and very poorly developed planning and control information. They wish to improve their information system to provide better information for planning and control.

Unstable processes	Adds
Management control changing	Adds
Low maturity in use of computers	Adds
Complexity and integration high	Adds
Experience of analysts low	Adds
Experience of users low	Adds

An evaluation of the characteristics suggests a high degree of uncertainty for existence and stability of requirements, user ability to specify, and analyst ability to elicit and evaluate. With this high level of overall uncertainty, the appropriate requirements strategy might be to use experimentation with an evolving system as the primary strategy for determining organizational requirements.

THE CONTINGENCY APPROACH APPLIED TO APPLICATION INFORMATION REQUIREMENTS DETERMINATION

The characteristics that may be considered in evaluating uncertainty of requirements processes for an application include the ones in Table 9.9.

TABLE 9.9 Characteristics for application-level requirements

Elements in process	Characteristics affecting requirements determination uncertainty
Utilizing system	Existence of a model of the system Stability of system Nonprogrammed versus programmed activity Stability in information use
Application	High-level versus low-level application Complexity Number of users
User	Experience with utilizing system Experience with application
Analyst	Experience with utilizing system Experience with application

The following examples illustrate the use of the contingency theory to select a requirements determination strategy for an application. In each example, the second column of the list indicates whether an item adds or reduces uncertainty.

1. A balance forward billing and accounts receivable application system for a retail store.

Utilizing system has stable, programmed activity	Reduces
Application has stable requirements with fairly small number of users (in accounting)	Reduces
User personnel familiarity with system is high	Reduces
Analyst familiarity and experience is reasonably high	Reduces

There is very little uncertainty with respect to the requirements themselves, little uncertainty with respect to user ability to provide requirements, and little uncertainty as to analyst ability to elicit requirements and evaluate their correctness and completeness. Given this overall low degree of uncertainty, the analyst may use a primary strategy of asking users to define requirements (using open or closed questions).

An alternative primary strategy is to derive requirements from an existing billing and accounts receivable system (existing system in this organization or in another organization).

2. An integrated on-line order entry transaction system and management order-tracking application to replace a traditional batch system having little management reporting.

Utilizing system is stable, mainly programmed activity	Reduces
Application has stable requirements for clerical users and moderately stable requirements for management users. Medium number of users.	Reduces
Well-defined model of requirements for order entry procedures;	Reduces
less well-defined model of tracking requirements	Adds
Complex system	Adds
User personnel are familiar with order entry requirements	Reduces
Analyst experience is at least moderate for on-line systems	Reduces

The overall uncertainty level is moderate, based on the evaluation of the three processes:

Little uncertainty with respect to the order entry functions to be performed and requirements related to these functions. Some uncertainty as to management functions to be supported.

Little uncertainty as to user ability to define transaction entry requirements and medium uncertainty as to ability to define management reporting. Because of on-line systems, there may also be new social system considerations and human behavior considerations that users cannot define clearly and completely.

Moderate uncertainty as to analyst ability to elicit requirements and evaluate their correctness and completeness.

Given this overall moderate degree of uncertainty, the analyst may choose to use synthesis from the characteristics of the utilizing system as the primary strategy. Examples of methods appropriate to this situation are

Input-process-output analysis

Socio-technical analysis for social and behavioral requirements

Decision analysis or critical factor analysis for management reporting

3. A management report application for problem identification and problem finding with respect to sales. It includes content of some existing informal, private information systems but does not replace an existing information system application.

Support mixture of programmed and nonprogrammed activities	Adds
Requirements not stable because they are dependent on experience and decision style of users	Adds
No well-defined model of utilizing system and its requirements	Adds
Users somewhat unsure of requirements	Adds
Analysts inexperienced in specific application because it is unique	Adds

Based on these characteristics, there is the following set of uncertainties with respect to requirements determination processes:

High uncertainty as to necessary and desirable requirements

High uncertainty as to user ability to specify requirements

High uncertainty as to analyst ability to elicit requirements and assess correctness and completeness

The high level of uncertainty suggests a discovery methodology in which requirements are identified iteratively as the application system evolves.

SUMMARY

The problem to which the paper has been directed is the selection of an information requirements determination strategy. In developing the concept of strategy selection, the paper defines two levels of requirements: organizational information requirements and application-level requirements. The constraints on humans as specifiers for information requirements are explored. Four broad strategies for information requirements determination encompass groups of methods. These strategies are (1) asking, (2) deriving from an existing information system, (3) synthesis from characteristics of the utilizing system, and (4) discovering from experimentation with an evolving information system application.

The selection of a strategy is based on uncertainties with respect to information requirements determination processes. The determination uncertainty focuses on (1) uncertainty with respect to existence and stability of a set of requirements, (2) uncertainty with respect to users' ability to specify requirements, and (3) uncertainty with respect to ability of analysts to elicit requirements and evaluate their correctness and completeness. These three uncertainties as to the information requirements determination process are associated with certain characteristics of the utilizing systems, the information system or application, users, and analysts.

The selection of a requirements determination strategy for both the organizational level and the application level is thus based on an evaluation of the characteristics that determine the three areas of uncertainty. The selection of a primary requirements determination strategy that satisfies the level of uncertainty points to a set of methods for use. An analyst may also choose to use other strategies and methods to supplement the primary determination strategy.

CITED REFERENCES AND NOTE

[1] G.B. Davis, *Management Information Systems: Conceptual Foundations, Structure, and Development,* McGraw-Hill Book Company, Inc., New York (1974).

[2] A. Newell and H.A. Simon, *Human Problem Solving,* Prentice-Hall. Inc., Englewood Cliffs, NJ (1972).

[3] G.A. Miller, "The magical number seven, plus or minus two: Some limits on our capacity for processing information," *The Psychological Review* 63, No. 2, 81–97 (March 1956).

[4] Davis, *op cit.*

[5] N.P. Vitalari, "An investigation of the problem solving behavior of systems analysts," unpublished Ph.D. dissertation, University of Minnesota (1981).

[6] Newell and Simon, *op cit.*

[7] Vitalari, *op cit.*

[8] *Ibid.*

[9] J.D. Naumann, G.B. Davis, and J.D. McKeen, "Determining information requirements: A contingency method for selection of a requirements assurance strategy," *The Journal of Systems and Software* 1, 273–281 (1980).

[10] G. Nadler, *Work Design: A Systems Concept,* Revised Edition, Richard D. Irwin, Inc., Homewood, IL (1970).

[11] M.C. Munro and G.B. Davis, "Determining management information needs —A comparison of methods," *MIS Quarterly* 1, No. 2, 55–67 (June 1977).

[12] W.M. Carlson, "Business Information Analysis and Integration Technique (BIAIT)—The new horizon," *Data Base* **10**, No. 4, 3–9 (Spring 1979).

[13] W.R. King, "Strategic planning for management information systems," *MIS Quarterly* **2**, No. 1, 27–37 (March 1978).

[14] J.F. Rockart, "Critical success factors," *Harvard Business Review* **57**, No. 2, 81–91 (March-April 1979).

[15] *Business Systems Planning—Information Systems Planning Guide*, Application Manual, GE20-0527-3, Third Edition, IBM Corporation (July 1981); available through IBM branch offices.

[16] R.L. Ackoff, "Management misinformation systems," *Management Science* **14**, No. 4, B147-B156 (December 1967).

[17] Munro and Davis, *op cit.*

[18] R.P. Bostrom and J.S. Heinen, "MIS problems and failures: A socio-technical perspective; Part I: The causes," *MIS Quarterly* **1**, No. 3, 17–32 (September 1977), and "Part II: The application of socio-technical theory," *MIS Quarterly* **1**, No. 4, 11–28 (December 1977).

[19] M. Lundeberg, G. Goldkuhl, and A. Nilsson, *Information Systems Development: A Systematic Approach*, Prentice-Hall, Inc., Englewood Cliffs, NJ (1981).

[20] The literature of data flow diagrams and structured analysis is fairly extensive. For example, see T. DeMarco, *Structured Analysis and System Specification*, Yourdon, Inc., New York (1978), and D.T. Ross and K.E. Schoman, Jr., "Structured analysis for requirements definition," *IEEE Transactions on Software Engineering* **SE-3**, No. 1, 6–15 (January 1977).

[21] H.J. Lynch, "ADS: A technique in systems documentation," *Data Base* **1**, No. 1, 6–18 (Spring 1969).

[22] T.R. Berrisford and J.C. Wetherbe, "Heuristic development: A redesign of systems design," *MIS Quarterly* **3**, No. 1, 11–19 (March 1979).

GENERAL REFERENCES

B. Bowman, G.B. Davis, and J. Wetherbe, "Modeling for MIS," *Datamation*, 155–164 (July 1981).

J.D. Couger, "Evolution of business systems analysis techniques," *Computing Surveys* **5**, No. 3 (September 1973).

G.A. Gorry and M.S. Scott Morton, "A framework for management information systems," *Sloan Management Review* **12**, 55–70 (Fall 1971).

R.H. Hayes and R.L. Nolan, "What kind of corporate modeling functions best," *Harvard Business Review* 52, No. 3 102–112 (May-June 1974).

B. Hedberg and E. Mumford, "The design of computer systems: Man's visions of man as an integral part of the systems design process," in *Human Choice and Computers*, E. Mumford and H. Sackman (Editors), North-Holland, Amsterdam, The Netherlands (1975), pp. 31–59.

A.M. Jenkins and R.D. Johnson, "What the information analyst should know about body language," *MIS Quarterly* 1, No. 3, 33–47 (September 1977).

W.R. King and D.I. Cleland, "The design of management information systems: An information analysis approach," *Management Science* 22, 286–297 (November 1975).

K. London, *The People Side of Systems*, McGraw-Hill Book Company, Inc., New York (1976).

J.C. Miller, "Conceptual models and determining information requirements," *Proceedings of the Spring Joint Computer Conference* 25, 609–620 (1964).

B. Shneiderman, *Software Psychology: Human Factors in Computer and Information Systems*, Winthrop Publishers, Inc., Cambridge, MA (1980).

The author is with the School of Management, University of Minnesota, 271 19th Avenue South, Minneapolis, MN 55455.

Discussion Questions for Part One

1. How do basic data processing, integrated data processing systems, management information systems, and decision support systems differ in terms of such key characteristics as:

    a. Ease of use
    b. Analytical problem solving ability
    c. Primary level of management supported
    d. Hardware and software resources required
    e. Degree of managerial interaction
    f. Flexibility in report format

2. EDP/MIS systems are said to be designed to automate record-keeping, transaction processing, and structured management reporting while decision support systems serve to assist managers in making and implementing strategic and tactical decisions. Which type of system is more likely to emphasize:

    a. Standardized information reporting
    b. Focus on past or current activities
    c. Efficiency in the use of system resources
    d. Participation by the decision-maker in searching for and displaying information
    e. Future impacts of alternatives evaluated
    f. Effectiveness in the accomplishment of human tasks
    g. Flexibility in meeting reporting requirements

Why? Explain briefly.

3. Why are data base management systems, financial planning models, and computer graphics systems key features of many decision support systems?

4. What major differences are likely to occur in the form of models used at operational, tactical, and strategical levels of management? How will these differences affect the manner and extent of use of such models?

5. What are the major similarities and differences between model base and model management software? How do major differences affect the operation of the total decision support system?

6. Why are command languages often used with decision support systems instead of procedural languages such as FORTRAN, COBOL, and PL/1? What are the major drawbacks of such languages?

7. How will the major characteristics and decision styles of specific decision-makers affect the operation of the data base and model base? How will key features of the model base and data base likely affect the extent and method of use of decision makers?

8. What impact will starting with the line manager and the nature of his job rather than with staff personnel have on the process of moving from MIS to DSS?

9. When is prototyping likely to be advantageous over full fledged iterative implementation in DSS Development?

10. Why must a system designed to improve management performance do more than provide fast, flexible access to data?

11. Many decision support system users are reluctant to use interactive computer systems because of lack of familiarity with system characteristics and languages, incompatibility with normal work styles, status conflicts, and fears of complex/technical operations. What enhancements can be added to decision support systems to overcome these obstacles?

12. For what decision-making activities (i.e., design, intelligence, choice, implementation) or functional problem areas (e.g., marketing, production, personnel, finance) are interactive decision support systems most likely to prove useful? Why?

13. Why is responsiveness in terms of power, accessibility, and flexibility rather than interactiveness frequently desired by users of information systems?

14. What capabilities must decision support systems have to increase personnel effectiveness, facilitate problem solving, improve interpersonal communication, promote learning, and increase organizational control over functional activities?

15. Why do some authorities argue that non-experts should be encouraged to use on-line, interactive systems with the help of expert intermediaries?

16. How can problems of unfamiliar representations, segmented decision-making activities, lack of memory and control aids, and indirect user control associated with many existing DSS be remedied?

17. What are the major differences in data-oriented and model oriented information systems? What types of decision processes is each type of system best suited for? Why?

18. How do the viewpoints of managers, builders, and toolsmiths differ toward DSS? How can these viewpoints be resolved?

19. What is the importance of dialog, data, and model management systems to the development of DSS?

20. Discuss the implications of DSS performance objectives from the standpoint of the types of decision-making tasks involved compared to the type of support needed?

21. What are the major differences between specific DSS, DSS Generators, and DSS Tools?

22. What impact do the DSS characteristics of decision support, flexible interface, and adaptive design process have on the decision-maker?

23. How can the human limitations of short-term memory, limited attention span, simplified models, focus on concreteness and regency, and intuitive statistical bias be overcome in designing DSS?

24. When should each of the common determining strategies (i.e. asking, deriving, synthesis, and discovery) be used for best results?

25. Which development steps and uncertainty categories are most likely to be important in a dynamic environment? In a static environment? Why?

PART TWO

Management Problem-
Solving Styles, Manager-
Analyst Interaction,
Interactive Model
Implications and
Successful Model
Applications

INTRODUCTION
William C. House

Many current decision support systems have some analytic characteristics which don't fit the thinking and problem-solving styles of typical managers. A second problem is the difference in decision-making styles and communication perspectives of managers and management scientists. A third difficulty is the fact that many analytic models and techniques embedded in decision support systems are not widely used for high-payoff, unstructured problems in uncertain environments. A better fit between the cognitive styles of decision-makers and their information collection and evaluation activities is needed, with enough flexibility in these systems to accomodate the most important needs of both intuitive and systematic managers.

Joint manager-management scientist development and implementation of decision models is desirable with more emphasis on problem determination than on problem solution and greater use of intermediaries in cases where there is a mismatch between DSS capabilities and the characteristics of intuitive managers. Greater involvement of decision-makers in model development and implementation will increase their data contributions, acceptance, use of, and confidence in such models. Model building is an evolutionary, iterative process with managerial judgment being a vital element in testing and adjusting the model for actual use.

Interactive, experience generalized models offer a greater opportunity for the user to structure his model and to generate a wide range of useful results than possible with experience based or staff developed, model optimized systems. Model quality, accuracy, and usefulness can often be improved through manager-model interaction. A high degree of interactive model usage can improve the decision-maker's understanding of the problem situation, the effectiveness of the problem solutions generated, and the fit of the model to the decision-maker's problem-solving style. Model-based decision support systems are finding increasing usage for such decision problems as new product planning, production-inventory planning, and corporate financial planning and simulation.

Flexible format, financial planning languages have provided an important foundation for wider and more intensive utilization of decision support systems. For the first time, many novice users are gaining invaluable hands on experience with simple planning models which lend themselves to providing quick answers to what-if questions. Further progress in efficient man-machine interaction will come as users progress from languages which require the user to explicitly state all necessary calculations and how data are to be retrieved to those which merely require statement of the problem to be solved along with the data to be used. Access to intelligent problem solver routines adapted from expert knowledge bases will also aid the decision-maker in the search for higher quality decision choices. Particular attention should be paid to the adequacy of software support for effective user-model, model-data, and user-data interfaces as well as for the integration of operational, tactical, and strategic management models into a unified whole.

McKenney and Keen discuss the difficulties of obtaining cooperation and communication between managers and management scientists, each group with its own goals, languages, and methods. Despite successes in such areas as logistics planning, resource allocation, and financial forecasting, management science techniques have not been widely used in decision areas with fuzzy problem formulation, ambiguous action criteria, and largely intuitive operations. One reason is that both groups have distinctly different styles of thinking and problem solving.

Training and experience will help to develop modes of thought which can be classified in terms of information gathering and information evaluation. *Information gathering* has two possible modes: perceptive thinking (relationship oriented) and receptive thinking (detail oriented). *Information evaluation* can be done systematically (problem structured) or intuitively (trial and error).

A better fit between the decision-maker's cognitive styles in information gathering/evaluation and the constraints of information processing tasks is needed if problem solution processes are to be improved. More attention should be paid to important decision processes such as problem finding, problem recognition, and problem definition. Research studies suggest that certain tasks are better suited to particular cognitive styles than others and that there is a consistent difference in problem solving approaches used by systematic and intuitive subjects.

Management scientists tend to be analytic problem solvers while many managers also tend to be systematic thinkers. This problem solving approach is suitable for many problems such as inventory control and price forecasting. However, intuitive styles may be more appropriate when tasks are unstructured, environments are uncertain, and information volumes are large. Tasks and problems can be assessed in terms of the problem solver's evaluation of his ability to recognize and act on relevant information and is viewed as falling in one of four classes: information acquisition (perceptual), known and unknown, and information manipulation (conceptual), known and unknown.

Intuitive managers and systematic managers should not be asked to change their natural styles. Both should be allowed to examine alternatives, test solutions, and validate models in a manner that fits their natural mode of problem solving. Especially in the case of the intuitive manager, model manipulation and testing should be simplified as much as possible. Recognition of differences in cognitive style is essential in developing successful methods of implementing analytic models.

Robey and Taggart emphasize the importance of a better and broader understanding of human information processing to improvement of the definition and design of decision support systems. Although many current systems are based on the assumption of logical, sequential, and quantitative data processing, several research studies question whether most humans process data in this manner. Effective systems should be flexible enough to allow both task requirements to be met and preferred processing styles to be utilized by system users.

Previous studies have indicated that the right and left brain hemispheres control intuitive and logical processing, respectively, and that most persons tend to favor one processing style or the other. However, even a "left brain" oriented person will utilize a "right brain" approach in some situations. Since present day electronic computers are not capable of performing right brain processing involving artificial intelligence, further hardware and software developments will be needed to make right brain machine processing feasible.

Both heuristic and analytical techniques are utilized in left brain processing. Right brain intuitive processing cannot be specified precisely as to the techniques used. Employing the Anthony framework for organizational decision levels, operational control systems are more automated, formally structured, and present oriented while middle and top level management systems are more flexible, informal, unstructured, and future oriented. A majority of information systems to date have been oriented toward operational control, left brain processing.

Structured tasks may best be performed by analytic individuals using structured data reports while less well structured tasks can best be performed by non-analytic, intuitive problem solvers using flexible, graphic, non-linear systems. Emerging decision support systems are beginning to provide flexibility and ease of communication adaptable to a user's decision style. Since most present day systems lack support for intuitive processing, intensive studies of right brain processing may be required before whole-brained man-machine systems can be fully developed.

Jones[1] maintains that designers of decision support systems too often design systems that don't fit the thinking styles of managers. Decision support systems with time sharing and graphic capabilities are best suited for nonprogrammed strategic and semistructured operational problems. Individual decision making styles vary from intuitive to analytical. Recent research studies indicate that the right and left sides of the brain operate independently with strategic planning activities occurring predominately on the right hemisphere and operational and management control activities occurring on the left hemisphere.

Analytic thinking managers will likely be more efficient at such structured operational tasks as credit control, inventory control, and production scheduling. Intuitive managers will be more efficient at strategic planning tasks such as developing marketing, research, and financial policies. Management control activities such as budget development, working capital planning, and new product evaluation can be performed efficiently by either type of manager. Intuitive managers who want to get a feel for the problem to be solved before proceeding to the solution stage, frequently have trouble with the analytic characteristics of many decision support systems.

Decision support systems should be keyed more closely to the thinking styles of managers. For intuitive managers, the use of an intermediary who can acquire analytically generated information and verbally transmit it to them for combination with qualitative data will be very helpful. This approach will allow the intuitive manager to use an unstructured approach to decision-making, to obtain information in a form compatible with his style of decision-making, to utilize simple but powerful models to test a wide range of alternative solutions, and to improve his understanding of problems to be solved.

Benbasat and Schroeder[2] conducted an experiment which related information system and decision-maker characteristics to cost, time, and report utilization performance in a simulated production/inventory environment. The information system characteristics analyzed included presentation form, decision aid and exception reporting availability, and amount of information furnished. The decision-making characteristics examined were decision-making style and knowledge of functional areas. Previous studies have indicated the importance of both the separate main effects and impact of the interaction of human and information systems variables in designing effective information systems. Consideration should also be given to conflicts among multiple performance measures.

Historical report information was presented in tabular or graphical form with statistical calculations such as the mean and variance being included. Decision aids available included an exponential smoothing routine, a production quantity algorithm using estimated average demand and probabilities provided by users, and a Hadley/Whitin optimum order point/quantity model. Decision makers were allowed to use decision aids by themselves or in conjunction with historical reports. Exception reports were made available to some groups and not to others. The number of reports was varied, based on a necessary number for some groups, and an extra number for overload groups.

Participants in the study were classified as having high or low functional area knowledge and low and high analytic ability. Performance was analyzed in terms of cost incurred, decision time required, and number of reports requested during twenty simulated time periods. Decision makers determined order points, order quantities, and daily production figures. The decision makers who used decision aids and graphical displays had the lowest total costs but took significantly longer to make decisions than nonaid and nongraph users. Individuals with graphical results and those with a high inventory knowledge used fewer reports and individuals with low analytical ability and low functional area knowledge used the most reports. Individuals with the overload report set used more reports than those with the necessary report set but did not have better performance.

Decision-making style and functional knowledge did not have a direct effect on time or cost performance. The analytic ability and functional knowledge of users should be considered in developing reporting systems and decision and graphical aids can be helpful in improving decision performance. Further experiments in this area should include both human characteristics and MIS design variables and also emphasize tactical and strategic level information systems.

King and Cleland[3] issue a clarion call for closer manager and operations analyst cooperation in developing decision models which can help managers improve their decision-making effectiveness. Increased understanding, learning, and effectiveness can be achieved through joint analyst-manager development of decision models as part of the management information system design process.

Sophisticated information systems should permit utilization of both formal and informal models and information collection for both high level strategic and lower level operational decisions. Data bases draw data from many data sources and provide data for informal models, for predictive models used to predict future events, and for optimization models which evaluate and select courses of action based on predicted values of key variables. Definition of information requirements for decision-making in terms of predictive variables, criterion, solution, and sensitivity information for the chosen model is the most critical question in information systems design.

Model-based MIS design increases the importance of managers and analysts explicating and verbalizing the mental models that managers use. Alternative models can be evaluated in terms of their accuracy, utility, and development/maintenance cost. As new information is collected, it can be used to evaluate that model's usefulness and the value of collecting additional information. The process of creating the decision oriented MIS is as important as the end product, in terms of the joint review and improved understanding of problem areas, models developed, and solution implications.

Bonczek, Holsapple, and Whinston raise important issues with regard to the extent to which computers can be made to emulate human perceptual and judgmental processes. Progress in this area can be made by increasing the computer's ability to recognize and execute tasks while decreasing the amount of human effort needed to specify tasks. A framework for decision-making is proposed, consisting of identification of abilities required in decision-making (i.e., a content rather than a process model) and the division of labor involved in organizational decision-making. An operational framework takes the form of a generalized intelligent decision support system which will support a wide variety of applications, understand English like queries, formulate and execute appropriate models, and develop problem solving information.

Decisions to be made range from highly structured to very unstructured ones. For unstructured problems, the GIDS problem processor contains general problem solving strategies in its information base which can be combined and modified to achieve a satisfactory problem solution. Usage tracking and utilization of programs that modify primary programs in the information base may allow the improvement of primary programs through experience.

Decision support systems have received more impetus from the expansion of data base management systems with query facilities than from improved understanding of decision-making processes. Addition of artificial intelligence to data base management systems allows nonprocedural operations and natural language processing to be carried out. A number of data base systems have been used in practical applications calling for unstructured processing.

The development of flexible decision support systems is facilitated by identifying the contents of decision-making situations. Division of labor in organizations can be represented by roles, definitional relationships among roles, and associated relationships among roles (with information passage) even for very complex organizations. Roles differ according to the nature of information processing tasks and the degree of control structure. Thus, organization planning resources can be modelled in a computerized information base by formalizing a set of roles and introducing problem reduction and problem solution methods. Unstructuredness in the man-machine decision making system can arise from user characteristics in terms of the nature, sequence, and manner of DSS interactions or from the availability of alternative problem solution methods.

Successful decision support systems should emulate cognitive capabilities by providing power to make decisions, perception for information collection, and design abilities to formulate models. From these basic abilities come other capabilities: analysis to adjust perceptions and formulations, valuations to modify perceptions and powers, organization to bring design and power into proper adjustment, and adaption in terms of a continual series of problem recognitions and adjustment, and adaption in terms of a continual series of problem recognitions and adjustments of the other abilities. All of these capabilities are incorporated into a generalized intelligent problem processor.

The generalized intelligent decision support system includes an information base and problem processor. The information base extends data base techniques to provide a complete semantic mechanism for storing knowledge, including the knowledge of experts in specialized fields. The problem processor collects user information, expressing user intentions in the form of models and interfaces models and data for execution. The AT&T Econometric Planning System is offered as a prototype GIDS example.

Keen and Wagner view decision support systems as personal tools for managers centered around data base management systems and financial planning models. Traditional computer systems often fail to adequately support managers in making personal decision choices. Standardized reporting systems, classical management science models, and traditional data processing systems lack the flexibility, scope, and fast response necessary for much of the ad hoc, adaptive, and unstructured decision making desirable at top and middle management levels.

Decision support systems should be easy to use, flexible, and adaptive if they are to be widely used by today's managers, reflecting the way managers think in an exploratory, evolutionary mode. It is also clearly evident that decision support systems can be more easily implemented with simple special purpose languages. Planning languages allow novice computer users to utilize simple, easy to learn commands to simulate the behavior of the organization over a specified time period and to ask what if questions in both deterministic and probabilistic modes. A wide variety of outputs, formats, and calculations can be generated easily in as many different reports as the user desires.

Considerable evidence exists that top and middle managers are beginning to obtain hands-on experience with computer terminals, that people-oriented benefits of planning systems are becoming to be regarded as highly as feature-oriented benefits, and that many users expect a lot from their decision support systems. However, it is quite clear that such systems are not automatic decision makers and that they amplify and expand but do not replace existing decision-making capabilities.

In their second article, Bonczek, Holsapple, and Whinston concur that while no clear cut line can be drawn between MIS and DSS, Decision Support Systems generally provide flexible report generation and computational modeling capabilities not found in most management information systems. Special emphasis is placed on issues of managerial problem solving and the interfaces between users, models, and data. Of particular importance is the incorporation of extensive data handling and modeling capabilities into an integrated single system with which the user can communicate easily.

Corporate planning models typically involve a modular financial simulation approach which allows later extensions and modifications. Software support of user-model, model-data, and user-data interfaces is also essential to overcome modeling problems of combination difficulties, inflexibility, lack of model bases, and updating complexities. Systems have been proposed that would include flexible and modular models, mechanisms for extracting model data from data bases, a conveniently accessible command language, and evolutionary model capabilities.

Some very primitive early decision support systems include project management systems and SPSS for statistical analysis. The Potlach Forest System incorporated models and data handling in a unified system, interrelating models in the same manner that organizational levels and activities are related. A bank Decision Support System, consisting of a data base, decision models, and a decision-maker, while allowing the independent utilization of operating, tactical, and strategic models, supports decisions at all three management levels. This system included both a model definition language and a simple command language. The Xerox Planning System incorporates a collection of simulation models that are more understandable and representative of actual decision processes than optimization models. The programmed models plus an online data base produce a combined man-model-machine system which many executives feel can be used to improve decision-making. For best results, managers must have both the expertise and motivation to use models.

Data management, modeling, and user interfaces are three key, interdependent topics that must be considered in examining decision support systems. Increased storage capacity and lower hardware costs have made possible storage of large volumes of complexly structured data. More comprehensive, integrated, and complex models can now be developed and utilized as compact chips and specialized languages come into widespread use. Hardware advances have also made possible user-oriented, higher level languages.

Direct retrieval languages include those in which the user explicitly states how the data are to be retrieved and those which require the user only to state the desired data with the system producing the necessary logic. Languages which direct computation range from those which require the user to explicitly state all calculations to those in which the user merely states the problem to be solved along with the data to be used.

Thus, languages for directing computation can state the model explicitly, invoke the model by name, or state the problem while languages for directing data retrieval can state the problem, invoke a report, or state retrieval procedures explicitly. Various combinations of the six types of retrieval and computational languages are possible, and these combinations suggest a classification scheme for decision support systems which may assist system designers and builders. The most common DSS's combine languages that invoke models and reports by name.

Emshoff[4] proposes a series of characteristics which the next set of managerial models should possess. A model is defined as a simplified representation of reality that can be manipulated to forecast the results of specified actions. Model building has evolved through three phases: Experience-based, model-optimized, and interactive decisions. Experienced based decisions were hampered by the slow pace of development of qualified decision-makers and model-optimized decisions frequently suffered from invalid assumptions, lack of acceptance by managers and worse results than decisions based on subjective judgments, in many cases.

Interactive computer terminals provide managers the opportunity to at least partially structure their own models, and to obtain a range of results which can be judged according to criteria such as risk, robustness, and performance. Interactive models promise to overcome at least some of the limitations of staff developed, model-optimized decisions, with greater emphasis on shared line-staff roles and responsibilities. In experience-generalized decisions, decision structures and key assumptions will be formulated by responsible decision-makers. Model-building staff work will consist of formalizing instead of formulating essential model relationships. Emphasis will also be placed upon obtaining wider, more general problem perspectives on a group basis, improving the quality of information filter activities, and developing better mental models of factors and relationships which affect decision processes.

Experience generalized decision processes should emerge most rapidly in strategic planning activities, where managerial modeling has been much less effective than in other areas. Such innovations as the *Delphi* process for technological forecasting, *Idealization* technique for removing self imposed constraints and redesigning organization structures from scratch, *Brainstorming* for generation and synthesis of diverse ideas, and *Dialectic Approaches* for creating generalized synthesis from conflicting views can aid in improving managerial interactions. Rules of thumb to test model assumption validity are sorely needed. Strategies for achieving changes include development of better models of problem environments, identifying weaknesses in current models, incorporating different decision styles into decision frameworks, and pinpointing background capabilities needed by management researchers to effectively develop experience-generalized decision processes.

Aaker and Weinberg point out that interactive marketing models are rapidly moving beyond the experimental stage.[5] This is happening because users can more easily obtain systems tailored to their needs from a wide variety of systems available and the emergence of a decision calculus model building philosophy lays out procedures for combining judgment and data to assist a manager in decision-making. Several such models have been used continually (a good measure of success) to allocate sales efforts and advertising dollars.

Interactive computer systems are defined as those in which the user interacts with the computer in a conversational mode. A model is a representation of a real world environment, which requires careful balancing of completeness and validity with simplicity and usability. Two major types of models are descriptive (which predict or permit understanding of processes) and decision (which are essentially descriptive models used to evaluate several decision alternatives).

Descriptive models involve determining input, output, and intervening constructs as well as development of relationships between these constructs. Constructs and relationships between constructs are typically developed by judgmental approaches, data-based approaches, or a combination of both methods. Models can be helpful in improving understanding of system operation, in summarizing and organizing information, and in identifying likely areas for further research.

Interactive systems contribute to wider managerial usage of models by reducing manager-model barriers, providing fast response to inquiries, producing computational procedures compatible with human thought processes, and by improving the efficiency of system operation. Decision-makers who become involved with interactive marketing models tend to build higher quality models which are more likely to be widely accepted by organization members than uninvolved managers who depend upon analyst developed models for decision support.

Involved decision makers will normally provide more valid, relevant data and will often contribute more to model development and refinement than uninvolved managers. Involvement in model development also tends to increase usage and confidence levels, the likelihood that the decision-maker will sell the model to his associates, and the probability of appropriate and effective use of the model. Interactive, model-based systems do have the disadvantages of higher costs, lower reliability, and greater complexity than batch processed systems. Interactive, model-based, marketing information systems are most effective when line personnel must make decisions, fast response times are needed, judgmental data is important, decision-makers are widely dispersed, and data/processing capabilities are adequate for model support. In essence, interactive marketing models will contribute the most to decision-making processes when they are compatible with decision-making situations to which applied and to the decision-making styles and philosophies of users.

Konczal[6] emphasizes that model-building is an iterative process requiring continual reevaluation of a model in the light of new insights and experience with the process being modelled. Managerial input and guidance is important in formulating model construction philosophy, ensuring model methodology objectiveness and accuracy, and in administering model development/implementation activities efficiently. Computer business models should help managers improve their decision-making effectiveness by minimizing the impact of surprise events and bad decisions, by coping more efficiently with increased complexity and rapid change, and capitalizing on the systems approach. Managers should be highly involved in stating objectives, logical system definition, model adjustment, and implementing/using results, and at least, moderately involved in data analysis, model construction, and model solution.

Managerial input is particularly important in adjusting the model during model construction and after the model is run. Since no model can ever completely capture all relevant aspects of a real-life situation, judgment should be used to refine the model and highlight non-quantitative factors. Managerial judgment is also important during model verification for logical correctness, and validation to determine if the model agrees with the real system. Validation can take the form of parametric or non-parametric evaluation and models are not likely to have much impact on decision-making until verification/validation is complete. Good management of the model-building activity requires careful planning of operations, coordinating efforts of managers and quantitative analysts, and careful documentation of model activity. Successful use of computer models will occur only as managers increase their involvement in model building activities.

Hudson, Chambers, and Johnston[7] illustrate how management science models can be used to assist decision makers in planning purchasing, production, and development activities for a new product in an unfamiliar, high technology market. Sales, costs, product/process development outcomes, etc., were subject to considerable uncertainty. Particular emphasis was placed on methods by which management scientists can assist decision makers rather than concern with the accuracy and validity of the models and techniques used.

Alternative marketing and economic outcomes were simulated using volume and capacity models, functional organizational units provided information on the range and likelihood of input variables, the sensitivity of various variables to reasonable variations in input values was determined, and results were presented to managers to assist in determining plant sizes, purchase quantities, and alternative components and processes. The system developed was particularly valuable in providing more reasonable demand forecasts, in improving the understanding of the economic consequences of component costs and performance, in laying the basis for improved contract terms, and in enabling faster decision making and negotiations to take place. Discounted present values and expected values of alternatives were developed and provided decision makers with a good indication of the relative benefits and risks of the various proposals.

The model results produced significant cost savings, changed the emphasis from component cost reduction to performance improvement, accelerated decision-making processes, demonstrated explicit consideration of uncertainty in alternative evaluation was feasible, and permitted quantifying intuitively determined insights. Experience with this project also underscored the importance of systematic information structuring, explicit value determination, and subjective encoding of probabilities in complex decision-making situations.

Sprague[8] describes the process of developing a financial planning model for a commercial bank. The process of planning practiced in this case includes goal setting, competitive assessment, market forecasting, and internal assessment. Information from each of these phases is submitted to a planning model. The model can be a mental process or a staff developed, computer-based model. The model output is the simulated performance of the firm under a given set of assumptions, forecasts, guidelines, and decisions. Eventually a set of projections is produced which satisfies the firm's goals and objectives. These model outputs must be periodically compared with actual results to permit refining the model and its forecasting techniques.

In the bank's financial planning system, goals, objectives, and forecasts were phased in specific terms. Model outputs take the form of a set of financial statements. After the initial simulation, managers can use the system to test the potential results of changes in decisions or forecasts. The system structure includes the data matrix, the financial simulator, and the executive access system. The data matrix holds input and output variables and has an historical and future section. The financial simulator includes endogenous (internal) variables and exogenous (outside) variables which are combined to produce total bank performance, and has three sections: A projection model, an asset allocation module, and a report generator module. The executive access system enables managers and analysts to access the data base, analyze it, and enter changes. The system can be operated on a regular, periodic or conversational, ad hoc basis. A key feature of the system is the ability of the planner to run the model to determine, on an immediate access basis, the results of alternative decisions and plans.

As Keen illustrates, Decision Support Systems shift the emphasis from large scale, complex computer projects to individual user access to analytic models and tailored information systems. A DSS should support managers in nonroutine tasks, provide flexible and easy access to desired data, and become an integral part of the individual's decision-making process under his personal control. Such systems can be developed, using technological building blocks in an evolutionary fashion, based on the manager's understanding of the decision-making process and organization structure. The available technological building blocks include decentralization of computing activities, differentiation of software and hardware components, and diffusion of technical expertise.

The example of a brand manager, who must determine prices, promotion outlays, and advertising budgets, is used to illustrate how DSS can support but not replace judgment. For a given product, the manager and a systems analyst develop response curves for price, promotion, advertising, and sales force levels, which help to pinpoint feasible alternatives. Emphasis is placed on producing more effective decisions rather than improving the efficiency of the decision-making process.

Managers who utilize DSS effectively must understand the decision process to be supported and should be able to use commands that correspond to the verbs they normally use. Analytic methods can be imbedded in familiar commands (e.g., PLOT can activate a linear regression routine). A DSS may include optimization models but still rely on judgment as in the case of a linear programming routine used in a simulation mode to aid in redesigning school boundaries. In essence, complex analytic models can be translated into useful decision-making approaches by utilizing decision support systems.

Successful implementation of a DSS requires the assistance of a technician to help identify the task to be supported, project objectives, and extensive knowledge of the characteristics of the current decision process being considered. A software interface must be provided to handle commands developed by users and to allow evolutionary development of the total system as experience is gained in its use. Understanding the decision process is also an essential development requirement. While Decision Support Systems can reduce operating costs, improved decision effectiveness and better communication patterns are the acid tests of its true worth.

Larreche and Srinivasin indicate that more attention is being paid to development of strategic models that will allocate marketing resources to product lines or business units in an optimal fashion, with less emphasis being placed on traditional functional models that focus on narrower problem areas (e.g., brand management). STRATPORT is an online computerized model, incorporating both empirical and judgmental data, used to evaluate and select business portfolio strategies. Careful development of and resource allocation to a balanced portfolio of business units is considered vital to long term survival and growth by many authorities. Current portfolio approaches are limited by portfolio representation shortcomings, implicit relationships between business unit position and cash generation or consumption rates, and the scope of the analysis.

STRATPORT extends the scope of the strategic analysis and makes explicit certain marketing, investment, and cash flow and profit relationships in order to overcome the limitations of earlier models. It allows integration of empirical and managerial judgment, evaluation of strategies for different financial requirements, and determination of the effect of changes in underlying assumptions upon portfolio mixes.

Managerial inputs for internal and external resources determine the total size of the investment portfolio. Market share and sales volume for each business unit is determined for planning and post planning periods. Specific strategies can be evaluated for each business unit in terms of marketing investments or target market shares and strategies can also be formulated to allocate resources among business units to meet specific cash flow requirements. Both business portfolio analysis and financial portfolio theories are incorporated in the model.

The principal functional relationships of the STRATPORT model include the market response, maintenance marketing, capacity expenditure, working capital, cost, and price functions. Optimum allocations to ten business units for eleven cash flow levels can be determined in a few seconds. A sample set of six business units is evaluated for a planning period of three years and a post planning period of five years in terms of profits and cash flows to illustrate the power of the model.

STRATPORT extends and makes operational current business portfolio approaches but is limited by its restricted scope, structural assumptions, and external aggregation requirements. Successful use of the STRATPORT model requires a good understanding of its basic structure, capabilities, and limitations, and allows the user to concentrate on the qualitative aspects of strategic decision making.

Wagner points out that an executive support system permits the coupling of a user's intellectual resources with those of computer systems. The availability of financial planning languages enables non-data processing personnel to develop competency in building and solving models in an interactive, exploratory manner. In a rapidly changing environment, it is important that managers anticipate, detect, and counter changing conditions as rapidly as possible.

Decision support systems extend human memory and logical reasoning capabilities. Some data base management systems permit information retrieval in such a manner that significant patterns and correlations can be discovered. Simulation models help managers outline future possibilities, forsee consequences, and pinpoint alternative courses of action. Financial planning languages are an integral part of many decision support systems.

For best results, computer models should allow statements to be expressed in a users normal vocabulary, follow the normal thought patterns of users, and permit real time response to user inputs. It is very helpful to the user if statements can be expressed in any order he may desire. A sample set of outputs is provided to illustrate how a typical model might be used to answer what if questions concerning how sales, expense, or profit goals can best be met.

The use of Monte Carlo Risk Analysis, in conjunction with business models, to express intuitive patterns of uncertainty is also demonstrated in the form of sample outputs. By using a clearcut, crisp set of directives as contraints, it is possible to optimize the number of sales personnel or other variables. The greatest benefit of interactive planning languages plus optimization may be in effective resource allocation among diverse future alternatives.

Durway emphasizes the usefulness of two methods of minimizing uncertainties and evaluating risk—sensitivity analysis and simulation. The lack of software packages easily understood by managers and sophisticated enough to handle complex calculations as well as inadequate managerial exposure to risk analysis techniques has inhibited its acceptance as a decision-making tool. Some companies have long used standardized reporting forms or even manual calculations to perform project analyses. A new generation of financial modeling and planning languages now provides significant advantages over earlier versions, including natural language modes, nonprocedural statements, interactive responses, and the ability to handle both what if and goal seeking calculations.

When evaluating a package, its ease of use, nonprocedural, flexibility, and direct interaction characteristics should be carefully considered. The new systems can be used to run a multitude of cases to answer what if questions, reducing the numerous variables down to the most critical ones through a process of continuous iteration. Another approach which can be used is to run a risk analysis using Monte Carlo methods and then to narrow the focus to a specific variable for sensitivity analysis. The most significant effect of the new systems is to provide the means for combining theoretical knowledge of risk analysis with practical means of implementing it through the use of an interactive computer.

Footnotes

[1] See Jack W. Jones, "Making Your Decision Support Systems Pay Off," COMPUTER DECISIONS, July 1979, pp. 46–47 for a brief but excellent discussion of how different decision making styles affect DSS use.

[2] Izak Benbasat and Roger G. Schroeder discuss the experiment and its result in detail in "An Experimental Investigation of Some MIS Design Variables," *MIS Quarterly*, March 1977, pp. 37–49.

[3] See William R. King and David R. Cleland, "Manager Analyst Teamwork in MIS," *Business Horizons,* April 1971, pp. 59–68 for a more complete discussion of this important topic.

[4] See James Emshoff, "Experience Generalized Decision-Making: The Next Generation of Managerial Models," *Interfaces,* August 1978, pp. 40–48, for a full-fledged treatment.

[5] David Aaker and Charles Weinberg discuss "Interactive Marketing Models" fully in *The Journal of Marketing,* October 1975, pp. 16–23.

[6] See Edward Konczal, "Models are for Managers not Mathematicians," JOURNAL OF SYSTEMS MANAGEMENT, January 1975, pp. 12–15 for a brief but very illuminating discussion of the importance of managerial participation in model building.

[7] Ronald G. Hudson, et al, in "New Product Planning Decisions Under Uncertainty," INTERFACES, November 1977, pp. 82–96 discuss in considerable detail an excellent example of a new product decision model which supports purchasing decision making.

[8] See Ralph H. Sprague, "Systems Support for a Financial Planning Model," *Management Accounting,* June 1972, pp. 29–34 for a more detailed discussion of how this banking model works.

10

How Manager's
Minds Work

by James L. McKenney
and Peter G. W. Keen

About the authors:

James L. McKenney is professor of business administration at the Harvard Business School where he teaches and studies management information systems.

Peter G. W. Keen is assistant professor of organizational psychology and management at the Alfred P. Sloan School of Management, Massachusetts Institute of Technology.

A number of researchers have pointed to particular aspects of thinking and personality that differ between the people who build models and those who use them. Obviously, management scientists and general managers think differently. In an effort to narrow this gap, the authors discuss their recent research on cognitive style, which provides a means of developing

Reprinted with permission from Harvard Business Review

strategies of action for the management scientist and
a useful way of focusing on the implementation of
analytic models for the general manager.

A common topic in management literature over the past few years
has been the difference between managers and management scientists,
usually in relation to the argument that their association has not been a
productive one. For example, a recent article by C. Jackson Grayson,
Jr., compares the situation with C.P. Snow's famous notion of the two
cultures of science and humanities:

"Managers and management scientists are operating as two separate
cultures, each with its own goals, languages, and methods. Effective
cooperation—and even communication—between the two is just about
minimal."[1]

Perhaps this is an overpessimistic viewpoint, but it is one that is expressed often and by individuals who have substantial experience with
the use of analytic methods in management.

Management science techniques have been very successful in such
areas of business as logistics planning, resource allocation, financial
forecasting, and so forth. It appears that, on the whole, these techniques have found the applications for which they are best suited, and
managers make substantial and continued use of them.

However, in other areas of business they have been unable to gain
any real foothold. Most obviously, they have had little impact on areas
of decision making where the management problems do not lend
themselves to explicit formulation, where there are ambiguous or over-
lapping criteria for action, and where the manager operates through
intuition.

The major issue for management science as a discipline now seems
to be to get managers in such situations to make use of the formal
techniques that can clearly be so helpful to them but have not yet been
so in practice. There seem to be two main factors affecting this problem.

One concerns the actual techniques available. Obviously, process
chemists use linear programming because it suits the constraints and
natures of the problems they deal with.

The primary factor, however, is the differences in approach and behavior between the two cultures. A feature under little control by

either manager or scientist is that each has a distinctive style of thinking and problem solving. In its own context, each style is highly effective but not easily communicated to the other. The differences in thinking are neither "good" nor "bad"; they simply exist.

In a way, it is platitudinous to state that managers and scientists are different, but a reason for focusing explicitly on this factor is to examine the argument, maintained by management writers, that to bridge the gap between the two groups each should become a little more like the other. In this view, the differences themselves are the problem, and education is generally recommended as the solution: the manager should be trained in elementary quantitative techniques, and the scientist, in interpersonal and managerial skills.

Yet it is this very differentiation of thinking style that makes each of them successful in his chosen specialization. But the cost of differentiation is the increased difficulty it presents in integration. Therefore, the issue for both manager and scientist is complex: how to communicate with each other; how to complement each other's strengths without sacrificing too much of one's own.

In this article, we are explicity concerned with these differences in thinking between the two cultures. We shall offer suggestions as to how the manager and the scientist can best work together in the development and use of analytic models and decision aids.

We suggest that such aids must be designed to amplify the user's problem-solving strategies. Thus it seems that the central factor determining whether a manager will use a model to reach a decision is the extent to which it "fits" his style of thinking. The main body of this paper largely defines what we mean by "fit."

Over the past four years, we have developed and tested a model of cognitive style, drawing on the developmental psychology that has in recent years reinvigorated the whole study of thinking and problem solving.[2] Our main aim has been to better understand the cognitive aspects of the decision-making process.

In the first section of this article, we shall provide a statement of our model in terms applicable to problem solving and decision making in general, rather than just to analytic techniques. Next, we shall discuss the experimental data we have gathered in validating the model. Finally, we shall extend our findings to the implications of cognitive style for implementing formal analytic models.

We view problem solving and decision making in terms of the processes through which individuals organize the information they perceive in their environment, bringing to bear habits and strategies of thinking. Our model is based on the dual premise that consistent modes of thought develop through training and experience and that these modes can be classified along two dimensions, information gathering and information evaluation, as shown in Figure 10.1.

Information gathering relates to the essentially perceptual processes by which the mind organizes the diffuse verbal and visual stimuli it encounters. The resultant "information" is the outcome of a complex coding that is heavily dependent on mental set, memory capacity, and strategies—often unconscious ones—that serve to ease "cognitive strain." Of necessity, information gathering involves rejecting some of the data encountered, and summarizing and categorizing the rest.

Preceptive individuals bring to bear concepts to filter data; they focus on relationships between items and look for deviations from or conformities with their expectations. Their precepts act as cues for both gathering and cataloging the data they find.

Receptive thinkers are more sensitive to the stimulus itself. They focus on detail rather than relationships and try to derive the attributes of the information from direct examination of it instead of from fitting it to their precepts.

Each mode of information gathering has its advantages in specific situations; equally, each includes risks of overlooking the potential meaning of data. The preceptive individual too easily ignores relevant detail, while the receptive thinker may fail to shape detail into a coherent whole. In management positions, the former will be most successful in many marketing or planning roles, and the latter in tasks such as auditing.

Information evaluation refers to processes commonly classified under problem solving. Individuals differ not only in their method of gathering data but also in their sequence of analysis of that data. These differences are most pronounced in relation to formal planning.

Systematic individuals tend to approach a problem by structuring it in terms of some method which, if followed through, leads to a likely solution.

Intuitive thinkers usually avoid committing themselves in this way. Their strategy is more one of solution testing and trial-and-error. They are much more willing to jump from one method to another, to dis-

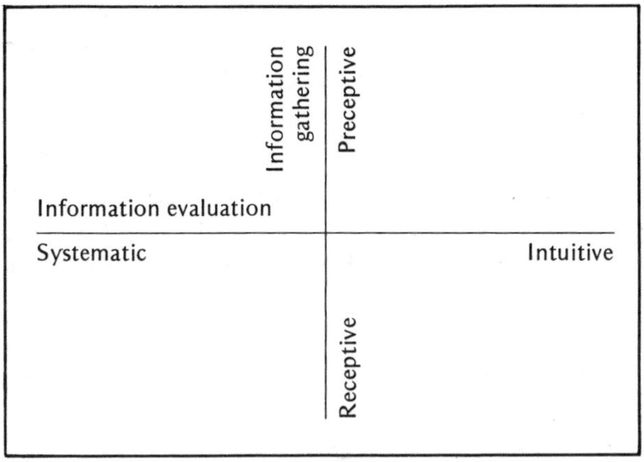

FIGURE 10.1 Model of Cognitive Style

card information, and to be sensitive to cues that they may not be able to identify verbally.

Here again, each mode of information evaluation has advantages and risks. In tasks such as production management, the systematic thinker can develop a method of procedure that utilizes all his experience and economizes on effort. An intuitive thinker often reinvents the wheel each time he deals with a particular problem. However, the intuitive person is better able to approach ill-structured problems where the volume of data, the criteria for solution, or the nature of the problem itself do not allow the use of any predetermined method.

FOCUS ON PROBLEM FINDING

Most modern theories of the decision process stress "rationality." Mathematical decision theory and game theory, for example, are both mainly concerned with defining the basics of rational behavior. Accounting for the discrepancies between it and observed behavior is only a secondary aim. Other theories, particularly those concerning organizational decision making, include factors of motivation, personality, and social forces but still treat decision making as essentially equivalent to problem solving.

In our model of cognitive style, we focus on problem solving, but our central argument is that decision making is above all situational and, therefore, includes problem finding. The manager scans his environment and organizes what he perceives. His efforts are as much geared to clarifying his values and intents as to dealing with predefined problems.

Obviously, some problems do force themselves on his awareness; this is particularly true in crisis situations. Nonetheless, he generally has some discretion in the selection of problems to deal with and in the level of aspiration he sets for himself. (His aspiration often determines the extent to which he involves himself in tems of effort and risk.)

The manager's activities are bounded not only by the formal constraints of his job, but also by the more informal traditions and expectations implicit in his role. Because of this, the decision-making activity is strongly influenced by his perception of his position. A decision "situation" exists when he sees some event or cue in his environment that activates him into a search-analyze-evaluate sequence that results in a decision. This sequence is initiated by and depends on his environment assessment.

Our cognitive-style model provides some explanation of the processes affecting the manager's assessment of this environment. It thus includes an important aspect of behavior omitted in most theories on decision making—namely, that of problem finding, problem recognition, and problem definition. Generally, other theories assume that the situation has already been defined; the manager is presented with a neatly packaged problem and instructions on what he should try to do.

Implicit in the focus on problem finding is the concept that particular modes of cognition are better suited to certain contexts than others. As we mentioned earlier, the central argument of our study is that there needs to be a fit between the decision maker's cognitive style and the information-processing constraints of his task. Given this fit, the manager is more likely to gather environmental information that leads to successful (or at least comfortable) problem finding. He should also be able to evaluate that information in a way that facilitates successful problem solving. Perhaps the implications of a misfit are easier to indicate.

We mentioned earlier that a receptive thinker focuses on detail rather than pattern. But a receptive field sales manager who receives a wide range of information may well be flooded by it. He probably cannot examine all the sales reports, orders, phone calls, and so on. Instead, he should try to filter his information and be alert to trends and discrepancies. Thus a combination of the sales pattern in a particular region and a recent salesmen's report of several customers' comments may lead him to recognize signs of change in consumer taste.

The preceptive individual is particularly suited to those tasks where he must have a concept of his environment. A preceptive manager would not be very successful in a task such as editing.

Similarly, it is easy to envisage tasks in which the intuitive thinker cannot come to terms with the data that are required in his decision making because he is unable to think in terms of a methodical sequence of analysis.

We have chosen the term "style" rather than the more common one of "structure" to stress the fact that modes of thinking relate more to propensity than to capacity. An individual's style develops out of his experience. For example, there is a tendency, particularly in late high school and college, for a student to increasingly choose courses that build on his strengths. This reinforcing pattern further develops those strengths and perhaps atrophies the skills in which he is less confident.

This suggests not only that tasks exist that are suited to particular cognitive styles, but also that the capable individual will *search* out those tasks that are compatible with his cognitive propensities. In addition, he will generally approach tasks and problems using his most comfortable mode of thinking.

Our model indicates some important differences in the ways in which individuals of particular styles approach problems and data. The accompanying list summarizes the main characteristics of each style:

Systematic thinkers tend do—

. . . look for a method and make a plan for solving a problem.
. . . be very conscious of their approach.
. . . defend the quality of a solution largely in terms of the method.
. . . define the specific constraints of the problem early in the process.
. . . discard alternatives quickly.
. . . move through a process of increasing refinement of analysis.
. . . conduct an ordered search for additional information.
. . . complete any discrete step in analysis that they begin.

Intuitive thinkers tend to—

. . . keep the overall problem continuously in mind.
. . . redefine the problem frequently as they proceed.

. . . rely on unverbalized cues, even hunches.
. . . defend a solution in terms of fit.
. . . consider a number of alternatives and options simultaneously.
. . . jump from one step in analysis or search to another and back again.
. . . explore and abandon alternatives very quickly.

Receptive thinkers tend to—

. . . suspend judgment and avoid preconceptions.
. . . be attentive to detail and to the exact attributes of data.
. . . insist on a complete examination of a data set before deriving
conclusions.

Preceptive thinkers tend to—

. . . look for cues in a data set.
. . . focus on relationships.
. . . jump from one section of a data set to another, building a set of
explanatory precepts.

Our research supports the concept that particular tasks and roles
are more suited to one cognitive style than to another. Figure 10.2
shows careers that seem to be especially compatible with the skills and
predispositions implicit in each of the cognitive modes of style.

Production & logistics manager Statistician Financial analyst	Preceptive	Marketing manager Psychologist Historian
Systematic		Intuitive
Auditor Clinical diagnostician	Receptive	Architect Bond salesman

FIGURE 10.2 Tasks and Roles Compatible With Each
Cognitive Style

EXPERIMENTAL RESULTS

We have carried out a range of experiments over the past four years aimed at validating the assertions made in the preceding statements.[3] The main effort in the experiments has been to identify and measure cognitive style. In the spring of 1972, a set of 12 standard reference tests for cognitive factors, developed by the Educational Testing Service, was administered to 107 MBA students. Each test was specifically chosen to fit one particular mode of style. The results confirmed most of the main characteristics of each style summarized earlier.

INITIAL TESTS

In our first set of experiments, 70% of the sample showed distinct differences in performance level between the systematic and the intuitive tests or between the receptive and the preceptive. This supports our basic contention that individuals tend to have a definite style.

We chose a conservative approach for our tests classifying a subject as "intuitive," "systematic," and so on, only when the scores on tests requiring, say, an intuitive response were substantially different from those measuring capacity for the other mode of style along the same dimension. The comparisons focused on relative, not absolute, performance. The numeric scores were converted to a 1 to 7 scale, with a "1" indicating that the subject scored in the lowest seventh of the sample and a "7" corresponding to the top seventh.

From our main sample of 107 MBA students, we selected 20 whose test results indicated a distinct cognitive style for a follow-up experiment. This made use of a "cafeteria" set of 16 problems from which the subjects were asked to choose any 5 to answer. In individual sessions, which were tape recorded, the subjects were invited, though not required, to talk aloud as they dealt with each problem. The results pointed to distinct differences in the ways in which individuals of particular styles repond to problems.

As expected, the systematic subjects tended to be very concerned with getting into a problem by defining how to solve it. They were conscious of their planning and often commented on the fact that there were other specific ways of answering the problem.

In contrast, the intuitive subjects tended to jump in, try something, and see where it led them. They generally showed a pattern of rapid solution testing, abandoning lines of exploration that did not seem profitable.

More important, each mode of response was effective in solving different kinds of problems. In one instance, which required the decoding of a ciphered message, the intuitive subjects solved the problem—sometimes in a dazzling fashion—while none of the systematics were able to do so. In this particular case, there seemed to be a pattern among the intuitives: a random testing of ideas, followed by a necessary incubation period in which the implications of these tests were assimilated, and then a sudden jump to the answer.

There were often unexplained shifts in the reasoning of the intuitives, who were also much more likely to answer the problems orally. The latter tendency provided some confirmation for the idea that intuitive individuals use their own talking aloud to cue their activities and to alert themselves to possible lines of analysis.

There were distinct differences in the problems chosen by each of the groups, and their ratings of which problems they enjoyed most were remarkably consistent. The systematics preferred program-type problems, while the intuitives liked open-ended ones, especially those that required ingenuity or opinion.

The overall results of the initial experiments provided definite evidence to support both our model of cognitive style and the classification methods we developed through the main-sample test scores. The verbal answers in particular highlighted the degree to which these subjects consistently and distinctively respond to problems. There seems little doubt that, in these extreme cases at least, the individual maps himself onto the problem, rather than matching his behavior to the constraints and demands of the particular task.

SECONDARY SAMPLING

In another set of tests, again using the main sample of 107 subjects, we examined the relationship between cognitive style and personality. We did this through comparisons of our test results with the Myers-Briggs scales used to classify individuals in relation to Jungian theories of psychological type.[4]

The most striking result of our experiment was that, while the scores on the Myers-Briggs scales showed virtually no correlation with absolute performance on our tests, there was a relationship between cognitive style and those scales. In particular, the systematic subjects were very likely to be of the "thinking" type and the intuitives much more likely to be at the other end of the scale, "feeling." R.O. Mason and I.I. Mitroff provide a useful summary of the difference between the thinking-feeling types:

"A Thinking individual is the type who relies primarily on cognitive processes. His evaluations tend to run along the lines of abstract true/false judgments and are based on formal systems of reasoning. A preference for Feeling, on the other hand, implies the type of individual who relies primarily on affective processes. His evaluations tend to run along personalistic lines of good/bad, pleasant/unpleasant, and like/dislike. Thinking types systematize; feeling types take moral stands and are interested in and concerned with moral judgments."[5]

We found a more modest relationship between systematic style and "introversion" and similarly, between intuitive style and "extroversion." Thus our findings mesh well with Mason and Mitroff's predictions (they did not report any experimental data) about psychological type and information systems.

FINAL STUDY

A year after the first two sets of experiments, we examined the relationship between style and career choice, using a sample of 82 MBA students. The results showed consistent differentiations between systematic and intuitive subjects. We compared the career preferences of the two groups and also looked at the test scores of those individuals who showed strong preference for particular careers.

In this experiment, the systematic students were attracted to administrative careers, to the military, and to occupations involving production, planning, control, and supervision. The intuitive group's choices centered around the more open-ended business functions; they preferred careers in psychology, advertising, library science, teaching, and the arts.

The overall result of the three sets of student experiments supports the validity of our conceptual model as a useful and insightful framework for examining the role of cognitive processes in decision making. More important, now that we have established such proof, we plan to extend our research to the study of business managers and especially to model builders and model users.

ANALYTIC MODELS

One of our major conjectures, which partly underlay the whole development of our model, has been that computer systems in general are designed by systematic individuals for systematic users. Although management science has lost its early tones of missionary zeal, of bringing "right" thinking to the ignorant, the implementation of analytic techniques not unreasonably reflects the scientist's own distinctive approach to problem solving.

Model building, from the viewpoint of the management scientist, involves making the causal relationships in a particular situation explicit and articulating the problem until he gets a reasonably predictive model; he will then generally refine that model. He has a faith in his own plan and process, and his specialized style of thinking enables him to literally build a model, shaping ideas and concepts into a methodological whole, and above all articulating relationships that the manager may understand but may not be able to make explicit.

The management scientist's skill is indeed a specialized one; the powerful organizing and systematizing capacity he brings to model building is his special contribution. But, obviously, that can be a vice rather than a virtue in specific situations. What Donald F. Heany calls the "have technique, will travel"[6] banner really amounts to the rigorously systematic individual's preference for a methodical approach to all problems in all contexts.

Fortunately, there are many systematic managers. Our assumption is that most general managers who use management science techniques are likely to be systematic in style. The techniques match their own innate approach to problems, and they gravitate to occupations that are suited to their style.

For example, since inventory control is a task that can be systematized, it will attract systematic managers, and it will therefore be an area in which management science techniques will find fruitful ground.

However, there are just as many management positions not filled by systematic thinkers. For example, advertising, which is not so easily systematized, will attract intuitive people. If management scientists want their techniques used in these more loosely structured business areas, they must try both to make their models less awesome to the intuitive managers they will be working with and to support the managers in their decision-making processes.

This requires understanding the intuitive approach to problem solving in general and developing models which will amplify and complement that approach.

CLASSES OF PROBLEMS

We have found it useful to categorize tasks—and problems in general—in terms of the problem solver's assessment of his ability to first recognize and then act on relevant information.[7] This process provides four basic classes of problems, as in Figure 10.3.

The classes are easily illustrated. If, for example, a manager encounters a problem of inventory control in which he feels that he knows both what data are relevant and what mental operations and analysis are required to deal with that data, the problem is one of planning (Type I in Figure 10.3.). His whole effort then involves merely arranging the data into a form which can be used as input to a defined sequence of evaluation.

Another class of problem (Type 2) exists when the required operations and methods are known, but the data involved are not. Price forecasting in complex markets is an example of this situation. Before a forecast can be made, a mass of data on economic, price, and mar-

| | | Information acquisition, perceptual process | |
		Known	Unknown
Information manipulation, conceptual process	Known	Planning, Type 1	Intelligence-search, Type 2
	Unknown	Invention, Type 3	Research, Type 4

FIGURE 10.3 Classification of Tasks and Problems

ket variables must be organized and sifted. Once this has been done, the forecasting procedure is simple.

A very different state of affairs exists when the individual understands the data but does not know how to manipulate them. Many production-scheduling problems fall into this class, invention (Type 3.) The relevant data are known and the problem consists of finding a way to achieve the desired end.

The fourth class of problem exists when both information and operations are unknown. In this situation, there is a conscious search for cues and a generation of explanatory concepts, together with the development of a method for manipulating the data thus organized. The development of new products is a typical research problem.

SPECIALIZED STYLES

Many management-science projects start as research. For example, modeling a complex environment such as the housing market in order to make industry or demand forecasts generally requires a complicated first step in which two areas of the problem are worked on in parallel: (1) the generation of concepts to "explain" reality and identify the most relevant variables, and (2) the definition of the outputs, aims, and implementation of the model.

Systematic individual

In our cafeteria experiment, the one problem rated most enjoyable by well over half the systematic group was a basic planning task. The systematic management scientist can often take a research problem and shift it to one of planning. The methodological formalization he provides helps translate unknown states of perception and conception into known ones.

However, there is sometimes the danger that he will force the translation; he may insist on some objective function that does not really fit the situation, partly because his preference for planning leaves him unwilling to accept "unknown" states. He needs to make the implicit explicit.

Intuitive manager

Just as the systematic management scientist's specialized style of thinking provides very definite strengths in specialized tasks, so too does the intuitive manager's. It is important to again stress that the intuitive mode is not sloppy or loose; it seems to have an underlying discipline at least as coherent as the systematic mode, but is less apparent because it is largely unverbalized.

There are many situations where the volume of information, the lack of structure in the task, and the uncertainty of the environment defy planning and programming. In such situations the intuitive manager's style can be highly effective.

For example, there is no way for any manager to systematically forecast consumer tastes for funiture styles. He can, however, build a set of cues and flexible premises that may alert him to shifts in taste. He may also use the rapid scanning and testing (the main characteristic of the intuitive) for a sense of fit among disparate items of information. More important, he need never make his concepts and methods explicit.

Unlike the model builder, the intuitive manager can act without making any conscious articulation of his premises. An amusing instance of this fact occurred in many of the early efforts to use process-control computers in paper making. The computer experts "knew" that paper makers knew how to make paper; the experts' only problem was articulating the decision processes that the paper makers used, which turned out to depend mainly upon the operators' "tasting the broth" and controlling the paper flow.

For a long time, this well-established and highly effective human decision process defied conversion into formal and explicit terms. The operators were not too helpful. They "knew" what worked; they had built up out of their experience a clear but not conscious sense of the process, but this sense often varied with the individual. Thus, when a shift changed, the new crew chief, for example, might reset the valves and modify the whole operation, asserting that the changes were needed because of the time of day. There was no articulated set of concepts or methods by which this assertion could even be tested.

The decision makers here—and they merit the term, since controlling the paper-making process is a constant series of evaluations, assessments, and actions—were able to act efficiently even though they could not articulate their own procedures. This lack of articulation became a problem only when it was necessary for the computer experts to build a model of that process.

APPROACH DIFFERENCES

Systematic and intuitive individuals often treat the same project as two entirely different problems. The systematic management scientist may try to structure the problem to reduce the unknowns and to define very explicitly all the constraints in the situation. He aims at a model that is complete and has predictive power, which he can then improve and refine. That, essentially, is how he regards problem solving.

However, consciously or not, the intuitive manager is most concerned with using the model to give him a better sense of the problem. He focuses on and enjoys playing with the unknowns until he gets a feeling for the necessary steps for completion. Then he is ready to delegate the process of dealing with the problem to some individual in his organization who can systematically handle it in a more routine fashion.

The intuitive manager may also approach a task for which a model is to be built not with a need to understand the analytic process, but with a desire to discover what he can trust in order to make useful predictions. This can be of value to the systematic scientist, in that, if he can build a model which "works," the manager may well be ready to use it even though he does not understand it.

The central issue, however, is the validation of the model. The scientist validates his model formally and methodologically; he can test it in relation to known inputs and outputs. In general, he will have faith in his plan and in his own systematic process. The manager will validate the model experientially and test it against some of his own concepts and expectations. He places much less faith in external "authority."

RECOMMENDATIONS FOR ACTION

If our line of argument is valid, it is clear that the solution to the difficulties intuitive managers and systematic management scientists have in working together will not be obtained by trying to blur the differences. The intuitive manager may learn what network optimization is, but that is unlikely to make him think in the same systematic mode as the management scientist, who, in turn, is unlikely to develop intuitive responses through any form of education.

(This is not to assert that cognitive style is fixed, but to reinforce the point that individuals with very distinctive styles in specialized areas of activity have strengths that are directly related to their styles. It seems unlikely that the cognitive specialist will change easily—or that he should do so in any case.)

The real solution seems to lie in two areas: (1) in defining the model's role within the larger decision-making process of the particular situation, and (2) in determining how to validate the model.

From this, the manager and scientist together can better control both the process of building the model structure and their mutual expectations and actions. At the root of both these areas of concern is the whole question of trust and communication, less in the interpersonal than in the cognitive sense.

ROLE DEFINITION

The management scientist's role can be one of either product or service. It is important that he decide which it is in a particular situation.

On the one hand, if his model will mainly help clarify a manager's sense of the issues and options, then there is no point in the scientist's trying to provide a meticulous and complex simulation. The manager does not intend to use the model as the basis for any decision. In fact, the model may simply help him decide what the problem is and can then be thrown away.

On the other hand, the manager may need a product rather than a service; for example, a financial forecasting model, once validated, may be used by a manager as the main basis for ongoing decisions.

The degree and direction of the scientist's efforts will be very different, depending on how he perceives the manager's needs in the situation. The scientist can only identify those needs by asking questions: How does this manager approach problems? How does he define his problem, given the four different classifications in *Exhibit III*? Does he want the model to further his own learning or to help him make a specific decision?

The answer to each question has distinct consequences. For example, if the manager's response to problems is systematic, the model should explicitly reflect this fact. The scientist should explain to him the underlying assumptions as to method; the two can afford to invest substantial time and discussion on how to deal with the problem. Here, the manager is essentially looking for a technique and the scientist is the expert, with a catalog of methods.

However, if the manager is intuitive in style, the scientist should recognize that the model must allow the manager to range over alternatives and test solutions in the fashion that fits his natural mode of problem solving.

In this context, J. W. Botkin has used the paradigm of cognitive style in designing an interactive computer system for intuitive subjects.[8] He has identified five necessary features for such a model:

1) The user should have the ability to create an arbitrary order of processing; the system should not impose a "logical" or step-by-step sequence on him. In Botkin's words, "This lack of set sequence allows the intuitive user to follow his instinct for developing his ill-defined information plan directly from environmental cues."

2) The user should be able to define, explore, and play out "scenarios" that may either generate cues or test solutions.

3) The user should be able to shift between levels of detail and generality.

4) The user should have some control over the forms of output and should be able to choose visual, verbal, and numeric displays at varying levels of detail.

5) The user should be able to extend his programming, providing input in an irregular and unspecific form (i.e., he should be able to provide commands such as, "Repeat the last step, increasing X by 10%").

Botkin's experiment showed fairly clearly that intuitive and systematic subjects used his model in greatly differing ways. The differences corresponded on the whole to those found in our cafeteria experiment. The intuitive group seemed to learn from the system and to enjoy using it as much as the systematic group.

Even though Botkin's model was a special case, his results suggest that an effort on the part of the model builder to consider how the manager will use the model—in terms of process rather than output— will provide large dividends.

Here again, there is a distinction between service and product. Where the manager is most concerned with the recommendations he can derive from the model, the sort of cognitive amplifiers Botkin provides are unnecessary. However, where the manager wants the model to help him clarify his own understanding of the situation, it may well be essential to build them into the formal structure of the model.

Thus the management scientist needs to consider what a "good" a model is . For himself, goodness is largely a quality of predictive power and technical elegance. For the manager, it is more a concern of compatibility and comfort—that is, the fit between how he approaches the problem and how the model allows him to do so.

MODEL VALIDATION

Perhaps even more important than either recognizing the relevance of the user's own problem-solving process or determining how that person will use the model is the whole question of trust. Often, the manager does not get involved in the model itself; he simply asks for the outputs. He may well wish to validate the model by testing out some scenarios for which he has some expectations of the outcome.

However, John S. Hammond suggests that the model builder should recognize that in a large and complex model the user will have neither the desire nor the ability to understand its mechanics. The designer must, therefore, provide the user with some other way of testing out— of building trust in—the model. Hammond recommends, therefore, that the management scientist should aim—

". . . to get something simple and useful up and running as soon as possible. By skillfully manipulating the resultant model, the management scientist should be able to obtain results that will give great insights about the problem, its nature, and its alternatives to the manager. These insights should cue the mind of the manager and cause him to perceive the problems and alternatives differently, which will in turn affect the priorities and direction of the management science effort. . .

"Thus the management scientist, too, will learn about the nature of the problem and also about the nature of the manager's perception of it."[9]

This recommendation seems particularly relevant in cases where the manager's cognitive style is highly intuitive. For relatively little effort and minimal commitment to a particular definition and design, the manager can obtain the initial exploration and trial testing that may enable him to articulate his assessments of the problem—or, better, that may enable the scientist to deduce them for him.

Our recommendations are fairly modest. Essentially, they argue that if both manager and scientist alike will look at the process instead of the output the techniques will look after themselves. It seems of central importance for the manager and scientist to recognize that each has a distinctive style of problem solving, and that each should accept the other's difference.

If the management scientist can anticipate the fact that the manager may not use in his decision-making process the conscious planning that is so natural for the scientist himself, he will be less likely to assume that the manager's reluctantly given statement of what the problem is has any permanent force. The intuitive manager can recognize a good plan, if he can validate it at some point on his own terms; the scientist's responsibility is to provide the plan and also the validation.

The manager's responsibility is to make very clear, first to himself and then to the scientist, what he wants the model to do and to be. If he asks for an optimization program for a facilities planning project, he should decide well in advance what he will do with the results. If he knows that he will not make his decision on the basis of the model's output, he should make sure that the design process and the model structure allow him to use the model to amplify his own thinking.

The intuitive manager is very happy to relinquish the mechanics of formal analytic techniques to the expert, but only after he has developed confidence and trust in that expert. It is in this sense that the common recommendation of educating the manager in quantitative skills seems so inadequate. The intuitive manager will learn to make use of these skills supplied by others; but this learning is internal, experiential, and informal.

More than anything, the manager needs to learn how to tell a good model from a bad one. For him, a good model is one that he can, by testing his own scenarios, make sense of. However sloppy this may seem to the systematic scientist, his model will be used only if it allows the manager to make such tests or if the process of designing it has done so on a more ongoing basis.

CONCLUDING NOTE

People in general tend to assume that there is some "right" way of solving problems. Formal logic, for example, is regarded as a correct approach to thinking, but thinking is always a compromise between the demands of comprehensiveness, speed, and accuracy. There is no best way of thinking. If the manager and the management scientist can recognize first that each has a different cognitive style, and thus a different way of solving the same problem, then their dialogue seems more likely to bear fruit.

Our model of cognitive style is not necessarily either complete or precise. We suggest, however, that it does provide a useful way of focusing on the implementation of analytic models for decision making and of developing strategies of action that are much more likely to succeed than those based on concepts of technique, education, and salesmanship.

Footnotes

[1] "Management Science and Business Practice," HBR July-August 1973, p. 41.

[2] See Jerome S. Bruner, Jacqueline J. Goodnow, and George A. Austin, *A Study of Thinking* (New York, John Wiley & Sons, 1956).

[3] These experiments are described in detail in Peter G.W. Keen, "The Implications of Cognitive Style for Individual Decision Making," unpublished doctoral dissertation, Harvard Business School, 1973.

[4] See Isabel Briggs Myers and Katharine C. Briggs, "The Myers-Briggs Type Indicator," Educational Testing Service, New Jersey, 1957.

[5] "A Program for Research on Management Information Systems," *Management Science*, January 1973, p. 475.

[6] See "Is TIMS Talking to Itself?" Management Science, December 1965, p. B-156.

[7] See James L. McKenney, "A Taxonomy of Problem Solving," working paper, Harvard Business School, 1973.

[8] "An Intuitive Computer System: A Cognitive Approach to the Management Learning Process," unpublished doctoral dissertation, Harvard Business School, 1973.

[9] "The Roles of the Manager and Analyst in Successful Implementation," paper presented to the XX International Meeting of the Institute of Management Sciences, Tel Aviv, Israel, 1973.

11

Human Information Processing in Information and Decision Support Systems

by Daniel Robey and
William Taggart

About the authors:

Daniel Robey, D.B.A., is an Associate Professor of Management at Florida International University. He has also served on the faculties of the University of Pittsburgh and Marquette University.

William Taggart is a Professor in the Department of Management of the School of Business at Florida International University.

INTRODUCTION

This article explores the relevance of human information processing to the development and use of computer based information and decision support systems. Since all information systems make implicit assumptions about user cognitive characteristics, a broader understanding of human information processing may contribute to the more effective

Reprinted with permission from MIS Quarterly

definition and design of such systems. Many present systems assume that users are logical, use sequential routines in solving problems, rely on causal connections, and only value quantitative data. Recent research into MIS user behavior and MIS failures leads one to reconsider these assumptions. In particular, studies relating user cognitive characteristics to use and performance in computer supported decision tasks suggest the importance of human differences to the success of such systems.[1, 8, 37]

In this article the authors speculate on the relevance of cerebral hemispheric specialization as a means of conceptualizing differences in information processing. Awareness of the *biological* basis for decision behavior yields insights into interpersonal differences in decision styles, the prospects for personal flexibility in decision styles, and the differences between electronic computers and human "biocomputers." Knowing how humans process information should be a major consideration in the development of systems to support human decision making in organizations.

The authors first explain the basic ideas of hemispheric specialization in lay terms, drawing from medical and clinical research. The relationships between cerebral activity and psychological tests for cognitive style are briefly explored along with the concept of style dominance. Secondly, the limitations of the electronic computer in comparison with the biocomputer are examined. Despite fictional accounts of computers with intuition and wisdom, the bio-computer's right hemisphere abilities cannot be duplicated with present technology. The ethical question of whether such capabilities *should* be developed is also discussed briefly. Finally, the implications of human information processing for the definition and design of decision support systems are developed. Systems which fit both the task requirements and the user's preferred processing style are likely to be most effectively used. For complex decision areas, this means the design of support systems for both the right and left hemispheres of the decision maker.

HEMISPHERIC SPECIALIZATION IN HUMAN INFORMATION PROCESSING

The qualitative differences in processing style on either side of the brain are summarized in Figure 11.1. While the research supporting this dual perspective of human nature is quite recent, philosophical

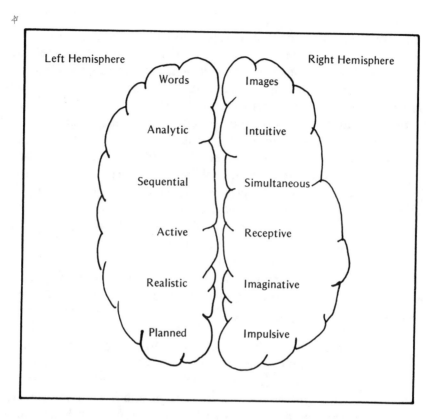

FIGURE 11.1 Summary of Clinical and Experimental Evidence About Hemispheric Specialization

explanations have existed for much longer.[30] Discovery of these two minds in each of us has profound implications for the behavioral sciences and the applied areas that depend on them.

Substantial clinical evidence of hemispheric specialization has grown out of studies of patients undergoing brain surgery or suffering various forms of brain damage. In one of the radical procedures for preventing epileptic seizures, the corpus callosum, which is the main connection between the two brain hemispheres, is severed. Behavioral studies of patients after this surgical procedure reveal the distinct functions of each hemisphere.[6, 14] In "normal" people it is, of course, more difficult to detect hemispheric specialization because the corpus collosum maintains communication between both halves of the brain. We are not usually conscious of the separation of word and image processing, for example, or that one side of the brain is rational and the other intuitive. However, analysis of electroencephalograms (EEG) shows that the strength of brain waves emitted from either hemisphere does vary with the task being performed.[24]

In one EEG study with direct relevance to management, Doktor [10] monitored the brain waves of fourteen subjects who held professional positions as business executives and/or operations research analysts. Two different kinds of problems were presented to each subject: one requiring analytic-verbal skills, the other requiring intuitive-spatial skills. Overall, the analyst tended to use *less* right hemisphere processing than the executives on *both* tasks, although the intuitive-spatial task did generate more right hemisphere activity in all subjects than did the analytic-verbal task. Doktor concluded that problem solving is conditioned by one's professional experience, but that people also adopt a processing style that is appropriate for the task they face.

Doktor's findings suggest the notion *dominance* in human information processing. In spite of the fact that we are all biologically equipped with two hemispheres, our educational and occupational experiences lead us to favor one side over the other. Psychological tests for cognitive style also yield this conclusion by generally classifying respondents into one psychological type or another.[1] However, dependence on psychological tests to measure cognitive style may reinforce the idea of dominance to such an extreme that the potential for flexibility and style change is overlooked. Biological models, on the other hand, point to the inherent potential for flexibility in human decision makers. Given the variety of situations which many decision makers face, cognitive style flexibility becomes an important personal asset. Development of "dual dominance" has also become a prominent theme of writers describing the human potential movement.[11]

It is difficult to capture the full range of implications that hemispheric specialization holds for human behavior in a single article, and doing so is certainly not the authors' purpose. Excellent nontechnical reviews of this work and its philosophical and practical extensions are available elsewhere.[5, 24] The objective is to characterize the nature of human information processing so that the role of computer systems that support human decisions might be better understood. Having briefly described some features of the biocomputer, the electronic computer will now be examined.

PROCESSING CAPABILITIES OF ELECTRONIC COMPUTERS

In his book *Giles Goat Boy*, John Barth describes two massive computer systems that confront each other across the cold war line. On one front is WESCAC (West Campus Automatic Computer), and on the other sits EASCAC (East Campus Automatic Computer). WESCAC figures prominently in the story:

> . . .whereas EASCAC (larger but cruder than its West-Campus brother) was employed almost solely in the cause of military science and heavy engineering, WESCAC had been trained to do virtually the whole brainwork of the "Free Campus.". . .Of necessity, WESCAC and EASCAC shared the common power source. . .and a certain communication. . .went on between them; from a special point of view it might be argued that they were brothers, or even the hemispheres of a single brain.[2]

A significant issue in this story involves extending WESCAC's MALI (manipulative analysis and logical inference) capability to include NOCTIS (non-conceptual thinking and intuitional synthesis). Together the MALI and NOCTIS systems of WESCAC pose a truly miraculous potential, capable of solving the most subtle problems not only of scientists, mathematicians, and production managers, but also of poets, philosophers, and theologians.[2]

Current computer systems do not include NOCTIS capabilities; they rely solely on MALI skills. Furthermore, it is debatable whether we should try to develop computer systems that simulate NOCTIS capabilities. Raphael poses the optimistic view by claiming that computer intelligence is not a threat but rather "...a promising hope for the future of mankind".[26] In contrast, Weizenbaum says that since we do not have ways of making computers wise,we should not give them tasks that require wisdom.[34] The issue of giving computers the ability to perform right hemisphere processing is probably moot. Regardless of one's stance on the desirability of computer intelligence, true *judgment* remains the realm of the more highly evolved human biocomputer. We cannot, to paraphrase Weiner, cast our responsibility to the winds by throwing the problem of judgment on the machine.[35]

An illustration of the computer's limitations is a test developed by Thurstone, shown in Figure 11.2. Identifying which hand is shown in the pictures is a simple task for most human beings because they can draw upon the powerful spatial processing abilities and visual memory

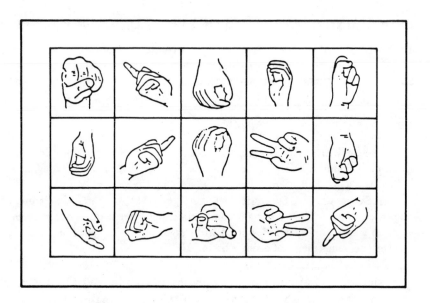

FIGURE 11.2 Thurstone's Hand Test—Which of these Hands are Left Hands and Which are Right?*

of the right hemisphere. The electronic computer cannot do this problem nor any other "creative" tasks. It is in one sense a large and efficient left brain, superb at sequential calculation of digitally encoded information, but devoid of the capabilities that all human beings house in their right hemispheres. Fictional accounts of creative, sensitive, wise, or intuitive computers are just that—fiction. Nonetheless, computers may play a role in creativity when their talents are combined with those of the biocomputer. This issue shall be addressed later in this article.

IMPLICATIONS FOR INFORMATION AND DECISION SUPPORT SYSTEMS

Three major implications can be drawn from this discussion. While the first does not really deal with information systems per se, it does sug-

*Reprinted from L.L. Thurstone, *Primary Mental Abilities,* University of Chicago Press, 1938, pp. 55.

gest an extension of cognitive style concepts to include more explicity the right hemisphere's abilities. Those attempting to relate cognitive style to information system use may benefit by this extension. The second and third implications deal more directly with the development of information and decision support systems.

EXTENSION OF THE COGNITIVE STYLE CONCEPT

Much of the literature which relates cognitive style to decision making behavior draws from Huysman's distinction between *analytic* and *heuristic* styles.[17] Several instruments, including Vasarhelyi's [32] and the "Minnesota questionaire" [9], determine respondents' preference for analytical procedures that provide optimal solutions (heuristics). Conceptually, analytic and heuristic styles are treated as polar opposites on the continuum of processing styles. As one moves from analysis to heuristics, mathematical elegance is replaced by approximate procedures for obtaining "good" solutions that may not be optimal.

An inadvertent consequence of this conceptualization of styles is the virtual exclusion of intuitive processing from studies of decision making. As heuristic procedures and decision rules have become central to operations research and computer modeling, it is tempting to conclude that these models accurately capture human decision processes. Since virtually all heuristic models can be described in computer programs, however, none of them successfully capture right hemisphere processing. Even a cursory examination reveals that heuristics involve detailed sequential operations and the heavy use of mathematics. Thus, heuristics as well as analytical techniques are both left hemisphere types of activities to the extent that they rely upon specific programmable procedures.

By contrast, intuition implies an inability to specify precisely how information is being processed. Intuition may be a distinct type of processing that cannot be described on the same continuum as analysis and heuristics. However, an understanding of intuition seems important to those who study and seek to improve decision making. Because intuition does not depend on verbal or mathematical processing, we are unlikely to be able to model what goes on in the right hemisphere with traditional approaches. Those engaged in human decision research must come to grips with this prospect and move away from traditional measures of processing style that depend, for example, on verbal protocols.[23] Perhaps cognitive style research will increasingly use more direct measures of processing styles like EEGs [13, 27] and other physiological indicators. Those concerned with the definition and design of information systems should also recognize that some managers may use few systematic, and therefore describable, processes in making decisions.

DIVISION OF LABOR BETWEEN ELECTRONIC COMPUTERS AND BIOCOMPUTERS

Our recognition that electronic computers and biocomputers do different things well leads directly to implications about the division of labor between them. The framework by Gorry and Scott Morton [16] assists understanding the typical tasks at various levels of the organization and the type of information support suitable for those tasks. Figure 11.3 depicts the basic argument concerning the man-machine division of labor. Management information systems designed for operational control can be more automated and less dependent on the biocomputer, as can decision support systems for structured tasks. As we move toward unstructured tasks and strategic planning systems, the biocomputer plays a more dominant role. Here intuition plays a more significant role in generating solutions to complex problems.

Another perspective is gained by thinking about the orientation of decision makers in *time*. Figure 11.4 shows three types of systems oriented to the past, present, and future. Operational control systems deal with past events about which there is little uncertainty. Transaction processing systems deal in the present, also the known quantities. Systems oriented to the future deal with uncertainty and unstructured tasks involving prediction. Here intuition as well as statistical forecasting models serve the decision maker. Intuition can generate assumptions and hypotheses about the future which may be more suitable because they are not tied explicitly to past data and assumptions. This ability to divorce forecasts from the past is of critical importance for decision makers faced with considerable uncertainty. [33] For more predictable futures, statistical models that do not require intuition may be more appropriate.

Further distinctions can be made between *formal* and *informal* information requirements. Formal information can be encoded unam-

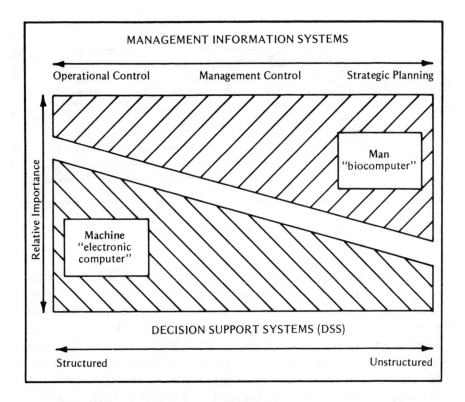

FIGURE 11.3 Decision Support Systems in Computer Based Applications

biguously for machine processing. The format in which the information is presented is less important because the "facts speak for themselves." A simple example of formal information is a stock status report indicating the quantity of various items in inventory. Informal information is not so easily encoded, and meaning depends more on the context in which the information is presented. Personal communication carries many nonverbal cues to meaning that greatly affect information content. The right hemisphere's capacity for visual organization, recognition of emotional content, and holistic construction plays a major role in processing informal information. Again, the relative importance of informal and formal information requirements varies with the degree of task structure, organization level, and orientation in time.

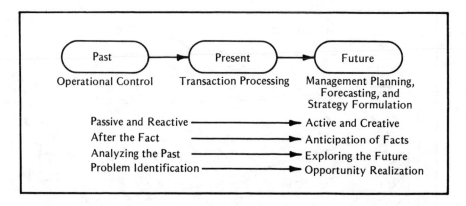

FIGURE 11.4 Information System Orientations in Time

The arguments for an appropriate division of labor between bio-computers and electronic computers grow out of a general awareness of each one's capabilities. However we should not conclude that computer systems have no relevence for unstructured decision making. Non-analytic decision makers *do* use information to make decisions; in fact they may use *more* information than highly analytic persons. [3] Intuitive processes can be supported, but care must be taken in the definition of such systems. In the next section of this article some principles for "wholebrained" information systems design are developed.

IMPLICATIONS FOR SYSTEMS DESIGN

Not surprisingly, academic and applied advances in management information and decision support systems have dealt primarily with the technical problems of supporting left hemisphere decision making. This is the easier task and one well-suited for routine control decisions. However, it would be erroneous to extend the design principles for these systems into more complex tasks where decision making is less structured. Rather, complex decisions require richer information support that engages the right *and* left cerebral hemispheres. As Keen and Wagner[18] have suggested, a decision support system should be a natural extension of managers' normal methods for exploring problems. For many successful managers at top levels this implies the balanced use of both hemispheres.

Research supports the notion of fitting information support to the decision at hand and to the processing style of the user. For the sample task of extracting specific data from a quantitative report, Lusk has found that tabular reports produce more accurate performance for all users.[19, 20] In addition users rated as higher analytic outperformed less analytic subjects, regardless of the complexity of report format. On more complex tasks, like the setting of production and inventory policies, the need for a fit between user style and information support becomes more critical. Benbasat and Dexter [3] report a significant interaction effect between cognitive style and the nature of information support in a production inventory simulation game. Highly analytic users achieved greater success with a more flexible interactive system for information retrieval.

These findings suggest that information support should fit both the objective demands of the task and the cognitive style of the user. Sprague points to two key performance objectives for decision support systems. "...the concept of 'structure' in decision making is heavily dependent on the cognitive style and approach to problem solving of the decision maker" and "...a very important characteristic of a DSS is that it provide the decision maker with a set of capabilities to apply in a sequence and form that fits his/her cognitive style".[28]

Figure 11.5 suggests that structured tasks are best performed by analytical persons operating with structured data reports, consistent with both sets of findings discussed above. Figure 11.5 also suggests that less structured tasks are best performed by non-analytic, intuitive problem solvers using a flexible, nonlinear, graphic system. These systems offer more potential for trying out intuitive insights and sparking creativity in the manager. The idea of a three-way fit potentially resolves an important issue raised by DeWaele.[8] He questions whether information systems should be designed with the user's *preferences or needs* in mind. In other words, should information support be fit to the demands of the task or the style of the user? Figure 11.5 answers this question by saying that *both* criteria for a fit should be satisfied for optimal results.

In many cases an optimal, three-way fit is not achieved because one of the three variables does not mesh with the other two. In one case, the information system might be well designed for the task but the manager's style might not fit. In this case the manager might not use

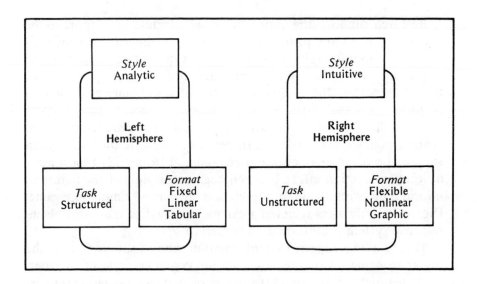

FIGURE 11.5 Fit Among User Style, Decision Task, and Information Support

or understand the information. For example, intuitive managers who are assigned the job of scheduling production might ignore computer generated analyses and schedule according to their "feel" for the situation, resulting in poor allocation of production resources. A second type of mismatch involves a correct fit between the manager's style and the task structure, but a failure of information support to fit. For example, an intuitive manager engaged in planning market strategy might not use detailed historical sales reports. The third mismatch occurs when the user's style and information system fit together but neither is appropriate for the task to be performed. This perhaps results in the worst performance since neither of the decision making resources are appropriate to the task.

Of course, these ideas are oversimplified. As noted earlier, human decision makers are potentially quite flexible and can shift their styles to fit the problem and/or information support provided. Further, most problem situations cannot easily be categorized as structured or unstructured. Most contain elements of both. The identification of mismatches among tasks, systems, and decision makers is unlikely to be as "structured" as implied in Figure 11.5. However, the idea of fit can be a guiding principle for system design, particularly when the authors address the problems of designing systems which support both right- and left-brained processes.

Perhaps the greatest challenge to developers of information systems is to create systems that truly support intuition in the manager. Systems failure often occurs because the decision maker perceives report format, timing, and content as irrelevant to the problem, and therefore does not process the information. While some would attribute this failure to the manager, who should have used the information, often the information system is to blame because of the way the information is presented. It does little good to assign highly analytic managers the task of creative policy making just because they are the ones who can read the computer generated reports! Rather, systems should be tailored to both the intuitive styles that can more successfully understand possibilities and relationships, and to the analytic styles which value facts and details.

Some of the specific features of such "wholebrained" support systems are already evident in the literature. Keen and Wagner specifically see the need for:

- a flexible development language that allows rapid creation and modification of systems for specific applications,

- a system design architecture that allows quick and easy extensions and alterations,

- an interface that buffers users from the "computer" and allows a dialogue based on the manager's concepts, vocabulary, and definition of the decision problem, and

- communicative display devices and output generators.[18]

They state: "A manager will not use a system lacking these attributes. It is hard to see any reason why he should".[18]

Flexibility and ease of communication in the manager's intuitive style underlie these recommendations. It is also possible to see some other development implications that relate even more directly to the right hemisphere's unique processing abilities. Use of color, graphics, and human verbal communication are key features of the "executive window" system being developed at AT&T. Vivid pie charts summarize divisional profits in cool green and losses in bright scarlet. A talking head of a real executive delivers a report so that significant nonverbal meaning is not lost in a page of words and figures. The video display unit for this system is always "on," showing the four programs available in each corner of the screen.

Facilities like the "war room" [15] and the management communication center of the First National Bank of Chicago [12] achieve decision support for intuitive decision makers on complex tasks. In combination, four characteristics contribute to the distinctive quality of these facilities. The display formats are varied. The traditional tabular presentations of columns of numbers are supplemented by graphic representations of trends, comparisons, and other performance patterns. Further, in an advanced facility the display can be generated in online, real-time, full color along with traditional hand prepared outputs. In addition, the semicircular arrangement of the decisions center with swivel chairs supports dynamic reconfiguration of the meeting interaction by allowing the display screen or any other position in the room to become the focus of attention as needed. Finally a control console is available to the meeting facilitator. With this technology the group leader manages the message by managing the medium. Together these characteristics provide whole-brained support for the group decision making process.

One characteristic feature of creative problem solving is the need for "surprise" or nonsensical alternatives to be generated. Techniques like brainstorming and Synectics thrive on the playful generation of silly ideas which can later be subjected to critical analysis[24]. Perhaps information systems could be designed to assist in creative idea generation rather than simply converging toward a solution which satisfies a predetermined objective function. Divination, oracles, and *The I Ching*[36], which rely on acausal, metaphoric, and nonlogical processes, have served as decision support systems for other cultures. In this vein, Mitroff, Nelson, and Mason [21] have proposed research on the use of "stories" as a means of presenting information for complex, unstructured tasks. Such information would appeal directly to the intuitive style of the right hemisphere's role in the decision process. While computers cannot create stories of their own, they may function as the story teller or oracle by producing "programmed" stories on a random basis. Just as older cultures use superstition to produce guidance that is *not* dependent on logical routines, modern cultures can use the computer's vast storage and retrieval capabilities to evoke "wisdom."

One applied example of the above theme is a modeling technique for water resources planning. Realizing the "optimal" solutions may violate real world assumptions and political constraints (not included in the model), Chang, Brill, and Hopkins [7] *randomly* generate changes in the model to produce "surprise" solutions. The decision maker can then choose among several "good" alternatives, i.e., ones which meet the known constraints of the model. The element of randomization introduces a creative element to the decision process. Models like this, when incorporated into decision support systems, could lead managers away from the obvious and toward new insights into the nature of the problem as well as its solution.

Incorporation of features like this may seem wasteful by traditional MIS design standards where premiums are placed on minimizing data redundance and maximizing programming efficiency. But such systems should be evaluated in terms of decision quality (effectiveness) rather than cost of decision support (efficiency). Creativity is a "wasteful" process in that many ideas are typically generated that are subsequently thrown away.[25] Computer programmers and system analysts are taught very early not to waste C.P.U. or output space with unnecessary steps. To support an intuitive decision process, however, it may be vital to supply seemingly irrelevant information because it may spark an idea in the decision maker's mind. Intuition support systems operate by evoking from decision makers something they already know. In contrast, traditional decision support systems provide information which the decision makers do not already know.

Clearly, individuals play the central role in intuitive decision making. Along these lines, Morris has noted that the most direct means of supporting intuitive process is to have individuals become more aware of their own intuition, to learn to trust and respect it.[22] To this end, perhaps MIS designers and management educators need to become more appreciative in general of the intuitive right hemisphere.

All of the suggestions made here are technically feasible. Development of "whole-brained" systems awaits only the joint commitment of systems professionals and managers. Awareness of the human information processing perspective provides the rationale for pursuing this kind of systems development.

CONCLUSION

Computers are powerful tools for certain kinds of tasks. Their potential to support intuitive, right hemisphere processing is just beginning to be developed. This article briefly introduces the differences between the right and left cerebral hemisphere as the first step in the more complete definition and design of management information systems to support human decision making.

For the understanding of cerebral functioning to influence systems design, it is helpful to examine the contrast between electronic computers and biocomputers. This leads the authors to conclude that the abilities of the right hemisphere cannot be duplicated electronically. Despite much talk about heuristic cognitive styles and heuristic computer models, it is unlikely that *intuition* can be successfully modeled. Thus we are better off focusing on the different but complementary roles which man and machine play in solving managerial problems.

While computer cannot be intuitive they can support intuitive processes in man if designed properly. Flexible interactive systems using natural language, color, visual images, graphics, and which generate random thoughts for managers to contemplate are better suited for complex tasks than routine processing systems. Use of these design principles may successfully extend human problem solving capacity in complex organizations. But success will depend on how well designers and managers comprehend the nature of the partnership between man and machine.

REFERENCES

[1]   Bariff, M.L. and Lusk, E.J. "Cognitive and Personality Tests for the Design of Management Information Systems," *Management Science*, Volume 23, Number 8, April 1977, pp. 820-829.

[2]   Barth, J. *Giles Goat-Boy*, Fawcett Crest Book, Greenwich, Connecticut, 1966, pp. 95, 97.

[3]   Benbasat, I. and Dexter, A.S. "Value and Events Approaches to Accounting: An Experimental Evaluation, " *The Accounting Review*, Volume 54, Number 4, October 1979, pp. 735-749.

[4]   Benbasat, I. and Taylor, R.N. "The Impact of Cognitive Styles on Information System Design," *MIS Quarterly*, Volume 2, Number 2, June 1978, pp. 43-54.

[5] Blakeslee, T.R. *The Right Brain*, Anchor Press/Doubleday, New York, New York, 1980.

[6] Bogen, J.E. "The Other Side of the Brain II: An Appositional Mind," *Bulletin of the Los Angeles Neurological Societies*, Volume 34, Number 3, July 1969, pp. 135-162.

[7] Chang, S., Brill, E.D., and Hopkins, L.D. "Use of Mathematical Models to Generate Alternative Solutions to Water Resources Planning Problems," Paper presented to the Joint ORSA/TIMS Meeting, Colorado Springs, Colorado, November 1980.

[8] DeWaele, M. "Managerial Style and the Design of Decision Aids," *Omega*, Volume 6, Number 1, 1978, pp. 5-13.

[9] Dickson, G.W., Senn, J.A., and Chervany, N.L. "Research in Management Information Systems: The Minnesota Experiments," *Management Science*, Volume 23, Number 9, May 1977, pp. 913-923.

[10] Doktor, R. "Problem Solving Styles of Executives and Management Scientists," *TIM Studies in the Management Sciences*, Volume 8, 1978, pp. 123-134.

[11] Ferguson, M. *The Aquarian Conspiracy*, J.P. Tarcher, Inc., Los Angeles, California, 1980.

[12] The First National Bank of Chicago. *Management Communications Center*, The First National Bank, Chicago, Illinois, n.d.

[13] Foa, U.G. and Turner, J.L. "Psychology in the Year 2000: Going Structural," *American Psychologist*, Volume 25, Number 3, March 1970, pp. 244-247.

[14] Gazzaniga, M.S. and Ledoux, J.E. *The Integrated Mind*, Plenum Press, New York, New York, 1978.

[15] Getz, C.W. "MIS and the War Room," *Datamation*, Volume 23, Number 12, December 1977, pp. 66-70.

[16] Gorry, G.A. and Scott Morton, M.S. "A Framework for Management Information Systems," *Sloan Management Review*, Volume 13, Number 1, Fall 1971, pp. 57-59.

[17] Huysmans, J.H.B.M. *The Implementation of Operations Research*, John Wiley & Sons, New York, New York, 1970.

[18] Keen, P.G. and Wagner, G.R. "DSS: An Executive Mind-Support System," *Datamation*, Volume 25, Number 12, November 1979, pp. 117-122.

[19] Lusk, E.J. "A Test of Differential Performance Peaking for a Disembedding Task," *Journal of Accounting Research*, Volume 17, Number 1, Spring 1979, pp. 286-294.

[20] Lusk, E.J. and Kersnick, M. "The Effort of Cognitive Style and Report Format on Task Performance: The MIS Design Consequences," *Management Science*, Volume 25, Number 6, August 1979, pp. 787–798.

[21] Mitroff, I., Nelson, J., and Mason R.O. "On Management Myth-information Systems," *Management Science*, Volume 21, Number 4, December 1974, pp. 371–382.

[22] Morris, W.T. "Matching Decision Aids with Intuitive Styles," in H.S. Brinkers, ed., *Decision Making*, Ohio State University Press, Columbus, Ohio, 1972.

[23] Nisbett, R.E. Aand Wilson, T.D. "Telling More Than We Can Know: Verbal Reports on Mental Processes," *Psychology Review I*, Volume 84, Number 3, May 1977, pp. 231–259.

[24] Ornstein, R.E. *The Psychology of Consciousness*, 2nd ed., Harcourt Brace Jovanovich, New York, New York, 1977.

[25] Prince, G.M. *The Practice of Creativity*, Collier Books, New York, New York, 1970.

[26] Raphael, B. *The Thinking Computer: Mind Inside Matter*, W.H. Freeman and Company, San Francisco, California, 1976, p. 3.

[27] Robey, D. and Taggart, W. "Measuring Managers' Minds: The Assessment of Style in Human Information Processing," *Academy of Management Review*, Volume 6, Number 3, July 1981, pp. 375–383.

[28] Sprague, R.H., Jr. "A Framework for the Development of Decision Support Systems," *MIS quarterly*, Volume 4, Number 4, December 1980, pp. 1–26.

[29] Taggart, W.M., Jr. *Information Systems: An Introduction to Computers in Organizations*, Allyn and Bacon, Inc., Boston, Massachusetts, 1980.

[30] Taggart, W. and Robey, D. "Minds and Managers: On the Dual Nature of Human Information Processing and Management," *Academy of Management Review*, Volume 6, Number 2, April 1981, pp. 187–195.

[31] Taylor, R.N. and Benbasat, I. "Cognitive Styles Research and Managerial Information Use: Problems and Prospects," Paper presented to the Joint ORSA/TIMS Meeting, Colorado Springs, Colorado, November 1980.

[32] Vasarhelyi, M.A. "Man-machine Planning Systems: A Cognitive Style Examination of Interactive Decision Making," *Journal of Accounting Research*, Volume 15, Number 1, Spring 1977, pp. 138–153.

[33] Weick, K.W. *The Social Psychology of Organizing*, 2nd ed., Addison-Wesley, Reading, Massachusetts, 1979.

[34] Weizenbaum, J. *Computer Power and Human Reasons: From Judgment to Calculation*, W.H. Freeman and Company, San Francisco, California, 1976, p.227.

[35] Wiener, N. *The Human Use of Human Beings*, Avon Books, New York, New York, 1954, p. 254.

[36] Wihelm, R. *The I Ching or Book of Changes*, Translated by C.F. Baynes, Princeton University Press, Princeton, New Jersey, 1969.

[37] Zmud, R.W. "Individual Differences and MIS Success: A Review of the Empirical Literature," *Management Science*, Volume 25. Number 10, October 1979, pp. 966-979.

12

Computer-Based Support of Organization Decision Making

by Robert H. Bonczek, Clyde W. Holsapple, and Andrew B. Whinstone

INTRODUCTION

Decision making constitutes the core of managerial activity. Both individual and collective decision makers (i.e., both managers and managerial systems) are essentially information processors. In this respect there is a common bond between decision makers and computers, for the history of computer science has been that of developing increasingly powerful techniques for information processing. Clearly, however, there are already differences in the natures and capabilities of human versus computerized information processing. The primary focus of this paper is on the extent to which the bond between decision makers and computers can be enhanced. Of particular interest is the computerized support of relatively unstructured, nonprogrammed decision activities such as those involved in strategic planning.[2]

The information-processing bond between decision makers and computers is strengthened by increasing the computer's ability to recognize and carry out requests while simultaneously decreasing the decision maker's effort in specifying those requests. Our examination of this issue is organized into three major parts. First, we review trends

Reprinted with permission from Decision Sciences

in the computer science field. Of special interest here is the emerging discipline of computerized decision support systems which draws upon the fields of computer science, psychology, artificial intelligence, and linguistics. Subsequent use of the phrase "decision support system" refers to a computer-based decision support system. It must be emphasized that computer-based support is not considered solely in the traditional sense of people writing and/or running application programs (e.g., math programming), nor in the sense of people writing and running programs to manipulate files of data.

There has been a trend in the planning area towards the study and development of more formal, more structured planning systems (e.g., [1] and [39]), whereas the emergence of the decision support discipline reflects a concern for finding techniques to support less formal, less structured decision activities. The emphasis in this exposition is upon the second consideration, with an eye to the possible contribution of decision support systems to the realization of formal planning systems.

The study of decision support systems must be based upon a conceptual framework of what constitutes decision making. The framework must be sufficiently abstract to be descriptive of the large variety of decision situations. But it must also have concrete implications for the design of a decision support system and its eventual operationalization in terms of computer code. The framework presented here is intended to provide a formalism for the study of decision support. This is introduced in the second major portion of the paper.

The proposed conceptual framework of organizational decision making has two major aspects. One aspect entails an identification of those abilities that are required in a decision-making process. These abilities constitute a content model, rather than a process model, of decision making. (A content approach deals with the nature of the decision maker, whereas a process approach is concerned with phases or stages of decision making.)[3] The elements of this content model may be used to hypothesize a variety of process models. One such process model is examined in detail as a basis for the implementation of a general decision support system.

The second aspect of the conceptual framework considers the division of labor involved in organizational decision making. The organization is viewed as a multi-level network of expert (specialized) information processors. The connecting links among these experts describe patterns of information transmission and effectively describe the organization's control structure. This aspect of the framework models an organization both from the artificial intelligence viewpoint of problem reduction and from a data-base schema perspective.

The dual framework is introduced as a conceptual, theoretical device for modeling organizational decision making. The final portion of this paper is a description of how the framework can be operationalized in the design of a generalized intelligent decision support (GIDS) system. This system is general in the sense of its ability to support decision activities regardless of the application area (e.g., urban planning, water quality planning, corporate planning). It is intelligent in the sense of its ability to comprehend English-like requests and subsequently formulate models, interface appropriate data with these models, and execute the models to produce some facts or expectations about the problem under consideration.

DECISION SUPPORT

COMPUTERS AND DECISION MAKING

We begin with a few general remarks about computers and decision making. These are followed by a survey of the emerging discipline of decision support systems. It is well known that the capabilities of computers are constrained principally by elementary processing speeds and by memory sizes (subject to real-time retrieval). It has been argued that all limits on the potential scope of "computer intelligence" are also restrictions to human intelligence and that "the scale of available computer memories is increasing rapidly, to the point where memory size may not be much longer an effective limit on the capacity of computers to match human performance".[41, p. 1187]

If these assumptions are rejected, then the practical viability of a general computerized decision support system (not to mention a general computerized decision-making system) must be severely limited. (The term general system, as it is used throughout this discussion, indicates a system whose design does not restrict it to consideration of problems in a single application area or in a small class of application areas.) On balance, however, the study of a general computerized decision support system can offer insights that are useful in the study of specialized systems. It can also offer an operational framework for the implementation of specialized decision support systems or of general decision support systems having more modest "intelligence" (e.g., [23]) than the GIDS system described in this paper. If time shows the above assumptions to be correct, then the practicality of general decision support (and decision-making) systems is greatly enhanced. Thus, the basic research presented here posits a conceptually viable framework for studying and discussing decision support systems (that are general and "intelligent") in terms of implementable techniques.

Decisions fall along a continuum that ranges from highly structured to highly unstructured. These two endpoints are also referred to as programmed and nonprogrammed, respectively. [22] The former refers to routine and repetitive decisions, whereas the latter describes situations where there is not a "cut-and-dried method for handling the problem because it hasn't arisen before, or because its precise nature and structure are elusive or complex, or because it is so important that it deserves custom-tailored treatment". [40, p. 6] A program is a strategy for processing information. The psychological perspective taken here is that human memory contains "programs" or strategies for processing information [17], even though one may be unable to articulate (or be unconscious of) the strategy employed in a given decision-making instance. A discussion of this view and the contrasting behaviorist position appears in [18].

A question arises concerning what governs a decision in the unstructured, nonprogrammed situation. Simon [40] maintains that the governing agent is a set of rules of procedure and that the individual has some general problem-solving strategies (i.e., programs) in addition to specialized strategies. This approach is adopted in the design of the GIDS system itself. Specialized (varying degrees of specialization are permitted) strategies are maintained, along with more conventional kinds of data, in a memory mechanism called the information base. The most general problem-solving strategies comprise the GIDS problem processor. When confronted with a problem, this processor can combine and modify the available specialized strategies in the effort to reach a solution. This is a step in the direction of matching human flexibility. With respect to the trait of flexibility, humans hold a definite advantage over extant decision-making (and decision support) systems. Simon's view is also adopted at the system-user interface.

That is, the user's own general problem-solving capacities are used to pose a series of requests, each of which evokes specific skills and specific knowledge of the system.

A related issue that is not directly addressed, but that is of interest as a topic for future research, concerns the extent to which the proposed GIDS systems can learn. Human strategies can be improved by instruction and experience. In the system to be considered here, instruction can be accomplished by adding to, modifying, and deleting from procedural information existing in the information base (just as the same operations can be applied to more traditional data). The notion of program improvement through experience suggests the need for usage tracking and a program that can modify the programs existing in the information base (according to protocols involving past usage).

DECISION SUPPORT SYSTEMS

With this background we can consider more precisely what is meant by computerized decision support. The broad outlines of this emerging discipline have only recently begun to take shape. It has been estimated [41] that, to date, 95 percent of all computer power has been consumed in record keeping and in performing large-scale scientific and engineering computations. But computerized decision support involves a good deal more than this. A survey of the small, but rapidly growing, literature concerned with decision support reveals comparatively little practical experience and an absence of fundamental theory. It further reveals that the primary impetus for interest in this area comes from advances in the field of data-base management rather than from any advance in our understanding of the mechanisms of decision making.

The various definitions that have been suggested for decision support (e.g., [4], [5], [19], [21], [28], and [31]) agree that the system must aid a decision maker in solving unprogrammed, unstructured (or "semi-structured") problems. A review of the definitions also shows a widespread agreement that the system must possess an interactive query facility, with a query language that resembles English (or is at least easy to learn and use). It has been argued[28] that the main reason that computerized information systems have not been used for decision support is their inaccessibility to nonprogramming decision makers.

An examination of existing systems which have been called decision support systems (e.g., [5], [28], [31], and [30]) shows that each is composed of a data-base management package plus some sort of query facility. The query facility typically permits ad hoc queries for retrieval and in some cases handles ad hoc analyses.

The perspective on decision support held in this presentation is that it can (and should) be approached as a synthesis of both data-base management techniques and artificial intelligence techniques. That is, the data base and query facilities can make use of artificial intelligence techniques. In a rather exhaustive survey, Wong and Mylopoulos [46] have shown that there is a strong relationship between recent research in artificial intelligence and topical issues in the data-base management area. These two can be compared and contrasted with respect to three questions: How is knowledge represented? What is the nature of the system-user interface? What applications are dealt with?

Regarding the representation of knowledge, artificial intelligence (AI) has concentrated upon the modeling of abstract, rather than concrete knowledge. Abstract knowledge is knowledge that is disassociated from any specific instance (e.g., companies supply parts). Concrete knowledge deals with specific instances (e.g., ACME supplies BOLTS). The way in which AI models have been implemented is "often haphazard and rarely formalized to the point where they could be duplicated with any degree of success".[46, p. 33] In contrast, data-base management has been primarily concerned with representing large volumes of concrete knowledge, and its treatment of abstract knowledge has been comparatively meager. As one traces the evolution of data-base management, however, there is a discernible trend in the direction of representing more and more complex types of abstract knowledge. For example, the notion of an information base [9] provides an added dimension to the customary representation of abstract knowledge in a data base. Moreover, the data base management approaches to knowledge representation are considerably more formal with respect to implementation [46] than those of artificial intelligence.

Proceeding to the second question of user-system interface, the trend in data-base management has been a progression from procedural, programming languages towards nonprocedural, English-like interface languages [9] based on the myriad language translation and compiling techniques developed by computer scientists.

The emphasis in artificial intelligence has been on nonprocedurality and on natural-language processing. This nonprocedurality is accomplished by evaluating queries with predicate calculus theorem-proving methods.[35] These methods have been used for special purpose systems (e.g.,[37]) by inserting inference rules into the system's programs. The resolution principle [38] has been used to build more general systems (e.g.,[20]) that are independent of predicate calculus rules that they use. Others [34] [6] have suggested interaction with the user in order to select the rules needed to execute a proof.

Another method for answering queries involves search and backtracking mechanisms such as those used in PLANNER.[24] In this case, the query is taken as an assertion to be proven by searching (with backtracking) a data base. Automatic path determination in the GPLAN system[11] bears a strong resemblance to the PLANNER technique, despite GPLAN's data-base management origins. GPLAN can also be characterized as using the state space problem-solving method from the field of artificial intelligence.[24] Yet another artificial intelligence technique for question-answering is problem reduction. The GIDS problem processor can be characterized as performing problem reduction.

Artificial intelligence research also involves natural-language processing. This may be viewed as a type of automatic code generation. Existing studies in this area (e.g., [47], [7], and [45]) are concerned with allowing human-computer interaction via some subset of the English language. The desirability and utility of strictly natural-language discourse is a point of controversy.[33] [27] From the user's viewpoint, the incremental benefit of natural-language processing diminishes as we approach a strict natural-language capability, while marginal cost of the implementation increases sharply.

With respect to the third question raised previously, data-base systems have been extensively used in practical applications. Most natural-language systems (and other artificial intelligence query-answering systems) deal only with toy problems and are application-specific. There are exceptions. The NLP system [26] is used for constructing and executing simulation models. More general systems, in terms of application areas supported, are REL [43] and REQUEST [36] ; but these systems are primarily for retrieval. Descriptions of natural-language processing systems typically detail various schemes of knowledge representation and describe specific implementations of semantic nets. It has been shown [9] how known constructs (with certain extensions) from the data-base management discipline can be utilized to provide a single mechanism for data storage (consisting of both programs and traditional data) and abstract semantic representation. In summary, the convergence of data-base management with artificial intelligence, culminating in systems for decision support, should be kept in mind throughout the ensuing discussion.

FRAMEWORK FOR ORGANIZATIONAL DECISION MAKING

Having established a decision support perspective, we proceed to develop a conceptual framework that addresses organizational decision making. The objective is a framework that can be used to develop a flexible decision support system for managing the complex information requirements of decision makers. A content approach is taken in specifying the framework. The attempt is to identify the "contents" of decision-making situations. That is, specific process models may be built in terms of the content framework. The importance of such flexibility is pointed out in [44] and [29]. This flexibility is incorporated into the GIDS system design.

DIVISION OF LABOR

Organizations are processors of materials and information.[32] Our principal concern here is with their information-processing aspects. The nature of organizational information processing depends upon organizational structure and style. but what are the components in an organizational structure, and how can we characterize their inter-relationships? It has been remarked [13] that an organization is a structure of roles tied together with lines of communication. This view holds that the essential units of an organization are roles, not persons. That is, there may be several persons, each of whom could fill a certain role; a person may be capable of filling several roles; and the person actually filling a role may change from time to time. Whereas organizational structure is given by the information channels among roles, organizational style refers both to the *way* in which roles are filled and to the *selection* of particular lines of communication in the face of a given problem.

As the problems encountered by an organization become increasingly complex, the organization tends to exhibit division of labor, greater specialization of roles, and a hierarchic structure of communication and structural complexity. Another phenomenon is that some roles are created that are filled by other roles. For instance, role A may be played by B or C or D, where each of these three is itself a role that could be filled by yet other roles.

Several conventions are adopted in the discussion of roles and their interrelationships. First, our attention is confined to those roles that are information processors (i.e., problem solvers). Thus each role can be described in terms of the nature of information processing that it performs, or in terms of the problem that it solves. Secondly, roles that do not fill any other roles are said to be the most abstract roles in the organization. Symmetrically, roles that are not filled by any other role are said to make up the most concrete level of organizational structure. There is a range between the most abstract level and the most concrete. A "concrete" role, then, is either a person or an information-processing mechanism (e.g., a computer program). Persons or programs are not abstract roles capable of being filled by anything that is more concrete. It could be argued that persons and programs are not roles at all, although for ease of exposition they will be treated as the most concrete of roles. Finally, if two roles are not identical in terms of the information processing they perform, they are referred to as distinct.

The framework for representing division of labor in organizational decision making utilizes three constructs: the role, definitional relationships among roles, and associative relationships among roles. It is helpful to think of roles and their interrelationships in a theatrical sense. A definitional relationship between roles A and B indicates that role B is capable of playing role A. Suppose that C (where C is distinct from B) is also capable of filling role A. Then role A may be "defined" in terms of either of the more concrete roles B or C. An associative relationship between roles D and E indicates that role D must "associate" with (receive information from) role E in order to carry out its information-processing task.

An example is used to illustrate these constructs in more detail. In addition, a pictorial formalism is used to depict each construct. Consider a system whose most abstract role is Divisional Planning (DP̂). This role can be filled (i.e., defined) in any one of several ways. That is, a request to perform Divisional Planning could be a reference to planning performed by Division 1 (DP1), or planning performed by Division 2 (DP2),..., or planning performed by Division K (DPK). With respect to a particular context, one of these must play the role of Divisional Planning.

In Figure 12.1, roles are denoted by nodes. The K definitional relationships just described are denoted by the K directed arcs emanating from DP̂. The arc from DP̂ to DP1 indicates that DP1 can define (play the role of) DP̂; planning performed by Division 1 is a particular instance of DP̂. This arc does *not* indicate a flow of information between DP̂ and DP1. The entire group of definitional arcs departing from DP̂ describe the various ways in which Division Planning can be performed. Recognition of a divisional planning problem confronting the organization results in DP̂ being played by either DP1, or DP2, . . . , DPK.

As the foregoing example suggests, a role can be defined (filled) in no more than one way with respect to a particular context. Taking a theatrical analogue, a role cannot be cast in more than one way for a particular performance, although the casting may change from one performance (context) to the next. Definitional relationships, by themselves, are clearly inadequate for representing the nature of organizational decision making. They do not account for the passage of information between roles involved in a particular decision process. Such relationships, therefore, do not address the issue of interaction among roles, as in the case of group activities. This nondefinitional type of relationship between roles is represented by the aforementioned associative construct.

It must be emphasized that, unlike a definitional relationship, an associative relationship involves a passage of information between two roles. One role, in order to execute its information-processing task, may need the assistance of other roles. The relationship between the assisted role and a role that provides assistance (an assisting role) is termed associative. The association consists of a transferral of information from an assisting role to the assisted role.

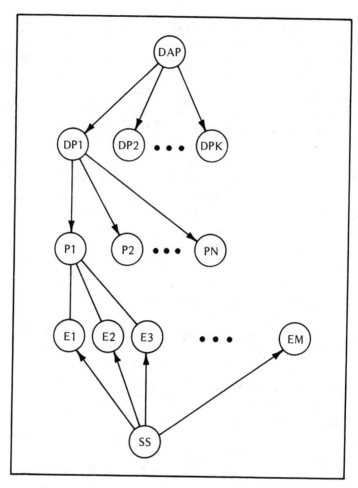

FIGURE 12.1 Structure of Roles in a Hypothetical
Planning Situation

Assistance is given according to the needs of the assisted role. That is, the assisted role controls the initiation and sequencing of information transferrals. Furthermore, the assisted role gives the assumptions under which an assisting role is to operate in its attempt to provide the needed information. The role being assisted also has control over how to use the information it receives from other roles. The particular character of the information received may affect subsequent initiation and sequencing of information transferrals, as well as the set of assumptions under which assisting roles must operate.

Roles differ not only according to their information-processing tasks but also with respect to the structuredness of control that they exhibit. Where control is highly structured, an algorithm can be written depicting all sequencing of requests for assistance and depicting the assumptions that accompany each request. When control is highly unstructured, such algorithms cannot be written. We can only indicate which roles are available to provide assistance. The manner in which these assisting roles are controlled in order to solve the problem of the assisted role is unknown a priori.

Some assisted roles may be interpreted as being persons (or mechanisms) that request information from other roles in order to solve their problems. Mechanisms are examples of highly structured roles, whereas the information processing performed by a person may or may not be highly structured. To the extent that unstructuredness enters, the information processing is called creative or intuitive. Other assisted roles may be interpreted as "group" processes that may involve persons and/or mechanisms. The group is not a mere sum of individual problem solvers. But in the course of solving its problem, the group utilizes individual problem solvers in its own particular way. It is this particular method of utilization (specifying the nature of the group's information processing), along with the problem being attacked, that defines the group. A group may be viewed as a multi-argument function with individual (or other group) processors as its arguments. Participation in a group problem-solving process is akin to the associative connections between an assisted role (group) and assisting roles (other groups, persons, or mechanisms).

The "group" process may be highly structured or relatively unstructured. In the former case, the "group" process consists of rigid, well-defined, formal procedures that control the participation of assisting roles. In the latter case, procedures are informal and are not well defined; the assisted role's control over assisting roles is manifest through the use of associative connections to solve the assisted role's problem. In other words, the nature of interaction among assisting roles is not known (a priori), but the interaction is governed by the problem to be solved.

Associative connections are pictorially represented by arcs emanating from the node of the assisted role to the nodes of the assisting roles; associative arcs are joined by a semi-circle. In Figure 12.1, for instance, the role Planner 1 (P1) receives assistance from Expert 1 (E1), Expert 2 (E2), and Expert 3 (E3) in the course of solving its problem. Planner 1 (P1), Planner 2 (P2), ..., Planner N (PN) are capable of filling the role of Division 1 Planning (DP1). Similarly, E1, E2, ..., EM are experts capable of filling the role of Staff Support (SS). The only flows of information shown here are between the first three experts and the first planner. More complex communication patterns may exist among the roles. One planner, for instance, may make requests upon other planners. Specialist E6 may need an assist from E8. There may also be recursion such as E8 assisting E6 and being assisted by E9, where E9 needs the assistance of E6. Each of the experts could be filled by a role that is capable of being filled by other roles.

The three simple constructs presented above (the role, definitional relationships among roles, and associative relationships among roles) permit us to describe very complex organizational structures. The description furnishes a flexible tool with which to model roles and their associative connections as a pattern of passing messages among the roles. The structures of control among the roles is embedded in this pattern. This modeling technique says nothing about the previously noted control mechanisms within a role that govern the sequencing and conditioning of message passing. In the passage of messages, it is necessary to have a means for translating the information that one role is attempting to convey into a form that is comprehensible to the other role. Otherwise there is misunderstanding or non-understanding. This translation issue is not incorporated into the modeling technique shown in Figure 12.1. If both roles have the same "world view" and the same terminology, then the translation problem is trivial. If their views and terminology differ (e.g., a local view versus a more global view), then the issue of mapping information from one to the other becomes important.

In a subsequent section we shall show that there is a direct correspondence between the proposed framework for representing the division of labor in organizations and the problem reduction method of classical artificial intelligence. There is also a correspondence between the framework's definitional and associative constructs on the one hand and computerized information base schemas on the other hand. The implications of these correspondences are that (1) an organization's planning resources and methods can be modeled in a computerized information base; (2) to the extent that information processing within each of a group of roles can be formalized, that processing can be automated; and (3) the problem reduction technique gives a way to automatically find solution method(s) for a given problem.

Thus far we have a framework for representing the patterns of control and information flow among roles (e.g., experts) in a decision-making system. Suppose that we have a means for automating the information processing performed by the various experts. This information processing includes the sequencing of requests for information, the specification of assumptions within each request, and the transformation or manipulation of available information. If this processing is automated for each of a sizable number of roles, a question arises concerning how to coordinate (manage) these automated roles. In particular can we computerize this coordination activity such that, in response to a problem statement, the problem is automatically solved?

If the answer is affirmative then we have a joint human-computer decision-making (e.g., planning) system in which the human instigates the decision-making process and in which the computer supports the process by furnishing pertinent information. Since the computer manages a network of "experts" or "specialists," it may be viewed as a sort of collective expert with which the human user can interact in the effort to make a decision. The user has no need to interact directly with the more specialized experts (i.e., with specific computer programs); this is handled by the collective expert that is a decision support system.

Unstructuredness is accommodated (1) in the nature of and sequencing of requests made upon the decision support system, (2) in the manner in which decision support system responses are utilized, and (3) in the decision support system's recognition of alternative methods for satisfying a given request. (It is possible to have a mixed system of programmed experts and experts who are not programs, but who must be consulted by the system in the course of problem solving.)

Thus there are two varieties of unstructuredness in the joint human-computer decision-making system. One variety is addressed by the system's user (see items 1 and 2 above). The other, which is treated by the decision support system, is of principal concern here. This variety of unstructuredness derives from the existence of alternative methods for solving a problem (as suggested by definitional relationships among information processing roles). In completely structured problems there is only a single "alternative" way for finding a solution. Structured problems are routine and repetitive precisely because they are unambiguous (because each problem has a single solution method). A less-structured problem has more alternative solution methods and the solutions given by these methods may not be equivalent. A "completely" unstructured problem has n solution methods where $n \to \infty$.

ABILITIES INVOLVED IN DECISION MAKING

Prior to closer examination of this joint human-computer decision-making system, it is useful to have a conceptual framework of decision making that identifies the basic abilities needed in order to make a decision. We can then describe a decision support system in terms of those abilities that it possesses. The decision support system can be viewed as emulating (in some degree) human cognitive abilities. Those abilities that it does not possess must lie with the system's user. Taken together, the decision support system and its user constitute a decision-making system. The framework of decision-making abilities is given in the form of postulates that identify seven abilities required for decision making.

The central postulate is that decision making has three facets that are basic in the sense that no one of the three can be expressed in terms of the other two. We shall call these facets (1) Power, (2) Perception, and (3) Design. In other words, a decision-making process necessarily involves (1) the ability to exercise some power, authority, or directive force; (2) the ability to collect information; and (3) the ability to formulate models.

A second postulate states that the existence of the three basic abilities implies the existence of four additional abilities called (4) Analysis, (5) Valuation, (6) Organization, and (7) Adaptation. Analysis may be described as a continuing adjustment between perceptions and formulations; and it results in beliefs, expectations, or "facts." Valuation is describable as a continuing adjustment between perceptions and powers. Values (ideals, standards, utilities, etc.) are based on available information and available powers. If there is no information about X, it is meaningless to speak of the value of X; similarly, if there is no power with respect to X, then it is irrelevant to speak of the value of X. The ability to organize may be viewed as a continuing adjustment between design and power resulting in the imposition or execution of plans. Finally, the facet of adaptation may be described as a continuing adjustment among the other six facets. As such, it involves the activity of problem recognition which is constrained by the natures of the other six facets. Adaptation may be considered to be a sequence of problem recognitions that, as a result of the activity of the other facets, tends toward a problem that is minimal; that is, the minimal problem consists of a single alternative.

If these postulates are accepted as accurately portraying the functional aspects of decision making, then they furnish a framework for designing an intelligent problem processor for decision support. The processor supports (rather than makes) decisions because some of the facets are not accounted for in the processor. For instance, the processor has no intrinsic power or authority; it has authority only in proportion to the weight that the decision maker attaches to its activities. For each of the abilities, the processor can participate in the joint human-computer decision activity only to the extent that the ability can be formally expressed. For example, the facet of valuation may involve some nonformalizable subjective processes.

An overview of those functions that have been incorporated into the processor design is given in Figure 12.2. The arrows roughly indicate flows of control (and information). This should not be confused with the previously described flows of control and information within a "society" of experts. Rectangles within the problem processor do not indicate distinct components but rather distinct abilities that are operationally related to one another. Throughout this paper the problem processor is discussed more on this functional level of detail than

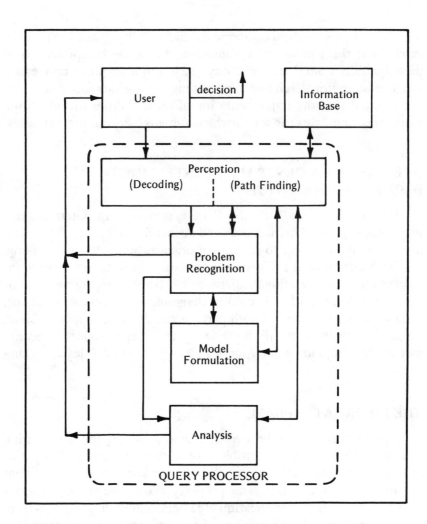

FIGURE 12.2 Overview of Abilities Incorporated into a Generalized Intelligent Problem Processor

on the level of structural components. Each ability (function) may be carried out through several components; but some components may participate in more than one ability [32], and in so doing they establish the operational relationships among the various functions. It is not claimed that the implementation of these abilities within a problem processor mirrors the way in which humans carry out these abilities.

OVERVIEW OF A GENERALIZED INTELLIGENT DECISION SUPPORT SYSTEM

As depicted in Figure 12.2, the GIDS system described here has two major parts: an information base and a generalized intelligent problem processor. With respect to support of organizational decision making, the information base utilizes the previously outlined framework for representing organizational division of labor; the framework of decision-making abilities is used in designing the problem processor. Following this overview of both parts of the decision support system, we shall illustrate its details by showing how it can support an econometric planning model for American Telephone and Telegraph Company.

THE INFORMATION BASE

A point that cannot be overemphasized is that the information base is *not* a part of the problem processor. It may be thought of as a single device that contains all available knowledge independent of interaction with a user. This property allows the problem processor's invariance to the application area being considered since the processor can access the knowledge of any information base regardless of its structure and content. For instance, the information base structure can be tailored to store knowledge about an organization's role structure (e.g., Figure 12.1).

The information-base notion is an extension of well-known data base techniques to provide a more complete semantic mechanism for storing knowledge.[9] From the data-base management viewpoint, the information base furnishes a fundamentally new technique for structuring information. It has all of the capabilities afforded by network data structures, but it also provides a means for integrating networks of varying levels of semantic resolution into a single structure. Here network structures are referred to in the CODASYL sense [15], subject to some important extensions and modifications detailed in [8]. The information base also incorporates another departure from data base management as it is customarily practiced: namely, the integration of program modules (i.e. formalized information processors or 'experts") into the information base so that they can be managed just like the more traditional type of data.

THE PROBLEM PROCESSOR

Consideration of the problem processor begins by recalling that it is intended to *support* decision makers, rather than to *make* decisions. This support is furnished by virtue of the processor's abilities (1) to collect information from the user and from a central repository called the information base, (2) to recognize the intentions of the user (even though they are not explicitly stated) and express those intentions as a set of solvable primitive problems, (3) to formulate models by combining modules of computer code, and (4) to interface formulated models and desired data for subsequent execution. As the term is used here, a model consists of a specification of how each role pertaining to the problem being solved is to be filled.

The problem processor is said to be general in the sense that it can support decision making in a wide variety of application areas (e.g., water-quality planning, nuclear power plant siting, corporate planning, etc.). Indeed, the problem processor is itself invariant to the application area being supported, to the kinds of formal models ("experts") that are to be used, to the ways in which (i.e., the assumptions under which) a model may be used in carrying out desired analysis, and to the vocabulary that the system's user desires to utilize in conversing with the processor. That is the problem processor's two sources of information (i.e., the user and the information base) may undergo many changes, but no change in the problem processor's code is required.

The problem processor could be said to be intelligent because of its generality which enables it to successfully cope with new situations. In this discussion, the term "intelligence" should be considered in the sense of artificial intelligence. Thus the problem processor endeavors to emulate certain human cognitive abilities, namely the four abilities enumerated above.

With respect to the information gathering ability, the problem processor has two sources of information, just as a human information processor also has two sources: external discourses and memory. The method for obtaining information from one source is different from that of the other. Information is obtained from the user by decoding the user's English-like requests into an internally comprehensible form called an intermediate structure. (The user's request is said to be in a form called the surface structure.) This decoding may be characterized as an application of inverse transformations (in the sense of Chomsky [14]) to the surface structure query. Information is obtained from the information base by finding paths through a semantic network.[11] This path searching is a way of implementing the problem reduction concepts [35] that are well known in artificial intelligence (and that are directly analogous to the previously outlined framework for representing organizational role structures.[10]

The second ability (i.e., problem recognition) forms the core of the query processor in that it makes extensive use of the ability to formulate models and the ability to gather information from the two sources. Its primary function is to "understand" a query, thereby discovering the model and the data that the user desires to have interfaced and executed; that is, it finds the intended type of analysis. The user is not required to provide an explicit statement of how the problem is to be solved, nor even a precise statement of the problem.

In intelligent inter-human discourse, implications are frequently attached to messages by both recipients and senders (i.e., implications that are not explicitly stated). In order to recognize the intent of a message, the recipient must examine that message in the light of stored information about the sender and the problem area (i.e., the context) under consideration. Discourse between an intelligent query processor and its user should also address these economies of expression. Thus during the problem recognition activity, the processor utilizes pertinent stored information (and possible interaction with the user) in order to precisely determine the user's intent. Parenthetically, just as there may be a misinterpretation of intent during inter-human discourse, so is there the possibility of the same type of misinterpretation during human-computer discourse.

The third ability, that of model formulation, involves the generation of potential data-analyzing algorithms. This is accomplished by modifying and combining various known program modules. Rules for the permissible modifications and combinations are incorporated into the structure of the information base, and the modules themselves are treated as data in the information base. Thus, program modules may be added and deleted from the information base just as easily as other sorts of data.

The model formulation activity for a given query begins in concert with a query. Before the problem recognizer can produce the explicit statement, it must have available to it a description of the models that could possibly have been intended by the user. It is through the model-formulation activity that these descriptions are generated.

One way to view the formulation activity is as a problem-reduction process.[10] Briefly, a portion of the decoded query is viewed as an initial problem description that can be reduced to one or more sets of directly solvable primitive subproblems. The structure of the information base is used to specify permissible reductions. If it occurs that more than one set of primitive subproblems is generated (i.e., more than one model is formulated), then the problem recognizer resolves the ambiguity through interaction with the user or through the use of pertinent stored information. The problem recognizer must also eliminate any ambiguity as to the data that the user intends to be accessed by the model.

Once the explicit statement of a user's intention has been produced, it is used to direct the fourth ability of the problem processor. This ability is referred to as analysis since it involves the interfacing (and execution) of the desired model and the desired data in order to provide some facts or expectations for decision support. The "explicit statement" that governs the analysis process is directly analogous to the JCL (Job Control Language) that a typical computer-user submits to that computer's operating system. The analysis process corresponds to a limited sort of operating system in that it sequences the job steps, assigns I/O locations, performs data mappings, loads code, and executes.

To conclude this overview, it is useful to summarize the major contributions of this work. We have described a mechanism for generating information to support organizational decision-making activities. This information is generated in response to nonprocedure, English-like requests made by the mechanism's user. We refer to this mechanism as a generalized intelligent decision support system. This system is founded upon a conceptual framework that (1) accounts for the division of labor within a decision-making organization and (2) addresses the kinds of abilities that are typically required for decision making. It is this first aspect that leads to the system's generality, allowing the information base to be tailored to fit a given situation. So the decision support system is in a sense "ready-made"; all that is required is that we fill in its memory (i.e., the information base). On the basis of the second aspect of the presented framework, the problem processor is designed to emulate certain human cognitive activities: two types of information collection, model formulation, problem recognition, and analysis. It is in this sense that the query processor is said to be "intelligent."

APPLICATION TO AN ECONOMETRIC PLANNING SYSTEM

In this section we illustrate some of the details of the GIDS system in the context of an econometric planning model for the American Telephone and Telegraph Company. This model had been developed at A.T. & T. [16] to show that "for present day corporate planning modeling, the state of applied economics and the availability of planning technology is such that comprehensive and informative models can be constructed on simple economic theory".[16, p. 29] In other words, it is possible and practical to formalize some of the information-processing roles involved in planning. The GIDS approach is to build a repertoire of available modules without foreknowledge of how this repertoire will be used for particular problems. The same overall repertoire is used in a variety of planning situations, although the way in which it is used in one situation differs from the way in which it is used in another situation. Role-structuring techniques are used to capture the possible ways in which the repertoire can be used. The reason for including alternatives within the role structure is that, in most planning situations, the way in which a role is to be filled is unknown in advance. It is the joint task of the management scientist and the decision support systems analyst to decide upon the appropriate role structure for a given application area.

It is with this task that the fields of management science (MS) and decision support systems (DSS) meet on a common ground. A primary function of the management scientist is the development of formal models. The organization and interrelation of these models is a joint MS-DSS task. And the management of the resultant organization of interrelated modules is a primary function of the DSS analyst.

The focus of the following example is not upon the detailed workings of the various parts of the A.T. & T. model, but rather upon how it can be described as a structure of roles that can be used by the GIDS problem processor. Although the information processing for each role is formalized in this example, it should be clear that one could also represent role structures with roles whose information processing is not formalized. The difference is that in the latter case the decision support system cannot automatically perform the information processing, although it can still exercise its information collection, problem recognition, and model formulation abilities.

INFORMATION BASE FOR A.T.& T.

At its most abstract level the A.T. & T. planning system consists of three roles: environment modeling (EM), corporate modeling (CM), and management modeling (MM). The three kinds of environmental modeling—national economy forecasting (NE), price forecasting based on governmental regulation (RG), and modeling the effects of possible actions by the Federal Cost of Living Council (WP) –are depicted in Figure 12.3. Although it was not mentioned in descriptions of the A.T. & T. model, it is possible to have alternative methods for performing national economy forecasting. Such alternatives effectively serve as alternative definitions of the concept "national economy forecasting"; they are different ways in which the role "national economy forecasting" can be filled. Which of these alternatives should be used depends upon the nature of the problem statement furnished by a user.

Suppose that a planning situation is encountered in which there is a need for some type of environmental modeling not already included in the information base and that this type of environmental modeling is available in the guise of a computer program. This program can be incorporated into the formation base, as described in [11]. The result is an increase in the knowledge available to the problem processor. No change in the problem processor's code is needed.

As shown in Figure 12.3, there are six varieties of corporate modeling. Price modeling (PR) involves the calculation of price indices. An-

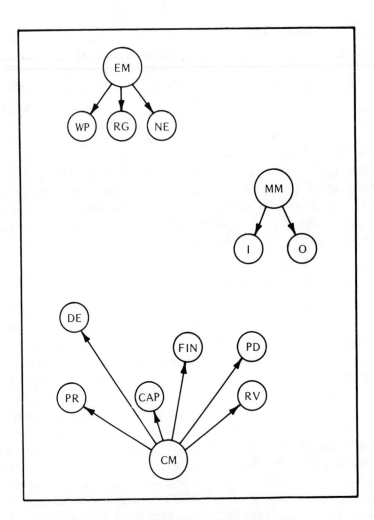

**FIGURE 12.3 Roles and Definitional Arcs for the
A.T. & T. Example**

other variety results in forecasts of demand (DE). Determinations of revenue (RV), of production levels (PD), of total expenses (FIN), and of the cost of capital (CAP) are the remaining kinds of corporate modeling. Each of these six may itself be viewed as a role capable of being filled by other roles. For instance, there may be a variety of ways to forecast demand, each of which is relevant in a particular planning context.

These are not depicted in Figure 12.3.

Management modeling is a role that can be filled in one of two ways. The first (I) is used to generate managerial policy with respect to finance mix and factor mix. The second (O) produces quantitative indicators of corporate performance for a stated strategy. Here again one can conceive of alternative methods for generating managerial policy (or for generating performance indicators); however, these are not displayed in Figure 12.3.

The other type of relationship that can exist among roles, namely one role assisting another role, is shown for the A.T. & T. example in Figure 12.4. For instance, forecasting demand (DE) requires information directly from national economy forecasting (NE) and price determination (PR). But DE can be "asked" to supply information directly to PD and to RV.

The notation of Figure 12.4 is akin to that used for specifying an AND/OR graph. Such graphs are used in artificial intelligence to depict problem reduction processes. In Figure 12.4, EM could be called an OR node because, in order to solve an environment modeling problem, we must solve either a wage-price (WP) problem *or* a regulatory (RG) problem *or* a national economy (NE) forecasting problem. Definitional arcs emanating from a node indicate an OR node. Associative arcs emanating from a node indicate an AND node. For example, DE is an AND node; in order to produce a demand forecast, information is required from both the price index determination (PR) and the national economy forecast (NE).

In problem reduction, no node is permitted to be both an AND node and an OR node. This is not a serious restriction since it can be satisfied by creating artificial nodes. Each node is viewed as a problem to be solved. The objective is to reduce this problem to a group of di-directly solvable primitive problems; that is, solvability of all primitive problems within the group implies a solution to the original problem.

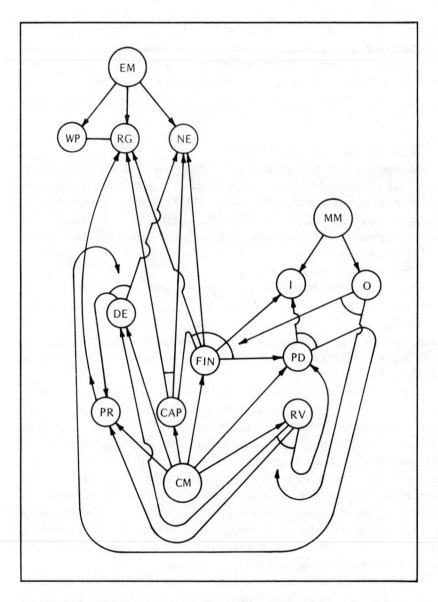

**FIGURE 12.4 All Roles and Their Interrelationships for the
A.T. & T. Example**

TABLE 12.1 Correspondence Between Organizational Role Structure and Problem Reduction

Structure of Roles	AND/OR Graph
Node	Node
Expert at solving problem	Problem to be solved
Expert Role (Problem Solver Role which can be filled in alternative ways)	OR Node (Problem with alternative solutions)
Expert Person (or Mechanism) that consults other experts	AND Node (Problem which requires solution of other problems)
Expert Person (or Mechanism) that consults no other expert	Primitive Node (Problem which is directly solvable)
Arc	Arc
Definitional Arc points to a way in which an Expert Role can be filled (i.e., defined)	Arc emanating from an OR Node points to one of a number of alternative problems (one of these alternatives must be solved)
Associative Arc points to an Expert from whom information is required	Arc emanating from an AND Node points to a problem which must be solved

A primitive problem is one that has no departing arcs. The correspondence between organizational role structure and problem reduction is summarized in Table 12.1. As was indicated earlier, AND/OR graphs can be implicitly stored in the logical structure of an information base. [10] Introduction of information-base terminology [9] is avoided here.

THE PROBLEM PROCESSOR

In order to understand the manner in which the problem processor works we trace the effect of the user submitting the following request: FORECAST DEMAND. Details of the syntax of the request language may be found in [11]. Upon receipt of this request the problem processor decodes it into an internally comprehensible form. The processor recognizes that a demand model is needed. Utilizing its model formulation ability, the processor proceeds to generate the possible demand models implicit in the information-base structure. In the present case (A.T. & T.) we have only one demand model. This can be visualized by consulting Figure 4. In order to solve the demand problem (DE) there must be a solution of price (PR) and national economy problems. Stated in another way, the demand expert needs information from the price expert and the national economy expert. NE represents a primitive problem (an expert problem solver that consults no others). The price expert must consult the regulatory (RG) expert that must in turn request information from the wage-price (WP) expert. If there had been alternative models, the ambiguity would be resolved by interaction with the user and by consulting the information base for information about the intended type of analysis.[10] The problem processor proceeds to recognize the needed information inputs for this model and where to obtain them. Finally, the analyst's ability is used to interface the demand model with pertinent data and to automatically carry out the execution.

Suppose that the problem processor is presented with a less explicit request, such as PERFORM ENVIRONMENTAL MODELING. The first step is again a decoding into an intermediate structure. By utilizing its model formulation ability, the problem processor recognizes that there are three possible meanings for this request (either wage-price modeling or regulatory modeling or national economy forecasting). This may be visualized in Figure 12.4.

The problem processor attempts to eliminate this ambiguity by searching the information base for an indication of which of the three types of analysis is intended. This indication can be in the form of a history of the user's past intentions for the same query or in the form of axioms that state conditions under which one of the alternatives is to be chosen.[12] If ambiguity is not entirely eliminated with this procedure, interaction with the user occurs. The problem processor presents to the user the alternative meanings that it has determined for the query. The user makes the final selection. Needed inputs are recognized and the analysis proceeds.

What does the GIDS system user gain beyond "going next door" and asking an expert? First, there may not be an expert available to perform the desired information processing. Second, suppose such human experts are available; then the desired information processing is typically of such complexity that the expert(s) relies on a computer program(s) to perform the processing. This requires that the expert supervise the writing and/or running of programs to manipulate data and programs to execute analyses. This cumbersome task is eliminated by the GIDS system. The principal asset of an expert human information processor is the capacity to perform nonformalizable information processing, not the capacity to supervise the writing and/or running of computer programs.

Finally, a more complex request is examined: DETERMINE EARNINGS-PER-SHARE FOR FACTOR-MIX= . . . In this case, recognition of the intended model is make on the basis of the requested output (E-P-S) and the stated assumptions in the conditional clause (that part of the request following the "FOR"). These are used by the problem processor as "hints" as to what model is intended. The processor must consult its "memory" (information base) to ascertain what is to be done in terms of model formulation when these hints are received. Upon selection of a model, all inputs to that model must be located. Inputs to a model (expert) are the assumptions under which that model (expert) is to perform. Some of these assumptions may be stated by the user, whereas others may be obtained from the information base.

The model that results from the above request consists of module O requesting information from FIN and RV, each of which makes its own requests upon other expert information processors, and so forth (see Figure 12.4). An important issue is the passage of information between two experts or, in this case, between two modules. In the event that modules have been developed independently it is quite probable that the data structures used by two modules are different. Thus there must exist a means for correctly translating information organized according to the data structure of one module into the data structure of another module. This issue is examined in [10] and is analogous to the issue of two experts being able to understand each other.

CONCLUSION

The major focus of fields such as operations research, management science, and normative economics has been the development of models to determine the best or optimal decision. In contrast, the focus here has been to develop tools for modeling the process of decision making in organizational settings. In the framework discussed here, this involves the selection of appropriate experts that are able to solve more specialized problems than the original. It involves the coordination of these expert problem solvers. Each expert may break its subproblem into further subproblems, each of which is solved by other experts. We have centered our attention on experts that are application programs and upon a decision support system that makes these information processing resources available to a decision maker. The conceptual framework and decision support system outlined here should not be viewed as a complete or final statement, but rather as an initial effort pointing out directions for future development of computer-based support of decision makers.

REFERENCES

[1] Allen, S. A. "Environment, Organization and the Design of Formal Planning Systems." *Formal Planning Systems—1971.* Edited by R. F. Vancil. Boston, Mass.: Harvard Business School, 1971.

[2] Anthony, R. N. *Planning and Control Systems.* Boston, Mass.: Harvard School of Business Administration, 1965, pp. 13 -43.

[3] Behling, O., and C. Schriesheim. *Organizational Behavior.* Boston, Mass.: Allyn and Bacon, Inc., 1976, p. 15.

[4] Benbasat, I. "Cognitive Style Considerations in DSS Design." *Data Base,* Vol. 8, No. 3 (1977), pp. 3–8.

[5] Berger, P., and F. Edelman. "IRIS: A Transactions-Based DSS for Human Resource Management." *Data Base*, Vol. 8, (1977), pp. 10–14.

[6] Bledsoe, W. W., and P. Bruell. "A Man-Machine Theorem Proving System." *Artificial Intelligence,* Vol. 5 (Spring 1974), pp. 51–72.

[7] Bobrow, D. G. "Natural Language Input for a Computer Problem Solving System." *Semantic Information Processing.* Edited by M. Minsky. Cambridge, Mass.: M.I.T. Press, 1968.

[8] Bonczek, R. H.; C. W. Holsapple; A. B. Whinston. "Extensions and Corrections for the CODASYL Approach to Data Base Management." *International Journal of Information Systems,* Vol. 2 (1976), pp. 71–77.

[9] Bonczek, R. H.; C. W. Holsapple, A. B. Whinston. "Design and Implementation of an Information Base for Decision Makers." *Proceedings of the National Computer Conference—1977*, Dallas, June 1977.

[10] Bonczek, R. H.; C. W. Holaspple, A. B. Whinston. "Processing Deep Structures in a Generalized Intelligent Query Processor for Decision Support." West Lafayette, Ind.: Krannert Graduate School of Management, Purdue University, July 1977. (Krannert Institute Paper No. 612.)

[11] Bonczek, R. H., and A. B. Whinston. "A Generalized Mapping Language for Network Data Structures." *International Journal of Information Systems*, Vol. 1 (1977), pp. 171-185.

[12] Bonczek, R. H.; C. W. Holsapple; A. B. Whinston. "The Integration of Data Base Management and Problem Resolution." West Lafayette, Ind.: Krannert Graduate School of Management, Purdue University, February 1978.

[13] Boulding, K. E. *The Image.* Ann Arbor: University of Michigan Press, 1956, pp. 1-30.

[14] Chomsky, N. *Aspects of the Theory of Syntax.* Cambridge, Mass.: M.I.T. Press, 1965.

[15] CODASYL: *Data Base Task Group Report.* ACM, April 1971.

[16] Davis, B. E.; G. J. Caccappolo; M. A. Chandry. "An Econometric Planning Model for American Telephone and Telegraph Company." *Bell Journal of Economics and Management Science* (April 1973), pp. 29-56.

[17] Ebert, R. J., and R. R. Mitchell. *Organizational Decision Processes.* New York: Crane, Russak & Co., 1975, pp. 15-17.

[18] Forehand, G. A. "Constructs and Strategies for Problem Solving Research." *Problem Solving.* Edited by B. Kleinmuntz. New York: Wiley, 1966.

[19] Grace, B. F. "Training Users of a Prototype DSS." *Data Base*, Vol. 8, No. 3 (1977), pp. 22-24.

[20] Green, C. C., and B. Raphael. "Research on Intelligent Question-Answering Systems." *Proceedings of National Computer Conference.* Princeton, N.J., 1968.

[21] Hackathorn, R. D. "Modeling Unstructured Decision Making." *Data Base*, Vol. 8, No. 3 (1977), pp. 27-30.

[22] Harrison, E. F. *The Managerial Decision Making Process.* Boston, Mass.: Houghton Mifflin Co., 1975, pp. 11-15.

[23] Haseman, W. D. "GPLAN: An Operational DSS." *Data Base*, Vol. 8, No. 3 (1977), pp. 80-85.

[24] Haseman, W. D., and A. B. Whinston. "Problem Solving in Data Management." *Proceedings of Fourth International Conference on Artificial Intelligence.* Tbilisi, Georgia, U.S.S.R., September 1975.

[25] Haseman, W. D., and A. B. Whinston. *Introduction to Data Management.* Homewood, Ill.: Irwin, 1977.

[26] Heidorn, G. E. "English as a Very High Level Language for Simulation Programming." *Proceedings of Symposium on Very High Level Languages,* SIGPLAN Notices, Vol. 9 (1974).

[27] Hill, I. D. "Wouldn't It Be Nice If We Could Write Computer Programs in English or Would It?" *Computer Bulletin,* Vol. 16 (1972), pp. 306-312.

[28] Joyce, J. D., and N. N. Oliver. "Impacts of a Relational Information System on Industrial Decision." *Data Base,* Vol. 8, No. 3 (1977), pp. 72-75.

[29] Lorange, P. "Towards a Situational Design of Formal Systems for Capacity Expansion." *Formal Planning Systems—1971.* Edited by R. F. Vancil. Boston, Mass.: Harvard Business School, 1971.

[30] Mantey, P. E., and J. A. Sutton. "Computer Support for Management Decision Making." *IBM Research Report,* RJ 1893, 1976.

[31] McLean, E. R., and T. F. Riesing. "MAPP: A DSS for Financial Planning." *Data Base,* Vol. 8, No. 3 (1977), pp. 50-58.

[32] Miller, J. "Living Systems: The Organization." *Behavioral Science,* Vol. 17 (January 1972), pp. 1-182.

[33] Montgomery, C. A. "Is Natural Language an Unnatural Query Language?" *Proceedings of the ACM Annual Conference,* New York, 1972.

[34] Nevins, A. J. "A Human Oriented Logic for Automatic Theorem Proving." *Journal of ACM,* Vol. 21 (October 1974), ppl 606-621.

[35] Nilsson, N. *Problem Solving Methods in Artificial Intelligence.* New York: McGraw-Hill, 1971.

[36] Plath, W. J. "Transformational Grammar and Transformation Parsing in the REQUEST System." *IBM Research Report 4396,* 1973.

[37] Raphael, B. "SIR: A Computer Program for Semantic Information Retrieval." Cambridge: Massachusetts Institute of Technology, 1964. (Doctoral dissertation.)

[38] Robinson, J. A. "A Machine-Oriented Logic Based on the Resolution Principle." *Journal of ACM,* Vol. 12 (January 1965), pp. 23-41.

[39] Rothschild, W. E. *Putting It All Together.* New York: AMACOM, 1976.

[40] Simon, H. A. *The New Science of Management Decision.* New York: Harper & Brothers, 1960, pp. 1–8.

[41] Simon, H. A. "What Computers Mean to Man and Society." *Science,* Vol. 195 (March 1977), pp. 1186–1190.

[42] Sussman, G. J.; T. Winograd; E. Charniak. "Micro Planner Reference Manual." Artificial Intelligence Memo No. 203A. Cambridge: Artificial Intelligence Laboratory, Massachusetts Institute of Technology, 1971.

[43] Thompson, F. B.; P. C. Lockemann; B. Dostert; and R. S. Deverill. "REL: A Rapidly Extensible Language System." *Proceedings of National Computer Conference,* 1969.

[44] Vancil, R. F. (ed.) *Formal Planning Systems—1971.* Boston, Mass.: Harvard Business School, 1971, pp. 1–3.

[45] Winograd, T. *Understanding Natural Language.* New York: Academic Press, 1972, pp. 23–27.

[46] Wong, H. K. T., and J. Mylopoulos. "Two Views of Data Semantics." Toronto, Ont.: Department of Computer Science, University of Toronto, December 1976.

[47] Woods, W. A. "Transition Network Grammars for Natural Language Analysis." *Communication ACM,* Vol. 13 (1970), pp. 591–606.

13

DSS: An Executive Mind-Support System

by Peter G.W. Keen and G.R. Wagner

About the authors:

Peter G.W. Keen is an associate professor at the MIT Sloan School of Management, and has served on the faculties of Stanford and Harvard. He is a coauthor of the book *Decision Support Systems: An Organizational Perspective* and a founding partner of CGK Associates, Washington, D.C. He holds a Ph.D. in business adminstration from Harvard.

G.R. Wagner is president of EXECUCOM Systems Corp. in Austin, Texas. He has been professor of operations research at the University of Texas, vice president of MRI Systems Corp., and corporate director of operations research for Swift & Co. He received a Ph.D. in statistics from Iowa State University.

When one asks a senior manager, "What do you use computers for?" the dialog is often predictable:

"Oh, we use them for everything. Why, we have systems on-line, interactive thus-and-so's. We're putting in a distributed such-and-such."

"Yes, but what do *you* use computers for?"

"Well, I get a lot of reports. Some of them are very helpful ... "

Reprinted with permission from Datamation

"Yes, but what do you *use* computers for?"

"Well, actually—very little."

The importance of data processing to the organization and the feverish growth in demand for hardware and software hide an inescapable reality: even now, many managers feel that the computer is only of peripheral value.

But a new concept in computer use is afoot that promises to improve this situation. New approaches are being taken that represent an entirely different philosophy. As a result, in many organizations, computers are being used by managers as *personal tools*—as extensions of the executive mind. Wrapped up in this change are some monumental implications for dp professionals.

The new managerial uses of computers are being brought about by inexorable trends in hardware, software, and business needs. This is not a single, clean-cut innovation that occurred overnight, but is more like a tide moving in many currents and eddies over a period of time. What is happening is manifested in a variety of new software packages for interactive use by managerial personnel. This software is centered around two broad classes of applications: data base management (information systems) and financial planning (modeling, analysis, etc.).

Several years ago, one of us (Keen, in association with others at the Sloan School of Management) began describing the emerging new philosophy and gave it a name: decision support. A decision-support system (DSS) is a computer-based system (say, a data base management system or a set of financial models) which is used personally on an ongoing basis by managers and their immediate staffs in direct *support* of managerial activites—that is, *decisions*. Another term for DSS might be "executive mind-support system."

The other one of us (Wagner, working independently) created a planning or modeling language which is an expression of the decision-support concept. Called interactive financial planning system (IFPS), this software package is a method of creating a DSS in the form of one or more models, and then using the system on a continuing basis by manipulating the models and improving them in a learning process. The models may be linked to a data base management system to form an even broader expression of the DSS philosophy.

Here, we will elaborate on the movement toward personal use of a computer by managerial personnel in terms of decision support. We will draw on IFPS as an example of DSS philosophy.

First, it is well to explore the discouraging situation reflected in the opening dialog. What does it mean when a senior manager admits computers are of little use to him? And why is this so?

For one thing, many technical specialists have little understanding of managers. They assume the products they offer are useful to executives. Data Processing views its role as improving the operations and data flows of the organization, MIS as providing the information needed by managers, and OR/MS (operations research/management science) as developing analytic methods for decision-making. Each group works forward from technology (the means) to applications (the end). For some, the end *is* the means.

No one can deny these traditional approaches have been fruitful. Even though we have often jumped ahead only to scuttle back, computer systems and models are indeed a central component of most functions of business.

But regardless of how indispensible such computer-based systems have become, they are incomplete from the viewpoint of the manager. Benefits of the systems are often limited to matters peripheral to the center of the manager's activities, such as reporting and control systems, delegated activities that mainly involve procedures and rules, and delegated decisions that—although they involve judgment—are of minor importance.

The central managerial activities not touched by traditional computer systems are those involving personal choices—matters that cannot be performed routinely or delegated: planning for the future, "fire fighting," and providing fast responses to unanticipated situations. Even though much of the analysis is provided by staff, the final choice must be made by the manager.

Henry Mintzberg [1] aptly characterized the senior manager's job as one of brevity, fragmentation, and variety. Managers rarely spend more than an hour at a time on any one activity; they deal with a typical problem in fragments of time scattered over a period of weeks or months; and they cover many different tasks in a given day. Furthermore, they prefer obtaining concrete information and rely on face-to-face discussions; yet they often depend on intuition.

In light of a senior manager's real job and how he does it, one may discern several reasons why computer-based systems useful to the manager's organization may provide no help at all to him personally:

1. Since his decision-making is often ad hoc and addressed to unexpected problems, standardized reporting systems lack scope, flexibility, and relevance.

2. Many classical OR/MS models that are *conceptually* useful often do not adequately fit a specific situation. Decision-making involves exceptions and qualitative issues.

3. While plenty of computer power is available, the lead time is too long for writing programs and getting answers.

4. Managers cannot specify in advance what they want from programmers and model builders. Decision-making and planning are often exploratory. Information needs and methods of analysis evolve as the decision-maker and his or her staff learn more about the problem.

SUPPORT FOR MANAGERIAL DECISIONS

However, systems are appearing that do provide direct, personal support for managerial decision: decision-support systems. What capabilities must such a system have to be useful to a manager? A DSS should be able to reflect the way managers think, be flexible and adaptive through ease of modification, support managers in a complex process of exploration and learning, and evolve to meet changing needs, knowledge, and situations.

In many ways, such a system is defined by its uses, and not by any specific technology. The goal is to provide managers with tools they will choose to adopt and that mesh with their own decision-making and judgment processes. The means are whatever software and hardware tools are suitable and available.

This is the essence of DSS philosophy. As far as computer systems are concerned, the foregoing capabilities translate into some specific design criteria:

- A flexible development language that allows rapid creation and modification of systems for specific applications.

- A system design architecture that allows quick easy extensions and alterations.
- An interface that buffers the users from the "computer" and allows a dialog based on the manager's concepts, vocabulary, and definition of the decision problem.
- Communicative display devices and output generators.

The key words to this system are flexibility, ease of use, and adaptivity. A manager will not use a system lacking these attributes. It is hard to see any reason why he should.

Decision-support systems are used for many purposes, but there are certain common features. Direct, personal support of managerial decisions requires either the elements of an information system (a DBMS) for storing and retrieving data, or modeling and analysis capabilities, or both. Of course, the systems are interactive—usually on a time-shared basis.

Systems with these characteristics are becoming more prevalent as interactive processing spreads and as the software tools become available. Some decision-support systems are created by means of canned models that provide many functions. Others are developed from scratch by close staff members of the managers whose decisions are to be supported—or, in some cases, by the managers themselves.

Although it is possible to use a general purpose language, such as APL, DSS can be more easily implemented by using any of several simple special-purpose languages. For example, EXPRESS is a development language used for marketing analysis applications. A language called RAMIS is suitable for data base-oriented decision support. In addition, there are several financial planning languages.

Of course, it's not in any particular software package that the DSS philosophy is realized—it's in the way the software is used.

Of all managerial tasks, strategic planning is the least amenable to the traditional computer system approach, because it is least subject to predictability, delegation, and automation. The more continuous, ongoing aspects of planning (budgeting, capital investment analyses, and forecasting) are obvious candidates for decision-support applications. But perhaps the most spectacular use of a DSS is in a quick-turnaround, ad hoc situation. Here is a case in point. [2]

Houston Oil and Mineral Corp. was interested in a proposed joint venture with a petrochemicals company, with respect to developing a chemical plant. The executive vice president responsible for the decision wanted a Monte Carlo analysis of the risks involved in the variables of supply, demand, and price. David Simpson, manager of planning and administration, and his staff built a DSS model in a few days by means of a planning language. The results strongly suggested the project should be accepted.

Up to this point, any traditional simulation model might well have been adequate for providing answers to the expressed problem. The genuine decision-support capabilities of the model were mainly latent. They were reflected principally in the speed with which the problem statement was translated into a model the executive vp could readily understand and trust.

Then came the real test. Although the executive vp accepted the validity and value of the results, he was worried about the potential downside risk of the project—the chance of a catastrophic outcome. As Simpson tells it, his words were something like this: "I would like to see this in a different light. But I realize the amount of work you have already done, and I am 99% confident with it. I know we are short on time and we have to get back to our partners with our yes or no decision."

In short, Simpson replied that the executive vp could have the risk analysis he needed in less than an hour's time. Simpson concludes, "Within 20 minutes, there in the executive boardroom, we were reviewing the results of his 'what-if?' questions. Those results led to the eventual *dismissal* of the project which we otherwise would probably have accepted."

This was decision support in action. The particular situation is one that occurs again and again in top-level decision-making. The process began with what was really a first cut, based on the decision-maker's best initial definition of what was needed. The executive vp then responded to the results—his judgment alerted him to the need for additional analysis, so that the model needed to be modified, and *quickly*. In a sense, the first model—the one he asked for—was either incomplete or incorrect. It performed well, but the executive vp's broader sense of the situation told him something was wrong—even though he did not realize that the computer tools at hand were flexible and responsive enough to allow this result of his own learning to be followed up. In the end, he was using the system as an extension of his own mind.

In this and countless other specific applications for which decision-support systems are being created, one sees the necessary capabilities we listed earlier—reflection of the way managers think, flexibility, and ease of use, exploration, and evolution. The importance of these features is apparent in studies of DSS development and use.[3] Without them true DSS is impossible.

LANGUAGES FOR DECISION SUPPORT

The foregoing example may leave some people incredulous. In such a short time, how can a thorough risk analysis be performed for a proposed major chemical plant? How can all the judgment factors be elicited, quantified, and worked into a model? How can the results be presented meaningfully and convincingly to the manager? And how could a worthwhile model for such an undertaking be created and validated as quickly as it was in the first place?

To provide an idea of how these things—and more—are being done, we should study the planning language used for such applications.

Although a planning language is often used in systems supporting a wide range of managerial activities, its basic design reflects its original purpose—corporate planning by the use of models for simulation purposes. It allows a user—often without prior programming expertise —to set up a model that operates on a rectangular array of numbers. The numbers represent characteristics of a business entity over a series of time periods. The model consists of mathematical formulas or relationships for calculating the numbers of the array. These formulas are specified so as to stimulate the behavior of the entity as time passes. In operating the model, certain numbers in the array are provided and the remaining numbers are automatically calculated.

The commands that comprise some of these languages are easy to learn and use, and each command is powerful in terms of the results. To this end, the commands often resemble familiar business terminology and may be phrased with a great deal of latitude. Moreover, these languages allow highly nonprocedural descriptions of the problems, in that the user may key in a model's characteristics in whatever order he thinks of them. The system, in turn, comes up with a specific procedure (invisible to the user) for getting the desired results.

Because of these features—and because the language use is interactive —models may be built, modified, and applied quickly. Simple models can be created in a few minutes; complex ones rarely take more than a few days. A modification can be made in a few seconds, and the new results obtained a few seconds later.

Other features of planning languages vary widely, but a few of the more important ones may be named. A "what-if?" command allows the results of changed conditions to be revealed quickly, without losing the original base case. A "goal-seeking" or "reverse what-if" command similarly calculates the change that would be required in one variable to produce specified results in another variable.

Besides the expected sort of algebraic and trigonometric functions, a number of sophisticated mathematical techniques are usually provided. For example, there is often a choice of several types of curve-fitting for smoothing and extrapolation of data. There are logic-condition expressions of the "if . . . then . . . else" type. Routines are often provided for standard business purposes such as net present value, depreciation, and so forth. Functions may sometimes be specified in terms of interpolation along straight segments between given points. Sometimes the user is able to define his own subroutines and functions in various programming languages such as FORTRAN and incorporate them into the model.

A STUDY OF DECISION-MAKERS

From 1970 to 1974, a research group at IBM in San Jose developed one of the first decision-support systems. The project centered around a system for geographic allocation of resources and people, and was used both by IBM, to determine, for example, how many reps to put where, when, and how, and by customers, on a test basis. IBM provided the software free—and temporarily— while the customer paid operational costs and provided the data.

One of the most impressive aspects of the General Analysis and Display System—GADS, as it was known—was its proven flexibility. Over 200 people at 17 different organizations used the same version of GADS. And none of them were computer experts.

IBM learned a great deal about end-user problem solving from the GADS project. For one thing, the way organizations do business is very likely to change once automation begins to be applied to decision-making. Behavorial studies of the manager and the organization thus become newly important.

For another thing, the nature of decision-making itself presented a serious design problem for which traditional systems analysis isn't really very well suited. The user interface is one of the least mature aspects of system design.

Also, in order to attack the business user market, the nature of the business would have to be examined. The most obvious finding IBM made along these lines was that decision-making is almost entirely unstructured. Managers don't really know how they make decisions, and, on top of that, they don't want to reveal the details of decision-making of which they *are* aware, as these tend to be important specifics.

IBM's DSS research group decided it was necessary to start with the assumption that they didn't know what was needed, and then piece together the answer from the clues. They got the clues by asking simple questions of decision-makers. "What do you look at when you are making a decision?" "What do you need to have on hand?" "How do you manipulate these tools?" "What are the standard operating procedures you have that you know you want to keep?"

With the answers to these questions, the research group came up with a set of variables that made sense for use in a decision-support system. The success of GADS was probably due to the wisdom of this simple analysis.

The significance of the user interface lent weight to two more research directions for IBM. Having discovered that the nonprogrammer user wants a completely interactive system, the importance of a menu-driven system with good display capabilities became obvious. Neither the hardware nor the software available were geared to these characteristics. IBM realized that it was going to have to design a system to really involve the people. Improving the user interface would need a better terminal.

It was also going to require a better language. In an interactive program, screen management—putting up the option or the information, manipulating it, taking it down, and quite possibly keeping it handy for later use—takes up much of the code, about 60%. Because IBM believes the major new applications will be interactive, research is being done on a language discipline tailored to the heavy use of the display. What is needed is a language that goes beyond the subroutine—coroutines make more sense when a lot of information needs remembering (and only ALGOL and one version of PASCAL use coroutines).

Another important aspect of decision-making surfaced in IBM's examination of its successful research effort. The final ingredient of decision-making is communication. The social acceptance involved in presenting a decision or solution and the feedback generated from those people the decision involves must be considered part of the process.

Sarah Rolph

Some planning languages allow variables to be specified probabilistically, using a choice of several intuitive formats including normal, triangular, and uniform random distributions. Deterministic values may often be called from a probabilistically specified variable in terms of high, low, mean, or most probable. At least one language allows a Monte Carlo solution for specified variables, based on probabilistic inputs. That is, the probabilities of various outcomes of a particular scenario can be calculated.

Arrays of data may usually be stored apart from the actual models (the numerical framework and formulas). Such arrays are created as outputs of models or called from storage as inputs. Arrays (data files) resulting from several different models may in some cases be consolidated—as for various divisions of a company—either by simple addition of corresponding entries or with the inclusion of weighting or post-consolidation processing.

Finally, the contents of many of the array files (say, the results from a model being investigated) may be reported in any desired arrangement of rows, columns, and headings. Report formats may be called from storage or specified as needed. As for all other capabilities of certain languages, report generation is accomplished by simple, easily remembered, English-like commands.

From this brief generic description it can be seen that the potential exists for the more sophisticated planning languages to create a system suitable for genuine decision support. Referring to our earlier list of necessary DSS capabilities, some particular instances immediately come to mind.

Familiar and flexible syntax allows models to be specified in terms of the way a particular user or manager thinks. The same may be said of intuitive expressions for probabilities and risks, and of output formats variable to suit the manager's style. Simple, powerful commands and rapid interactive processing allow the model or given data to be changed quickly and easily to adapt flexibly to new situations or assumptions.

If desired, the senior manager may put hands to the keyboard for instant feedback on various scenarios. In any event, the manager need be only one step removed from the machine—which may be a dedicated installation right in the executive suite, with no need for traditional forms of dp support. (More on dp's new role later.) Obviously, a system application built and used through a planning language can support exploration and learning by the manager with respect to the problem at hand. Furthermore, an ongoing system will readily evolve to meet inevitable changes.

USES CORRESPOND TO PHILOSOPHY

More than a potential, DSS is a recognized reality, although not necessarily by that particular name. For evidence, we turn to IFPS, one of several planning languages. The question is, "Do the actual uses of a planning language correspond to the philosophy of DSS?" The results of a recent survey of IFPS users shed a great deal of light on this question.[4]

The survey was conducted among 24 medium-to-large companies. The reported model applications covered a broad range of purposes, as diverse as predictions of long and short term financial positions, product line studies, pricing analysis, facilities planning, and contract negotiations. Table 13.1 is a summary of the responses to four questions with regard to the persons connected with each application.

From these responses, it is apparent computer power has been placed in the hands of upper and middle management. Although staff analysts are understandably heavily involved in the actual keyboard work, a significant percentage of upper-management people are actually sitting down at the terminal.

On the other hand, it would appear that so-called "data processing" personnel are almost never involved. In this category were placed sys-

TABLE 13.1 Planning Language Use Summary

		Percent of Total		
Question	Dp	Staff Analyst	Middle Management	Upper Management
Who initiates requests to build models?	0	4	30	66
Who built the model?	3	53	22	22
Who uses the output?	0	6	42	52
Who uses the terminal to ask "what-if?" questions?	0	70	21	9

TABLE 13.2 Number of Days to Build Model

1 to 5	6 to 10	11 to 15	16 to 20	Beyond 20
62%	13%	4%	6%	15%

TABLE 13.3 Benefits of IFPS

People-Oriented	Feature-Oriented
1. Easy to learn and easy to use	1. Quantify risk in a sensible manner
2. "What-if?" capability	2. Goal-seeking (reverse what-if)
3. Low hurdle entry—speed of being effective	3. Consolidation of levels of data
4. Flexibility of use	4. Sensitivity analysis
5. Complete, accurate output in a few minutes	5. Power, simplicity, and flexibility of report writing
6. Communication with management	6. Variety of functions and applications
7. Model itself readable in English	7. Simultaneous equations
8. Ability to respond quickly to user requests	8. Quick updates
9. Decision-makers can easily build own models	9. FORTRAN user interfaces

tems analysts and programmers. As we will see later, this finding need not imply that the dp function and organization drops out of the picture when DSS comes in.

Table 13.2 shows the responses with regard to the number of days required to build each model.

Bearing in mind that the models reported were real-life and moderately complex, it may seem startling that the majority were created in five days or less. Five days would correspond to a cost (principally the employee's time) of perhaps $2,300. That is the sort of performance to be expected of a true DSS.

The respondents were asked to describe the most important "people-oriented" benefits and the most important "feature-oriented" benefits of the language. Table 13.3 is a partial rank-ordered summary according to the number of times various classes of benefits were mentioned.

These responses could be analyzed and categorized, but it takes only a cursory inspection to recognize echoes of DSS philosophy as we described it earlier. Leaping from the page are capabilities such as those we have been reiterating: flexibility, turnaround and responsiveness, meshing with managers' decision processes, and communicability. It is apparent managers not only want these attributes in a computer-based system, but that they are also getting them in the form of what we are calling decision-support systems.

A CLASSICAL DSS CASE STUDY

These findings are borne out in greater detail by a case study of the development and use of a set of models based on IFPS. The object was to develop a detailed proposal for a major new production plant for L.D. Shreiber Cheese Company of Green Bay, Wis. The proposal had to be accompanied by all the appropriate supporting information and by a list of feasible, if less desirable, alternatives. Variables included not only an uncertain sales volume forecast but also the configuration and flow pattern of the various equipment and peripheral facilities. The proposal was assigned to a team consisting of the prospective plant manager and various subordinate managers experienced in several fields.

The problems faced by the plant manager and his team before they began to apply IFPS to the problem were:

1. Estimates of sales volume might be revised at any time and in any category of product, depending on marketing plans.

2. Evaluation of any one alternative involved complex and largely manual calculations by each team member on the subject relevant to his own line responsibility. The calculations were called, appropriately enough, "homework." Meetings were needed to interpret the results and send them to top management.

3. The ground rules for the homework kept changing, so that previous analyses and data might become valueless.

4. Top management, who evaluated the succession of proposals that flowed from the team, were evolving their own criteria for acceptance, primarily in response to the stream of proposals.

In the published account, this situation was described as a classical problem. All growing companies involved in manufacturing have it, "... and some companies have it chronically because they are so successful." This is natural territory for DSS.

After a considerable amount of proposal development work had been done, IFPS was used to develop a family of models which became known as GYMJAC. Even though it was not characterized as such, it was a picture-book DSS. This fact is reflected in the explicit design criteria for the system, which emphasized that using computers and models must be a natural extension of a manager's normal methods for framing and exploring decision problems, and the system must be able to cope with a manager's need to change levels of sophistication in framing decisions.

CLEARING AWAY ACADEMIC DEBRIS

When a decision-support system is applied to the planning efforts of a school system—where limited public monies must be spent selectively—the support clears away academic debris to outline a solid program of definite answers and guidelines. Often these answers indicate necessary spending or educational needs, eliminating expensive dead ends or waste.

Such a program is Project Simu-School, developed by the Dallas Independent School District under a grant from the U.S. Office of Education. Simu-School is a computerized simulation of the school planning process: its three models predict enrollment (how many schools and what types of instructional programs will be needed); faculty requirements; and financial requirements.

Simu-School was one of the original projects to be funded through the National Diffusion Network (NDN), an end-product of a government program begun in the '50s to disseminate research information and materials to educators in the local districts.

The idea for Simu-School originated with an architect, Donald F. Burr, in 1974. He and a few other architects, attending a national convention, had the idea that if they had some scientific support for the requirements of the educational facilities they were planning, much time could be saved and unnecessary waste avoided. Over $10,000 in seed money was granted to see if such a project was feasible. It was—and in 1971, the first Simu-School Project began in Chicago, followed by others in Santa Clara County, Calif.; Ohio State Univ.; Washington State Univ.; and the Dallas Independent School District. Only the Dallas project survived. As part of NDN, it has been validated by the U.S. Office of Education as a sound, effective approach to educational decision-making, and has been made available to the 16,-000 school districts throughout the country.

The basic packages—enrollment and facilities projection (an interactive program written in COBOL), and faculty projection and financial projection (both batch programs written in FORTRAN)—can be combined in a comprehensive planning program or used individually. A fourth program, a forecast of energy requirements, will be added to the system shortly.

The models for Simu-School were originally developed on a Burroughs 5500; the programs require at least an 80K memory. Currently, the models in Dallas are running on a Burroughs 6700, but are being adapted to a variety of systems. Supporting programs for data entry and file updates are unique to each individual district.

As examples of how Simu-School has worked in real situations: in the Terrell Independent School District, near Dallas, an enrollment of 3,300 students was an unexpected, rapid growth. When a school bond issue passed, no one was certain precisely how to spend the money: How many schools did they need? Where should they build them? The enrollment and facilities model was fed historical data, current information, and some assumptions on the trends in the district. The model, forecasting needs over a 10-year period, provided statistics directing the construction of one new junior high school and the addition of several portable classrooms at other locations.

In Palo Alto, Calif., the district faced declining enrollment and a corresponding decrease in revenue. Using the faculty projection model, the educational planners were able to determine how many teachers were needed as a result of fewer students, and what specializations were needed as indicated by trends in student course selection.

In Dallas, the financial model's reports won a triple-A rating for a school construction bond issue.

School districts without computer systems for the Simu-School terminal to tie into can participate with other schools in an ad hoc consortium, or tie in with a regional service center. Texas, for example, has 20 regional school districts sharing five computer systems. Minnesota has a single system for the entire state—the Minnesota Educational Computing Consortium—which any school district in the state may join. A third alternative would be for a district to purchase a microcomputer in the $10K to $20K range to ensure the minimum system requirements for a single package are present.

Participation in Simu-School is described by its assistant project director, Jane Richardson, as "a snap." After several initial discussions and explanations, a user guide and a technical demonstration are provided for the interested district's staff. Once an adoption agreement is signed, the new district sends a scratch tape to Dallas, and the model is duplicated and returned to the district for implementation.

Richardson envisions a busy future for Simu-School, including the formation of users' groups, program sharing, computer planning conventions specifically for the educational field, and maybe, she adds, "We might even see every school superintendent with his or her own computer—either a time-sharing terminal or a microcomputer—on the desk."

William Pohl

The costs involved in completing the proposal to the point of acceptance are so unbelievable that we quote directly from the published account:

> The original family of models, MODs 1 to 9, was developed and put on-stream for about $4,000. Three-fourths of this amount derives from the time spent by the plant manager and one technician collaborating to develop the initial sets of variables and functions. The work required to build and test the modular hierarchy and scheme out MODs 10 and 11 was done for another $800. The operating costs over the nine months of GYMJAC activity totalled $5,800. About $3,000 of this amount went to time-sharing costs; the rest was the cost of labor at the computer keyboard terminal. Based upon pre-GYMJAC experience with manual homeworking, the same basic information would have cost over $300,000 to generate. However, we must point out that Monte Carlo style simulation and risk analysis are virtually impossible by hand.

The real user of GYMJAC was, of course, top management—through the intermediation of the proposal team. A major benefit expressed by the participants was improved communication between these two parties. Analysis was easier to understand and explain. Management had confidence in the results.

We may conclude that DSS is not only possible but has often been made a practical reality, recognized as valuable by top management. But what are the implications of this for the people who may be involved in such a process? This question may well be more significant than any other.

For the manager, the implication is not that he has an automatic machine that sits on his desk and cranks out decisions. A DSS is not the raven on Odin's shoulder whispering oracles in his ear. After all is said and done, the manager is still the source of the decisions. The DSS *supports* him in this process as a figurative extension of his own mind —as a tool that, like any other, must be properly used to be effective. It is not a fully automatic tool.

Here we begin to shade into the implications of DSS for the manager's close subordinates—the staff planners or analysts. It is really these people and not the DSS that constitute the top manager's mind support system. Far from competing with them, a capability for creating and operating decision-support systems augments their power in supporting the manager's decisions. In the words of a company president, "The human expertise that already existed within the company was amplified." As exemplified by the case of David Simpson's 20-minute risk analysis, a DSS tends to make the staff heroes.

What about the remaining people who have been traditionally involved with computers and their applications—the ones we earlier labeled as dp, MIS, and OR/MS? One might think—especially after noting the IFPS users' survey—that the new, easy-to-use development languages will leave them out entirely. But the fact is that DSS and the languages used can help these people make their products and services more complete. The technical specialists can work—almost for the first time—from the user's view of the world. They can become indispensible instead of peripheral to managers' activities and can move off the defensive. Like the staff analysts, they can become heroes.

This is written not in reassurance but in challenge. For dp, MIS, OR/MS, and related analytic disciplines, the urgent need is to bridge the gap between their specialized world and the manager's. Decision support exploits existing computer technology to meet the needs of decision-makers. As such, it is the basis for a refreshingly positive answer to the question, "What do managers *use* computers for?"

REFERENCES

[1] Mintzberg, H., *The Nature of Managerial Work*. New York: Harper & Row, 1973.

[2] Simpson, David J., "Making Business Models Easy To Use," Transcript of Panel Presentation of 1979 National Computer Conference, New York City, June 1979.

[3] Keen, P.G.W. and Morton, M.S. Scott, *Decision Support Systems: An Organizational Perspective*. Reading, Mass.: Addison-Wesley, 1978.

[4] Wagner, G.R., "Enhancing Creativity in Strategic Planning Through Computer Systems," *Managerial Planning*, July-August 1979.

14

The Evolving Roles of Models in Decision Support Systems

by Robert H. Bonczek, Clyde W. Holsapple, and Andrew B. Whinstone

INTRODUCTION

Although the management information systems (MIS) field generally implies computer-based systems for the storage, updating, and retrieval of information, where the retrieval is typically for a number of predetermined reports, there are alternative views as to what the MIS field entails.[16] More recently, the term decision support systems (DSS) has been used to refer to the expanding notions (vis-a-vis MIS) about what computer-based systems can or should be capable of doing.

Departing from the production of predetermined reports, the trend is toward systems that have more flexibility in the reports that can be produced. Due to the relatively unstructured nature of some decisions, neither the variety of reports needed to support an organization's decisions nor the order or frequency with which reports are desired are always known a priori (i.e., at the time of system design). The decision maker's interaction with computer-stored data can be exploratory [3] [4] [14] rather than being restricted to the repetitive and routine.

Another extension to the MIS notion further distinguishing DSS from systems that store, update, and retrieve data is their computational

Reprinted with permission from Decision Sciences

modeling capabilities. That is, a user's request for information may entail the interfacing of data with a computational model(s). The interfaces between user, models, and data are focal points of this article.

There is, however, no clear-cut line between MIS and DSS. A management information system, in furnishing a set of predefined reports, provides support for decision processes. Conversely, a system with flexible report generation capabilities and computational modeling capabilities furnishes information for management. A fairly broad view of DSS is developed in this presentation. The term "DSS" is used here to emphasize the relative newness of some of the ideas being considered.

The view of decision support systems expounded here is consistent with the DSS perspective offered by Keen and Morton: the "... key point for a DSS is to support or enhance the manager's decision making ability," and DSS "... shifts attention from the level of operations (an information system for job order status or accounts receivable) toward the issues of managerial problem solving".[16, pp. 57-58] (For more detailed discussions of the DSS field and its relationship to decision making see [16].)

Following a few brief observations on the incorporation of models into systems for decision support, the three major interfaces within a decision support system are examined. The importance of these interfaces is illustrated in a survey of several representative decision support systems containing computational models as integral components. This survey serves to indicate various usages of models within systems to provide enhanced, more facile decision support. The three interfaces lead us to a DSS classification scheme based upon the nature of interfacing languages. The scheme can be used as a framework for the study of existing decision support systems and for the development of new decision support systems.

THE INCORPORATION OF MODELS INTO SYSTEMS

Surveys [11] [18] have documented a marked growth in the use of corporate modeling in the past decade. These models, used as aids to planning activities, range from limited modeling to comprehensive modeling.[18] The development of computer-based modeling can be traced from an early stage characterized by a long communication chain between the decision maker and the computer, a concentration on operational control problems, and primitive data-handling methods.

Developments in the management science and information systems fields have led to the present recognition of the importance of incorporating extensive data-handling capabilities and models into a single system with which decision makers can directly communicate. Thus, the trend has been away from fragmented views of decision support, towards a workable integration of the two decision support functions of data handling and modeling. For instance, the Xerox corporate planning system described below integrates the retrieval of financial information and the use of models within a single system.

DSS INTERFACES AND MODEL USAGE

Most corporate planning models involve a financial simulation that allows the exploration of impacts of alternative plans. A modular approach to model development facilities later extensions and modifications to the model. We define a module as a model capable of being used in some configuration with other modules in order to form a larger or more comprehensive model; a module is always a model, and a model may or may not be used as a module.

Development of a corporate model is, however, only one prerequisite to the effective usage of models in planning process; another is software support of the various DSS interfaces. These include the user-model interface, the model-data interface, and the user-data interface (Figure 14.1). This interface framework for DSS suggests an approach for investigating various decision support systems. Faced with a particular decision support system we may begin to understand it (and its relationship to other decision support systems) by asking what language(s) is (are) used to accomplish each interface? Many descriptions of particular decision support systems in the literature do not fully explain one or more of these interfaces. Usage of the interface framework by DSS researchers and documentors should help to avoid the often underdeveloped treatment of such important DSS aspects as man-machine interactions. Later we present a DSS classification scheme based upon languages for interfacing with a system's data, and upon languages for interfacing with a system's models.

The predominant style of using models developed by the management scientist has been one of an ad hoc, fragmented nature. Sprague and Watson [21] have noted that models developed by the management scientist frequently fall into disuse because insufficient attention

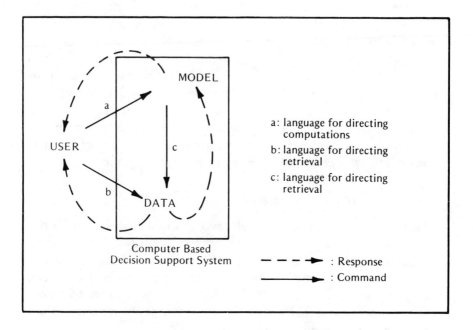

FIGURE 14.1 Crucial Interfaces in a Decision Support System

has been given to data sources and to the utilization of a model's outputs. The focus has been upon the models rather than upon the overall decision processes that potentially use the models.

Sprague and Watson [21] have observed that the principal problems are threefold. First, models are not easily combined. They are not developed as modules that can be combined to form other models as the need arises. Thus there is a lack of flexibility in dealing with new, unanticipated problems. Second, there is not an established data base that a model can use. Data must be repeatedly recollected and reorganized for each run of the model. A third problem is updating a model and modifying its uses.

Sprague and Watson [21] describe a new approach to handling data models that is beginning to be realized in practice. It is characterized by easily accessible models, mechanisms that permit models to be linked to form larger models, and the ability of models to draw the majority of their data needs from a data base. An important research issue is the discovery of systematic, general, and conceptually sound methods for addressing these points.

The design criteria for a decision support system, as proposed in [22], are:

- A set of models (modules) to support decisions in a variety of functional areas and at a variety of managerial levels.

- Models devised as modules that can stand alone or be used in conjunction with one another to form more expansive models.

- A mechanism whereby models extract data from a data base. A model, then, is a user of the data base and must have available some language to direct information retrieval (Figure 14.1, arrow c).

- A command language allowing convenient, direct access to the data base (Figure 14.1, arrow b) and allowing execution of available models (Figure 14.1, arrow a).

- Flexibility in modifying the procedural knowledge inherent in available models and in modifying ways in which modules can be used, permitting the system's modeling capabilities to evolve. The emerging perspective is one in which models are viewed as users of a common data base, where a given parcel of information may be used by several models. The decision maker is a user of both models and the data base.

With this background we now summarize the salient aspects of several representative computer-based systems that have been developed to aid decision makers. A common element to these systems is that all incorporate modeling capabilities in addition to more mundane data handling. For most, the degree of model formulation [4] is not particularly high. That is, the systems themselves do not formulate models, but they do make models available. Nevertheless, the inclusion of models into a system is but a step away from systems that do formulate models.

Descriptions of the systems are ordered to roughly reflect increasing sophistication and flexibility. The first two systems described are primitive decision support systems. It may be argued that they do not fit into the DSS category since neither one by itself is typically used to provide direct support to high-level decision makers. Nevertheless, they do fit into the broad view of DSS and may be regarded as forerunners of systems that can support higher-level decision making.

COMPUTER SUPPORT OF PROJECT MANAGEMENT

Computer support of project management is particularly applicable where the project's actions and events are numerous and where there is simultaneous management of several projects. The decisions supported are those that must be made in the course of project management. The multitude of computer-based systems (see, for example, [1]) for supporting project management have as common elements a data storage and handling system and a model based upon some PERT method.

Data storage and handling are specifically oriented towards treatment of the activity-event networks that comprise a project. The activity-event planning model is tied to the data storage and handling mechanisms in order to input the latest project status for analysis. Thus, computer systems to assist project management are usually highly specialized, addressing a very narrow aspect of corporate decision activities. Consult [1] and [13] for an enumeration of capabilities of various software packages.

The most important points concerning project management systems are:

- The successful utilization of management science and computer science to implement a decision support system.

- The very specialized nature of the resultant decision support system.

- The inflexibility of model usage.

The system is typically not designed to allow data sharing among models nor to treat a model as a module for use in tandem with other modules to build a model of broader scope. The same characteristics hold for other specialized decision support systems, such as material requirements planning systems (e.g., [15]).

Specialized decision support systems are practical and valuable within their narrow domains. It must be realized, however, that higher-level (e.g., strategic) decision making often cuts across (or encompasses) various functional levels. Development of decision support systems for higher-level management could reasonably be expected to model across functional lines and to require data from various functional areas. This is precisely the trend that can be observed in the evolution of decision support systems, as illustrated in the Potlatch and banking systems described shortly.

The evolution of information storage and retrieval systems has undergone a progression from situations of fragmented information storage with data in many places and in many forms, to increasingly unified and coordinated treatments of data. The same can be said of the treatment of modeling knowledge. Rather than numerous models, each dealing with a narrow functional area, there is a trend in management science and normative economics towards models that cut across functional areas and that encompass and coordinate model fragments (see [18]).

The trend from fragmentation to intergration is also seen in decision support systems. Instead of several independent, narrowly oriented decision support systems within an organization, the emerging pattern is one of decision support systems that can deal with a much broader domain of problems. Although these systems can cope with a much wider and more global class of problems, they are still specialized to the peculiarities of the type of organization within which they are used.

SPSS

The SPSS system [19] exemplifies another type of primitive decision support system. A collection of strictly independent statistical models is at the SPSS user's disposal; the user may invoke any model by simply stating its name. Data inputs to the invoked model are supplied from a file(s) of data that is maintained by the user. SPSS has no built-in data files. The user must indicate what data should be extracted from a file for input when stating the model to be executed.

As a system for decision support, SPSS differs in character from the project management (and inventory management, etc.) systems in that it may be used to support decision making in many functional areas. It may be viewed as a sort of "utility" decision support system. This support of many kinds of decision makers is directly attributable to the nature and widespread applicability of statistical models.

POTLATCH FORESTS, INC.

The Potlatch system described here is of 1970 vintage and is representative of early decision support systems. A more extensive description is given in [6]. This interactive system was used to support planning activities of Potlatch. It consists of a collection of data files and a large program that we shall call the "system program." The system program serves as an interface between a corporate planner and the data files. A set of assumptions, stated by the corporate planner, serves as input to the system program which proceeds to access data files in the process of generating projections. These system program outputs or projections are returned to the planner to be factored into a decision process.

A large portion of the system program consists of models of the Potlatch operations in the form of computer programs. On the basis of user-stated assumptions and stored data, the models can be executed to generate projections of the company's future position. Just as operations within the company are interrelated, so are the models. The entire set of interrelated models embedded within the system program result in the system's ability to generate many types of projection reports. The types of reports that can be generated are determined by the models incorporated into the system program. Finally, the system program has facilities for the maintenance of data files.

The important points that this system illustrates are:

- Incorporating models and data handling into a unified system.
- The interrelated nature of models mirroring the interrelated information processing roles in an organization.[4]

Other systems of the Potlatch type are surveyed in [6] and [7].

A DECISION SUPPORT SYSTEM FOR BANKS

The banking system [23] is a *conceptualization* of possible DSS features. It has three primary subsystems: a data base, decision models, and a decision maker. The available models may be be categorized as supporting strategic planning, managerial control, or operational control. Modules of code called "model building blocks" are used by the system designers in constructing these models. The models are constructed when the system is designed and are not constructed by the decision support system. The system's operations are directed with a "command language." It plays a dual role, allowing the decision maker to retrieve data from the data base and to request that some model be executed (Figure 14.1, arrows a and b).

The emphasis in this decision support system for banks is upon the decision models, integrated into a subsystem in which some models use other models. For instance, a strategic model could encompass the code of tactical models. But each tactical model can also be used on a stand-alone basis. Designers of this integrated decision model subsystem draw upon a pool of "model building blocks" in the process of specifying and coding those decision models to be invoked by a decision maker.

Each model requires certain types of data files as inputs. These are extracted from the data base. The needed retrieval procedure may be explicitly specified within a model, or the model might invoke input reports (i.e., execute predefined special report generators) without specifying how they are to be generated. In the former case, model code would depend upon data-base organization. In the latter model, code would be independent of, and invariant to, data-base organization. All dependencies would be embedded in the special report generators. Yet another way of directing retrieval would be through retrieval statements to a general report generator that is independent of the particular data organization for a problem domain. The generator would depend solely upon the constructs used to define data organizations.[2]

The mechanism for integrating the various models is founded on a philosophy of system design that realizes and plans for model interactions. Model linkages are specified in the guise of data flows, indicating that an output report of one model serves as an input report to other models. The process of actually coding the integrated system of models is outlined in [23], where a "model definition language" is proposed.

The proposed banking system was designed to encompass the various functional areas of management and to support decisions at all three levels of management. Another important issue illustrated by the system is the notion of a formal model definition language. It is also indicated [23] that the command language is simple enough to permit managers to direct the system's activities without reliance upon intermediate staff. Most decision support systems are not as comprehensive as the proposed banking decision support system.

DECISION SUPPORT SYSTEM FOR CORPORATE PLANNING

The Xerox corporate planning system [20] was founded only on a philosophy that it is possible to formally and theoretically describe the management process, that resultant models can be programmed, and that a combined "man-model-machine" system can be used to make better decisions.

The model design phase of system development involved the identification and replication of existing decision processes as well as alternative processes specified by a manager. Just as in the banking example, humans (not the decision support system) are in charge of model formulation. The major results of this model design phase were:

- A preponderance of simulation models more closely reflecting managerial decision processes and more easily understood than optimization models.

- Not a single planning model, but a collection of models that can be invoked to assist planning activities and that can change over time.

The programmed models, along with an on-line data base, are the two major components of the Xerox decision support system. The data base contains data describing actual operations and financial performance, as well as data concerning plans and forecasts that are generated by the execution of models.

It is indicated [20] that data is "made accessible" to models in either of two ways. The first involves establishing the linkage between modules. The output of one module (e.g., a forecast) is organized to be directly read into "decision tables" (i.e., data files) that have been defined in another module (e.g., a simulation). Secondly, a user's invocation of a model can state assumptions under which that model is to be executed. They are inserted into the model's decision tables before execution or entered during execution.

With respect to the user-data interface (Figure 14.1, arrow b), the user retrieves data by invoking a standard report generator. As for the user-model interface (Figure 14.1, arrow c), the decision maker directs the computational process by requesting a particular model to be executed; the information produced is stored such that it is immediately available to any other model that must use this information. The user must specify the sequence of model executions desired.

Advantages of this "man-model-machine" system vis-a-vis its predecessor (a manual system) were:

- Drastic decrease in analyst time required for manipulating data and a greater accuracy in the data.
- Better-defined forecasting logic.
- Drastic reduction in the time required to generate plans.
- Internally consistent forecasts.
- Increased time for more diligent, elaborate analyses.

Models must be devised to support managers that will be using them.[12] [17] It is important that managers have both motivation and some expertise in using the models. Not only must there be the right "man" and the right "models," but there must also be the right "machine." That is, the interfacing software must be effective, flexible, and user oriented. The Xerox experience has suggested that the previously mentioned philosophy is sound, that the scientific method can be usefully applied to a business situation, and that the decision maker can play an integral role in the design, implementation, and execution of on-line corporate planning models.

CLASSIFICATION SCHEME FOR DSS

The two major uses of computers are data handling and computation. An extremely important consideration in connection with each of these is the nature of the user's interface with the computer: how a user governs the data handling (Figure 14.1, arrow b), and how computation (Figure 14.1, arrow a) is directed. As the foregoing cases suggest, examination of a decision support system should at least address the three topics of *data management, modeling* (computation management), and the *user's interface* (i.e., the user's language). In many systems these three are intertwined and interdependent. We can, however, speak of these topics independently in order to indicate the way in which each has evolved in the past quarter of a century.

The *management of data* has been greatly affected by developments in computer hardware, including secondary storage devices and increased capacities at decreasing costs. This has made it practical to maintain large volumes of readily accessible data. A consequent area of development has centered more on the content than volume of data, and it involves methods of data structuring that have capabilities of representing more complex interrelationships among various data items. A progression has occurred from simple data structures, such as those used in lists, tables, and files, to the network structuring techniques of the artificial intelligence and data base management fields.[5]

With respect to the topic of modeling, the trend is toward increasingly complex or comprehensive models. Whereas early efforts dealt with modeling one or another particular problem area within an organization, present-day emphasis is upon a coordinated modeling of several problem areas. This integration of models is necessary if support of high-level decision making is to be enhanced, since high-level decision making (e.g., strategic planning) involves many problem areas. Current research in the management field aims at the discovery of formal techniques to aid planners.[24]

We can speculate about potential impacts of computer science on development and use of integrated models. With respect to hardware, the advent of computers on a chip may foreshadow the creation of libraries of inexpensive, more efficient modules. These modules may be logically organized in a variety of ways in order to specify a variety of models, each model being logically specified in terms of chips. With respect to software, the design of integrated models from a pool of modules may benefit from the development of languages particularly suited to such an activity.[5]

Turning to the third topic, that of *user interfaces* with the computer, we can again observe the influence of hardware advances. In the early days, a manager's communication with the computer was typically indirect, being mediated by a staff that in turn submitted instructions in batch mode to the computer. With the appearance of user terminals and on-line computing, turn-around times were shortened. But it was development in the software area that brought the computer "closer" to the manager. Specifically, methods for instructing the computer evolved from machine and assembly languages to more user-oriented, higher-level languages.

Thus there appeared successively more powerful methods of automatic code generation (some of which are interactive), culminating in languages with which a nonprogrammer can communicate with the computer. Software has taken the place of staff. The area of increasingly natural and facile interface languages is one of intense investigation. Some of these languages are highly structured to address a specific application. Others are less structured and more flexible with respect to the applications that can be addressed.

A person using a language to direct (or interact with) a computer does so with the objective of performing some computation and/or some data management (see Figure 14.1). It is instructive to examine these two major aspects of user languages. Each is discussed separately, and they are then combined to provide a rough classification scheme for guiding a study of various types of decision support systems.

LANGUAGES TO DIRECT RETRIEVAL

Languages used to direct data retrieval range between two extremes. One extreme is where the user explicitly states how the data are to be retrieved. Such languages vary from those in which a knowledge of physical data organization is assumed (e.g., FORTRAN) to those that deal with logical data organization (e.g., a DML-extended FORTRAN [3]). At the other extreme are languages where the user merely states the data desired and does not need to know how the data are organized (e.g., a generalized query language for retrieval [3]). Systems that process such languages must determine the logic of how to perform the retrieval. This may not always be straightforward, for the user's statement might be ambiguous with respect to the data available.[2] Thus the system may exhibit some problem recognition [4] ability. Determination of logic is followed by generation and execution of retrieval code.

Between the two extremes are those languages in which the user invokes one of a number of report generators. The logic of how to produce each report has been worked out during the design of the language processor and the code to generate each report is an integral part of the language processor. Such languages may be flexible enough to allow conditional retrieval in preparing a given report, but the types of report producible are predefined to meet users' anticipated needs.

LANGUAGES TO DIRECT COMPUTATION

Languages used to direct numerical computations also cover a range between two extremes. At one extreme are languages with which the user explicitly specifies all computations. That is, the user builds the programmed model. These languages vary from low-level (e.g., assembly) to higher-level general purpose (e.g., FORTRAN) programming languages and procedural problem-oriented languages (e.g., GPSS). At the other extreme are those where the user merely states the problem to be solved in terms of the data desired. Here, the language processing system must determine the model logic to be used. This may entail the formulation of model logic from more primitive modular logic. Once the model logic has been formulated, the corresponding model code must be generated and executed.

Between the extremes are languages that enable the user to invoke a model by name. Such languages allow the user to execute any one of some (possibly integrated) group of preformulated, preprogrammed models. Certain options within some model may be selected by the user through parameters associated with the model name. The models available are predefined to meet the anticipated needs of the users.

The distinction between these three types of languages is illustrated by considering the problem of finding a dividend projection for 1990. At one extreme the algorithm for projecting the dividend is explicitly stated in some language. At the other extreme, there is a simple statement such as LIST DIVIDEND FOR YR = 1990; the system determines the logic for accomplishing this. Between the two extremes are languages that permit the invocation of an already programmed model (PROJECTION) by statements such as CALL PROJECTION (1990, DIVIDEND), or the more stylized PROJECT DIVIDEND FOR YR = 1990.

RETRIEVAL AND COMPUTATIONAL LANGUAGES IN A SINGLE SYSTEM

A remaining question concerns the ways in which data handling and modeling can be combined into a single system. One approach commences by noticing that one extreme of the range of data retrieval languages looks very much like the languages at one extreme of the range of computational languages. In languages of the former type the user "states the data desired." In languages of the latter type the user also states the problem to be solved in terms of "the data desired."

There is little, if any, difference in the two statements. What is different is that a computational model is evoked by statements in one type of language, whereas a data retrieval procedure is evoked by statements in the other. Thus there are several distinct ways systems could react to a user's requests for some data (i.e., some report):

- The system could be designed to contain, in an explicit form, all reports that could be requested. Response time would be very fast, but storage requirements are potentially quite vast.

- It could be designed to extract a desired report from a data base that explicitly contains all data to be used in that report (although not in the report format); this might be termed a virtual report.[3] [14] Redundancy is reduced via data-base techniques, but response time is increased.

- It could be designed to generate a desired report from a data base that may explicitly contain some data to be used in that report and a set of axioms (rules) that indicate how to infer other necessary items.[5] Inclusion of axioms in the more traditional data base effectively gives a virtual data base from which reports may be extracted. Thus the system can determine what is implied by the data base in addition to what it explicitly contains.

- It could be designed to produce the desired data by executing (and perhaps building) an appropriate model that utilizes data extracted or generated from a data base (as in the three preceding methods).

A rough indication of possible approaches to the design of systems with embedded models is given in Figure 14.2. The horizontal axis represents the range of data retrieval languages. The range of languages for directing computations is represented by the vertical axis. The two axes meet where the distinction (in terms of appearance) between the two types of languages vanishes. This is the point where the user states the problem to be solved in terms of the data desired.

For explanation ease, the quadrant of Figure 14.2 has been partitioned into nine sections. The nature of systems in each of these nine categories will be described. The lines separating these categories are somewhat fuzzy; also, there can be fairly large differences among systems within a category. These differences are partially accounted for by language attributes not addressed within the classification scheme.

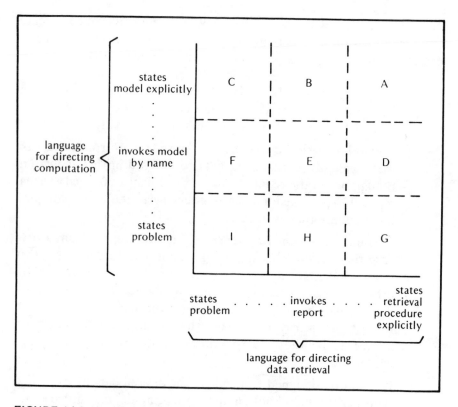

FIGURE 14.2 Classification Scheme

Examples are the nature of the grammar or syntax used and the extent
to which a language is English-like or natural from the user's viewpoint.
Such attributes could be used to augment the classification scheme,
giving it a higher dimensionality. While such issues are important, they
are beyond the scope of the present discussion.

The attribute used on the axes in Figure 14.2 might be called "procedurality." It reflects the flexibility of language in terms of the "richness" of procedures that can be used (a few simple procedures versus
many complex procedures). The dimensions also reflect how procedural a user's specification must be. So within any given category, systems may differ somewhat in terms of procedurality, and they may
also differ in terms of other language attributes such as those mentioned above.

Thus Figure 14.2 is a descriptive categorization suggesting possible ways in which the two primary uses of computers (data handling and computations) can be incorporated into a single system for the purpose of supporting decision activities. Most systems discussed in the literature are not described in sufficient detail to allow any more than a rough plot on the diagram of Figure 14.2. Systems reviewed earlier fall around the fringes of a central category.

As we examine the archetypal attributes of each category, it is also important to remember that we are considering only systems that execute models in addition to performing data retrieval (be it strict retrieval or the result of inference). Systems that do not involve execution of application models, but that deal with retrieval only, are briefly discussed later. It must be emphasized that the categorization is directed toward DSS builders and researchers rather than DSS users. The users may very well be unaware of the distinction between data handling and model handling.

Systems falling in category A require the user to explicitly specify the computational algorithm. The procedure for retrieving data required by the model must also be explicitly stated. A typical system of this category consists of a programming language, its associated compiler, and a data base. The system's user directs both the computations and data retrieval via the programming language. Depending upon the nature of the data base, some portion of the data retrieval procedure may need to be stated in a job control language.

In the FORTRAN programming language, for example, a user directs the desired computation by specifying the needed algorithm steps. If a library of modules (e.g., functions, subroutines) is available for this mode-construction process, then the system tends to fall lower in category A than systems without such libraries. The availability of such modules means that there are "submodels" that the user can invoke by name. The user, however, is still required to indicate the steps that constitute the overall model being built.

As for data-retrieval methods, these depend upon the nature of the data base being accessed. To obtain data required in the computational processes, it may be necessary to read, sort, merge, and extract from files. Where these are available as utility procedures in the language, the system is farther to the left in Category A than those systems where the user must program the sort, merge, or extraction. If an integrated data base, rather than a collection of files, is accessed, the user typically has available a group of commands for the manipulation of data in this data base. Such a system effectively extends the data-handling portion of the FORTRAN language (e.g., see [3]), so that a user can specify a procedure for retrieval from an integrated data base.

Languages in Category A run the gamut from the machine and assembly levels to "high-level" procedural languages. The most common in business applications are FORTRAN, COBOL, and PL/1. From the user's vantage point, computation and retrieval are directed from within a single language. The workings of systems in Category A may be visualized by joining the top of Figure 14.3 onto the right of the top of Figure 14.4.

Systems in Category B are accessed data by invoking a report (middle of Figure 14.3 with top of Figure 14.4). Rather than specifying how a particular set of data is to be retrieved for use by the model, the report is automatically generated. Consider for example, the extended FORTRAN language that allows integrated data base access. The systems with this language could be moved from Category A to B if all pertinent procedures for retrieval are preprogrammed and made available via subroutine calls. This approach is useful where types of reports needed are small in number and fairly stable, even though the number of models that need the data of one or more of these reports may be relatively large. The approach is limited since the need for a report differing from those producible by the predefined retrieval subroutine necessitates a return to Category A.

Systems in Category C eliminate the need for reliance upon a predefined group of report generators. At the same time they maintain the flexibility of report generation offered in Category A, but without resorting to procedural specification of retrieval processes. Such systems automatically generate code needed for retrieval in response to a statement of the desired data. Thus when the model requires some report, a statement of the data that should appear in that report suffices. There is no invocation of a special predefined report generating code, nor is there an explicit statement of how to produce the report. Such systems are especially useful where the types of reports needed by the various models being constructed are unstable, large in number, or unknown in advance of modeling. Rather than a group of special report generators, there is a single general report generation mechanism.

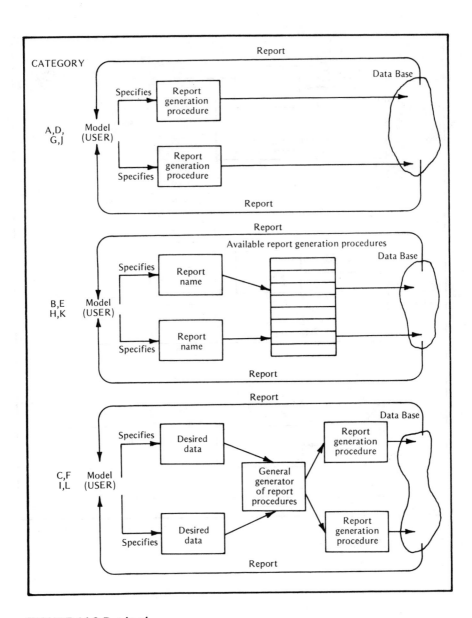

FIGURE 14.3 Retrieval

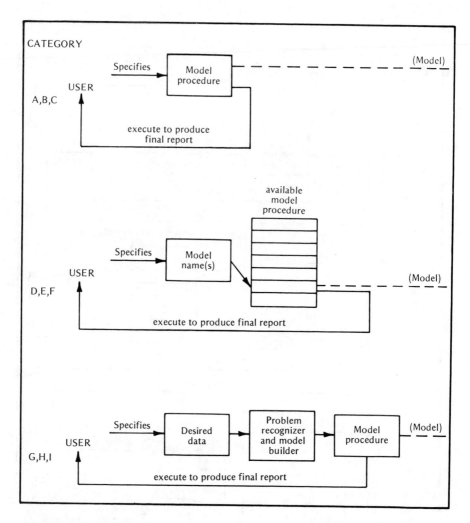

FIGURE 14.4 Computation

The distinctions among Categories A through C are the methods for directing data retrieval (top, middle, and bottom of Figure 14.3) when the model is explicitly stated (top of Figure 14.4). The same kind of distinctions hold for Categories D, E, and F. In these categories, however, computation is not directed by explicitly stating procedures (see middle of Figure 14.4). Systems in Category D enable the user to direct computations by stating a model's name; this model obtains needed data by explicitly specifying retrieval procedures. For instance, the user may invoke a simulation model by name, where the model code contains a procedural description of how to retrieve the data it requires.

In Category E, the invoked model acquires data by naming reports. Compared to that of Category D, the data retrieval language for E is less complex. It is useful in situations where reports needed by the various models are static in nature and few in number. Unlike Category D, the retrieval procedures are not intertwined with computational procedures. A predefined group of report types can be produced, each from a specialized report generator that has been preprogrammed. Several models may invoke the same report generator, and each model might call for several specialized reports.

On the boundary between Categories D and E are systems where specialized report generators are invoked, but where a resultant report contains more data than the calling model needs. In such systems the model explicitly specifies how to extract the required data. Although the specialized report generators produce excess data, they do reduce the data handling problem. Thus the problem becomes one of how to extract needed data from a few reports, rather than how to extract it from the entire body of available data.

An invoked model in systems of Category F retrieves data via language that merely states what data are desired. The processor of such a language may be viewed as a generalized report generator. Given a statement (possibly conditional) of data item types, it determines the logic for producing that report and proceeds to generate the code required to execute that retrieval logic.

In each of Categories D through F, the model may be thought of as the "user" of a language for directing data retrieval. These languages range from the procedural and flexible (D), to the nonprocedural and inflexible (E), to the nonprocedural and flexible (F). The languages

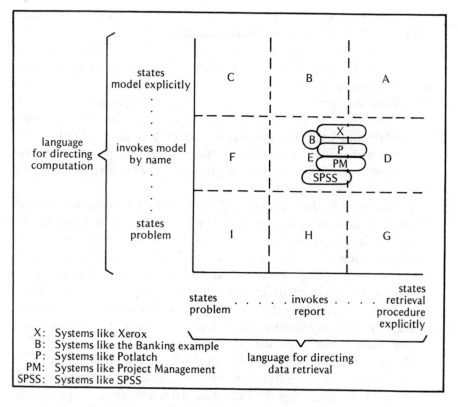

FIGURE 14.5 Approximate Decision Support System Placements

available to the user for model management in these three categories are less procedural and comparatively specialized or inflexible vis-a-vis those of Categories A through C.

This inflexibility of model management is reduced in systems of categories G through I. Here the user states a problem in terms of the data desired. On the basis of this statement, the system must determine a model (and generate its code) that can produce the desired data. The distinguishing characteristic among Categories G, H, and I is the nature of the language used by an inferred model to accomplish data retrieval. If the model code is punctuated with procedural specifications for data retrieval, then the system falls into Category G. If the model collects data by invoking one or more of a predefined group of specialized report generators, then the system is in Category H. A system in which inferred models access the data base via statements of the data types required would be in Category I.

Figure 14.5 shows roughly where systems reviewed earlier fall in the classification scheme. The state of the art in decision support has tended to move diagonally toward the "southwest." Present-day systems are in or around the fringes of Category E, whereas the earlier use of models was centered in Category A.

A SPECIAL CASE

A related special case of the system types depicted in Figure 14.2 involves those systems dealing exclusively with retrieval. Since such systems are not concerned with analytical models, they involve no notion of a language for directing computation and hence are not represented on the vertical axis in Figure 14.2. We can, however, classify these systems as shown in Figure 14.6.

Unless otherwise indicated, the term retrieval is used in a broad sense, meaning the extraction of data from some body of knowledge without intervening numerical computation. It involves the ability to collect information needed by a system's user or by the system itself. The extraction may be the reporting of data explicitly represented in the body of knowledge, or it may be a determination of data that are logically implicit in the body of knowledge. The nature of retrieval is closely related to the method chosen to represent a body of knowledge.[5]

In systems of Category J, the user states how the retrieval is to be accomplished. If the user is able to acquire any of a group of predefined report types by simply giving its name, then the system falls into Category K. Category L consists of systems that enable a user merely to state the data desired; the system then automatically generates the code required to produce the report. In Category J the user writes the report generator. In Category K, the report generator has already been written and is executed when invoked by a user. In Category L, the system automatically writes a report generator to retrieve data of the types specified by a user.

We have thus considered the horizontal axis of Figure 14.2 in isolation. Practical systems that involve modeling, but that possess no data-

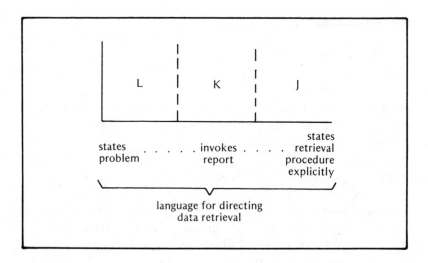

FIGURE 14.6 Classification for Systems that Treat Retrieval Only

handling capabilities, are rare and would depend upon all data having been declared in a model as a part of the model definition (perhaps with something like a FORTRAN DATA statement). Thus we shall not consider the vertical axis of Figure 14.2 in isolation; but there is an interesting correspondence between the three rows of categories in Figure 14.2 and the three categories of strictly retrieval systems described above. In Categories A, B, and C the user writes out the model in coded form. In Categories D, E, and F the model(s) has already been built and is executed when invoked by a user. In the last category row of Figure 14.2, the system automatically builds a model to retrieve data of the types specified. These descriptions should be compared to those of the preceding paragraph, and Figure 14.3 should be compared with Figure 14.4.

CONCLUSION

An important trait common to the decision support system developed in, or used by, the business community is their incorporation of models with information-handling capabilities. The significance of the user's interface with these systems has become increasingly apparent. Moreover, we saw that models themselves access the data bases of these systems, implying that *the model is a user* of the system's information-collecting abilities.

This led to a classification scheme for decision support systems in which humans used some language to direct computations. The computational model, in turn, used a language to obtain needed data from the system's data base. The "old" usage of models described in the second falls primarily in Category A.

The newer usage of models, often in conjunction with integrated data bases and exemplified by the representative systems discussed earlier, falls mainly in Category E. (For more examples of decision support systems, see [8] and [16].) The reader referring to the original literature on these systems will find that there is usually insufficient detail to determine the precise placement of these systems with respect to each other in Figure 14.2. We can say, however, that they fall largely into Category E, and possibly into D.

With regard to existing languages and software systems, the DSS field is presently centered in Category E. We can speculate that important advances in DSS software and languages may eventually come from experiences gained in artificial intelligence systems (e.g., [9], [10], and [25]). Although they do not stem from business contexts, they are useful in pointing out directions for future development of business-related decision support systems. Futhermore, the presently empty categories of the classification scheme suggest directions in which the current prevalent notions of decision support systems (Category E) can be expanded. If the DSS field has not advanced to the point of having systems in Category I, for instance, then how can this advance be made? This question should stimulate a good deal of research.

To summarize, the classification scheme is intended as an aid to the builders of decision support systems and to students and researchers in the field. It identifies the various design approaches that can be adopted by a DSS builder. It furnishes a broad perspective of DSS possibilities and, in view of the representative systems discussed, it shows where we stand today in terms of languages and system software. Finally, it hints at directions for future research in the DSS field.

[Received: March 28, 1979. Accepted: October 1, 1979.]

REFERENCES

[1] Archibald, R.D. *Managing High-Technology Programs and Projects.* New York: Wiley, 1976, pp. 204–215.

[2] Bonczek, R.H., and A.B. Whinston. "A Generalized Mapping Language for Network Data Structures." *Information Systems,* Vol. 2 (Spring 1977), pp. 171–185.

[3] Bonczek, R.H.; C.W. Holsapple; and A.B. Whinston. "Aiding Decision Makers with a Generalized Data Base Management System." *Decision Sciences*, Vol. 9 (April 1978), pp. 228–245.

[4] Bonczek, R.H.; C.W. Holsapple; and A.B. Whinston. "Computer-Based Support of Organizational Decision Making." *Decision Sciences*, Vol. 10 (April 1979), pp. 268–291.

[5] Bonczek, R.H.; C.W. Holsapple; and A.B. Whinston. "The Integration of Network Data Base Management and Problem Resolution." *Information Systems*, Vol. 4, No. 2 (1979), pp. 143–154.

[6] Boulden, J.B., and E.S. Buffa. "Corporate Models: On-line, Real-time Systems." *Harvard Business Review*, Vol. 48 (July-August 1970), pp. 65–83.

[7] Boulden, J.B., and E.S. Buffa. "A Systems Approach to Corporate Modeling." *Journal of Systems Management*, Vol. 24, No. 6 (1973), pp. 14–20.

[8] *Data Base*, Vol. 8, No. 3 (1977).

[9] Davis, R.; B. Buchanan; and E. Shortlife. "Production Rules as a Representation for a Knowledge-Based Consultation Program." *Artificial Intelligence*, Vol. 8 (1977), pp. 15–45.

[10] Fikes, R.E., and N.J. Nilsson. "STRIPS: A New Approach to the Application of Theorem Proving to Problem Solving." *Artifical Intelligence*, Vol. 2 (1971), pp. 189–208.

[11] Gershefski, G.W. "Corporate Models—The State of the Art." *Management Science*, Vol. 16, No. 6 (1970), pp. 303–321.

[12] Hammond, J.S., III. "The Roles of the Manager and Management Scientist in Successful Implementation." *Sloan Management Review*, Vol. 15, No. 2 (1974), pp. 1–24.

[13] Hansen, B.J. *Practical PERT*. Washington, D.C.: America House, 1965. Pp. 142–149.

[14] Holsapple, C.W., and A.B. Whinston. "A Decision Support System for Area-wide Water Quality Planning." *Socio-Economic Planning Sciences*, Vol. 10 (1976), pp. 265–273.

[15] IBM. *Wholesale IMPACT—Advanced Principles and Implementation Reference Manual*. GE 20-0173-1. White Plains, N.Y.: IBM, April 1971.

[16] Keen, P.G.W., and M.S. Scott Morton. *Decision Support Systems*. Reading, Mass.: Addison-Wesley, 1978. Pp. 33–59.

[17] McKenney, J.L., and P.G.W. Keen. "How Managers' Minds Work." *Harvard Business Review*, Vol. 52, No. 3 (1974), pp. 79–90.

[18] Naylor, T.H., and H. Schauland. "A Survey of Users of Corporate Planning Models." *Management Science,* Vol. 22, No. 9 (1976), pp. 927–937.

[19] Nie, N.H.; C.H. Hull; J.G. Jenkins; K. Steinbrenner; and D.H. Bent. *Statistical Package for the Social Sciences.* 2nd ed. New York: McGraw-Hill, 1975.

[20] Seaberg, R.A., and C. Seaberg. "Computer Based Decision Systems in Xerox Corporate Planning." *Management Science,* Vol. 20, No. 4 (1973), pp. 575–584.

[21] Sprague, R.H., Jr., and H.J. Watson. "MIS Concepts—Part I." *Journal of Systems Management,* Vol. 26, No. 1 (1975), pp. 34–37.

[22] Sprague, R.H., Jr., and H.J. Watson. "MIS Concepts—Part II." *Journal of Systems Management,* Vol. 26, No. 2 (1975), pp. 35–40.

[23] Sprague, R.H., Jr., and H.J. Watson. "A Decision Support System for Banks." *OMEGA,* Vol. 4, No. 6 (1976), pp. 657–671.

[24] Vancil, R.F. (ed.). *Formal Planning Systems.* Cambridge, Mass.: Harvard Business School, 1971.

[25] Van Emden, M.H. "Programming with Resolution Logic." In *Machine Intelligence,* Vol. 8. Edited by E.W. Elcock and D. Michie. New York: Halsted Press, 1977. Pp. 266–299.

15

DECISION SUPPORT SYSTEMS: Translating Analytic Techniques into Useful Tools

by Peter G. W. Keen

About the author:

Peter G. W. Keen is Associate Professor of Management Science at the Sloan School of Management, M.I.T. Dr. Keen holds the B.A. degree from Oxford University and the M.B.A. and D.B.A. degrees from the Harvard Graduate School of Business Administration.

Revolutions in technology and falling prices now make it possible to bring the computer to the user via terminals and desk-top computers. Personal systems to assist the manager must be built from the manager's perspective and must be based on a very detailed understanding of how the manager makes decisions and how the manager's organization functions. If one starts by looking at decision making and only then works back to technology, any manager can draw on a range of technical building blocks to develop systems that are usable and worth using. *Ed.*

Reprinted with permission from Sloan Management Review

Until recently, the main problems organizations faced in making use of computers were to get an adequate technology for the applications they wanted, and to learn how to manage large-scale, complex projects. As a result, many managers have come to view computers as important to the organization, but not to themselves, and as expensive and risky to be involved with.

The term "Decision Support Systems" (DSS) has been used by an increasing number of researchers and practitioners to define a very different view of computer technology and applications. DSS aims at providing access to information systems and analytic models directly to managers and challenges the assumption that computers are mainly valuable for data processing operations or the creation of standardized information systems.

The concept of Decision Support Systems began in the late 1960's, when a new technology was under development. This was time-sharing, which made the decentralized terminal a means of access to computer power and permitted a literal dialogue between system and user. Since then, the concepts and techniques of Decision Support, the end for which a DSS is the means, have been refined and extended. We now have a well-defined methodology for building systems for managers that:

1. Support them in their planning, problem solving, and judgment in tasks that cannot be routinized;

2. Permit ease of access and flexibility of use;

3. Are *personal* tools, under the individual's control and in most cases tailored to his or her modes of thinking, terminology, and activities.

The computer field has always been one of great expectations and rhapsodic promises. It is tempting for a True Believer once again to oversell a new idea. *Potentially*, DSS for the first time makes the computer an integral part of the decision-making and planning process, and provides a way for managers to get access to and really use information (instead of being buried under it, as over detailed, often irrelevant standardized reports are generated at 600 lines a minute [the 1960s], then 1,600, and now 30,000 or more). DSS also points towards a synthesis of the Management Information Systems field and Management Science.

Of course, realizing this potential is the issue. We now have substantial experience with DSS in a variety of settings and applications, so that we can demonstrate the practicality of the concept. More importantly, we also have an amazing range of technological building blocks that remove many constraints on developing useful systems quickly, cheaply, and responsively. In addition, the essential assumption underlying Decision Support is that DSS must be built from the *manager's* perspective and based on a very detailed understanding of the decision process and organizational context. This means that the application drives the technology and not, as too often before, the reverse. The available technology becomes an opportunity for *managers* to exploit, to help them in their own jobs and on their own terms.

The aim of this article is to justify these claims and give managers some guidelines for DSS development. The rest is up to the managers. The *criteria* for design must come from managers. The technical implementation depends on joint action between [1] a manager and his or her staff who accept that their insights, commitment, and involvement are essential in the development process, and [2] technical specialists who recognize that their task is to provide a service for the manager, rather than create a "state-of-the-art" product of interest to their professional peers.

TECHNOLOGICAL BUILDING BLOCKS

Over the past five years, there has been an increasing decentralization of computer resources, differentiation of software and hardware components, and diffusion of technical expertise. These trends in computer technology are of general relevance to managers.

DECENTRALIZATION

Traditionally, the computer has been kept in a centralized—and often jealously guarded—organizational location. Users go to it. Now, time-sharing, large-scale telecommunication networks, minicomputers, and (potentially at least) microcomputers bring the machine to the users. This obviously opens up whole new classes of applications.

DIFFERENTIATION

Traditionally, a computer has been a capital investment involving high fixed costs and relatively low marginal costs. There are many applications where it is still worth paying the fixed cost (of development time and managerial effort as well as dollars) to develop a system or computing facility, but organizations now have a wider range of options. The tradeoff is conceptually similar to the choice between buying and leasing; a public time-sharing utility which provides "packaged" financial planning software is expensive in terms of marginal cost but minimizes development time and setup cost. In addition, any organization can mix-and-match technical components. A front-end minicomputer can be linked to a large mainframe or, instead, a stand-alone mini purchased with intelligent terminals, CRTs, or hardcopy terminals. Explaining these jargon terms is unnecessary here. The key point is that a manager who has a clear and well-defined application can generally find a wide range of differentiated building blocks. (This is less true for software than hardware.)

This differentiation changes the whole nature of computer applications. Managers are not used to the idea that they can, within limits, develop an idea first and *then* look for the requiste technology. Effective R&D innovations in organizations are generally driven by "demand-pull" and not "technology-push"; now that this is true for computers as well, managers can play a fully active role in their use.

DIFFUSION OF EXPERTISE

The centralized computing facility of the past was a temple of worship served by a high priesthood of Delphic obscurantism. Today, even though computerese has increased to a point where the table talk of a convention of "hackers" sounds like a *Reader's Digest* version of James Joyce, there are many managers with a clear sense of what computers do and how development projects must be managed. There is also a growing supply of technical specialists with a managerial focus and business literacy. The days when the project leader for a major accounting system could wipe out his or her credibility in seconds by asking "Gee, what's a standard cost? Is that anything to do with overheads?" are passing. The main value of MBAs from the elite business schools is that they are either managerially fluent and technically literate or technically fluent and managerially literate; in either case, they can be effective implementers.

This process of decentralization, differentiation, and diffusion has begun only recently. It is important not to exaggerate its speed and impact. Nonetheless, it is now practicable for a manager with a clearly defined application, built around a simple and relatively specific task or decision, to realize it. Of course, identifying the application and providing clear and specific criteria for design are not at all easy. Too often. Big Ideas substitute for precise concepts. Being simple is very hard. It is far more appealing to come up with a grand scheme, such as an "integrated, on-line, interactive budget retrieval analysis and reporting system" (and then name it BOPSY or MEGAPLAN).

DECISION SUPPORT

Decision Support provides a means for managers to exploit this new technology—and any future developments in it. It focuses on assisting managers in tasks that cannot be routinized. It supports, rather than replaces, their judgment. The overall aim is to improve the effectiveness of their decision making. The vehicle for this is some type of interactive system that is flexible, adaptive, and under the user's control. How these objectives are translated into practice can be illustrated by a simple example from marketing management.

A brand manager must determine prices, promotion and advertising budgets, and sales force allocation for a product. Up to now, he has set advertising expenditures as a percent of the sales forecast. This is a convenient rule of thumb but obviously not the best approach, since advertising should surely influence sales.

The manager has computer reports and forecasts available, but most of his analysis is done informally. He has several years of experience in his job and feels he has a good sense of the market. He makes his decision sequentially: he determines price first, forecasts sales, and then perhaps adjusts the price and makes a new forecast. Next, he sets the advertising budget. He may make some tradeoffs between price and advertising, but on the whole he looks at only a few combinations, because he lacks the time for detailed analysis.

Brandaid is a DSS developed by J.D.C. Little to support this decision process. Conceptually, an analytic model could replace the manager's judgment and generate an optimal plan. That approach assumes the task can be structured, that with some effort parameters, constraints, and relationships can be identified and a single solution derived. It is the traditional viewpoint of Operations Research and Management Science.

The Decision Support approach argues that the decision is not structured. Parts of it can be delegated to the computer. But parts of the decision require the judgment of the manager to make qualitative

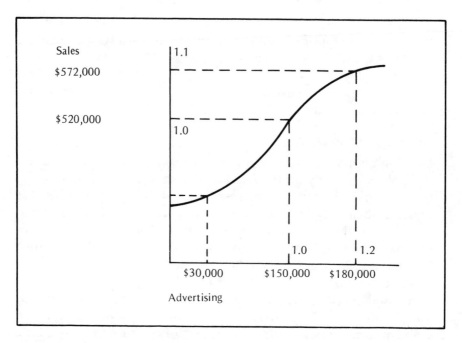

FIGURE 15.1 Response Curve for Advertising

tradeoffs and subjective assessments. For example, for a given product, there is no way of reliably identifying the relationship between advertising and sales.

Brandaid relies on the managers defining such a relationship. Figure 15.1 shows a typical "response curve." This states that for this product, the manager believes that an expenditure of $150,000 results in sales of $520,000. A 20 percent increase to $180,000 leads to a 10 percent increase in sales.

The response curve is specified by the manager with the analyst's help. It is a formalization of what may only be an intuitive concept in the manager's mind. His experience tells him that if less than $30,000 is spent, there is no consumer awareness; similarly, above $180,000 there is a saturation effect.

Response curves can be derived for advertising, promotion, sales force, and price (Figure 15.2). It is easy to represent them in computer code and then calculate the estimated sales and operating profit for, say, a price of $4.50, advertising of $135,000, promotion of $72,000, and a sales force of 15.

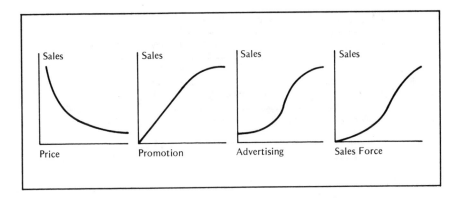

FIGURE 15.2 Response Curves for Price, Promotion, Advertising, and Sales Force

The manager's judgment is the basis for the individual assessments. In general, managers have a strong sense of the relationship between, say, price and sales, and between advertising and sales. They cannot easily, mainly for reasons of limited cognitive capacity, fit the pieces together. By contrast, a computer system can integrate them in seconds. Given the response curves, it can quickly assess a range of alternatives (see Table 15.1).

Of course, the manager may not be willing to use such a system. If it is cumbersome, unreliable, inaccessible, or hard to understand, there is no reason why he should abandon his reasonably effective rules of thumb or intuition. Building a DSS requires a variety of skills. First, and most importantly, the designer must understand the manager's decision process. The reason for using response curves as the basis for the system is that they make sense to the manager, who thinks in terms of a "reference point" (the $150,000 in Figure 15.1) and incremental changes (± 10 percent). A key assumption in Decision Supports is that one cannot help improve a process one does not understand. Brandaid was built by a *marketing* expert working with marketing managers. The key questions that must be resolved before any DSS can be built are:

1. What is the decision or task?

2. How does the manager carry it out?

3. What information does he or she use? In what way?

4. What would it mean to make this process more effective?

TABLE 15.1 Alternative Sales Plans

	PLAN 1	PLAN 2	PLAN 3	PLAN 4
Price	4.50	4.75	4.50	4.35
Advertising	135,000	148,000	120,000	178,000
Promotion	72,000	81,000	91,000	49,000
Sales Force	15	15	20	17

EFFECTIVENESS

The issue of effectiveness is central. Too often, computer systems improve *efficiency* by allowing the user to do something he or she already does, but cheaper, more quickly, or more accurately. That may be valuable but it does not in itself lead to more *effective* decisions. For example, a financial planning system may generate pro forma income statements, given sales figures and margins. That saves time and effort, but will not help a manager identify the best cash management plan.

Understanding the process to be supported creates *criteria* for developing a DSS. If a manager is to make direct use of it, it must be accessible; waiting even a day while the computer center processes the run is unacceptable. Time-sharing and terminals provide access.

The DSS must also be flexible; even in this oversimplified example, the manager will not follow exactly the same sequence of analysis each time. He might, for instance, wish to analyze a base case, with a price of $4.50 and advertising of $150,000 and fine tune it by making small tradeoffs between price and advertising. If he has to go through a repetitive process for each, he may stick with the base case and ignore variants. The left column of Table 15.2 shows such a base case; the right column shows the flexible "command-driven" dialogue that most DSS now use.

From the user's perspective, the quality of the DSS largely depends on the quality of the dialogue. More importantly, extremely complex analytic methods can be made easy to use by careful design of the user-system interface. If the DSS is structured in a "modular" fashion, new

TABLE 15.2 DSS User-System Dialogue

ENTER PRICE 4.50	PRICE = 4.50
ENTER ADVERTISING 150000	ADV = 150K
ENTER PROMOTION 72000	PROM = 72K
ENTER SALES FORCE 15	SALES FORCE = 15
SUMMARY OR DETAILED REPORTS? S	FORECAST
PRINT UNIT FORECAST? Y	SALES FORECAST
.	.
.	.
.	.
PRINT PROFIT FORECAST? Y	PROFITS
	PROFIT FORECAST
.	.
ANOTHER RUN? Y	.
ENTER PRICE 4.45	.
ENTER ADVERTISING 145000	PRICE = 4.45
ENTER PROMOTION 72000	ADV = 145K
	FORECAST
.	SALES FORECAST
.	
.	PRICE = 4.40
ETC.	FORECAST
	ETC.

Note: Output from the DSS is underlined; items not underlined are those typed in by the user.

TABLE 15.3 Expanded DSS User-System Dialogue

PRICE = 4.45

SALES FORCE = 15

PROM = 72K

COMPARE ADV = 150K. 160K

FORECAST

PROFIT FORECAST

ADV =	150.000	160.000
SALES =	538.625	549.802

ETC.

commands can easily be added. The commands ought to be based on verbs: "do this." New facilities are added to the system through new commands. For example, the command COMPARE could be added to the dialogue in Table 15.2 (see Table 15.3).

Similarly, if the manager wants the ability to display results in graphical form, commands such as PLOT or HISTO (gram) may be added. Complex systems can be evolved from simple basic structures in this way but still remain easy to use.

A key aspect of Decision Support is that the commands correspond to managers' verbs. Identifying those verbs requires careful and empathic understanding of the task and the manager. Paul Berry provides an excellent illustration of this point. He describes building a system for a planner whose job involved forecasting commodity prices and stocks. The economist saw his job as one that required complex analysis and explained all the data he needed and the calculations he made. After careful listening, Berry concluded that the planner intuitively exponentially smoothed historical data. He wrote a small-scale system in which the variables were assigned names, such as PRICE, STOCK, and PURCHASES. The command SMOOTH PRICES provided exactly the support the planner needed. It is easy to extend this system to make it a vehicle for several applications (see Table 15.4).

One valuable feature of this design structure is that an analytic method can be embedded in a command that makes sense to the man-

TABLE 15.4 Use of DSS Commands to Support Manager's Actions

---

1. *Analysis:*

   REGRESS PRICES WITH STOCK. GNP, SEASON
   (multiple linear regression)
   DESCRIBE PRICES
   (descriptive statistics, such as mean, median, range)

2. *Data Retrieval:*

   SELECT IF PRICE $>$ = 28.50

3. *Data Display:*

   PLOT PRICES. STOCKS
   LIST STOCKS BY PRICE

4. *Data Manipulation:*

   COMPUTE 100 X (PRICE – MEAN PRICE) ÷ MEAN PRICE

---

ager. For example, John or Joan Jones, vice-president of Marketing, routinely forecasts sales using a linear regression model with five independent variables, graphs the model forecasts for six quarters, computes the operating profits based on the forecast, and then does a sensitivity analysis varying the forecast plus and minus 10 percent. It may be useful to consolidate the sequence of commands—REGRESS, PLOT, FORECAST, PROFITS, and COMPARE—into one—PLAN or even JONES.

This article focuses on the manager's, not the technician's perspective. The reasons for discussing the technical design of DSS in some detail in this section are:

1. Managers have the right to ask that systems provide a JONES routine; in many ways, such DSS are easier to build than the complex, large-scale reporting systems managers find less helpful to themselves.

2. A DSS can be built around the manager's verbs. It is analogous to a staff assistant. In fact, if a command cannot be translated into the type of request—and phrasing—used by the manager in assigning a task to an analyst, it is unlikely to be used and probably incorrect.

3. The manager, not the technician, can be in charge of the development process. He or she can identify the key commands and help lay out the user-system dialogue.

DECISION SUPPORT SYSTEMS

There are at least thirty DSS used in real organizations that have been described in detail in published books or articles. Very few of them are "state-of-the-art." Most of them use the structure discussed below (Figure 15.3). None of them give "the" answer, but they respect the primacy of managerial judgment. If one can automate a task, there is no need for a DSS. Conversely, however, if one tries to *replace* the manager's judgment with an analytic model in a task that lacks a clear-cut objective and measure of quality of decision, the manager will not—should not—use it. DSS support "semi-structured" tasks, in which some functions can be best handled by the system and others by the manager.

Successful applications of DSS include: portfolio management, merger and aquisition analysis, the design of police force beats, the redesign of school districts, market planning, corporate planning, manpower planning, policy analysis in state government, R&D management, product planning, media selection, and budgeting.

What all these applications have in common is a focus on helping managers. This is a far more modest goal than looking for the "optimal" solution. A major difference between the DSS approach and traditional Operations Research is that a DSS may *include* an optimization model but still rely on judgment. For instance, Holloway and Mantey built a DSS for use by school supervisors and parents in redesigning school district boundaries. The DSS included a complex multi-objective linear programming (LP) routine which identified the optimal solution given particular constraints and goals (e.g., minimize the total travel time of school children and their transfers to new schools while making sure that all school buildings are used to the same level of capacity). As far as the users were concerned, the LP was really a simulation: "If you want to minimize travel time, etc., this is the best feasible solution." They could vary the goals and constraints and override the solution: "That plan is OK but you can't have the kids from the Soreno area being split up and all sent to different districts. Why don't we try it again adding a requirement that no more than, say, 25 percent of the children in any area should be bused to a new district."

The users of this DSS were nonanalytic but had no difficulty in accepting a highly complex analytic methodology because it was em-

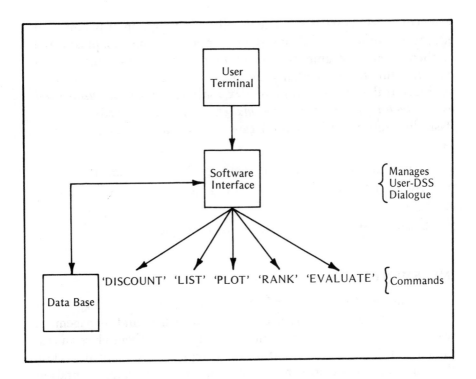

FIGURE 15.3 DSS Structure

bedded in a DSS that was under their control. They recognized the qualitative issues a formal model could not easily incorporate. At the same time they benefited from the LP; it went beyond the incremental, trial-and-error analysis they would otherwise have relied on. They could quickly check out imaginative alternatives, because:

1. The interactive, flexible structure of the DSS *encourages* questions like "what if . . . ?" or "why don't we take a look at . . . ?"

2. The DSS had been built to facilitate communication and understanding. The results of the linear program were displayed as maps on a TV-like screen.

3. The system did not impose a mode of analysis or a solution.

4. If users disagreed with the LP, they could simply change it and try again, or override it.

It is worth asking what the likelihood is that a group of parents and educators would accept a consultant's report based on "a sophisticated mathematical programming model that incorporates multi-criteria objective functions." Perhaps the most important aspect of the DSS approach is that it *translates complex analytic models into usable and useful techniques for decision makers.* This point needs stressing. Basically, any analytic method can be brought to the manager if it can be:

1. Related to his or her task and methods of problem solving;

2. Expressed in terms of the decision maker's commands to a staff assistant;

3. Made part of a dialogue between the user and the system.

IMPLEMENTATION OF DSS

DSS are not packages that can be bought off the shelf and plugged into the organization. Too often, computer specialists and management scientists have viewed their techniques as an end in themselves and assumed that design is equivalent to implementation. It is not at all clear that this approach works in any situation; effective implementation involves managing the organizational change implicit in technical innovations. For developing DSS, it is completely inadequate.

The overall implementation process for a DSS is as interactive as the tools it creates. Instead of a technical specialist building a "solution" to a managerial "problem" and then "signing off" on the "finished" system, DSS implementation iterates through the steps listed below.

THE IMPLEMENTER

A "hybrid"—a good technician with an interest in and understanding of the application (e.g., finance, planning, or marketing decision making) or, say, an MBA with solid technical skills—works with the manager to identify:

1. The specific task or decision to be supported (which narrows the application down from the planning model to supporting the capital budgeting decision process).

2. The objectives for the project. These must be defined in terms of the manager's assessment of better decision making, not the technical characteristics of the computer system.

3. The manager's current decision process. The DSS must mesh with this but also help extend it by suitable selection of analytic methods and models.

THE SOFTWARE INTERFACE

The software interface is built independent of the commands for the DSS; this handles the user-system dialogue. The manager can help evolve this if he or she can quickly be given a concrete system to interact with and respond to. The interface is the system from the manager's viewpoint and must be flexible, easy to use, reliable, reasonably self-explanatory, and responsive—just like a staff assistant. All these features can be provided by current software technology. That they are not characteristic of many "conversational" computer systems reflects the analytic specialist's general lack of awareness of any user.

DSS COMMANDS

Commands are developed. Many of these support the manager's existing verbs. Some of these are general. Virtually any DSS will include DISPLAY, GRAPH, SELECT, or REPORT. Some are specific. EVALUATE, for example, might apply a set of tests a particular financial manager uses to assess the earnings stability of a company. Some of the commands will extend the manager. SMOOTH, for instance, provides him or her with a forecasting technique based on exponential smoothing that replaces intuitive weighted averages.

DSS EVOLUTION

The DSS is evolved over time by adding new commands. The implementer's role is as an intermediary between the manager and the system. The manager may use him or her as a "chauffeur" to actually operate the DSS; while DSS are interactive, there is no assumption that the decision maker has to do the typing.

The evolutionary nature of a DSS is of central conceptual and practical importance. There can be no "final" system. In a sense, a DSS is a *base for learning,* not *solutions.* By definition, the task it supports is one where no programmed answer is available. If it is, the task does not involve decision making and ought to be delegated to a subordinate. Decision making involves dilemmas of choice and hence judgment. A well-designed DSS will stimulate learning. It encourages looking at more alternatives, experimenting, and probing. New tools create new uses. The main reason for flexibility in a DSS is that managers quickly find innovative ways of using it. New uses should also create new tools. This is why the command-based structure is so effective. The manager's learning leads to new ideas and willingness to try new methods; these are incorporated in new commands which can quickly be added to the DSS.

The key to effective implementation of DSS is simply understanding the decision process. This provides criteria for design, and without that it is hard to see how any tool can be developed which managers will choose to use. Of course, this understanding must be complemented by technical skill. DSS are almost invariably developed by extremely talented programmers and staff analysts. The importance of the software interface, the need to build commands around often complex analytic methods, and the central concern that the manager's perspective be translated into tools and vice versa, all make it essential that the builder of the DSS be far more than a computer "hacker" or "quant jock."

The availability of implementers is one of the two major constraints on DSS development. The other is the availability of managers who will commit time and effort to defining criteria for DSS design and work with the system builders to shape the tools.

THE COSTS AND IMPACT OF DSS

DSS will not save money or replace staff. The impact of DSS can be hard to assess, since they support managers and aim at helping to improve effectiveness. They facilitate but do not cause the improvement. Managers do that. In general, DSS cannot be justified in terms of costs and benefits. The benefits are often qualitative and not easily measured:

1. What is improved effectiveness?
2. How can it be recognized and a value put on it?

3. Is there a clear link between more effective decision making and better decision outcomes?

4. How much of the better outcome can be reliably ascribed to the DSS?

These questions are never easy to answer. DSS are a form of Research and Development. The real stimulus to DSS development has to be the manager's own assessment of value. If the DSS addresses a key decision or task in which improved effectiveness is important, and is designed in terms of the manager's needs and activities, it is likely that the potential value of the system will justify the investment. If there is no perceived value, *any* cost will be seen as disproportionate.

It is important to stress the R&D nature of DSS. Too often, computer specialists sell their wares as if they are guaranteed products. An innovative computer system is an invention; it cannot be defined in advance and there is always some degree of risk. No manager should get involved in a DSS venture if he or she does not view it as R&D. Innovations cannot be bought off the shelf.

Fortunately, the costs of DSS are often relatively small. By focusing on a specific decision, starting with a simple DSS that evolves with experience, and using the command-based structure, it is generally possible to deliver a system for under $20,000 in a few months. Johnson et al. estimate a cost of $12,000 to $18,000. Gambino and Keen have developed a DSS for policy analysts that includes a range of commands for data analysis, display, and retrieval for under $10,000. However, there was a prior investment of many months getting to understand how policy analysts do their job and the types of communication between analysts and policy makers. Understanding the process to be supported is essential and the direct technical costs of a DSS may be far easier to handle.

The benefits of a DSS can be hard to quantify, but not necessarily to recognize. There can also be hidden organizational costs in that it may take time and effort to embed the innovation in the organization. It can change communication patterns, the way the manager views his job and spends his time, and even the type of individual to be hired for the position. The more effective the DSS, the more likely it is to stimulate changes.

A major and often unanticipated impact of a DSS, which can be an immense benefit, is that it becomes a vehicle for communication. The following examples are typical.

PUBLIC EDUCATION

Parents and school supervisors use a DSS to explain their ideas to each other. It takes only a few minutes to generate a display, and the display requires no commentary.

PLANNING

Production and marketing planners use a DSS to work together to create a consensual plan from their two initial proposals; the DSS encourages cooperation—"let's see if we . . .," "Why don't we try . . —instead of competition. Without the DSS, it took substantial time and effort to change a plan, so that each side took fixed positions. When the marginal cost of generating another alternative is close to zero, the whole nature of the discussion shifts.

FINANCE

Portfolio managers make heavy use of a DSS in communicating the logic of their decisions and proposals to their customers: "The customer's perception of the information you're giving is much more concrete." "It's a confidence factor for the customer."

Some of the benefits of DSS are, as here, not anticipated. Of course, a DSS needs to be formally justified. Vague claims that it will lead to "better" planning are not enough. That said, in general DSS *do* seem to be of direct value to managers, often provide intangible benefits, and in many instances cost comparatively little.

CONCLUSION: FUTURE DEVELOPMENTS IN DSS

This article provides only a tentative summary of some complex research and practice in DSS development. In many ways, it does not matter if the reader completely discards its specific assertions. The central point is that managers can make effective use of computers in their own decision making. The current views of computers as limited to data processing and nonmanagerial operations are overconservative.

Similarly, the assumption by managers that most analytic models are unrealistic, abstract, and intimidating is probably correct; this does not mean they cannot be made practical, concrete, and useful. If one starts by looking at decision making and only then works back to technology, any manager can draw on a range of technical building blocks to develop systems that are usable and worth using. Usability implies some mesh with existing activities and modes of problem solving. Usefulness implies extending and adding to them.

The conceptual work in the DSS field was mainly carried out between 1970 and 1976. Scott Morton clarified the aims, Gerrity and Ness developed methodologies for design, and Keen and Scott Morton consolidated Decision Support as a field of study and rallying cry for action. All these individuals were then academics, though each has built DSS for use in the "Real World." They have made their point over and over; in the past three years, practitioners have responded to it.

There will be continuing research on DSS: current issues include developing methodologies for measuring the impact of graphics on problem solving, the use of microcomputers for Personal Support Systems, and strategies for implementing DSS. However, it is likely that the research will soon fall behind practice. Keen and Scott Morton's book on DSS includes only systems developed prior to 1976. Both authors admit that the book is now out of date. Practitioners have picked up the concept of Decision Support and used their own creativity and the resources provided by their organizations.

REFERENCES

[1] E. D. Carlson et al., "Proceedings of a Conference on Decision Support Systems," *Data Base*, Winter 1977.

[2] T. Johnson, J. Grajew, J. Tolovi, J-C. Courbon, and B. Oudet, "Cost-Benefit Analysis of and for the Evaluative Approach" (Decision Science Department Working Papers, The Wharton School, University of Pennsylvania, 1979).

[3] P. G. W. Keen, "Information Access Systems for Technology" (Paper presented to American Educational Finance Association, Washington, D.C., January 1979).

[4] P. G. W. Keen, " 'Interactive' Computer Systems for Managers: A Modest Proposal," *Sloan Management Review*, Fall 1976, pp. 1–17.

[5] P. G. W. Keen and M. S. Scott Morton, *Decision Support Systems: An Organizational Perspective* (Reading, MA: Addison-Wesley series on Decision Support, 1978).

[6] J. D. C. Little, "BRANDAID," *Operations Research* 23 (May 1975): 628–673.

[7] A. Vazsonyi, "Information Systems in Management Science: Decision Support Systems: The New Technology of Decision Making," *Interfaces*, November 1978, pp. 72–77.

16

STRATPORT: A Decision Support System for Strategic Planning

by Jean-Claude Larréché and V. Srinivasan

About the authors:

Jean-Claude Larréché is Associate Professor of Marketing, INSEAD, Fontainebleau, France.

V. Srinivasan is Professor of Marketing and Management Science, Graduate School of Business, Stanford University.

In the seventies, increasing environmental and competitive pressures have induced corporations to redefine to some extent the role of marketing in the firm. Instead of implementing the marketing philosophy mainly towards the achievement of growth objectives for individual products in a typical brand management organization, firms have given increasing importance to other factors such as profitability, market share, competition, product line management, and allocation of resources among products (see, for instance, Hopkins 1976).

Reprinted with permission from Journal of Marketing

The more strategic orientation of marketing has already been integrated, to some extent, in marketing education (Abell and Hammond 1979, Kotler 1980, Larréché and Gatignon 1977). This evolution is also reflected in the development of new marketing approaches and models to assist managers in the formulation of segmentation and positioning strategies in the context of a product line (Jackson and Shapiro 1979, Pessemier 1977, Shocker and Srinivasan 1979, Wind and Claycamp 1976). But marketing modeling has failed, so far, to assist top managers or corporate planners in the allocation of marketing resources across product lines or business units. This is reflected, in particular, by the poor quality of the marketing component in most corporate models (Larréché and Montgomery 1981). Naylor and Schauland (1976) identified close to 2,000 firms in North America and Europe that made use of some type of corporate model. Marketing modelers seem to have overlooked such wide use of corporate models.

Marketing modelers now face the challenge of adapting their efforts to the inceasing strategic orientation of marketing. The purpose of this paper is to present the result of such an effort, the STRATPORT (for STRATegic PORTfolio planning) decision support system, an on-line computerized mathematical model utilizing empirical and (managerial) judgment-based data. This system was designed to assist top managers and corporate planners in the evaluation and formulation of business portfolio strategies, and it represents both an operationalization and extension of the business portfolio analysis approaches developed in the seventies by a number of firms. This article will review and critique the main aspects of these approaches, present the basic structure of the STRATPORT model, describe a hypothetical example of its utilization, and discuss the contributions and limitations of the model in the allocation of resources among business units.

A BRIEF REVIEW OF BUSINESS PORTFOLIO
ANALYSIS APPROACHES

Following the pioneering work of General Electric in the late sixties, a number of business portfolio analysis approaches have been proposed and applied by various firms, including the Boston Consulting Group, McKinsey, Arthur D. Little, and Royal Dutch Shell (see, for instance, Hedley 1977; Robinson, Hickens, and Wade 1978). These different approaches have been compared by Boyd and Larréché (1978) and Wind and Mahajan (1981). Only their main characteristics will be reviewed here.

These approaches conceptualize the firm as a portfolio of business units and identify the major corporate strategic decision as being the allocation of resources among these business units. To aid top managers in this decision, they provide different procedures to cluster the business units into more homogeneous groups in terms of their expected contribution to the dynamic evolution of the portfolio.[1] In the Boston Consulting Group approach, relative market share and the market growth are used to classify business units as Question Marks, Stars, Cash Cows, or Dogs. In the General Electric/McKinsey approach, the business units are classified into nine groups according to company strength and industry attractiveness. The position of a given business unit on each of these dimensions is determined qualitatively from a number of market, competitive, environmental, and internal factors. The Royal Dutch Shell approach is somewhat similar although the two dimensions are called company's competitive capabilities and prospects for sector profitability, and the set of factors and their integration into these composite dimensions are also different.

The philosophy underlying these approaches is, however, similar. At a given point in time, each business unit has a specific role in the portfolio according to its short-term and long-term economic potential. This role determines the allocation of financial resources among elements of the portfolio. Minimum or maintenance investments will be made in a group of business units so that they generate a maximum cash flow in the short term. These may be business units that have a strong market position and are not vulnerable to competitive pressures, or do not represent satisfactory long-term potential. This generated cash flow allows investments in other business units, which will provide growth in the short and medium term. In the long term, these business units will, in turn, become net cash generators and will contribute to financing the growth of other units of the portfolio. The development and renewal of a balanced portfolio of business units through careful resource allocation is considered essential to the long-term survival and growth of the firm.

Business portfolio analysis approaches are being increasingly used in corporations (see, for instance, *Business Week* 1975, Kiechel 1979) for a number of reasons. They have effectively formulated the key strategic corporate decision as being the allocation of resources among business units. They provide a simple framework and language to classify business units into more homogeneous groups to facilitate this decision. From the position of a business unit on some dimensions, such as market growth and relative market share, they readily provide inferences on the cash requirements or cash generation of the business unit. These inferences are supported by past experience as well as empirical studies on cost and price dynamics (Boston Consulting Group 1972, Stobaugh and Townsend 1975) and on the relationship between market share and profitability (Buzzell, Gale, and Sultan 1975). Finally, they aid strategic thinking by graphically representing business units on two critical dimensions.

Different authors (Channon 1977, Day 1977, Wensley 1981, Wind and Mahajan 1981) have already discussed the limitations of these business portfolio approaches that stem from three main sources: the representation of the portfolio situation, the implicit relationships assumed in drawing inferences on desirable strategies, and the scope of the analysis. The representation of the current business portfolio situation involves a definition of the business units and the measurement of their position on the two dimensions considered. The analysis requires that business units should not share any cost or marketing interdependency. Implementation of the portfolio strategy, on the other hand, requires that delineation of business units should be coherent with the organizational structure of the firm. In practice, it is unlikely that all these conditions will be met simultaneously. The only safeguard available is to define business units in such a way as to minimize potential problems in analysis and implementation, and explicitly to consider the implications of the assumptions when interpreting a given portfolio strategy.

The definition of business units will also have a critical impact on the measurement of their position on the dimensions of analysis. The Boston Consulting Group approach considers two quantitative dimensions, relative market share and market growth, which can be determined based on the (difficult) definition of the relevant market and competitors for each business unit. The other approaches raise the additional issues of eliciting managerial judgments on the position of business units on qualitative factors, and of integrating these factors into composite dimensions.

Another commonly cited limitation of the business portfolio analysis approaches is the implicit relationship that they assume between the position of a business unit on the dimensions of analysis and its cash requirements or cash generation capabilities. In the Boston Consulting Group approach, cash flows are inferred from relative market share and market growth. For instance, a higher market growth is implicitly associated with a more unstable market structure and with higher marketing and production investments. A higher relative market share is implictly associated with a competitive cost advantage and higher profit margins. Combining the effects of these two factors, a business unit having a dominant posture in a high growth market will be expected to have a relatively small positive or negative cash flow, the high marketing and production investments being approximately financed by the high profit margin. These implicit relationships are generally valid and provide a basis to evaluate the overall balance of a business portfolio in a preliminary screening stage. They may, however, not hold under specific competitive and environmental conditions, and it is indeed possible to find business units that are highly profitable without enjoying a high relative market share (Hall 1980, Hamermesh, Anderson, and Harris 1978). Moreover, these implicit relationships can at best provide only an indication, but not a quantitive appraisal of the financial implications of a given portfolio strategy.

The use of these porfolio analysis approaches is also limited in practice by other aspects not given due emphasis in literature. The limitations are due to the fact that a number of important elements have been left out of the scope of the analysis. The previous approaches do not explicitly distinguish between cash flows and profits. In fact, cash flows represent constraints on the strategic options that may be adopted while profits are required to provide a satisfactory return to shareholders and to have further access to external financial sources. The previous approaches concentrate on total cash flow levels and do not explicitly distinguish between capacity, working capital, R & D, or marketing investments. As a result, they are valuable in diagnosing an existing situation but offer only an indication of the financial implications of changes in the market postures of business units. Furthermore, they center on existing business units while a long-term profit-ability of the firm may require investing in new business units (Wind and Saaty 1980, p. 648). Finally, these business portfolio analysis approaches do not explicitly consider the different financial risks in-volved in each business unit (Wind and Mahajan 1981).

The development of the STRATPORT decision support system was guided by two main considerations. The first one was to overcome some of the limitations of current business portfolio analysis approaches, especially by extending the scope of the analysis and by making ex-plicit some of the relationships on which these approaches are built. In particular, STRATPORT explicitly considers marketing, capacity and working capital investments, potential new business units, cash flows, profits, external financial resources, and financial risks. In addition, it provides an explicit specification of the relationship between changes in the market posture of a business unit and its cash flow requirements, as well as its long-term profit potential.

The second consideration in the development of STRATPORT was to provide an operationalization of the business portfolio analysis concept so that a number of alternative portfolio strategies and their underlying assumptions could be effectively investigated. In particular, STRATPORT allows:

- An integration of empirically based data with managerial judg-ments. The system may be used to study the sensitivity of out-comes to specific inputs and to guide accordingly the gathering of additional empirical data in areas where it is most valuable.

- A determination of business portfolio strategies appropriate for different financial requirements, on the basis of key quantifi-able factors.

- A rapid investigation of the robustness of a given business port-folio strategy to changes in the underlying assumptions.

The STRATPORT system does not resolve all of the limitations of the business portfolio analysis approaches. In particular, it assumes that the firm has appropriately defined its business units. Although progress is currently being made in this difficult area (Day, Shocker, and Srivastava 1979), no ideal solution will usually exist. The STRAT-

PORT system provides, however, a convenient support to test the robustness of a given portfolio strategy to alternative definitions of business units.

In addition, because of the complex and long-term nature of corporate strategy, top executives will continuously have to cope with incomplete and approximate data, imperfect knowledge of the outcome of alternative actions, uncertainties on market, competitive, and environmental dynamics, and factors that do not lend themselves to quantitative analysis. In this context, STRATPORT does not claim to determine *the* optimum business portfolio strategy. STRATPORT is a decision support system. It tries to extract relevant information from existing empirical data and managerial judgments and to integrate this information to assist decison making, while relieving corporate planners from fastidious computations. It provides a framework to investigate strategic factors and key assumptions. It identifies optimum portfolio strategies on the basis of critical quantifiable factors. Taking other qualitative considerations into account, top management may then concentrate on a more complete analysis of the proposed strategies, which may lead to the selection of a strategy or to further investigation of other alternative strategies.

AN OVERVIEW OF THE MODEL

STRATPORT is composed of a mathematical model and extensive input and output capabilities. Only the model will be described here, in the context of the portfolio planning framework represented in Figure 16.1.

At any point in time, the firm has internal cash resources from its equity and earnings required from past operations. It also has access to external financial sources. For a given dividend policy, the maximum sustainable growth that the firm may afford can be investigated from the current capital structure and an anticipation of profits and cost structure (see, for instance, Babcock 1970, Higgins 1977). The choice of a maximum substainable growth for the firm determines the maximum amount of external financial funds that it can attract. The sum of these external financial funds and of internal cash resources provide the maximum cash resources available.

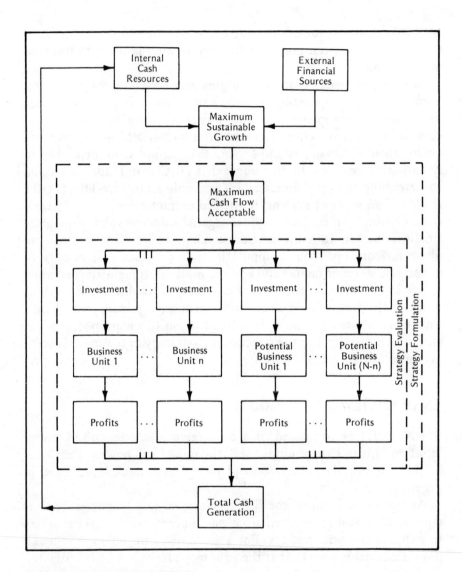

FIGURE 16.1 Overview of the Model

For a given amount of total cash resources available, the strategic portfolio problem is to determine how they should be allocated among the N business units considered in the firm's portfolio. These include ongoing operations of the firm as well as potential new business units that do not currently exist but may be either developed internally or acquired externally. The main investments considered will usually be in the areas of production capacity, working capital, marketing, and R & D. Over a certain period of time and for a given investment, a business unit will generate a level of profits and the resulting cash flow. This cash flow will affect the internal cash resources of the firm, which will in turn influence the maximum cash resources available. Thus the problem is highly dynamic.

In STRATPORT, the time horizon for the analysis is divided into two parts. The *planning period* is the one over which investments and cash constraints are explicitly considered. Marketing investments are expected to result in changes in market share and sales, which may require additional investments in the expansion of capacity and for working capital. The purpose of the *post-planning period* is to provide an evaluation of the long-term profit implication of actions taken during the planning period. For this reason, market shares are treated as if they remain constant during the post-planning period. Marketing investments are set at maintenance levels, while capacity expenditures and changes in working capital follow the evolution of sales.

The distinction between the planning and post-planning periods is illustrated in Figure 16.2 in terms of the evolution of the market share for different business units. The lengths of these two periods are chosen according to the characteristics of the industries considered and the confidence of management in the reliability of data for different time horizons. Typically, the planning period will cover from two to five years and the post-planning period from five to 15 years. The time horizon is further divided into time units typically representing quarters, semesters, or years and are the basis for representing different elements of the model.

The STRATPORT model may be used at two different levels represented by the dotted lines in Figure 16.1.

Strategy evaluation. The user of the model may evaluate a given portfolio strategy by indicating specific marketing investment levels (or, alternatively, market share objectives) for each business unit. The

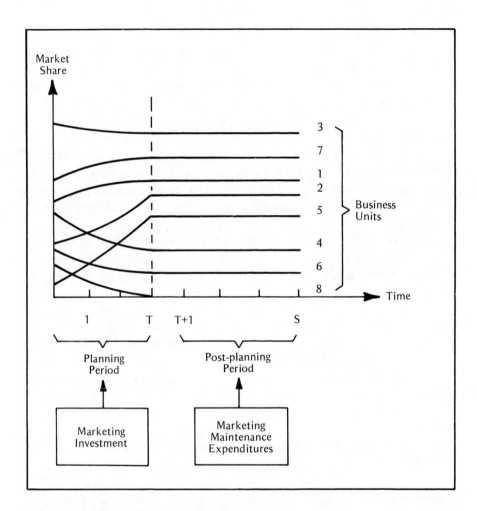

FIGURE 16.2 Planning and Post-Planning Periods

model will project for each business unit the expected market share (or marketing investment), capacity expenditures, working capital, profit, and cash flow resulting from such a strategy. Aggregation of these results over the business units provides an evaluation of the total profits over the planning and post-planning periods. The model may in particular be used in this fashion to project the long-term implications of a status quo strategy, or of incremental changes to the current strategy.

Strategy information. Given a specific cash flow requirement in the planning period, the model may be used to formulate a strategy in terms of the allocation of resources among business units that maximizes total profits over the planning and post-planning periods. The user may specify a range of values for the cash flow limit based on the maximum external financial funds available, or the maximum cash inflow that should be generated by the portfolio during the planning period. The optimum resource allocations recommended by the model may be used by the manager as a basis to formulate a portfolio strategy, taking into account factors not incorporated in the model.

Recognizing the inherent uncertainties in strategic planning, it is extremely important to analyze the sensitivity of the results of STRATPORT to changes in the data inputs. In fact, such sensitivity analyses may distinguish inputs where more accurate information is needed from inputs having relatively little impact on the results.

THE STRUCTURE OF THE STRATPORT MODEL

The core of the STRATPORT model is composed of a business unit module representing the cash flow and profit implications of a given marketing investment in a specific business unit. This module is used for both the evaluation of a specific portfolio strategy and the formulation of appropriate portfolio strategies. We will successively describe the overall structure of the business unit module, the key functional relationships in this module, and the principles of the optimization routine.[2]

OVERALL STRUCTURE OF THE BUSINESS UNIT MODULE

The structure of the model is common to all business units and is represented in Figure 16.3. The values of parameters and inputs are obviously specific to each business unit.

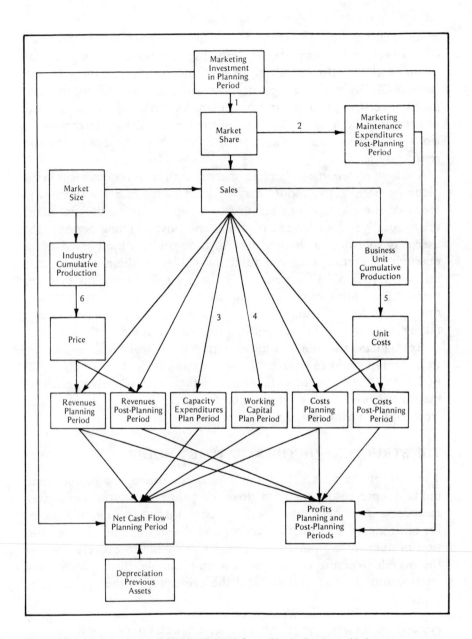

FIGURE 16.3 Structure of STRATPORT for a Single Business Unit

The marketing investment made in the business unit considered during the planning period results in an expected market share m_T for that business unit at the end of the planning period. This also determines the values for market share over the planning period and the marketing expenditures required to maintain market share in the post-planning period. The sales are obtained for each time unit by multiplying the market share by the market size. Different market growth rates for the planning and post-planning periods may be specified by the user.

At a given point in time, the market size determines the cumulative production of the industry, which influences the competitive price level for the firm. The revenues of the business unit are obtained from the sales volume and price level during each time unit. Similarly, the sales volume determines the cumulative production of the business unit at a given point in time, which influences the unit costs. The total costs of the business unit are computed directly from the sales volume and unit costs during each time unit. Finally, the sales level determines the capacity expenditures and working capital required during the planning period.

The cash flow during the planning period is computed as the after tax profits from the business unit (revenues minus costs minus marketing investments, adjusted by the appropriate tax rate), minus the portion of the increase in working capital not expensed during the planning period, minus the portion of the additional capacity investment not depreciated during the planning period, plus the depreciation during the planning period of assets acquired before the beginning of the planning period. The total after tax profits over time horizon considered are obtained from total revenues minus total costs, marketing expenditures during the post-planning period, adjusted by the appropriate tax rate.

All the financial entities in the STRATPORT model are expressed in constant dollars. Consequently, the model may be used to determine portfolio strategies that would maximize the total after tax profits in constant dollars cumulative over the planning and post-planning periods, subject to a cash flow constraint in the planning period. Although this approach may be desirable as a first step of the analysis, it does not take into account the time value of money, and thus discounted cash flows will usually be more appropriate. Consequently, the STRATPORT model allows a maximization of net present value over the planning and post-planning periods subject to a constraint on discounted cash flow during the planning period.

There is, for any given business unit, a level of risk associated with its projected profits and cash flows. To reflect this risk, the financial entities for that business unit should be discounted at a rate higher than the expected rate of return for risk free assets. Following the capital asset pricing model (see Van Horne 1980, Chapters 7 and 8), a different discounting rate can be specified in STRATPORT for each business unit to correspond to its level of systematic risk, which is the risk that cannot be avoided by diversification (Sharpe 1964). The discounting rate for a specific business unit can be estimated from the Beta coefficients published by various financial services for corporations operating in closely related industries (see Larréché and Srinivasan 1981 for details). The STRATPORT model consequently combines the strategic perspective of business portfolio analysis with the risk considerations of financial portfolio theory. (For other approaches to the incorporation of risk, see Corstjens and Weinstein 1981 and Mahajan, Wind, and Bradford 1981.) In addition to considering systematic financial risk, management may want to limit the activity of a business unit to reduce the total risks stemming from a variety of sources such as antitrust or competitive and labor reactions. These limits on total risk are incorporated in the model through upper and lower bound constraints on the market share of each business unit.

MAIN FUNCTIONAL RELATIONSHIPS

The six main functional relationships of the business unit module are (1) the market response function; (2) the maintenance marketing function; (3) the capacity expenditures function; (4) the working capital function; (5) the cost function; and (6) the price function. They are identified by the corresponding numbers in Figure 16.3 and illustrated graphically in Figure 16.4.

1. *The market response function.* The market response function specifies the market share m_T, on a quantity basis, which may be expected at the end of the planning period for a given marketing investment. It will generally be S-shaped, reflecting an increasing marginal response for small investments and a decreasing marginal response for large investments, but it may also assume a concave form. Since the market response function is strictly monotone increasing, it is feasible and

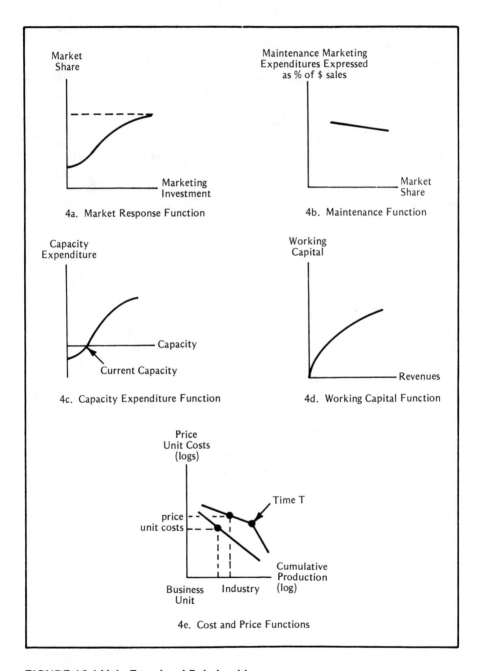

4a. Market Response Function

4b. Maintenance Function

4c. Capacity Expenditure Function

4d. Working Capital Function

4e. Cost and Price Functions

FIGURE 16.4 Main Functional Relationships

managerially more attractive to interpret this curve as a specification
of the marketing investments required to obtain different market share
levels. These marketing investments will typically include personal
selling and advertising expenditures, but also developmental costs to
improve product quality or to modify the product line within a business unit.[3]

Following a procedure proposed by Little (1970), the market response function is estimated from four managerial inputs: the market
share expected at the end of the planning period if no marketing investment is made, the marketing investment required to achieve a
reference market share level, the expected market share for a higher
marketing investment, and the maximum market share expected for
an unlimited marketing investment. For an existing business unit, the
reference market share is taken as the current market share, while for
a potential business unit, the minimum expected market share is set
to zero.

To provide the market response judgments, the manager should be
encouraged to think in terms of the best tactics (such as segmentation
strategy, consumer and trade promotions, product line changes including new products, improvements in product quality, acquisitions
of small competitors, advertising and personal selling) that can be used
in the product-market(s) corresponding to the business unit under
consideration. Substantial attention needs to be paid to likely competitive reactions, the strengths and weaknesses of the firm, and the
best ways to market to different segments constituting the product-
market(s). The market response function is likely to be a critical component of the proposed approach, and the quality of the results from
the model will reflect the intensity of analysis done before providing
the subjective judgments. The S-shaped market response function has
been successfully used in several decision calculus models (e.g., Little
1970, Lodish 1971).

2. *The maintenance marketing function.* This function specifies the
marketing expenditures required during the post-planning period,
expressed as a percentage of sales, to maintain market share at the level
reached at the end of the planning period. It will generally decrease
as market share increases, reflecting economies of scale in marketing,
although it may increase in some situations. This may, for instance,
be the case if a higher market share is anticipated to generate more than
a proportionate increase in competitive reactions. A linear functional
form was assumed in modeling the variation of relative marketing
maintenance expenditure as a function of market share. It is estimated
from managerial inputs corresponding to two market share levels.

3. *The capacity expenditure function.* This function represents the additional investment required to expand the current capacity to be consistent with the market share to be achieved. It also specifies the additional resources available if the activity level of the business unit is decreased. These additional resources represent the resale value of the freed capacity or the cash equivalent when transferred to other business units. The capacity expenditures are the proportion of the investment not accounted as depreciation in the computation of costs during the planning period.

The capacity expenditure function for an existing business unit is evaluated from five estimates provided by the user: the cash flow generated by a complete sale or transfer of the current capacity, the additional investment required for two expansion levels, and the investment required for a marginal expansion beyond a high capacity level. If the firm is not able to sell off a business unit or to use freed capacity for other activities, the cash flow corresponding to a complete sale may be set to a small value. The capacity expenditure function may be S-shaped or concave depending on the estimates provided by the user.

In the case of a business unit with no existing capacity, the capacity expenditure function has a concave form and is evaluated from estimates of the investment required for two capacity levels.

4. *The working capital function.* The working capital requirements (cash + inventory + equipment on lease + accounts receivable – accounts payable) are usually expected to differ for various levels of market share. Working capital is specified as a function of revenues. The parameters of this function are evaluated on the basis of estimates expressing the appropriate working capital as a proportion of revenues for two revenue levels. The working capital function may be expected to be generally concave, but it may also be convex when, for instance, an increase in market share will result in penetrating market segments requiring more favorable credit or delivery terms. Since the financing of working capital is already included under costs, additional working capital is defined as only that portion that is not expensed during the planning period.

5. *The cost function.* Following the works of the Boston Consulting Group on experience effects (1972), the STRATPORT model assumes that unit costs, expressed in constant dollars, decline as a function of the business unit's cumulative production. In STRATPORT, however, unit costs incorporate all costs (including depreciation) with the exception of marketing investments, which are accounted for separately.

The evaluation of the cost function is based on a loglinear regression of past data or, alternatively, on current unit costs and a managerial estimate of the cost reduction anticipated for an increase in cumulative production. If, however, the evolution of unit costs is estimated to be more a function of time than of cumulative production, the model can be extended to handle such cases. This extension may be particularly appropriate when raw materials costs are anticipated to evolve significantly and when they represent a substantial amount compared to value added.

6. *The price function.* The price function also assumes a decline in average industry unit price as a function of industry cumulative production, similar to the behavior of unit costs. The evolution of price may, however, be different in the planning and post-planning periods to reflect different patterns of price competition over time, which have been empirically identified by the Boston Consulting Group (1972). For instance, the average industry price may decline at a lower rate than unit costs for a new industry and decrease at a faster rate later as the market matures and competition intensifies.

This formulation does not assume that there is a market price followed by the firm. The price set by the firm may actually be above or below average industry prices according to the price positioning strategy adopted. Moreover, just as in the case of costs, the model can be extended to consider price as a function of time as opposed to a function of industry cumulative sales.

THE OPTIMIZATION MODULE

The business unit module described above is sufficient for the evaluation of a specific portfolio strategy. In addition, STRATPORT may be used to determine the allocation of resources among business units that provides the maximum net present value over the time horizon considered, subject to a constraint on the discounted cash flow during the planning period. This cash constraint may be evaluated over a range of levels as indicated earlier.

The optimization procedure follows the Generalized Lagrange Multiplier technique (Everett 1963) and transforms the simultaneous optimization of N variables to N univariate maximizations.[4] The univariate maximization algorithm is based on the decomposition of the Lagrangean derivative into a difference between two monotone increasing functions. It automatically provides the expected net present value for alternative cash flow constraints as well as an estimate of the marginal increase in net present value for an increase in the level of the cash flow constraint.

This optimization procedure is highly efficient, and the computer time required to find an optimum allocation goes up only linearly with the number of business units. It determines the optimum allocations to 10 business units for 11 different levels of the cash flow constraint in less than 20 seconds of CPU time on a DEC 2050 system. This high efficiency makes feasible the on-line interaction to conduct sensitivity analysis.

AN ILLUSTRATIVE USE OF THE MODEL

Figure 16.5 contains selected parts of a computer terminal printout corresponding to a hypothetical utilization of STRATPORT. The inputs provided by the user have been underlined to distinguish them from the text printed by the computer. In a previous utilization of STRATPORT, a data file had been created, containing the appropriate inputs for six business units over a planning period of three years and a post-planning period of five years. Without going into the detailed characteristics of the business units, we may summarize that, in terms of the Boston Consulting Group terminology, business units 1, 2, 3, and 4 are a Cash Cow, a Star, a Dog, and a Problem Child, with current market shares of 20%, 30%, 5%, and 5% respectively. Business units 5 and 6 are new opportunities that the firm is considering entering into.

The strategy evaluation and strategy formulation modes of STRATPORT are illustrated in Figure 16.5. For simplification, the financial entities in these examples are presented only before tax and without discounting. In the first part, the model is used to project the current situation over the time horizon. Over the planning period, the marketing investments required to maintain the current market share of each business unit are $45, $150, $40, and $30 million for business units 1, 2, 3, and 4, respectively. This status quo strategy implies that the firm will not make new entries into business units 5 and 6.

The results of this evaluation indicate that this strategy would generate a net cash flow of $297 million over the three-year planning period and profits of $1366 million over the total eight-year time horizon considered. The detailed results show that all business units

```
INDICATE MARKETING INVESTMENT FOR
  BUSINESS UNIT 1 : 45
  BUSINESS UNIT 2 : 150
  BUSINESS UNIT 3 : 40
  BUSINESS UNIT 4 : 30
  BUSINESS UNIT 5 : 0
  BUSINESS UNIT 6 : 0
OUTPUT SAVED IN FILE FOR OFF-LINE PRINTING.
DO YOU WANT TO PROCEED (0), OR TO DISPLAY RESULTS (1)? 1
```

EVALUATION OF PORTFOLIO STRATEGY
****

CASH NEEDS	−297.
PROFIT LEVEL	1366.
MARKET SHARE	
B. U. 1	.202
B. U. 2	.300
B. U. 3	.050
B. U. 4	.050
B. U. 5	.000
B. U. 6	.000

SOURCES AND USES OF FUNDS
****

B. U. NUMBER	1	2	3	4	5	6
CASH NEEDS						
REVENUE PL.	824.	1372.	345.	190.	0.	0.
COSTS PL.	551.	1082.	295.	127.	0.	0.
MKTG. IN.PL.	45.	150.	40.	30.	0.	0.
CAPA.IN.PL.	25.	79.	−11.	23.	0.	0.
TOTAL	−204.	−61.	−21.	−10.	0.	0.
PROFITS						
REVENUE PL.	824.	1372.	345.	190.	0.	0.
COSTS PL.	551.	1082.	295.	127.	0.	0.
MKTG. IN.PL.	45.	150.	40.	30.	0.	0.
REVENUE PP.	1623.	3838.	623.	468.	0.	0.
COSTS PP.	1089.	2969.	530.	302.	0.	0.
MKTG. IN.PP.	98.	460.	67.	84.	0.	0.
TOTAL	665.	550.	37.	115.	0.	0.

```
INPUT MINIMUM AND MAXIMUM LEVELS OF EXTERNAL CASH
AVAILABILITY: −600,200

OUTPUT SAVED IN FILE FOR OFF-LINE PRINTING.

DO YOU WANT TO PROCEED (0), OR TO DISPLAY KEY RESULTS
(1), PROFIT CONTRIBUTIONS (2), OR CASH FLOWS (3) 1
```

FIGURE 16.5 An Illustrative Run of the STRATPORT Model

KEY OPTIMIZATION RESULTS
****

OPTIONS	1	2	3	4	5	6
CASH NEEDS	206.	195.	185.	175.	165.	106.
PROFIT LEVEL	2911.	2894.	2877.	2860.	2842.	2735.
MARG. % YIELD	19.53	20.26	21.00	21.73	22.46	23.19
MARKET SHARE						
B. U. 1	.203	.201	.198	.195	.193	.150
B. U. 2	.394	.393	.391	.390	.389	.387
B. U. 3	.010	.010	.010	.010	.010	.010
B. U. 4	.171	.170	.170	.169	.169	.168
B. U. 5	.360	.358	.355	.353	.351	.349
B. U. 6	.000	.000	.000	.000	.000	.000
OPTIONS	7	8	9	10	11	
CASH NEEDS	-383.	-386.	-389.	-393.	-609.	
PROFIT LEVEL	1813.	1807.	1801.	1793.	1330.	
MARG. % YIELD	23.92	24.66	25.39	26.12	26.85	
MARKET SHARE						
B. U. 1	.150	.150	.150	.150	.150	
B. U. 2	.050	.050	.050	.050	.050	
B. U. 3	.010	.010	.010	.010	.010	
B. U. 4	.168	.167	.167	.166	.166	
B. U. 5	.346	.344	.342	.339	.000	
B. U. 6	.000	.000	.000	.000	.000	

PL. = Planning Period   B. U. = Business Unit
PP. = Post-Planning Period   IN. = Investment

FIGURE 16.5 An Illustrative Run of the STRATPORT Model (continued)

would, under this strategy, be net cash generators, although business unit 1 would account for close to 70% of the cash flow in the planning period. Over the long term, business units 1 and 2 would generate close to 90% of the total profits of the firm.

There are some indications that this status quo strategy may be far from optimum. There are obvious disparities between the marketing investments made in the business units and their long-term profit potential. It is possible, in particular, that more cash could be generated by business units 1 and 3 and invested more profitably into business units 2, 4, 5, and 6. Moreover, it is difficult to evaluate whether the total cash flow generated in the planning period corresponds to the appropriate level for the firm without knowing the long-term profit implications of alternative cash flow levels.

For these different reasons, in the second part of Figure 16.5 the strategy formulation mode of STRATPORT is used to investigate a range of portfolio strategies from a net cash generation of $600 million to a net cash need of $200 million. The detailed results of the optimization routine are saved in an output file for off-line printing. They can also be selectively displayed on-line, but only the key results of the optimization are presented here. They represent the profit, marginal percent yield, and market share for 11 portfolio strategies (options) corresponding to different cash flow levels. These cash flow levels correspond to constant steps in the marginal yield. At one extreme, option 1 would require $206 million of additional cash in the planning period and would provide a total profit of $2911 million. At the other extreme, option 11 would generate a net cash flow of $609 million and a total profit of $1330 million.

Business unit 6 does not appear to be an attractive opportunity over the whole range of cash flows considered. Similarly, the most appropriate strategy for business unit 3 in all options is a minimum marketing investment resulting in a minimum market share. At the other extreme, business unit 4 appears to warrant a substained market share increase under all options.

The optimum strategies for the remaining three business units appears to differ widely for different cash flow levels. These strategies vary from a sustained marketing investment for a given cash flow level to a minimum marketing investment when the cash flow requirement becomes very stringent. For instance, if a net cash generation of at least $383 million is required, a substained marketing investment cannot be made in business unit 2; its market share will drop to a minimum level of 5% at the end of the planning period (see option 7). The user could also look at the detailed cash flow and profit projections made available by the model for each option, although this capability is not presented here because of space limitations.

An analysis could be performed to compare the long-term profitability of different strategies with their cash requirements. Such an analysis is represented graphically in Figure 16.6 from the information obtained from the interaction with STRATPORT. The curve obtained by linking the points corresponding to different optimum strategies determines the profit/cash flow envelope of optimum strategies, and it increases at a declining rate. The slope of this envelope represents the marginal profit from the additional amount of investment involved

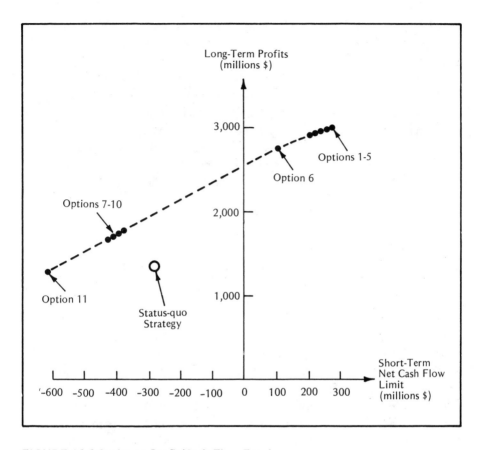

FIGURE 16.6 Optimum Profit/Cash Flow Envelope

in one option compared to the next. Comparing the marginal profit with the marginal cost of external financing can aid in the determination of a desirable cash flow level.

A more complete analysis would obviously require the incorporation of the effects of tax, discounting, and risk as well as a number of additional runs of the model to investigate the sensitivity of the results to changes in the input parameters. Final recommendations would also have to consider a number of factors not explicitly included in the STRATPORT model, such as implications for the labor force and financing possibilities. But this example clearly shows that the choice of an investment strategy may depend mainly on the characteristics of a business unit, as in the case of business units 3, 4, and 6, or be significantly affected by the net cash flow requirements of the firm, as in the case of business units 1, 2, and 5.

Finally, this analysis also provides a perspective on the adequacy of the status quo strategy. As represented in Figure 16.6, this strategy would be far from optimum. For the same cash flow level in the planning period, the profits of the firm could be increased by $500 million over the next eight years by a better allocation of resources among business units. Alternatively, the same level of long-term profits could be achieved while providing an additional $300 million surplus to the net cash flow during the planning period.

CONCLUSION

STRATPORT is a decision support system designed to assist top managers and corporate planners in the formulation of business portfolio strategies. The development of this system has been based on two specific research areas that have had a substantial impact on marketing in recent years: the decision calculus approach to marketing models (Little 1970) and strategic planning techniques.

The overall structure of the STRATPORT system is easy to understand and use. Yet it is reasonably complete in integrating the key aspects of the business portfolio problem. The complexities inherent in the mathematical formulation of the model, in the estimation of function parameters, or in the optimization procedure have been transferred to the computer so as to facilitate the use of the model by corporate planners and managers. The model attempts to make the best use of existing empirical data as well as managerial judgment. Judgmental inputs are elicited from managers on issues with which they are familiar and in a way that is coherent with managerial thinking. The model provides information readily interpreted by managers. These features are the result of an implementation-oriented decision-calculus approach to model design as advocated by Little (1970). Despite our best efforts, however, there remains the question of whether the present approach provides a valid representation of managers' beliefs and whether the approach would, in fact, improve management decisions. Research along the lines of Chakravarti, Mitchell, and Staelin (1979) and McIntyre (1980) may shed more light on these issues.

STRATPORT represents simultaneously an extension and operationalization of current business portfolio analysis approaches. The main extensions included in the model are the distinction made between specific types of investments, the inclusion of potential new business units in the analysis, the explicit specification of the relationship between changes in the market posture of a business unit, its short-term cash flow requirements and its long-term profit potential, and the incorporation of risk considerations. The operationalization of the business portfolio concept allows a more extensive and easier investigation of this complex problem, in particular by providing: a better exploitation of existing information, either empirical or judgmental, and guiding the gathering of additional data; a rapid evaluation and formulation of a large number of alternative business portfolio strategies; and an investigation of the robustness of a given portfolio strategy to changes in the underlying assumptions. A further benefit from the operationalization of the business portfolio concept into an interactive model is the potential linkage that one may anticipate, at least partially, between the STRATPORT decision support system and data bases as well as explanatory models developed by some firms in the context of the PIMS (Schoeffler, Buzzell, and Heany 1974) and ADVISOR (Lilien 1979) projects.

The appropriate use of the STRATPORT decision support system also requires an understanding of its key limitations, which stem from three main sources:

Restricted scope. The model centers uniquely on critical quantifiable factors in the formulation of business portfolio strategies. The main types of investments that it considers explicitly are capacity, working capital, and marketing investments (including product development). Other types of investments such as basic R & D are not directly incorporated in the model. Personnel, manufacturing, and financial policies (e.g., debt/equity, dividend) are not explicitly addressed. Nor are qualitative elements such as quality of management and political risks. The conclusions obtained from using the model have to be interpreted in the light of these missing factors.

Structural assumptions. The main assumptions in the structure of the model concern the specific forms selected for each function, the absence of market or cost interactions between business units, and the treatment of price behavior and market size as exogenous. The functional forms specified in the model are relatively general and will not usually represent a serious limitation. The other assumptions were made mainly because of the difficulty in obtaining reliable data, either empirically or through managerial judgments, to represent these more complex phenomena. The assumptions of cost and market independence of business units are usually quite reasonable when the model is used at the corporate or divisional level. In the context of a hierarchical approach (Wind and Mahajan 1981), they become less tenable at lower levels in the organization. Interactions between business units as well as the potential impact of marketing investments on price and market-size evolutions can, however, be taken into account by updating the values of the parameters in an iterative fashion in successive runs of STRATPORT.

External aggregation. Some aspects of the business portfolio problem that are kept outside the scope of the model have to be integrated in the formulation of the managerial judgments provided as inputs. In particular, the use of an aggregate response function of market share to marketing investment assumes that the manager providing the inputs for estimation will integrate such factors as the presence of multiple products and market segments, potential opportunities and threats, strengths and weaknesses of the firm, development of adequate marketing programs, and possible competitive reactions.

The adequate utilization of a model requires an understanding of its basic structure, capabilities, and limitations. We have attempted to provide such an understanding of the STRATPORT model. It is hoped that by providing a simple approach to comprehend better the quantitative aspects of corporate resource allocation, the model will enable top managers to give greater attention to the more qualitative issues involved in strategic decisions on business portfolios.

Footnotes

[1] These approaches are usually presented as classification procedures so that a finite number of typical strategies may be conveniently identified. In a more detailed analysis the posture of business units is more accurately defined in terms of continuous dimensions. The distinction between these two levels of analysis is particularly clear in the Boston Consulting Group approach.

[2] For a detailed mathematical formulation, see Larréché and Srinivasan (1981).

[3] A distinction is made between R & D investments concerning product development, which is an integral part of a business unit strategy, and more fundamental

research, which, because of the unpredictability and distant nature of its outcome, is unlikely to affect the market posture of the business unit during the planning horizon. The former is included as part of the marketing investment required to obtain a specific market share level. The latter reflects a policy decision made to protect the firm beyond the current planning horizon and is not directly incorporated in the model. The minimum cash flow acceptable for the firm should, however, be determined after allowing for the investments resulting from such policy decisions.

[4] For a mathematical description of the optimization routine, see Larréché and Srinivasan (1981).

GENERAL REFERENCES

Abell, Derek F. and John S. Hammond (1979), *Strategic Market Planning*, Englewood Cliffs, NJ: Prentice-Hall.

Babcock, Guilford C. (1970), "The Concept of Sustainable Growth," *Financial Analyst Journal*, 26 (May-June), 108–114

Boston Consulting Group (1972), *Perspectives on Experience*, Boston: The Boston Consulting Group Inc.

Boyd, Harper W., Jr. and Jean-Claude Larréché (1978), "The Foundations of Marketing Strategy," in *Review of Marketing 1978*, Gerald Zaltman and Thomas V. Bonoma, eds., Chicago: American Marketing Association, 41–72.

Business Week (1975), "Piercing Future Fog in the Executive Suite," April 28, 46–54.

Buzzell, Robert D., Bradley T. Gale, and Ralph S.M. Sultan (1975), "Market Share: A Key to Profitability," *Harvard Business Review*, 53 (January-February), 97–106.

Chakravarti, Dipankar, Andrew Mitchell, and Richard Staelin (1979), "Judgment Based Marketing Decision Models: An Experimental Investigation of the Decision Calculus Approach," *Management Science*, 25 (March), 251–263.

Channon, Derek F. (1977), "Use and Abuse of Analytical Techniques for Strategic Decisions," paper presented at the 23rd International Meeting of the Institute of Management Sciences, Athens, Greece (July).

Corstjens, Marcel and David Weinstein (1981), "Optimal Strategic Business Unit Portfolio Analysis," in *Marketing Planning Models*, A.A. Zoltners, ed., TIMS Studies in the Management Sciences, New York: North Holland, forthcoming.

Day, George S. (1977), "Diagnosing the Product Portfolio," *Journal of Marketing*, 41 (April), 29–38.

——, Allan D. Shocker, and Rajendra K. Srivastava (1979), "Customer-Oriented Approaches to Identifying Product Markets," *Journal of Marketing*, 43 (Fall), 8–19.

Everett, Hugh, III (1963), "Generalized Lagrange Multiplier Method for Solving Problems of Optimum Allocation of Resources," *Operations Research*, 11 (May-June), 399–417.

Hall, William K. (1980), "Survival Strategies in a Hostile Environment," *Harvard Business Review*, 58 (September-October), 75–85.

Hamermesh, R.G., M.J. Anderson, and J.E. Harris (1978), "Strategies for Low Market Share Businesses," *Harvard Business Review*, 56 (May-June), 95–102.

Hedley, Barry (1977), "Strategy and the Business Portfolio," *Long Range Planning*, 10 (February), 9–15.

Higgins, Robert C. (1977), "How Much Growth Can a Firm Afford?," *Financial Management*, 6 (Fall), 7–16.

Hopkins, David S. (1976), "New Emphasis in Marketing Strategies," *The Conference Board Record*, 13 (August), 35–39.

Jackson, Barbara B. and Benson P. Shapiro (1979), "New Way to Make Product Line Decisions," *Harvard Business Review*, 57 (May-June), 139–149.

Kiechel, Walter, III (1979), "Playing by the Rules of the Corporate Strategy Game," *Fortune*, 100 (September 24), 110–115.

Kotler, Philip (1980), *Marketing Management: Analysis, Planning and Control*, 4th edition, Englewood Cliffs, NJ: Prentice-Hall.

Larréché, Jean Claude and Hubert Gatignon (1977), *MARKSTRAT: A Marketing Strategy Game*, Palo Alto, CA: The Scientific Press.

———, and David B. Montgomery (1981), "Strategic Marketing and Corporate Modeling," unpublished paper.

———, and V. Srinivasan (1981), "STRATPORT: A Model for the Evaluation and and Formulation of Business Portfolio Strategies," Research Paper No. 572, Stanford, CA: Stanford University, Graduate School of Business.

Lilien, Gary L. (1979), "ADVISOR 2: Modeling the Marketing Mix Decision for Industrial Products," *Management Science*, 25 (February), 191–204.

Little, John D.C. (1970), "Models and Managers: The Concept of a Decision Calculus," *Management Science*, 16 (April), B466–B485.

Lodish, Leonard M. (1971), "CALLPLAN: An Interactive Salesman's Call Planning System," *Management Science*, 18 (December, Part II), P25–P40.

Mahajan, Vijay, Yoram Wind, and John W. Bradford (1981), "Stochastic Dominance Rules for Product Portfolio Analysis," in *Marketing Planning Models*, A.A. Zoltners, ed., TIMS Studies in the Management Sciences, New York: North Holland, forthcoming.

McIntyre, Shelby H. (1980), "The Leverage Impact of Judgment-Based Marketing Models," in *Market Measurement and Analysis,* David B. Montgomery and Dick R. Wittink, eds., Cambridge, MA: Marketing Science Institute, 551–573.

Naylor, Thomas N. and Horst Schauland (1976), "A Survey of Users of Corporate Planning Models," *Management Science,* 22 (May), 927–937.

Pessemier, Edgar A. (1977), *Product Management,* New York: John Wiley.

Robinson, S.J.Q., R.E. Hickens, and D.P. Wade (1978), "The Directional Policy Matrix—Tool for Strategic Planning," *Long Range Planning,* 11 (June), 8–15.

Schoeffler, Sidney, Robert D. Buzzell, and Donald F. Heany (1974), "Impact of Strategic Planning on Profit Performance," *Harvard Business Review,* 52 (March-April), 137–145.

Sharpe, William F. (1964), "Capital Asset Prices: A Theory of Market Equilibrium Under Conditions of Risk," *Journal of Finance,* 19 (September), 425–442.

Shocker, Allan D. and V. Srinivasan (1979), "Multi-Attribute Approaches for Product Concept Evaluation and Generation: A Critical Review," *Journal of Marketing Research,* 16 (May), 159–180.

Stobaugh, Robert B. and Phillip L. Townsend (1975), "Price Forecasting and Strategic Planning: The Case of Petrochemicals," *Journal of Marketing Research,* 12 (February), 19–29.

Van Horne, James C. (1980), *Financial Management and Policy,* 5th edition, Englewood Cliffs, NJ: Prentice-Hall.

Wensley, Robin (1981), "Strategic Marketing: Betas, Boxes or Basics?", *Journal of Marketing,* 45 (Summer), 173–182.

Wind, Yoram and Henry J. Claycamp (1976), "Planning Product Line Strategy: A Matrix Approach," *Journal of Marketing,* 40 (January), 2–9.

——, and Vijay Mahajan (1981), "Designing Product and Business Portfolios," *Harvard Business Review,* 59 (January-February), 155–165.

——, and Thomas L. Saaty (1980), "Marketing Applications of the Analytic Hierarchy Process," *Management Science,* 26 (July), 641–658.

17

Optimizing Decision Support Systems

by G. R. Wagner

About the author:

G. R. Wagner is president of EXECUCOM Systems Corp. in Austin, Texas.

Certain tools are commonly used as extensions of the human mind. An architect's ideas take shape on a sheet of drawing paper. An engineer works out a design with a sketch as his fingers fly over the keys of a calculator. Such tools can become as much a part of the mind as a tennis racket can become an extension of the body.

Computer-based decision support systems have been rather slow to arrive in the world of business management. The approach represents a radical departure from traditional business applications of computers, as executives are indeed augmenting mental powers in ways reminiscent of computer-aided design and interactive data analysis. In some cases, a manager sits at a terminal, although more often the same effect is achieved through an intermediate staff assistant. The process is not merely data compilation and reporting as in traditional mainstream applications; neither do users serve essentially as operators di-

Reprinted with permission from Datamation

recting the system. Executive support is more—it is a system that achieves a coupling of an individual's intellectual resources with those of the machine.

The recession of 1973-74 was the most important single stimulus in recognizing a manager's need for fast information updates and fast answers. By contrast with our former relative stability, it is now essential that business managers anticipate probable changes, detect change as it occurs, and take appropriate action—all very quickly. Managers also think strategically, using change and uncertainty to their advantage by planning to influence the future instead of performing reactively. The cycles of product life, competitive action, and other business realities are too short to allow the manager to have a wait-and-see attitude; the natural process is often too slow for business survival.

Decision support systems for executives can be categorized as corresponding loosely to the faculties of memory and reasoning. For example, certain data base management systems, providing the ability to retrieve information in such a way that meaningful patterns and correlations may be discerned, augment the memory. Simulation-based systems can be seen as extensions of an executive's reasoning powers. Models of the business environment help an executive envision possibilities for the future, foresee consequences, and identify and select alternative solutions. Most decision support systems contain elements of both data base management and modeling, but typically one element is dominant in a particular situation.

Most important innovations in computer-based modeling are financial planning languages—programming languages that enable non-dp people to become competent in building and solving models in an interactive, exploratory manner. For purposes of example, we will refer to one such language, called IFPS (Interactive Financial Planning System); however, most of what we will say applies to other languages of this type. The ways in which such a planning language are used are indicated by a survey of clients.[1] Among the results was the finding that 44% of the models were actually built by middle- or upper-level managers. By contrast, middle- and upper-level managers, performed only 21% and 9%, respectively, of the "what-if" analyses. Apparently, managers want to be involved in the building of their models—but once a model has credibility, they turn the mechanics of using a ter-

TABLE 17.1

10	COLUMNS 1980HALF1, 1980HALF2, 1981HALF1, 1981HALF2
20	* THIS MODEL IS FOR SIX MONTH PERIODS
30	* EXPENSE SECTION
40	PAYROLL = 19000*NUMBER OF SALESPERSONS, PREVIOUS* 1.05
50	NUMBER OF SALESPERSONS = 4
60	TRAVEL AND ENTERTAINMENT = 15000 * NUMBER OF SALESPERSONS
70	PROMO SUPPORT = 11000 * NUMBER OF SALESPERSONS
80	ADMINISTRATIVE SUPPORT = 53000, PREVIOUS*1.05
90	COMMISSIONS = 15%*SALES REVENUE
100	TOTAL EXPENSES = SUM(PAYROLL THRU COMMISSIONS)
110	* REVENUE SECTION
120	SALES REVENUE = NUMBER OF SALES*SALES PRICE
130	NUMBER OF SALES = 5*6*NUMBER OF SALESPERSONS
140	SALES PRICE = 4350 FOR 2,4695
150	* SUMMARY SECTION
160	GROSS CONTRIBUTION MARGIN = SALES REVENUE-TOTAL EXPENSES
170	EXPENSE RATIO = TOTAL EXPENSES/SALES REVENUE

---

minal over to a staff assistant. The key persons actually performing "what-if" analyses tend to be intermediaries such as secretaries and MBA assistants—after the model has been aligned with the thinking processes of the executive.

For a model to provide true decision support, its statements must resemble the business person's vocabulary and track unstructured and continually changing thought processes. Furthermore, the model must react in real time, while the person's attention remains focused on the subject. Decision support is further promoted by permitting the model statements to appear in any order—to this extent, the language is "nonprocedural." This example is not intended to be complete or even realistic, but it does demonstrate that anyone who understands English or any other natural language can understand our model. Building a

TABLE 17.2

?SOLVE				
ENTER SOLVE OPTIONS				
?ALL	1980	1980	1981	1981
	HALF1	HALF2	HALF1	HALF2
EXPENSE SECTION				
PAYROLL	76000	79800	83790	87980
NUMBER OF				
SALESPERSONS	4	4	4	4
TRAVEL AND				
ENTERTAINMENT	60000	60000	60000	60000
PROMO SUPPORT	44000	44000	44000	44000
ADMINISTRATIVE				
SUPPORT	53000	55650	58433	61354
COMMISSIONS	78300	78300	84510	84510
TOTAL EXPENSES	311304	317754	330737	337848
REVENUE SECTION				
SALES REVENUE	522000	522000	563400	563400
NUMBER OF SALES	120	120	120	120
SALES PRICE	4350	4350	4695	4695
SUMMARY SECTION				
GROSS CONTRIBUTION				
MARGIN	210696	204246	232664	225552
EXPENSE RATIO	.5964	.6087	.5870	.5997

real model for a real company involves a more thorough description but not any more complex programming.

The model as it would appear after being typed into the terminal in interactive fashion appears in Table 17.1.

To get an automatic report the user need only type the command SOLVE, and receive the report depicted in Table 17.2.

To answer "what-if" questions, the user types in the command WHAT IF along with the questions he wants to consider, as shown in Table 17.3.

What sales price would result in an expense ratio of .57? To answer this type of question, the user can use the GOAL SEEKING command (see Table 17.4).

TABLE 17.3

```
?WHAT IF
WHAT IF CASE 1
ENTER STATEMENTS
?COMMISSIONS = 16% *SALES REVENUE
?SALES PRICE = 4450 FOR 2,4750
?SOLVE
ENTER SOLVE OPTIONS
?SALES REVENUE THRU EXPENSE RATIO
```

WHAT IF CASE 1

2 WHAT IF STATEMENTS PROCESSED

	1980 HALF1	1980 HALF2	1981 HALF1	1981 HALF2
SALES REVENUE	534000	534000	570000	570000
NUMBER OF SALES	120	120	120	120
SALES PRICE	4450	4450	4750	4750
SUMMARY SECTION				
GROSS CONTRIBUTION				
MARGIN	215556	209106	232574	225462
EXPENSE RATIO	.5963	.6084	.5920	.6045

TABLE 17.4

```
ENTER SOLVE OPTIONS
?GOAL SEEKING
GOAL SEEKING CASE 1
ENTER NAME OF VARIABLE TO BE ADJUSTED TO ACHIEVE
PERFORMANCE
?SALES PRICE
ENTER COMPUTATIONAL STATEMENT FOR PERFORMANCE
?EXPENSE RATIO = .57
```

GOAL SEEKING CASE 1

	1980 HALF1	1980 HALF2	1981 HALF1	1981 HALF2
SALES PRICE	4623	4751	4885	5026
EXPENSE RATIO	.57	.57	.57	.57

USING RISK ANALYSIS

One particularly noteworthy aspect of decision support is that Monte Carlo risk analysis is being applied to business models through the modeling language. Although the classic paper on the Monte Carlo method was published in 1964,[2] this technique has been slow to reach its potential in routine planning. To see how the Monte Carlo technique is implemented in IFPS, the foregoing model has been modified to include the uncertainties shown in Table 17.5.

Now the decision-maker can express intuitive patterns of uncertainty and immediately gain insight into how much various outcomes might swing. For example, with the given assumptions, it is reasonable that the expense ratio in the last period could swing between 57.9% and 67.1%. Probably the most important tool in the operations research/management science kit is optimization. Optimization is now available; it may be applied interactively to an IFPS model through an optimization system called IFPOS. See Table 17.6.

The following example is simple but realistic. It represents a project or activity module that could be included in an overall corporate planning model. This particular module entertains possible expansions of a company's field sales force and its customer support group (consultants). First, IFPS is used to describe expenses, revenues, billing ratios, fees, and other variables, as shown in Table 17.7.

For the present example, this separate and standalone model will be optimized. However, in practice this would be just another activity added to the total corporate planning model and the total model would be optimized. The point of the demonstration is to show how easy it can be to use optimization without the hindrance of complexity, jargon, and other distractions.

After building the IFPS description of the business the user accesses IFPOS, and using *its* language he constructs a set of "directives" or rules. The objective of the exercise is to maximize cumulative corporate contribution as defined in the IFPS model. This is indicated as follows:

10 MAXIMIZE CUM CORP CONTRIBUTION (1981HALF2)

This means we want to maximize the *cumulative* contribution in the last period. This is a resource-allocation problem, where we want

TABLE 17.5

	Low Value	Most Likely Value	High Value
TRAVEL AND ENTERTAINMENT	$12,000	$15,000	$18,000
PROMO SUPPORT	9,500	11,000	13,000
ADMINISTRATIVE SUPPORT	45,000	53,000	62,000
NUMBER OF SALES	4	5	5.5

Each of these variables will be represented by a triangular statistical distribution which in a picture looks like the following:

PROBABILITY
PESSIMISTIC VALUE
MOST LIKELY VALUE
OPTIMISTIC VALUE

The IFPS word to represent the triangular distribution is TRIRAND. It is used as follows

VARIABLE NAME = TRIRAND (LOW VALUE, MOST LIKELY VALUE, HIGH VALUE)

All that's needed is to replace lines 60, 70, 80, and 130 in the IFPS model with the following:

60 TRAVEL AND ENTERTAINMENT = TRIRAND (12000, 15000, 18000)* NUMBER OF SALESPERSONS
70 PROMO SUPPORT = TRIRAND (9500, 11000, 13000)* NUMBER OF SALESPERSONS
80 ADMINISTRATIVE SUPPORT = TRIRAND (45000, 53000, 62000), PREVIOUS *1.05
130 NUMBER OF SALES = TRIRAND (4, 5, 5.5) *6* NUMBER OF SALESPERSONS

The user gets probabilistic answers by typing the command MONTE CARLO:

?MONTE CARLO
ENTER MONTE CARLO OPTIONS
?ALL GROSS CONTRIBUTION MARGIN, ALL EXPENSE RATIO
ENTER MONTE CARLO OPTIONS
?NONE

TABLE 17.6

FREQUENCY TABLE

PROBABILITY OF VALUE BEING GREATER THAN INDICATED

	90	80	70	60	50	40	30	20	10
GROSS CONTRIBUTION MARGIN									
1980HALF1	152753	165740	179519	190729	196567	203796	211951	220087	230485
1980HALF2	146302	159248	173053	184261	190067	197160	205534	213886	224032
1981HALF1	170571	184433	198993	211024	217528	225132	234254	242984	253822
1981HALF2	163526	177291	191806	203841	210500	217800	227201	235877	246707
EXPENSE RATIO									
1980HALF1	.576	.586	.596	.604	.613	.621	.632	.649	.688
1980HALF2	.588	.598	.608	.617	.625	.634	.646	.662	.682
1981HALF1	.567	.577	.586	.595	.603	.611	.622	.638	.657
1981HALF2	.579	.589	.598	.607	.616	.624	.636	.652	.671

TABLE 17.7

```
10    COLUMNS 1980HALF1, 1980HALF2, 1981HALF1, 1981HALF2
20    *  PROPOSAL FOR NEW SALES PEOPLE
30    SALES HIRINGS = 5,0
40    SALARY = 19000, PREVIOUS *1.05
50    FIELD OFFICE EXPENSE PER PERSON = 22000, PREVIOUS *1.05
60    NUMBER OF SALESPEOPLE = PREVIOUS + SALES HIRINGS
70    PAYROLL = NUMBER OF SALESPEOPLE *SALARY
80    FIELD OFFICE EXPENSE = NUMBER OF SALESPEOPLE *FIELD
      OFFICE EXPENSE PER PERSON
90    COMMISSION = 18% *TOTAL REVENUE
100   TRAVEL AND ENT = L60*10000
110   OTHER EXPENSES = L60*6000
120   TOTAL SALES EXPENSES = SUM(PAYROLL THRU OTHER EXPENSES)
130   INITIAL SALES QUOTA = 50000
140   SUBSEQUENT SALES QUOTA = 120000
150   TOTAL REVENUE = SALES HIRINGS *INITIAL SALES QUOTA +
160      PREVIOUS NUMBER OF SALESPEOPLE *SUBSEQUENT SALES
      QUOTA
170   CONTRIBUTION MARGIN NEW SALES FORCE = TOTAL REVENUE-
      TOTAL SALES EXPENSES
180   CUM CONTR MARGIN SALES = L170, PREVIOUS + L170
190   EXPENSE RATIO SALES = TOTAL SALES EXPENSES/TOTAL
      REVENUE
200   *  PROPOSALS FOR NEW CONSULTANTS
210   CONSULTANT HIRINGS = 10,0
220   CONSULTANT SALARY = 19500, PREVIOUS *1.07
230   FIRST PERIOD BILLING RATIO = 0.45
240   SECOND PERIOD BILLING RATIO = 0.48
250   THIRD PERIOD BILLING RATIO = 0.52
260   FOURTH PERIOD BILLING RATIO = 0.54
270   FIRST PERIOD PER DAY RATE = 600
280   SECOND PERIOD PER DAY RATE = 650
290   THIRD PERIOD PER DAY RATE = 700
300   FOURTH PERIOD PER DAY RATE = 750
310   NUMBER OF CONSULTANTS = PREVIOUS + CONSULTANT HIRINGS
320   PAYROLL CONSULTANTS = NUMBER CONSULTANTS *CON-
      SULTANT SALARY
330   TRAVEL AND ENT CONSULTANTS = NUMBER CONSULTANTS *5000
340   MISC EXPENSE = NUMBER CONSULTANTS *3000
350   ADMIN SUPPORT CONSULTANTS = 22000, PREVIOUS *1.05
```

TABLE 17.7 (continued)

---

360   CONSULTANT REVENUE = CONSULTANT HIRINGS*L390*FIRST
PERIOD BILLING RATIO* FIRST PERIOD PER DAY RATE + PRE-
VIOUSL210*L390*L240*L280 + PREVIOUS 2 L210*L390*L250*
L290 + PREVIOUS 3 L210*L390*L260*L300
390   DAYS AVAILABLE FOR CONSULTING = 120
400   TOTAL EXPENSES = SUM (L320 THRU L350)
410   CONTRIBUTION MARGIN CONSULTANTS = CONSULTANT
REVENUE TOTAL EXPENSES
420   CUM CONTR MARGIN CONSULTANTS = PREVIOUS + L410
430   CORPORATE CONTRIBUTION = L170 + L410
440   CUM CORP CONTRIBUTION = PREVIOUS + L430

---

decisions for (1) when and how many new salespersons to add, and
(2) when and how many new consultants to add. These decisions and
their limits are expressed as follows, where the total number of new
salespersons over the two-year period cannot exceed 10 and the total
number of consultants over the two-year period cannot exceed 15.

15   DECISIONS
20   SALES HIRINGS (ALL) BETWEEN 0 AND 5
25   CONSULTANT HIRINGS (ALL) BETWEEN 0 AND 5

The management constraints on the decisions are:

(1) Financial contribution in any period cannot be negative;
(2) No more than five new consultants per period, where a period
is six months;
(3) No more than five new salespersons per period, where a period
is six months.

These limitations or constraints are expressed as follows:

30   CONSTRAINTS
35   NUMBER OR SALESPEOPLE (1981HALF2) .LE. 10
40   NUMBER OF CONSULTANTS (1981HALF2) .LE. 15
45   CORPORATE CONTRIBUTION (ALL) .GE. 0

Once again, these natural language "directives" were built using the
IFPOS language, and the user is now on-line using IFPOS. He retrieves

TABLE 17.8

	1980 HALF1	1980 HALF2	1981 HALF1	1981 HALF2
?SOLVE				
ENTER SOLUTION OPTIONS				
?OPTIMAL				
ENTER SOLVE OPTIONS				
?SALES HIRINGS, CONSULTANT HIRINGS, CUM CORP CONTRIBUTION				
SALES HIRINGS	0	2	5	0
CONSULTANT HIRINGS	5	5	5	0
CUM CORP CONTRIBUTION	2500	3850	65694	455063

the stored IFPS model and simply types in the command SOLVE, thereupon receiving from IFPOS the standard reports that he is accustomed to seeing from IFPS, as depicted in Table 17.8.

Thus the optimal strategy is no new salespeople in the first and last six months, two in the second period, and five in the third period. The optimal strategy for consultants is to add five in each of the first three periods and none in the last period.

The constraints are typical of those which might be suggested by management. An important aspect of mind support in this example was the intuitive or subjective constraints expressed in the IFPOS language, yielding immediate answers that reside within these constraints. This can be especially useful if nonobvious answers lead to more insight to the problem. For example, an interesting "what-if" question or sensitivity analysis might be to permit a negative corporate contribution of up to $100,000, but not change any other constraints. This would be done as shown in Table 17.9.

This relaxation to allow a negative contribution of up to $100,000 significantly changes the optimal strategy. Instead of making only one pass to get "best" answers, the manager can see the results of multiple scenarios and gain more confidence and knowledge to support decision processes.

Of course, interactive optimization within the scope of a planning language will not necessarily supersede classical large scale optimization systems such as those applied to complex distribution problems

TABLE 17.9

```
?WHAT IF
WHAT IF CASE 1
ENTER STATEMENTS
?LIMIT CORPORATE CONTRIBUTION .GE. -100000
?SOLVE
ENTER SOLUTION OPTIONS
?OPTIMAL
ENTER SOLVE OPTIONS
?SALES HIRINGS, CONSULTANT HIRINGS, CUM CORP
CONTRIBUTION
```

	WHAT IF CASE 1			
	1980 HALF1	1980 HALF2	1981 HALF1	1981 HALF2
SALES HIRINGS	5	5	0	0
CONSULTANT HIRINGS	5	5	5	0
CUM CORP CONTRIBUTION	-77500	66450	526887	1021068

and allocation of production capacity. These and similar historical uses have usually been for the optimal utilization of already-committed plant and people resources. On the other hand, optimization in decision support has its greatest potential in the allocation of resources among a diverse variety of alternative futures—that is, strategic planning: doing the right things as opposed to doing things right. After all, the strategic issues are where executive minds excel, and it is there that support will be the most fruitful.

REFERENCES

[1] Wagner, G.R., "Enhancing Creativity in Strategic Planning Through Computer Systems, " *Managerial Planning*, July-August 1979.

[2] Hertz, David B., "Risk Analysis in Capital Investment," *Harvard Business Review*, January-February 1964.

18

Sensitivity Analysis and Simulation

by Jerry W. Durway

About the author:

Jerry W. Durway is a planning consultant at EXECU-COM Systems Corp., Austin, Texas.

It has long been said that there are only two absolute certainties—death and taxes. This old saying implies that everything else has some degree of uncertainty attached to it. In the business world, at least, that proposition is certainly true. The resulting, natural desire to minimize these uncertainties, and, therefore, risk, has led to the development of numerous methods which attempt to quantify and, thus, to evaluate this risk. Two of the more common methods are sensitivity analysis and simulation.

PROBABLISTIC SIMULATION

In this context, sensitivity analysis might be defined as the change in results brought about by varying an input assumption(s) over a given range. Similarly, simulation might be defined as the limiting case of a sensitivity analysis in that a very large number of data points, within the range under study, are considered. The theory underlying these

Reprinted with permission from Infosystems

two analytical methods is readily available; and, for this reason, I will not be discussing any new principles. I will, however, be discussing a new means for applying these principles to practical, everyday business problems.

First, however, I would like to interject a qualifying note. The word simulation has many different meanings to many different people. For purposes of this discussion, I shall define simulation to be probabilistic simulation, or risk analysis. It is also often referred to as Monte Carlo simulation. Certainly, many very fine papers have been written on this subject. Of these, one which comes to mind very quickly is David Hertz's 1964 article entitled "Risk Analysis in Capital Investment" as published in *Harvard Business Review*. Although Hertz's article of 14 years ago clearly described the Monte Carlo simulation method, particularly as applied to capital investment analysis, the method is still not widely used within the business community as a basis for real decision making. There are many reasons for this.

It is quite likely, however, that risk analysis' difficulty in gaining general acceptance stems from two major obstacles. For a long time there was no adequate computer software package available for developing a model which was 1) easily read and understood by those managers directly responsible for decisions and 2) sophisticated enough to handle the complex calculations required. Thus, risk analysis results could not be comfortably integrated into the management decision support process. A second major problem is that top managers have not had adequate exposure to risk analysis, and do not feel comfortable in relying on results obtained by risk analysis.

Let's start with the first problem area—getting appropriate computer software into managers' hands—and consider its effect on the use of risk analysis. Before the computer, companies used a single value for each critical variable and made hand-calculated, deterministic analyses of their capital investment problems. Then, along came the computer—no magic was added, but speed was. At that point, users got rapid feedback but still were limited to very rigidly defined programs. Modifications to those programs did not come easily and changes required data processing personnel for implementation. This multilayered procedure became a major impediment to timely analysis. In addition, there was no opportunity to ask "WHAT IF" questions on anything approaching an interactive basis. Finally, the technical languages used to write the programs were not understood by managers responsible for decisions based on their results; and at the same time the manager's business language was not understood by the programmers. They couldn't communicate.

One result was that sensitivity analyses were normally limited to using the most likely value for each input variable and then looking at cases perhaps 10-20 percent over and 10-20 percent under these most likely values.

ANALYSES BY FORM

At one major chemical producer, for example, project analyses in precomputer days were done by completing a form which had all the calculations built into it. When the form was properly completed, the analysis was finished. Once the appropriate data was collected, it became a routine operation. With computers, analyses followed the same rigid form but were prepared more quickly. It still was extremely difficult, however, to ask non-routine questions and get answers back within a reasonable time frame.

At another large diversified manufacturing company, precomputer analyses were also done by hand but there was no prescribed format: each analysis was done on an individual basis. When the computer arrived, a series of programs, each of which stood alone, was developed. These programs were not tied together in any way as a single package. This meant that the output from the first program had to be physically entered into each succeeding program. The results of this system, while better than doing it by hand, still left much to be desired. Even with its inefficiencies, it was used for a broad range of feasibility studies and served as a basis for presentations to top management. In those instances, the computer studies were supplemented with accounting statements which could not be programmed at that time.

In each case, everyone always kept saying "there must be a better way." And now, there is a better way. That better way is the new generation of financial modeling and planning languages. These software packages are distinguished by being user-oriented. This means that they have some rather significant advantages. For example, they allow models to be written in a natural language—English, Spanish or whatever one's natural language is. They are non-procedural, which means that statements in the model may be entered in any order. The system itself determines the order of solution.

INTERACTIVE RESPONSES

Another advantage is that they provide interactive responses. The user can modify the base model, get a modified solution, ask another question and get a second, third or fourth solution, all on an immediate basis. Finally, they have the ability to handle "WHAT IF" questions and to make "GOAL SEEKING," or reverse calculations.

One significant point must always be remembered. Although there are many financial modeling packages currently available, the characteristics and features associated with these different packages vary significantly. Therefore, when considering a package, it is very important to evaluate carefully that system's characteristics, such as its ease of use (is it non-procedural or procedural), its flexibility and its ability to provide direct interaction with managers. These characteristics have to be considered along with whatever specific features it offers.

And now that languages having these characteristics are available, let us take a quick look at how they might be used for sensitivity analysis and risk analysis. First, there is what might be called the "strong arm" method. This method depends on running a multiplicity of cases based on "WHAT IF" questions to an original model. It has flexibility and provides an enormous amount of information.

In one joint-venture situation a large international petroleum company used this method to prepare a grid of discounted cash flow solution rates. They selected a series of variables, each of which was to be assigned two or three separate values. Then, beginning with a base model, a given variable was given two or three possible values and tested against each reasonable combination of the other variables. This process was repeated for each variable such that all required points on the grid were calculated. Analysis of this grid allowed the company to zero in on those variables, or combination of variables, which were shown to have a significant impact on the results. Through this analysis, attention could be limited to these more critical variables.

The preceeding example is a situation in which sensitivity analyses were run to such an extent that they tended toward a risk analysis. A reverse approach could also have been taken. That is, run a risk analysis and then narrow the focus to a particular variable for sensitivity analysis. As an example, let's consider a typical analytical problem—new product analysis. The input information for our analysis is shown in Figure 18.1. As can easily be seen, this is a very simple, straightforward problem.

Product Life—
   Five Years

Overhead—
   High $15,000
   Most Likely   12,000
   Low   10,000
   May Be Different Each Year

Production Costs—
   $7.00, 7.15, 7.25, 7.40, 7.50

Investment—
   Between $90,000 And $100,000

Total Market—
   500,000 Units, Increasing At
   10 Percent Per Year

Market Share—
   Mean Value Is 5 Percent
   95 Percent Probability Of Being
   Between 3 And 7 Percent

**Remains Constant After
Establishment in First Year**

Product Price—
   High $9.25
   Most Likely   9.00
   Low   8.50

**Remains Constant After
Establishment In First Year**

Discount Rate—
   15 Percent

**FIGURE 18.1 Diversified Products Inc.
New Product Analysis**

Figure 18.2 shows a simple financial planning model for this situation. From a brief look at this model, it is easy to see that it really does reflect the input assumptions specified in Figure 18.1. At the same time, it should be noted that the model contains three different types of distributions—normal, uniform and triangular. Special attention should be given to the specification of the overhead variable. The function TRIRANDR is simply a triangular distribution which is serially independent. The other distributions—NORRAND (normal), TRIRAND (triangular) and UNIRAND (uniform)—remain constant at the values established in the first year. The model also contains two financial evaluation functions—net present value and internal rate of return.

As suggested earlier, there are many ways to approach the solution of this model. For example, each stochastic variable might be set at its most likely value. As shown in Figure 18.3, this would yield a 27.4 percent rate of return. The pessimistic approach yields a rate of return of −39.7 percent, a value which, besides being extremely low, certainly raises a number of interpretative questions. Alternatively, the optimistic case yields 81.2 percent. You will, of course, recognize that each of these approaches yields a deterministic solution. If, however, we were to perform a Monte Carlo simulation, or risk analysis, consisting of say, 500 iterations, the results would be as follows: there is a 10 percent that the rate of return will be less than 5.5 percent. It is equally likely that the rate of return will be above or below 24.9 percent; and there is only a 10 percent probability that the rate of return will be greater than 44.1 percent. It might be interesting to note that all the above results can be obtained within a matter of some five minutes elapsed time, using the model specified in Figure 18.2.

Given these results, let's go one step further. Assume that we can define one variable, say market share, much more closely. Applying this to our model, let's assume we know that our market share will be about five percent, or the mean value in the base case. To analyze this situation, we simply ask our model a "WHAT IF" question. "WHAT IF" market share equals five percent? After about one more minute elapsed time, while running 500 Monte Carlo iterations on this "new" model, we get the results shown in Figure 18.4. This provides us with a substantially greater amount of information than we had before. The 10 percent probability point has risen from 5.5 to 17.9 percent. The 90 percent probability point has dropped from 44.1 to

```
MODEL DIVERSE VERSION OF 08/15/78  17:12
 1   COLUMNS YEAR 1, YEAR 2, YEAR 3, YEAR 4, YEAR 5
 2   *
 3   * DIVERSIFIED PRODUCTS, INC.
 4   *
 5   TOTAL MARKET = 500000, PREVIOUS TOTAL MARKET*
     1.10
 6   MARKET SHARE = NORRAND (.05, .01)
 7   SALES VOLUME = MARKET SHARE*TOTAL MARKET
 8   *
 9   SALES PRICE = TRIRAND (8.5, 9.00, 9.25)
10   GROSS PROFIT = SALES PRICE*SALES VOLUME
11   *
12   OVERHEAD = TRIRAND (10000, 12000, 15000)
13   UNIT COST = 7.00, 7.15, 7.25, 7.40, 7.50
14   COST = UNIT COST*SALES VOLUME
15   *
16   NET PROFIT = GROSS PROFIT - COST - OVERHEAD
17   *
18   INITIAL INVESTMENT = UNIRAND (90000, 100000), 0
19   *
20   DISCOUNT RATE = .15
21   *
22   NET PRESENT VALUE = NPVC (NET PROFIT, DISCOUNT
     RATE, INITIAL INVESTMENT)
23   RATE OF RETURN = IRR (NET PROFIT, INITIAL INVEST-
     MENT) END OF MODEL
```

FIGURE 18.2 Financial Planning Model

35.8 percent. Therefore, we can easily see that by better estimating market share, we can significantly reduce the uncertainty, and thus the risk, in our new product decision.

Now, how might we actually use all the information just obtained? First, let's review just what information we do have. We know that if everything goes right, the IRR will be 81.2 percent. We know that if everything goes wrong, we will have a negative rate of return of 39.7 percent. Furthermore, we know that the probability of the project's yielding less than our 15 percent discount rate is almost 30 percent in the base case. However, we also know that if our market share is very close to five percent, we can feel confident that we have reduced

Assumptions About Stochastic Variables	Calculated Rate of Return (In Percent)
Most Likely: All	31.0
Mean: All	27.4
Pessimistic:	
Low Market Share	
Low Sales Price	
High Overhead	
High Initial Investment	-39.7
Optimistic:	
High Market Share	
High Sales Price	
Low Overhead	
Low Initial Investment	81.2
Risk Analysis:	
500 Iterations	
10 Percent Probability	
Of Being Less Than	5.5
50 Percent Probability	
Of Being Less Than	24.9
90 Percent Probability	
Of Being Less Than	44.1

FIGURE 18.3 Calculated Rate of Return for
Stochastic Variables

our risk of earning less than the discount rate to something in the
range of 5-10 percent. This information about the sensitivity of rate
of return to market share certainly does give us a substantial opportunity to reduce our risk in undertaking this project. The next question that we might wish to consider is how much value this information has to us. Or, to put it another way, how much might we afford
to invest in additional market research if this investment could help
us determine much more precisely what our market share would be?

In summary, let's review the major issues discussed here. First, we
touched on a recent advance in implementing risk analysis methods—
the use of powerful financial modeling and planning languages to incorporate risk analysis techniques into planning models. We then
looked at a simple analytical example, one for which we constructed
a model in one of these planning languages. And using that model,
we prepared a simple sensitivity analysis on a deterministic basis.

```
What If:
    Market Share = 5 percent
Risk Analysis:
    500 Iterations


                                Calculated
                                Rate of Return
Probability                     (In Percent)
  10 Percent Of
      Being Less Than     17.9
  50 Percent Of
      Being Less Than     29.1
  90 Percent Of
      Being Less Than     35.8
```

FIGURE 18.4 Monte Carlo Results

Going one step further, we used Monte Carlo simulation, or risk analysis, techniques to obtain results. Finally, we asked a significant "WHAT IF" question and got an immediate response. There are, of course, many similar situations in which planning models can be used to obtain equally critical information, again all within a very short time frame.

SIGNIFICANT IMPLICATION

Perhaps the most significant implication of this new process is that we can now combine our theoretical knowledge of risk analysis with a practical means for implementing these principles on a computer and on an interactive basis. Equally important, this analysis may be performed in a language understood by both the decision maker and by the computer. As a result, we are now ready to direct our attention to the final step in the process of making risk analysis a valuable business decision aid. That step is to help business management understand risk analysis and to remove their fears about integrating it into their everyday decision support system.

Discussion Questions for Part Two

1. What are the most significant differences between systematic and intuitive thinkers? Between perceptive and receptive thinkers? What types of problems seem best suited for each type of thinker?

2. What are the major differences in thinking and decision-making characteristics of analytic and intuitive managers? Which characteristics are most likely to encourage the use of computer-based decision-making systems? Why?

3. What major characteristics commonly posessed by decision support systems are likely to reinforce the decision processes of an analytic manager and possibly impede those of an intuitve manager? Impede decision processes of an analytic manager and reinforce those of an intuitive manager?

4. How do theories of right and left brain processing of information relate to systematic and intuitve decision-making styles?

5. In what types of problems is the fit among user style, decision type, and format of information support most critical? Least critical? Why?

6. Essential differences in decision-making approaches of a typical manager and an operations analyst include such characteristics as intuitive versus analytical approaches to decision-making, mathematical versus non-mathematical backgrounds, and broad vs. narrow perceptions of managerial problems. How can these differences be reconciled or at least minimized?

7. The major decision processes in managerial decision-making include such steps as problem finding, problem recognition, problem definition, criteria determination, alternative evaluation, alternative selection, and solution implementation. For which of these stages is a decision support system most likely to be helpful? Least likely to be helpful?

8. Of what value are surprise alternatives likely to be in creative problem solving? What contribution can decision support systems make in generating and evaluating such alternatives?

9. What major problems must be overcome if capabilities of existing decision support systems are broadened from concentration on specific

problem areas to generalized intelligent decision support systems capable of handling a wide variety of problem types at different management levels?

10. How do generalized intelligent decision support systems differ in terms of key characteristics and features from typical decision support systems in existence today?

11. How can data base management systems and artificial intelligence techniques be incorporated efficiently and effectively into decision support systems?

12. Explain how a problem processor can support generalized decision-making and exhibit intelligence in its operations.

13. What problems are likely to be encountered by the problem processor in emulating human cognitive activities such as information collection, model formulation, problem recognition, and problem analysis? What approaches can be employed to overcome these problems?

14. Distinguish between the information base and problem processor. How can the frameworks for representing organizational division of labor and decision-making abilities be used to design these major components of a GIDS?

15. What are the major benefits of interactive decision models as compared to staff developed model-optimized decision models? What barriers must be overcome if interactive decision models are to be successfully implemented?

16. What major benefits are likely to be achieved by encouraging managers to participate in the design of decision support systems? How can the obvious problems of increased system cost, excessive demands on managerial time, and lack of familiarity with modeling concepts and techniques be overcome in such cases?

17. What problems are typically encountered in using ad hoc single purpose models? Describe the characteristics and advantages of an integrated approach designed to help overcome these problems.

18. What major developments in data management, modeling, and user interfaces have contributed to an evolution of DSS to its current status?

19. What advantages do models such as STRATPORT have over conventional strategic models? On what basis can the increased cost and complexity be justified?

20. What benefits do model-based Monte Carlo risk analyses have over simulation driven sensitivity analyses? What typical situations is each technique best suited for?

Bibliography

ARTICLES

A

Aaker, David A. and Weinberg, Charles B., "Interactive Marketing Models," *Journal of Marketing,* October 1975, pp. 16-23.

Ackoff, Russell, "Management Misinformation Systems," *Management Science,* December 1967, pp. 147-156.

Adams, C.K., "How Users View Management Information Systems," *Decision Sciences,* April 1975, Vol. 6, No. 2, pp. 337-345.

Ahituv, Niv and Wand, Yair, "Information Evaluation and Decision Makers Objectives," *Interfaces,* June 1981, pp. 24-33.

Akoka, J.A., "A Framework For Decision Support Systems Evaluation," *Information and Management,* July 1981, pp. 133-141.

Alav, Maryam and Henderson, John C., "An Evolutionary Strategy For Implementing a Decision Support System," *Management Science,* November 1981, pp. 1309-1323.

Alexander, Tom, "Teaching Computers the Art of Reason," *Fortune,* May 17, 1982, pp. 82-92.

____, "Practical Uses for a Useless Science," *Fortune,* May 31, 1982, pp. 138-146.

Allen, James L., and Scher, Marvin, "Risk Analysis for Non Mathematicians," *Management Accounting,* October 1979, pp. 55-58.

Alexander, Tom, "Computers Can't Solve Everything," *Fortune,* October 1969.

Alter, Steven, "A Taxonomy of Decision Support Systems," *Sloan Management Review,* Fall 1973, pp. 37-56.

____, "Development Patterns for Decision Support Systems," *MIS Quarterly,* September 1978, pp. 33-41.

____, "How Effective Managers Use Information Systems," *Harvard Business Review,* November–December 1976, pp. 97-104.

____, "Why is Man Computer Interaction Important for Decision Support Systems," *Interfaces,* Vol. 7, No. 2, February 1979, pp. 109-115.

Alter, Steven and Ginsberg, Michael, "Managing Uncertainty in MIS Implementation," *Sloan Management Review,* Fall 1978, pp. 23-31.

Amstutz, Arnold E., "Market-Oriented Management Information Systems—The Current Status," *Journal of Marketing Research,* November 1969.

445

Anderson, John C. and Janson, Marius A., "Methods for Managerial Problem Cause Analysis," *Interfaces*, November 1979, pp. 121-128.

"APL and Decision Support Systems," *EDP Analyzer*, May 1976, pp. 1-12.

Argyris, Chris, "Interpersonal Barriers to Decision-Making," *Harvard Business Review*, March-April 1966, pp. 84-97.

____, "Management Information Systems: The Challenge to Rationality and Emotionality," *Management Science*, Vol. 17, No. 6, February 1971, pp. 3275-3292.

Archer, Earnest R., "How To Make A Business Decision: An Analysis of Theory and Practice." *Management Review*, February 1980, pp. 55-61.

"Artificial Intelligence: The Second Computer Age Begins," *Business Week*, March 8, 1982, pp. 66-75.

Assmus, Gert, "Newprod: The Design and Implementation of a New Product Model," *Journal of Marketing*, January 1975, pp. 16-23.

Avramovich, Dan, Thomas M. Cook, Gary D. Langston and Frank Sutherland, "A Decision Support System For Fleet Management: A Linear Programming Approach," *Interfaces*, June 1982, pp. 1-9.

B

Bacot, Eugene R., "Logical Decision-Making," *Chemical Engineering*, September 3, 1973, pp. 112-114.

Barbosa, L.C., and R.G. Hirko, "Integration of Algorithmic Aids Into Decision Support Systems," *MIS Quarterly*, March, 1980, pp. 1-12.

Barton, Richard F., "A Decision Support System to Enhance Rationality of Simulation Game Play," *Journal of Experiential Learning and Simulation*, December 1980, pp. 253-260.

Begeo-Dov, Aharon G., "An Overview of Management Science and Information Systems," *Management Science*, 13, No. 12, August, 1967.

Benbasat, Izak and Roger G. Schroeder, "An Experimental Investigation Of Some MIS Design Variables," *MIS Quarterly*, March 1977, pp. 37-49.

Benbasat, Izak and Ronald N. Taylor, "The Impact of Cognitive Styles On Information Systems Design," *MIS Quarterly*, June 1978, pp. 43-54.

Berger, Roger W., "Use Risk Analysis For Decision-Making," *Computer Decisions*, March 1972, pp. 13-22.

Berhold, Marvin and John Coffman, "Decision Science Concepts—Foundation For the Future," *Business* (Formerly Atlanta Business Review), January-February 1979, pp. 9-16.

Blakeney, Susan, "DSS Seen Moving Ahead in Information Area," *Computerworld* May 10, 1982, pp. 16-23.

____, "Speaker Warns Against Dependence on DSS," *Computerworld*, March 29, 1982, pp. 16-27.

Blanning, Robert W., "The Sources and Uses of Sensitivity Information,"*Interfaces*, August 1974, pp. 32-38.

____, "Information Systems for Model Based Planning," *Proceedings, tenth Annual Conference, Society for Management Information Systems*, 1978, pp. 132-140.

____, "Model-Based and Data-Based Planning Systems," *Omega*, Vol. 9, No. 2, 1981, pp. 163-168.

____, "Information Systems for Model-Based Planning," *MIS: The Universal Organizational Resource*, Proceedings Tenth Annual Conference SMIS, Washington, D.C., September, 18-22, 1978. [SMIS—Society for Management Information Systems.]

____, "The Functions of a Decision Support System," *Information and Management*, No. 2, 1979, pp. 87-93.

Bonczek, Robert H., Clyde W. Holsapple, and Andrew B. Whinston, "Computer-Based Support of Organizational Decision-Making," *Decision Sciences*, April, 1979, pp. 268-291.

____, "Aiding Decision Makers with a Generalized Data Base Management System: An Application to Inventory Management," *Decision Sciences*, 1979, pp. 228-235.

____, "Future Directions For Developing Decision Support Systems," *Decision Sciences*, October 1980, pp. 616-631.

Bonczek, Robert, Clyde Holsapple, and Andrew B. Holsapple, "Development Tools for Decision Support Systems," *Computer World*, September 14, 1981, in depth, pp. 25-26+.

Boehm, George A.W., "Shaping Decisions With Systems Analysis," *Harvard Business Review*, September-October 1976, pp. 91-99.

Bonoma, Thomas V. and Dennis P. Slevin, "Management and the Type II Error," *Business Horizons*, August 1978, pp. 61-67.

Borje, Langford, Discussion of "Determining Management Information Needs: A Comparison of Methods" (Appearing in the *MIS Quarterly*, June 1977), *MIS Quarterly*, December 1977, pp. 53-56.

Boulden, James B. and Elwood S. Buffa, "Corporate Models: On-Line Real Time Systems," *Harvard Business Review*, July-August 1970.

Boulden, James B. and E.R. McLean, "An Executive's Guide to Computer Based Planning," *California Management Review*, Fall 1974, pp. 58-67.

Brady, Rodney, "Computers in Top Level Decision Making," *Harvard Business Review*, July-August 1967, pp. 67-76.

Briggs, Warren G., "Decision Support Systems: An Evaluation of DSS Packages," *Computer World*, March 1, in depth, 1981, pp. 30-35.

____, and C.L. Meador, "Distributed DSS," *Computer World*, October 1981.

Brightman, H. "Differences in Ill-Structured Problem Solving Along the Organizational Hierarchy," *Decision Sciences*, Vol. 9, 1978, pp. 1-8.

Brown, Rex V., "Do Managers Find Decision Theory Useful," *Harvard Business Review*, May-June 1970, pp. 78–89.

Bruce, James W., "Management Reporting System: A New Marriage Between Management and Financial Data Through Management Science," *Interfaces*, November, 1977, pp. 54–63.

Bucatinsky, Julio, "Ask Your Computer 'What if...,'" *Financial Executive*, July 1973.

Bucatinsky, Julio, "Improve Your Decision-Making," *Automation*, July 1973, pp. 34–38.

Bunn, Derek and Howard Thomas, "Decision Analysis and Strategic Policy Formulation," *Long Range Planning*, December 1977, pp. 23–30.

C

Carbonnel, F.E. and R.G. Dorrance, "Information Sources For Planning Decisions," *California Management Review*, XV, (4), pp. 42–53.

Carlson, Eric D., Barbara F. Grace, and Jimmy A. Sutton, "Case Studies of End User Requirements for Interactive Problem Solving Systems," *MIS Quarterly*, March 1977, pp. 51–63.

____, "An Approach for Designing Decision Support Systems," *Data Base*, Winter 1977, pp. 3–15.

____, "Decision Support Systems: Personal Computing Services For Managers," *Management Review*, January 1977, pp. 4–11.

____, [Editor], "Proceedings of a Conference on Decision Support Systems," *Data Base*, Vol. 8, No. 3, Winter 1977.

Casey, Cornelius J., "Coping With Information Overload: The Need for Empirical Research," *Cost and Management*, July-August 1982, pp. 31–37.

Chorba, Ronald W. and Joan L. New, "Information Support for Decision-Making in a Competitive Environment," *Decision Sciences*, October, 1980, pp. 603–615.

Comer, James M., "The Computer, Personal Selling, and Sales Management," *Journal of Marketing*, July 1975.

"Computer Support for Managers," *EDP Analyzer*, May 1979.

"Computers That Think Are Here," *Dun's Review*, October 1981, pp. 111–112.

Conhagen, Amy Ellis, "Decisions Support Systems In Banking," *Bankers Magazine*, May-June 1982, pp. 79–84.

Cook, Victor, "Computers Pay Off in Marketing," *Business Horizons*, April 1972, pp. 25–34.

Cooper, D.O., L.B. Davidson, and W.K. Denison, "A Tool For More Effective Financial Analysis," *Interfaces*, February 1975, pp. 91–103.

Couger, Daniel J., "Computers and the Schools of Business: Evolution of MIS Course to Include DOS," *Decision Line*, Vol. 10, No. 3, May 1979, p. 6. See also *Computing Newsletter*, Oct., Nov., Dec. 1978, March 1979.

____, "Computers and The School of Business," II, *Decision Line*, November/December 1979, pp. 9–10.

Courtney, James F., and Ronald L. Jensen, "Teaching DSS with DBMS," *Data Base*, Spring 1981, pp. 7–11.

____, "Incorporating MIS/DSS Into Policy Courses Via Simulation," and Raymond McLeod and Jack W. Jones, "Introducing Decision Support Systems Into Business School Curricula," *Journal of Experiential Learning and Simulation*, December 1981, pp. 203–212 and 213–228.

Cowey, A. and D. Green, "A Marketing Model For a Price Promoted Consumer Good: A Case Study," *Operational Research Quarterly*, Vol. 26, No. 1, 1975, pp. 3–14.

"Corporate War Rooms Plug Into the Computer," *Business Week*, August 23, 1976, pp. 65-66.

D

"Data Processing: 'What If' Help For Management," *Business Week*, January 21, 1980, pp. 73–74.

Davidson, Lynn B. and Dale O. Cooper, "Implementing Effective Risk Analysis At Getty Oil Company," *Interfaces*, December 1980, pp. 62–75.

Davis, K. Roscoe, "The Process of Problem Finding: A Production-Marketing Example," *Interfaces*, November 1977, Vol. 8, No. 1, pp. 82–85.

____, and B.W. Taylor, "Terminal Based Systems: A Key To Putting The Computer in Marketing," *Industrial Marketing Management*, (1976), pp. 197–207.

Davis, K.R. and R.A. Leitch, "Improving Marketing-Production Through On-Line Modeling," *Production & Inventory Management*, 2nd Quarter, 1976, pp. 79–92.

Davis, Charles K., and James C. Wetherbe, "DSS For Chargeout System Planning, Control in Large-Scale Environment," *Data Base*, Summer 1980, pp. 13–20.

Davis, Richard K., "Strategic, Tactical, and Operational Planning and Budgeting: A Study of Decision Support System Evolution," *MIS Quarterly*, December 1979, pp. 1–19.

DeNeufville, Richard, "Systems Analysis—A Decision Process," *Industrial Management Review*, Spring 1970, pp. 49–58.

De Waele, M., "Managerial Style and the Design of Decision Aids," *Omega*, Vol. 6, No. 1, 1978, pp. 5–13.

Delbecq, A., "The Management of Decision-Making in the Firm: Three Strategies for Three Types of Firms," *Academy of Management Journal*, 10 (4), 1967, pp. 329–339.

Dickson, Gary W., "Management Information – Decision Systems," *Business Horizons*, December 1968, pp. 17–26.

De, Prabudda and Arun Sen, "Logical Data Base Design in Decision Support Systems," *Journal of Systems Management*, May 1981, pp. 28-33.

Digman, Lester A., "A Decision Analysis of the Airline Coupon Strategy," *Interfaces*, April 1980, pp. 97-101.

Doktor, R.H. and W.F. Hamilton, "Cognitive Style and the Acceptance of Management Science Recommendations," *Management Science*, April 1973, pp. 884-894.

Donovan, J.J. "Database System Approach to Management Decision Support," *ACH Transactions on Database Systems*, Vol. 1, No. 4, December 1976, pp. 344-369.

Dresser, Michael, et al, "What the Hot Marketing Tool of the '80s Offers You," *Industrial Marketing*, March 1983, pp. 51-60.

E

Edelman, Franz, "They Went Thataway," *Interfaces*, May 1977, pp. 39-43.

Edelson, Edward, "Expert Systems: Computers That Think Like People," *Popular Science*.

Eilon, Samuel, "Goals and Constraints in Decision Systems," *Operational Research Quarterly*, March 1972, pp. 3-15.

____, "Mathematical Modelling For Management," *Interfaces*, February 1974, pp. 28-32.

____, "What is a Decision," *Management Science*, 16, No. 4, December 1969.

Ein-Dor, Phillip and Eli Segen, "Strategic Planning for Management Information Systems," *Management Science*, November 1978, pp. 1631-1641.

Elam, Rich, "General Purpose Simulation System: A Management Tool," *Managerial Planning*, May/June 1977, pp. 29-34.

Emery, Douglas R., and Francis D. Tuggle, "On the Evaluation of Decisions," *MSU Business Topics*, Spring 1976, pp. 42-48.

Erwing, D.W., "Discovering Your Problem Solving Style," *Psychology Today*, December 1977.

Emshoff, James R., "Experience Generalized Decision-Making: The Next Generation of Managerial Models," *Interfaces*, August 1978, pp. 40-48.

Emery, James C., "Decision Models," Parts 1, 2, *Datamation*, September 1, 1970, pp. 32-36, and September 15, 1970, pp. 59-64.

Enrick, Norbert L., "Development of Models for Marketing Decisions," *Journal of Academy of Marketing Science*, Summer 1974, pp. 465-477.

F

Farwell, David C. and Ted Farwell, "Decision Support System for Ski Area Design," *Journal of Systems Management*, March 1982, pp. 32-38.

Fey, Curt F., "Putting Numbers Where Your Hunches Used To Be," *IEEE Spectrum*, July 1974, pp. 34-40.

"Financial Modeling Software: Tools For the Overworked Manager," *Personal Computing*, June 1981, pp. 22–28, 59–62.

"Financial Planning Models," Special Issue, *IBM Systems Journal*, Vol. 12, No. 2, 1973.

Fischer, Robert A., "Decision Support Systems: Don't Look Back," *Computer World*, October 29, 1979, 5/16.

"Focus on Planning," Special Issue, *Management Focus*, Peat, Marwick, Mitchell, January-February 1979.

Frank, Jonathan and Jaques Schnabel, "Timing of Borrowing Decisions—A Decision Support System," *Journal of Systems Management,* April 1983, pp. 6–9.

Fudge, William D., and Leonard M. Lodish, "Evaluation of the Effectiveness of a Model Based Salesman's Planning System by Field Experimentation," *Interfaces*, November 1977, No. 1, Part 2, pp. 97–106.

Fuehrer, Walter, "Corporate Modeling: A Selective Focus Will Make It Work," *Managerial Planning*, November/December 1976, pp. 20–23.

Fuller, Don, "Decision Making: A Little Technique Goes a Long Way," *Machine Design*, July 22, 1976, pp. 64–68.

Fuller, Jack A. and Roger M. Atherton, "Fitting in the Management Science Specialist," *Business Horizons*, April 1979, pp. 14–17.

G

Getz, C.W., "MIS and the War Room," *Datamation*, December 1977, pp. 66–70.

Geoffrion, Arthur M., "Better Distribution Planning With Computer Models," *Harvard Business Review*, July/August 1976, pp. 92–99.

___, "A Guide To Computer-Assisted Methods For Distribution Planning," *Sloan Management Review*, Winter 1975, pp. 17–41.

Gerrity, T.P., "Design of Man-Machine Systems: An Application to Portfolio Management," *Sloan Management Review*, Winter 1971, pp. 59–75.

Geschika/Horst, et al, "Modern Techniques for Solving Problems," *Chemical Engineering*, August 6, 1973, pp. 91–97.

Gibson, L.D., C.S. Mayer, C.E. Nugent, and T.E. Vollman, "An Evolutionary Approach to Marketing Information Systems," *Journal of Marketing*, April 1973, pp. 2–6.

Gilliver, Alan and Harvey Gordon, "An Analytic Information System for a Representative Sales Force: A Case Study," *Operational Research Quarterly*, August 1978, Vol. 29, No. 8, pp. 717–730.

Ginzberg, J.J., "Steps Toward More Effective Implementation of MOS and MIS," *Interfaces*, May 1978, pp. 57–63.

Ginzberg, Michael J., "Redesign of Managerial Tasks: A Requisite for Successful Decision Support Systems," *MIS Quarterly*, March 1978, pp. 39–52.

____, "Steps Towards More Effective Implementation of MS and MIS," *Interfaces*, May 1978, pp. 57-68.

Ghymn, K. and W.A. King, "Design of a Strategic Planning Information System," *Omega*, Vol. 4, No. 5, 1976, pp. 595-607.

Glover, Fred, Gene Jones, David Karney, Darwin Klingman, and John Mote, "An Integrated Production, Distribution, and Inventory Planning System," *Interfaces*, November 1979, pp. 21-35.

Gorry, G.A. and Scott Morton, Michael, "A Framework for Management Information Systems," *Sloan Management Review*, Fall 1971, pp. 55-77.

____, "The Development of Managerial Models," *Sloan Management Review*, Winter 1971, pp. 1-16.

Grayson, C. Jackson, "Management Science and Business Practice," *Harvard Business Review*, July/August 1973, pp. 41-48.

Green, Thad B., "An Empirical Analysis of Nominal and Interacting Groups," *Academy of Management Journal*, Vol. 18, No. 1, 1975, pp. 63-73.

Greer, Willis R., "Value Added Criterion for Decision Support System Development," *Journal of Systems Management*, May 1980, pp. 15-19.

Griffin, Marvin A., "Information Processing Systems," *Alle Transactions*, September 1976, pp. 307-313.

Gross, Andrew C. and Samuel A. Wolpert, "New Information Technology Impacts Business Hierarchy," *Infosystems*, October 1979, pp. 128-132.

H

Hackathorn, Richard D. and Peter G.W. Keen, "Organizational Strategies for Personal Computing in Decision Support Systems," *MIS Quarterly*, September 1981, pp. 21-27.

Hahn, Gerald J., "Some Uses of Time-Sharing Computers in Statistical Analysis," *American Statistician*, December 1968, pp. 14-18.

Hall, Jay, "Decisions, Decisions, Decisions," *Psychology Today*, November 1971.

Hamilton, William F. and Michael A. Moses, "A Computer-Based Corporate Planning System," *Management Science*, October 1974, pp. 148-159.

Hamilton, William F. and Michael A. Moses, "An Optimization Model for Corporate Financial Planning," *Operations Research*, May/June 1973, pp. 677-692.

Hammond, John A., "Better Decisions With Preference Theory," *Harvard Business Review*, November/December 1967.

____, "The Roles of the Manager and Management Scientists in Successful Implementation," *Sloan Management Review*, Winter 1974, pp. 148-159.

____, "Do's and Don'ts of Computer Models for Planning," *Harvard Business Review*, 1974, Vol. 52, No. 2, March/April 1974, pp. 110-125.

Hansen, James, L.E. Heitger, and Lynn McKell, "Computer Aided Modelling of Decision Support Systems," *Operational Research Quarterly*, August 1978, Vol. 29, No. 8, pp. 789-802.

Hax, Arnoldo C., "Planning a Manufacturing Information System for a Distributing and Manufacturing Company," *Sloan Management Review*, Spring 1973, pp. 85-98.

Hayes, R.H. and R.L. Nolan, "What Kind of Corporate Modelling Functions Best," *Harvard Business Review*, May/June 1974, pp. 102-122.

Heckerman, Donald A., "Financial Modelling: A Powerful Tool for Planning and Decision Support," *Managerial Planning*, March/April, 1982, pp. 21-25.

Heenan, David A. and Robert B. Adelman, "Keeping Informed—Quantitative Techniques for Today's Decision Makers," *Harvard Business Review*, May/June 1976, pp. 32-36, 40, 46, 51, 56, 62.

Hellriegel, Don and John W. Slocum, "Managerial Problem Solving Styles," *Business Horizons*, December 1975, pp. 29-37.

Henderson, John C. and John M. West, Jr., "Planning for MIS: A Decision-Oriented Approach," *MIS Quarterly*, June 1979, pp. 45-58.

Henderson, John C. and Paul C. Nutt, "On the Design of Planning Information Systems," *Academy of Management Review*, October 1979, pp. 774-785.

Herbert, Theodore T. and Edward B. Yost, "A Comparison of Decision Quality Under Nominal and Interacting Consensus Group Formats: The Case of the Structured Problem," *Decision Sciences*, Vol. 10, 1979, pp. 358-370.

Hoard, Bruce, "Decision Analysis Promises Success," *Computerworld*, October 5, 1981, pp. 24.

Hocking, Ralph T. and Joan M. Hocking, "The Evolution of Decision Systems," *MSU Business Topics*, Summer 1976, pp. 55-59.

Hoffman, Gerald M. "The Contribution of Management Science to Management Information," *Interfaces*, November 1978, pp. 34-39.

Howard, Niles, "Decisions, Decisions, Decisions," *Dun's Review*, May 1981, pp. 98-101.

Huber, George P., "The Nature of Organizational Decision-Making and the Design of Decision Support Systems," *MIS Quarterly*, June 1981, pp. 1-10.

Hudson, Ronald G. and John C. Chambers and Robert G. Johnson, "New Product Planning Decisions Under Uncertainty," *Interfaces*, November 1977, Vol. 8, No. 1, Part 2, pp. 82-96.

Hunsaker, Phillip L. and Johanna S., "Decision Styles—In Theory, In Practice," *Organizational Dynamics*, Autumn 1981 pp. 23-36.

I

"Interesting Decision Support Systems," *EDP Analyzer*, March 1982.

Issaack, Thomas S., "Intuition: An Ignored Dimension of Management," *Academy of Management Review*.

Ives, Brian D., "Ideational Items: Decision Theory and the Manager," *Business Horizons*, June 1973, pp. 38-40.

"Improvements in Man-Machine Interfacing," *EDP Analyzer*, April 1975, B pp.

J

Jacob, Jean-Paul and Ralph H. Sprague, "Graphical Problem Solving in DSS," *Data Base*, Fall 1980, pp. 33-39.

Jackson, Barbara and Benson P. Shapiro, "New Way to Make Product Line Decisions," *Harvard Business Review*, May/June 1979, pp. 139-149.

Johnson, J. "The Implementation of Computer Assisted Underwriting," *Interfaces*, February 1976, pp. 2-13.

Jones, Curtis H., "At Last: Real Computer Power for Decision Makers," *Harvard Business Review*, September/October 1970, pp. 75-90.

Jones, Jack William, "Making Your Decision Support System Pay Off," *Computer Decisions*, June 1979, pp. 46-47.

K

Kabas, Irwin, "You Can Bank on Uncertainty," *Harvard Business Review*, May/June 1976, pp. 95-105.

———, "Risk Analysis: The Forgotten Tool," *Management Review*, June 1981, pp. 42-50.

Kanter, Jerome, "Putting Management Into Management Information Systems," *Infosystems*, 12/79, pp. 48-53.

Kaplan, Sheldon, "Computer Modeling Plans For The Future," *Administrative Management*, September, 1981, pp. 43-44-54, 56.

Keen, Peter G.W., "Adaptive Design for Decision Support Systems," *Data Base*, Fall 1980, pp. 15-25.

Keen, Peter, "Computer-Based Decision Aids: The Evaluation Problems" *Sloan Management Review*, Spring, 1975, pp. 17-29.

Keen, Peter, "Interactive Computer Systems for Managers," *Sloan Management Review*, Fall 1976, pp. 1-17.

Keen, Peter G.W. "Value Analysis: Justifying Decision Support Systems," *MIS Quarterly*, March 1981, pp. 1-16.

Keeney, Ralph L. "Decision Analysis: How To Cope With Increasing Complexity," *Management Review*, September 1979, pp. 24-40.

Kennedy, Miles H. and Jeffrey A. Hoffer, "Real-Time Data Processing and Real-Time Decision-Making," *Journal of Systems Management*, October 1978, pp. 21-25.

Kilmann, Ralph H. and Ian I. Mitnoff, "Qualitative versus Quantitative Analysis For Management Science: Different Forms For Different Psychological Types," *Interfaces*, February 1976, pp. 17-27.

King, John L., "Cost Benefit Analysis For Decision-Making," *Journal of Systems Management*, May 1980, pp. 24-29.

King, R.H. and R.R. Love, Jr., "Coordinating Decisions For Increased Profits," *Interfaces*, December 1980, pp. 4-19.

King, William R., "Strategic Planning For Management Information Systems," *MIS Quarterly*, March 1978, pp. 27-37.

King, William R., Biplab K. Dutta, and Jaime T. Rodriguez, "Strategic Competitive Information Systems," *Omega*, Vol. 6, No. 2, pp. 123-132.

King, William R., and David Cleland, "The Design of Management Information Systems: An Information Analysis Approach," *Management Science*, November 1975, pp. 286-297.

____ and ____, "Environmental Information Systems For Strategic Marketing Planning," *Journal of Marketing*, October 1974, pp. 35-40.

King, William R. and David I. Cleland, "Manager Analyst Teamwork in MIS," *Business Horizons*, April 1971, pp. 59-68.

King, William R., and David I. Cleland, "The Design of Management Information Systems: An Information Analysis Approach," *Management Science*, November 1975, pp. 286-297.

King, William R., "The Intelligent MIS: A Management Helper," *Business Horizons*, October 1973, pp. 5-12.

King, William R. and Jamie I. Rodriguez, "Participative Design of Decision Support Systems: An Empirical Assessment," *Management Science*, June 1981, pp. 717-726.

Kingston, Paul L., "Generic Managerial Support Systems," *Managerial Planning*, March-April 1981, pp. 7-11.

Kingston, Paul L., "The Anatomy of a Financial Model," *Managerial Planning*, November-December 1977, pp. 1-7.

Klein, Richard, "Computer Based Financial Modeling," *Journal of Systems Management*, May 1982, pp. 6-13.

Kling, Rob, "The Organizational Context of User-Centered Software Designs," *MIS Quarterly*, December 1977, pp. 41-52.

Kolb, D.A. and A.L. Frohman, "An Organizational Development Approach to Management Consulting," *Sloan Management Review*, Fall 1970, pp. 51-60.

Kolb, David A., "Management and the Learning Process," *California Management Review*, Spring 1976, pp. 21-31.

Koncazc, Edward F., "Models are for Managers, Not Mathematicians," *Journal of Systems Management*, January 1975, pp. 12-15.

____, "New Demand for Managing Management Science," *Journal of Systems Management*, November 1979.

Kosaka, Takeshi and Tetsuo Hirouchi, "An Effective Architecture for Decision Support Systems," *Information and Management*, No. 5, 1982, pp. 7-17.

Kotler, Philip, "Corporate Models: Better Marketing Plans," *Harvard Business Review*, July-August, 1970, pp. 135-152.

Kuebel, Charles H. "The Future MIS," *Business Automation*, June 1972, pp. 18–19, 42–46.

Kull, David J. "Group Decisions: Can Computers Help?," *Computer Decisions*, May 1982, pp. 70–84, 106.

L

La Brecque, Mort, "On Making Sounder Judgments: Strategies and Snares," *Psychology Today*, June 1980, pp. 33–42.

LaBriola, Peter, "Corporate Planning Systems: A Decade of Evolution," *Infosystems*, 11/79, pp. 68–69.

Lambin, Jean Jacques, "A Computer On-Line Marketing Mix Model," *Journal of Marketing Research*, May 1972.

Lang, James R., John E. Dittuch, and Sam E. White, "Managerial Problem Solving Models: A Review and A Proposal," *Academy of Management Review*, October 1978, pp. 854–866.

Lankau, Walter E., "Decision Support Systems Clearly Explained," *Computer World*.

Lasden, Martin, "Computer Aided Decision-Making," *Computer Decisions*, December 1982, pp. 156–172.

Leavitt, Harold J., "Beyond the Analytic Manager," *California Management Review*, Spring 1976, pp. 5–12.

Leighton, Robert T., "Decision Support Systems," *Journal of Systems Management*, February 1981, pp. 40–41.

Lewis, Walker, "What The Computer Can Do For The Planner," *Journal of Business Strategy*, 1981, pp. 70–72.

Lindgren, Richard K., "Justifying a Decision Support System," *Data Management*, May 1981, pp. 30–32.

Little, John D.C., "Brandaid," *Operations Research*, May 1975, pp. 628–673.

——, "Models and Managers: The Concept of A Decision Calculus," *Management Science*, April 1970, pp. 466–485.

Little, John D.C., Lakshmi Mohan, and Antoine Hatoun, "Banking Knowledge From the Numbers: How Marketing Decision Systems Can Work For You," *Industrial Marketing*, March 1982, pp. 46–50, 52–56.

Locander, William B., H. Albert Napier, Richard Napier, Richard W. Scamell, "A Team Approach to Managing the Development of a Decision Support System," *MIS Quarterly*, March 1979, pp. 53–63.

Lodish, Leonard M., "Call Plan: An Interactive Salesman's Call Planning System," *Management Science*, Part II, December 1976.

Lois, Paul, "Study Probes Efficient DSS Development," *Computer World*, November 23, 1981, pp. 35.

Loye, David, "The Forecasting Mind," *The Futurist*, June, 1979, pp. 173-177.

Lucas, Henry C., "Unsuccessful Implementation: The Case of a Computer-Based Order Entry System," *Decision Sciences*, January 1978, pp. 68-79.

Luhring, "Personal Computer Spread Sheets," *Machine Design*, June 10, 1982, pp. 79-83.

Lusk, E.J. and M. Kensnick, "The Effect of Cognitive Style and Report Format on Task Performance: The MIS Design Consequences," *Management Science*, August 1979, pp. 787-798.

M

Magee, John F., "Decision Trees For Decision Making," *Harvard Business Review*, July/August 1964, pp. 126-138.

Maley, Al, "Guidelines for Selecting a Statistical System," *Infosystems*, June, 1977, pp. 66, 68, 70.

Mann, Herschel, "Sensitivity Analysis and Decision-Making," *Cost and Management*, September/October 1973, pp. 19-24.

Marenghi, Catherine, "Executives DSS as Invaluable Support—Not Replacement —For Decision-Making," *Computerworld*, June 28, 1982, pp. 16-31.

Martin, Merle P., "Decision-Making: The Payoff Matrix," *Journal of Systems Management*, January 1979, pp. 14-18.

Martin, M.J.C. and S.G. Penose, "Transactional Analysis: Another Way of Approaching OR/MS Implementation," *Interfaces*, February 1977, pp. 91-98.

Mason, Richard and Ian I. Mitroff, "A Program for Research on Management Information Systems," *Management Science*, 19 (s), 1973, pp. 475-483.

_____ and E. Burton Swanson, "Measurement for Management Decision: A Perspective," *California Management Review*, Spring 1979, pp. 70-81.

_____, "Basic concepts for designing Management Information Systems," AIS Research Paper No. 8, October 1969. Reprinted in *Information For Decision-Making Quantitative and Behavioral Dimension's*, Alfred Rapaport, Editor, 1970.

McCarthy, Daniel J. and Charles A. Morrissey, "Using the Systems Analyst in Preparing Corporate Financial Models," *Financial Executive*, June 1972.

McFarlan, F. Warren, "Portfolio Approach to Information Systems," *Harvard Business Review*, September/October, 1981, pp. 142-150.

McKenney, J.L. and Peter Keen, "How Managers Minds Work," *Harvard Business Review*, May/June 1974, pp. 79-90.

Meador, Charles L., and D.N. Ness, "Decision Support Systems: An Application to Corporate Planning," *Sloan Management Review*, Winter 1974, pp. 51-68.

Methue, Leif B., "Data Management for Decision Support Systems," *Data Base*, Fall 1980, pp. 40-46.

Miller, Irvin M., "Economic Art Speeds Business Decision-Making," *Computer Decisions*, July 1972, pp. 18-21.

——, "Computer Graphics for Decision-Making," *Harvard Business Review*, November/December 1969, pp. 121-132.

Miller, Robert B., "Archetypes in Man-Computer Problem Solving," *Ergonomics*, July 1969, pp. 559-581.

Mintzberg, Henry, "Managerial Work: Analysis From Observation," *Management Science*, 1971, Vol. 18, No. 2, pp. B 97-B 110; and "The Manager's Job: Folklore and Fact," *Harvard Business Review*, July/August 1975.

Mintzberg, Henry, "Planning on the Left Side and Managing on the Right," *Harvard Business Review*, July/August 1976, pp. 49-58.

——, "Strategy-Making in Three Modes," *California Management Review*, Winter 1973.

—— and Raisinghani D., and Thoret, A., "The Structure of Unstructured Decision Processes," *Administrative Science Quarterly*, June 1976, pp. 246-275.

Montgomery, David B., and Clen L. Urban, "Marketing Decision Information Systems—An Emerging View," *Journal of Marketing Research*, May 1970, pp. 226-234.

Morris, William T., "On the Art of Modeling," *Management Science*, August 1969, pp. 707-717.

Munro, Malcolm R., "Determining The Manager's Information Needs," *Journal of Systems Management*, June 1978, pp. 34-39.

Munro, Malcolm R. and Gordon B. Davis, "Determining Management Information Needs: A Comparison of Methods," *MIS Quarterly*, June 1977, pp. 55-67.

Murnighan, J. Keith, "Group Decision Making: What Strategies Should You Use?," *Management Review*, February 1981, pp. 55-62.

N

Napier, H. Albern, "The Utilization of Financial Planning Systems in Decision Support Systems," *Journal of Data Education*, July 1980, pp. 13-18.

Naylor, Thomas H., "Decision Support Systems or Whatever Happened to M.I.S.?" *Interfaces*, August 1982, pp. 92-94.

——, "Why Corporate Planning Models?," *Interfaces*, Vol 8, No. 1, November 1977, pp. 87-94.

——, "The Future of Corporate Planning Models," *Managerial Planning*, March/April 1976.

Ness, David and C.R. Sprague, "An Interactive Media Decision Support System," *Sloan Management Review*, Fall 1972, pp. 51-61.

Neumann, Seev and Michael Hadass, "DSS and Strategic Decisions," *California Management Review*, Spring 1980, pp. 77-84.

Nolan, Richard L. and James C. Weath Erbe, "Toward a Comprehensive Framework for MIS Research," *MIS Quarterly*, June 1980, pp. 1–20.

Nutt, Paul Charles, "Influence of Decision Styles on Use of Decision Models," *Technological Forecasting and Social Change*, 14, 17, 77–93, 1979.

O

Oelberg, P.O., "Unprogrammed Decision Making," *Industrial Management Review*, Spring 1967, pp. 19–29.

Olson, Philip P., "Notes: Decision Making: Type I and Type II Error Analysis," *California Management Review*, Fall 1977, pp. 81–83.

Oren, Samuel S. Michael H. Rothkopf, and Richard D. Smallwood, "Evaluating a New Market: A Forecasting System for Nonimpact Computer Printers," *Interfaces*, December 1980, pp. 76–87.

Oxenfeldt, Alfred R., "Effective Decision-Making for the Business Executive," *Management Review*, February 1978, (Condensed in Management Digest, August, 1978, pp. 4–8).

Ozernoy, Vladmir M., Dennis R. Smith and Alan Sicherman, "Evaluating Computerized Geographic Information Systems Using Decision Analysis," *Interfaces,* October 1981, pp. 92–99.

P

Peck, Stephan C., "Communicating Model Based Information for Energy Debates: Two Case Studies," *Interfaces*, October 1980, pp. 42–48.

Pukempner, Stanley, "Management Information Systems—A Pragmatic Survey," *Conference Board Record*, May 1973, pp. 49–54.

Pounds, W.F., "The Process of Problem Finding," *Industrial Management Review*, Fall 1969, pp. 1–20.

R

Radford, K.J., "Decision Making in a Turbulent Environment," *Operational Research Quarterly*, Vol. 29, No. 7, 1978, pp. 677–682.

——, "Information Systems and Managerial Decision Making," *Omega*, Vol. 2, 1974, pp. 235–242.

Raiborn, Mitchell H. and William T. Harris, "Systems Approach to Model Design," *Cost and Management*, May/June 1974, pp. 33–42.

Rakes, Terry and Lori Franz, "Model Procurement and Development Decision in MIS," *Journal of Systems Management*, July 1981, pp. 30–35.

Rappaport, Alfred, "Management MIS Information Systems—Another Perspective," *Management Science*, December 1968, pp. B133–B136.

Raudsepp, Eugene, "Nuturing Managerial Creativity," *Administrative Management*, October 1980, pp. 32–33, 55–56.

Ranin, J. and M. Schatzoff, "An Interactive Graphics System for Analysis of Business Decisions" *IBM Systems Journal*, No. 3, 1973, pp. 239-256.

Reed, Stanley Foster, "On the Dynamics of Group Decision Making in High Places," *Directors & Boards*, Winter 1978, pp. 40-56.

Reeser, Clayton, "Making Decisions Scientifically," *Machine Design*, June 29, 1972, pp. 52-57.

Richman, Eugene and Dennis Coleman, "Monte Carlo Simulation for Management," *California Management Review*, Spring 1981, pp. 82-94.

Robey, Daniel and William Taggart, "Measuring Managers Minds: The Assessment of Style in Human Information Processing," *Academy of Management Review*, July 1981, pp. 375-383.

Rockart, John F., "Chief Executives Define Their Own Data Needs;" Richard L. Nolan, "Managing the Crisis in Data Processing," *Harvard Business Review*, March/April 1979, pp. 81-93 and 115-126.

Roberts, Edward B., "Strategies for Effective Implementation of Complex Corporate Models," *Interfaces*, November 1977, Vol. 8, No. 1, pp. 26-33.

Roy, Asim, Emma E. De Falomir, and Leon Lasdon, "An Optimization-Based Decision Support Systems for a Product Mix Problem," *Interfaces*, April 1982, pp. 26-33.

Roy, Herbert J.H., "Using Computer Based Control Systems for Decision-Making," *Advanced Management Journal*, January 1971, pp. 57-62.

Rucks, Andrew C. and Peter Ginter, "Strategic MIS: Promises Unfilled," *Journal of Systems Management*, March 1982, pp. 16-19.

Russo, Joseph A., "What To Look For In Computer Assisted Planning Systems," *Managerial Planning*, July/August 1976, pp. 5-8.

S

Saipe, Alan L., "Conditional Risk Analysis," *Decision Sciences*, January, 1978, pp. 19-36.

Sanderson, I.W., "An Interactive Planning System in the Chemical Industry," *Operational Research Quarterly*, August 1978, Vol. 29, No. 8, pp. 731-740.

Schaffir, Kurt H., "Marketing Information Systems," *Management Informatics*, February 1974, pp. 29-36.

Schendel, Dan, "Designing Strategic Planning Systems," *Academy of Management Journal*, October 1978.

Schneyman, Arthur H., "Management Information Systems for Management Sciences," *Interfaces*, May 1976, pp. 52-59.

Schonberger, Richard J., "MIS Design: A Contingency Approach," *MIS Quarterly*, March 1980, pp. 13-20.

Schrage, Michael, "DSS: What to Make of What-If Software," *Business Computer Systems*, September 1982, pp. 25-26.

Schrenk, L.P., "Aiding the Decision-Maker—A Decision Process Model," *Ergonomics*, July 1969, pp. 204–218.

Schuler, C.O., "How Good Are the Decision Makers?," *Business Horizons*, April 1975, pp. 89–93.

Schultz, Brad, "MIT Developing Concepts for a Successful EIS," *Computerworld*, June 29, 1981.

Seabolg, Ronald A. and Charlotte Seaberg, "Computer Based Decision Systems," *Management Science*, (Part II), December, 1973, pp. 575–584.

Seils, Harold L., "Do Decision Support Systems Really Support," *Computerworld*, June 28, 1982, 16: Sr/38.

Shaffer, Richard A., "Judgment Day: The Thinking Computer Arrives," *Wall Street Journal*, 9/3/82.

Shneiderman, Ben, "Human Factors Experiments in Designing Interactive Systems," *Computers*, December 1979, pp. 9–19.

Shycon, Harvey, "All Around the Model: Perspectives on MS Applications (Computer Graphics)," *Interfaces*, August 1975, pp. 70–73.

Slovic, Paul, Baruch Fischhoff, and Sarah Lichtenstein, "Risky Assumptions," *Psychology Today*, June 1980, pp. 44–48.

Small, Michael, "Business Planning Needs Computer Models Too," *Infosystems*, December, 1976, pp. 44, 47, 63.

Sprague, Ralph and Hugh Watson, "A Decision Support System for Banks," *Omega*, Vol. 4, No. 6, 1976.

———, "MIS Concepts: Parts 1 and 2," *Journal of Systems Management*, January 1975, pp. 34–37; February 1975, pp. 35–40.

———, "Bit by Bit: Toward Decision Support Systems," *California Management Review*, Fall 1979, pp. 60–68.

Smart, Phillip C., "Ingredients for a Successful Decision Support System," *Data Management*, January 1983, pp. 26–33.

Sprague, Ralph H. "A Framework for the Development of Decision Support Systems," *MIS Quarterly*, No. 4, pp. 1–26, December 1980.

———, "System Support for a Financial Planning Model," *Management Accounting*, June 1972, pp. 29–34; and "A Conceptual Description of a Financial Planning Model for Commercial Banks," *Decision Sciences*, Jan./March 1971.

Ralph Sprague and Ronald L. Olson, "The Financial Planning System At Louisiana National Bank," *MIS Quarterly*, September 1979, pp. 35–45.

Sprague, Ralph H., Laurence T. Burden, Ronald L. Olson, Louis Contreros, "Decision Support Systems," *MIS and the Bottom Line: Satisfying Senior Management Expectations*, Proceedings of the Eleventh Annual Conference of the Society for Management Information Systems, Minneapolis, Minnesota, September 10-13, 1979, pp. 45–56.

Sprague, Ralph H., "Attribute Analysis of Information Technology Support for Managerial Tasks," *Proceedings American Institute of Decision Sciences*, New Orleans, Louisiana, 1979, 3 pp.

Stephenson, Blair Y. and Stephen G. Franklin, "Better Decision-Making for a Real World Environment," *Administrative Management,* July 1981, pp. 24-26, 36-38.

Swanson, E.B., "Management Information Systems: Appreciation and Use," *Management Science,* No. 21, 1974, pp. 189-198.

T

Taplin, J., "AAIMS: American Airlines Answers the What Ifs," *Infosystems,* February 1973, pp. 40-41.

Tersine, Richard J., "Organization Decision Theory—A Synthesis," *Managerial Planning,* July/August 1972, pp. 18-26, 40.

Thayer, Richard P., "Statmod: An Integrated Package of Computer Programs for Statistical Analysis," *Western Electric Engineer,* April 1970, pp. 11-15.

Theil, Carol T., "DSS Means Computer Aided Management," *Infosystems,* 3/83, pp. 38-44.

Thompson, John M. and Thomas P. Gerrity, "The Strategic Development of DSS in Investment Departments," *Best's Life,* March 1982, pp. 74.

Tydeman, J. and R.B. Mitchell, "Subjective Information Modeling," *Operational Research Quarterly,* Vol. 28, No. 1, 1977. pp. 1-19.

"Tools for Building an EIS," *EDP Analyzer,* August 1979.

Tummala, V.M. Rao, "Decision Analysis in Retrospect and Implications for the Future," *Managerial Planning,* May/June 1978, pp. 20-24.

U

Ulvolua, Jacob W., Rex V. Bilown, and Karle A. Packard, "A Case In On-Line Decision Analysis for Product Planning," *Decision Sciences,* Vol. 8, 1977. pp. 598-615.

Urban, Glen L., "Building Models for Decision-Makers," *Interfaces,* May 1974, pp. 1-11.

Urban, Glen L. and Richard Karash, "Evolutionary Model Building," *Journal of Marketing Research,* February 1972, pp. 193-199.

Ungson, Gerado Rivera, Daniel N. Braunstein, and Phillipp Hall, "Managerial Information Processing: A Research Review," *Administrative Science Quarterly,* March 1981, pp. 116-133.

"User Friendly Package Lets Avon Execs Access Data Easily," *Computerworld,* January 11, 1982, pp. 24.

V

Van de Ven, A. Noren and A.L. Delbece, "Nominal Versus Interacting Group Processes for Committee Decision Making Effectiveness," *Academy of Management Journal,* June 1971, pp. 203-212.

——, "Effectiveness of Nominal, Delphi, and Interacting Group Decision Making," *Academy of Management Journal,* December 1974, pp. 605-621.

Vazsonyi, Andrew, "Computer Supported Gedanken Experiments," *Interfaces*, August 1982, pp. 34–41.

——, "Decision Support Systems, Computer Literacy, and Electronic Models," *Interfaces*, February 1982, pp. 74–78.

——, "Decision Support Systems: The New Technology of Decision-Making," *Interfaces*, November 1978, pp. 72–77.

——, "The Decision To Inquire," *Interfaces,* November 1976, pp. 73–80.

——, "The Calculus of Information," *Interfaces,* August 1976.

——, "Predicate Calculus and Data Base Management Systems," *Interfaces*, February 1980, pp. 64–71.

——, "The Use of Mathematics for Management Information Systems, I, II," February 1976, pp. , May 1976, pp. 42–46.

Vroom, Victor, "A New Look at Managerial Decision-Making," *Organizational Dynamics*, Spring 1973, pp. 66–80.

W

Wagner, Gerald R., "DSS: Dealing With Executive Assumptions in the Office of the Future," *Managerial Planning*, March/April 1982, pp. 4–10.

——, "Decision Support Systems: Computerized Mind Support for Executive Problems," September/October, *Managerial Planning*, 1981, pp. 9–16.

——, "Enhancing Creativity in Strategic Planning Through Computer Systems," *Managerial Planning*, July/August 1979, pp. 10–17.

——, "Decision Support Systems: The Real Substance," *Interfaces*, April 1981, pp. 77–86.

Wagner, Harvey M., "A Manager's Survey of Inventory and Production Control Systems." *Interfaces*, August 1972, pp. 31–39.

Waltz, David L., "Artificial Intelligence," *Scientific American*, October 1982, pp. 118–133.

Williamsen, James S. and G.R. Wagner, "Cymjac: One Company's Solution to a Classical Problem in Group Planning and Decision-Making," *Interfaces*, August 1976, pp. 65–78.

Watson, Charles E., "The Problems of Problem Solving," *Business Horizons*, August 1976, pp. 88–94.

"What if Help for Management," *Business Week*, January 21, 1980, pp. 73–74.

Winer, Leon, "Putting the Computer to Work in Marketing," *Business Horizons*, December 1974, pp. 71–79.

Winter, Frederick W. and Kenorith M. Rowland, "Personnel Decisions: A Bayesian Approach," *California Management Review*, Spring 1980, pp. 33–41.

"What Information Do Managers Need," *EDP Analyzer*, June 1979.

Wright, Charles R., "Decision Trees: Computer Modeling Facilitates Their Use To Improve Managerial Planning," *Managerial Planning*, September/October 1982, pp. 30–34.

Wynne, B.E. and Gary W. Dickson, "Experienced Manager's Performance in Experimental Man-Machine Decision System Simulation," *Academy of Management Journal*, 1975, pp. 25–40.

Wynne, BYE, "Decision Support Systems–A New Plateau of Opportunity or More Emperor's Clothing?," *Interfaces*, February 1982, pp. 88–91.

Y

Young, Lawrence F., "Another Look at Man-Computer Interaction," *Interfaces*, February 1978, pp. 67–69.

Z

Zalud, Bill, "Decision Support Systems–Push End User in Designs Build Stage," *Data Management*, January 1981, pp. 20–22.

Zand, Dale E. and Robert E. Sorenson, "Theory of Change and Effective Use of Management Science," *Administrative Science Quarterly*, December 1975, pp. 532–545.

Zeleny, Milan, "Managers Without Management Science," *Interfaces*, August 1975, pp. 35–42.

BOOKS

A

Alter, Steven A., *Decision Support Systems: Current Practices and Future Challenges.* Reading, Mass.: Addison-Wesley, 1979.

B

Bennett, John L., *Developing Decision Support Systems.* Reading, Mass.: Addison-Wesley, 1982.

Bonczek, Robert H., Clyde W. Holsapple, and Andrew B. Whinston, *Foundations of Decision Support Systems.* New York: Academic Press, 1981.

C

Churchman, C. West, *The Design of Inquiring Systems.* New York: Basic Books, 1971.

E

Ebert, Ronald J. and T.R. Mitchell, *Organizational Decision Processes.* New York: Crane, Russak and Company, 1975.

F

Frick, G., and R.H. Sprague, editors, *Decision Support Systems: Issues and Challenges.* New York: Pergammon Press, 1980.

H

Harrison, E. Frank, *The Managerial Decision Process.* Boston: Houghton Mifflin, 2nd Edition, 1981.

K

Keen, Peter G.W., and Michael Scott Morton, *Decision Support Systems: An Organizational Perspective.* Reading, Mass.: Addison-Wesley, 1978.

M

Mason, Richard O., and E. Burton Swanson, *Measurement for Management Decision.* Reading, Mass.: Addison-Wesley, 1981.

N

Nevison, John M., *Executive Computing.* Reading, Mass.: Addison-Wesley, 1981.
Newell, Allan and Herbert A. Simon, *Human Problem Solving.* Englewood Cliffs, N.J.: Prentice-Hall, 1972.

O

Oxenfeldt, Alfred R., *A Basic Approach to Executive Decision Making.* New York: ANACOM, 1978.

S

Shneiderman, Ben, *Software Psychology: Human Factors in Computers and Information Systems.* Cambridge, Mass.: Winthrop Publishers, 1980.
Sprague, Ralph H., Jr., and Eric D. Carlson, *Building Effective Decision Support Systems.* Englewood Cliffs, N.J.: Prentice-Hall, 1982.

T

Thierauf, Robert J., *Decision Support Systems for Effective Planning and Control.* Englewood Cliffs, N.J.: Prentice-Hall, 1982.